Helmut Schwägermann, Peter Mayer, Ding Yi (Eds.)
Handbook Event Market China

Handbook
Event Market China

Edited by
Helmut Schwägermann, Peter Mayer and Ding Yi

DE GRUYTER
OLDENBOURG

ISBN 978-3-11-057856-0
e-ISBN (PDF) 978-3-11-036677-8
e-ISBN (EPUB) 978-3-11-039862-5

Library of Congress Cataloging-in-Publication Data
A CIP catalog record for this book has been applied for at the Library of Congress.

Bibliographic information published by the Deutsche Nationalbibliothek
The Deutsche Nationalbibliothek lists this publication in the Deutsche Nationalbibliografie; detailed bibliographic data are available on the Internet at http://dnb.dnb.de.

© 2016 Walter de Gruyter GmbH, Berlin/Boston
This volume is text- and page-identical with the hardback published in 2016.
Printing and binding: CPI books GmbH, Leck
Bildnachweis: Zhudifeng/iStock/Thinkstock

♾ Printed on acid-free paper
Printed in Germany

www.degruyter.com

Table of Contents

Preface	VII
Editorial	IX
Introduction	1
The event market: An introduction	3
Schwägermann, Helmut	
The event market China: A global view	27
The development of Asia-Pacific's meetings industry	29
Hamid, Noor Ahmad, Lu, Margaret Kwai Ting	
China's MICE industry: Advancement through reform and opening	41
Chen, Zeyan	
Raising the level of market-orientation in the Chinese exhibition industry – based on international experience	55
Chen, Xianjin	
The role of China in Germany's exhibition industry	65
Koetter, Harald, Spinger, Marco	
China's meetings industry: A future market for Germany	77
Schultze, Matthias	
Externalities, market potential and tourism development: Empirical evidence from China	91
Zhao, Lei, Quan, Hua, Xie, Jia	
Internationalisation of trade fair organisers – Theoretical considerations and practical implications	109
Kaur-Lahrmann, Ravinder, Mayer, Peter	
The role of the state in the exhibition industry in Germany and China – A reflection based on the varieties of capitalism-approach	123
Mayer, Peter, Ding, Yi	
Green economy and tourism	139
Frey, Andreas, Gervers, Susanne	
China outbound: How China will affect the international meetings industry	155
Schwägermann, Helmut, Zhang, Li	

Table of Contents VI

Management aspects in China's event industry — 179

Green meeting standards: A conceptual review 181
Cai, Meng, Griese, Kai-Michael, Große Ophoff, Markus, Tang, Jiani

Probe into the Chinese event venue market – From an outside perspective 195
Gaida, Hans-Jürgen

The Role of a Destination Management Organisation (DMO) in China,
taking the example of Shanghai 217
Chen, Patrick

Opportunities and challenges for Shanghai Disneyland – A stakeholder analysis 229
Du, Jiayi

The challenges posed by international trade fair projects 237
Kamphus, Manfred

Chinese companies at European trade fairs 249
Müller-Martin, Rolf

Why China needs more Professional Congress Organisers (PCOs) 257
Seifert, Frank, Ding, Yi

How to organise successful meetings in China 267
Gao, Frankie

The evolution of the Chinese events market – An agency perspective 277
Dams, Colja M.

A City Brand Personality Model for international event marketing:
An empirical research across multiple cultures 291
Milewicz, Chad, Griese, Kai-Michael, Ding, Yi

Education for China's event industry — 303

Fit for the future? Some thoughts on event education in a changing world 305
Schwägermann, Helmut

The event industry and its human resources: A view based on
the characteristics of the industry 323
Mao, Daben

Education of event management in Germany and China: A comparison 333
Ding, Ye, Gaida, Hans-Jürgen, Schwägermann, Helmut

Where do they want to go? Expectations of Chinese talents
from their future employer 349
Schinnenburg, Heike, Walk, Marlene, Jin, Quan

Learning style of Chinese event management students 361
Louw, Mattheus J., Louw, Lynette, Li, Yanxia

Lecturing key competencies in China and the challenge of transnational education 385
Steinkuhl, Claudia, Gray, Clare, Metz, Annette

Authors — 399

Preface

序言

This book is the outcome of an intellectual discourse, which started many years ago and finally culminated in this handbook.

这本书是智慧探讨的结晶，发端于多年之前并最终在此凝结。

The editors like to thank all the authors who contributed to this publication. All articles have been written specifically for this book. The research results presented are the result of work specifically done for this project.

本书编辑对所有作者表示感激。书中的文章都是为这本书特意撰写，所呈现的研究成果都是为本项目量身定制。

The editors like to express their gratitude as well to the two organisations which run the joint study programme International Event Management Shanghai (IEMS): Hochschule Osnabrück, University of Applied Sciences and Shanghai University of Business and Economics, formerly: Shanghai Institute of Foreign Trade (SIFT). The programme, which started in 2004 allowed for numerous interactions between scholars from China and Germany.

本书编辑还想对运营中德合作国际会展管理（IEMS）项目的两个机构表示感谢，它们是德国奥斯纳布吕克应用技术大学和上海对外经贸大学（前上海对外贸易学院）。这个创始于 2004 年的项目为中德两国的学者提供了大量合作的机会。

This handbook is also the first major publication in the framework of IEMS. On occasion of the 10th anniversary of IEMS, the International Research Institute for the Event Industry has been founded in Shanghai and Osnabrück. We are looking forward to more publications on the Chinese event market initiated by this new research institution.

这本工具书也是 IEMS 合作体系下的第一本主要出版物。在 IEMS 十周年活动的庆典上，上海与奥斯纳布吕克的中德合作会展研究所成立。我们期待这个崭新的研究所将引领出版更多有关中国会展市场的出版物。

This book would not have been possible without the excellent work of those who helped in bringing manuscripts into a publishable shape. The work of Cai Yanwen who studies international business and management in Osnabrück was particularly helpful. Her diligence in working with the submitted drafts, harmonizing the approach towards structure and referencing was extremely useful. The book has been published in English which is not the mother tongue of most of the authors. Teresa Gehrs and Clare Gray in Germany did an outstanding work. Isaac Aamidor, Xiang Shujie, Guo Zi'ang, Yang Siqi, Chen Tianqi, Tan Qingzhu, Jiao Jie, Qiu Wenqian, and Zhu Wanling in Shanghai contributed as well towards the translation or the polishing of the English of Chinese authors. Last but not least we would like to thank Anja Cheong, De Gruyter Oldenbourg, for her invaluable support.

如果没有下列人员在从初稿到可交付出版的成稿中所付出的卓绝努力，本书不可能出版。在奥斯纳布吕克学习国际商务与管理的蔡妍雯的工作尤其可圈可点，她对提交的初稿进行了结构和参考文献方面的协调与整理，这些辛勤的工作对本书的出版大有裨益。该书以英语出版，对大多数作者来说这不是他们的母语。在翻译和文章的润饰上，德国的特蕾莎·格尔斯，克莱尔·格蕾工作相当出色，上海的伊萨克·阿米多,向书杰，郭子昂，杨思琪，陈天琦，谭庆珠，矫洁，邱文倩，朱婉玲也贡献了他们的力量。最后，我们还要衷心感谢来自德格鲁伊特出版社的编辑，昌安雅女士宝贵的支持和协助。

Given the enormous potential of China's event market, the editors of this handbook hope that the articles of this handbook find many readers and stimulate further academic work on the development of this market.

鉴于中国会展市场的巨大潜力，本书编辑希望这些文章能吸引众多读者并激发有关中国会展市场发展的学术研究更上一层楼。

Berlin, Osnabrück and Shanghai, July 2015

柏林，奥斯纳布吕克，上海，2015 年 7 月

Helmut Schwägermann, Peter Mayer, Ding Yi

海尔默特·史怀格曼，皮特·马亚，丁忆

Editorial

编者按

China's event market has witnessed unparalleled development in recent decades. There is a thriving event market, full of dynamic development, innovation, new players and novel ideas. This new and huge market is interesting for the event industry in China and beyond. The aim of this handbook is to analyse the Chinese event market; reflect on emerging trends; scrutinise the key players; and identify the implications for the education of future professionals in this industry.

在最近的几十年间，中国的会展市场见证了无与伦比的发展。这是一个欣欣向荣的会展市场，充满活力，创新，新成员和新点子。无论是中国国内还是国外的会展行业都对这个崭新和巨大的市场充满兴趣。本书旨在分析中国的会展市场，反映其新兴趋势，仔细分析市场中的主要参与者，并揭示在行业中培养未来专业人才的意义。

This handbook is the first of its kind on the Chinese event market written in English. The authors are not only from universities, but also from national and international event organisations and corporations. Many also lecture at universities or vocational schools. The handbook is a collection of 27 articles written by 41 authors from China, Germany, Malaysia, South Africa, the United Kingdom and the United States of America.

这本书是用英语撰写的第一本有关中国会展市场的工具书。作者来自大学、国家级或全球性的会展机构和会展公司，其中许多作者还在大学或职业院校任教。本书共收录27篇文章，由41位作者完成，分别来自中国、德国、马来西亚、南非、英国和美国。

The contributions embrace a mix of theoretical and practical reflections, written by academics/lecturers and practitioners alike. Some very specifically describe a certain trend or development; others focus on overall trends.

本书兼顾了理论与实践两种类型的思考。文章由在大学授课的学者以及行业从业者撰写。有些文章专注于具体态势或新生事物的描述，而另一些则聚焦于大趋势的勾画。

The handbook is divided into four chapters. Following an introductory chapter on the event market, the second chapter focuses on the event market in China from a global perspective. The third chapter reflects on management aspects in China's event industry. The fourth and final chapter addresses the issue of educating professionals for the event industry.

本书共有四个章节。第一章为会展市场的介绍，第二章为全球视角下的中国会展市场。第三章为中国会展市场的管理。最后一章为中国会展市场的人才培养。

Chapter 1: Introduction

第一章 引言

The international event industry is relatively young compared to other industries. In addition, the event market is a highly fragmented market with many facets. H. Schwägermann introduces the event market from an international perspective, and comments on a number of special Chinese approaches.

与其它行业相比，国际会展行业还相对年轻。而且，会展市场具有多面性和高度零散的特点。史怀格曼教授从国际化视角介绍了会展市场，并对中国的一些特有做法进行了评价。

Chapter 2: The event market China: a global view

第二章 中国会展市场：基于全球的观点

N. Hamid and M. Lu provide an overview of the international meeting market. By using existing statistical data, the authors succinctly show in Article 2.1 how the market developed in various Asia-Pacific cities and regions.

哈米德和玛格丽特陆对国际会展市场进行了概览。通过相关统计数据，文章2.1言简意赅地描述了亚太地区不同城市和地区之间会展市场的演化。

In Article 2.2, Z. Chen outlines the Chinese market and describes how governmental policies shaped the MICE industry in China. The second half of the article focuses on China's policy towards restructuring the market and the role played by foreign enterprises.

在文章2.2中，陈泽炎描述了中国会展市场的发展概况，分析了政府制定的政策如何影响了中国会展市场的形成。文章在最后聚焦于市场的改革以及外资企业在市场中的角色。

Article 2.3 explores the evolution of the approach taken by the Chinese Government with a particular emphasis on the role of market mechanisms. X. Chen describes China's overall transformation from a tightly controlled state-led economy to a more diverse and complex economy, which is mirrored in the event industry. Further steps must be taken to fully exploit the potential of the exhibition industry.

文章2.3在强调市场机制的作用下审视了中国政府行事方法的演变。陈先进以会展市场为例，描述了中国从一个严格控制的国有经济体向更为多元、综合经济体改革的概况。文章最后还提出了一些必要的步骤可尽最大可能开发会展市场的潜力。

Thousands of exhibitors and visitors from China come to Germany every year, and the same is true in the other direction. In Article 2.4, H. Koetter and M. Springer provide valuable information about the role and structure of AUMA, the key association of the German trade fair industry. This article provides valuable input for the discussion on establishing a Chinese trade fair association.

每年有成千上万的参展商和专业观众赴德国参展,同样也有诸多的德国参展商和观众来到中国。科伊特和斯普林格在文章2.4中提供了有关德国核心展览业协会AUMA的作用和结构的有价值的信息。这篇文章还对建立中国展览业协会的讨论提出了有价值的思考。

Germany has been one of the world's leading destinations for meetings and congresses for many years. It is incumbent upon the German Convention Bureau (GCB) to secure this position for the future. As a future market with outstanding potential, China is a major focus of GCB's marketing activities. M. Schultze highlights major aspects in this specific area (2.5).

多年以来,德国一直是世界最重要的会议目的地之一。德国会议旅游局(GCB)的作用就是帮助德国在未来也保持这样的地位。作为具有杰出发展潜力的未来市场,中国是德国会议旅游局的市场推广重点。在文章2.5中,舒尔茨强调了该领域中的若干重要事实。

In Article 2.6, L. Zhao, H. Quan and J. Xie show that diversification in the development of tourism in China is conducive to the overall development of the industry, given the existence of externalities. Based on a theoretical model and national data, the authors demonstrate how externalities, the market potential and the development of tourism interact.

赵磊,全华和谢佳在文章2.6中提出,在外部性存在的情况下,中国旅游发展的多样化有助于行业的总体发展。基于理论模型和全国性的数据,作者揭示了外部性、市场潜力以及旅游发展之间如何相互作用的机理。

The motives and rationales behind internationalisation can be very diverse, sometimes even contradictory. It is important for all actors in this field to have a clear view of the advantages of internationalisation; the options available; and the type of internationalisation that occurs in the case of event organisers. P. Mayer and R. Kaur-Lahrmann address theoretical and practical issues (Article 2.7).

国际化的动机和依据可以非常多元,有时甚至相互矛盾。对所有的参与者来说,看清国际化所带来的好处,国际化的不同选择,以及国际化在会展策划者的具体案例中的表征相当重要。在文章2.7中,马亚和卡拉玛从理论与实践两个方面对国际化进行了探讨。

In their article (2.8), P. Mayer and Y. Ding explain the different roles played by the government in the exhibition industry in Germany and China. The authors demonstrate the potential of an established theoretical model for analysing the role of government in greater detail, going beyond the simplistic views of "more government" or "less government".

马亚和丁忆在文章2.8中描述了中德会展行业中政府所扮演的不同角色。作者采用了一个被广为接受的理论模型来分析政府角色,使用这种方法的潜在好处在于能逾越"增加政府力量"或"减少政府力量"的简单思考方式。

Sustainability issues are becoming increasingly important. In this respect, the event industry can learn from the tourism industry. In Article 2.9, A. Frey and S. Gervers explore sustainability with respect to business and leisure travel. They provide an in-depth reflection of the challenges facing the event industry in China and beyond.

可持续性问题日趋重要。在这方面，会展行业可以向旅游行业学习。在文章2.9中，弗雷和格弗斯审视了商务和休闲旅游中的可持续性。他们对中国以及其它国家会展行业面临的挑战提出了深刻的思考。

In Article 2.10, H. Schwägermann and L. Zhang focus on the future influence of China on the meetings industry in all major countries and cities active in the meetings business. They develop a forecast model and report about the results of a survey conducted among ICCA members.

在文章2.10中，史怀格曼和张丽聚焦于会议业活跃的主要国家和城市，探讨了中国对其会议业的影响。他们开发了一个预测模型并发布了对ICCA成员调查问卷的计算结果。

Chapter 3: Management aspects in China's event industry

第三章：中国会展产业的管理

The connotation of organising "green meetings" is positive. But what is a "green" meeting? Do any national and international standards exist that provide useful, sound and robust guidance? In Article 3.1, M. Cai, K.-M. Griese, M. Große Ophoff and J. Tang introduce important concepts and explain what to look for when stakeholders are serious about addressing green issues.

组织'绿色会议'的内涵是积极的。但什么是'绿色'会议？是否有有用的、合理的，有力的国内、国际的标准？文章3.1中，蔡萌，格里斯，格劳塞奥弗夫和唐佳妮介绍了重要的概念并且揭示了当利益相关者认真对待绿色问题时该如何对他们进行引导。

H.-J. Gaida provides a detailed description of popular types of event venues and considers them from an event management perspective. The author of this article (3.2) makes suggestions about how to ensure that facilities in China meet the growing requirements.

盖达从会展管理的角度详细介绍了通常使用的会展场馆类型。文章3.2对中国的场馆建设如何与不断发展的标准相符合提出了建议。

Following the example of many other cities, Shanghai has commissioned a specific department to promote the city as an attractive MICE destination. In his contribution in Article 3.3, P. Chen shows what this task entails, for example in terms of coordinating stakeholders' activities and providing training.

与许多其它城市一样，上海也设有旨在把上海推广成有吸引力会展目的地的专门部门。陈平在文章3.3中描述了其任务的内容，比如协调利益相关者的活动以及提供培训。

In her paper (3.4), J. Du takes a critical look at the potential effects of the Shanghai Disneyland Park and analyses the opportunities and challenges involved from the perspective of different stakeholders.

杜佳毅在文章3.4中辩证地探讨了上海迪士尼乐园的潜在影响，并从不同利益相关者的角度分析了其带来的机会与挑战。

In Article 3.5, M. Kamphus identifies some of the key challenges facing companies when they participate in international trade fairs. With China in mind, he emphasises the importance of stand design. In his contribution, he focuses on the importance of deciding which trade fairs to attend and how to identify the right cooperative partners.

堪弗斯在文章3.5中指出公司在参加国际展会中所面临的主要挑战。以中国为例，他强调了展台设计的重要性。同样，选择哪个展览会以及找到正确合作伙伴也相当关键。

One important function of trade fairs is to build brand awareness. In Article 3.6, R. Müller-Martin emphasises the role played by trade fairs in establishing brands. Participation in trade fairs is an important channel for many global players to communicate their success stories. Chinese companies can learn from this.

参加展览会的一个重要作用在于建立品牌知名度。文章3.6中，穆勒马丁强调了展会在建立品牌上的作用。对许多国际化的企业来说，参加展览会是通向成功的重要手段。这值得中国公司学习。

F. Seifert and Y. Ding draw attention to the role of professional congress organisers in the MICE industry. They argue in Article 3.7 that China needs more professional congress organisers, and show what action needs to be taken to develop them.

赛福特和丁忆强调了会展行业中专业会议组织者（PCO）的作用。他们在3.7中提出中国需要更多的PCO并且提出了发展PCO所须采取的步骤。

In Article 3.8, F. Gao provides suggestions on how to organise successful events in China, ranging from the bidding process to issues such as sustainability.

高峰在文章3.8中对在中国组办成功的会展活动提出了建议，包括从会展活动的竞标到会展活动的可持续性发展等事项。

C. Dams shows in Article 3.9 that event management is, in essence, communication. He emphasises that communication needs to be authentic, emotional and relevant, and must offer some kind of added value.

达姆斯在文章3.9中提出会展管理的实质是沟通。他强调沟通应该是真实的、有情感的、相关联的并且还得具备附加值。

In Article 3.10, C. Milewics, K.-M. Griese and Y. Ding reflect on the theory of branding, which can be applied to the branding of cities, regions or countries, demonstrating the potential for the event industry. Major investments in the development of the event industry require a clear perspective on the requirements for local government officials seeking to enhance the image of their community.

文章3.10中，
麦尔维可思，格里斯和丁忆进行了品牌理论应用于城市、地区和国家品牌化的思考，并显示了其应用于会展业的潜力。会展业发展的主要投资取决于当地政府以提升社区形象为目的的清晰需求。

Chapter 4: Education for China's event industry

第四章：中国会展业的教育

H. Schwägermann reflects on the long-term challenges in higher education in the specific field of event management. With possibly 40 years of work ahead of them when students graduate, education should not only focus on the challenge of employability immediately after graduation, but on the general skills that graduates require to enable them to succeed many years later, too, after repeated phases of transformation within the industry. Lifelong learning will be an important aspect (Article 4.1).

史怀格曼对会展管理高等教育所面临的长期挑战进行了思考。学生毕业之后也许需要工作40年，因此教育面对的挑战不仅仅是让学生具备毕业后即时的就业力，而且要让学生掌握通用的技巧。这些技巧可以让学生在毕业后许多年间在行业内不断转型并获得成功。因此，终身学习很重要（4.1）。

In Article 4.2, D. Mao reveals what practitioners in event management need to know, and which skills and competencies are required to succeed. It provides ample food for thought for academic institutions, which need to ensure that their graduates are "employable" and successful in the long run.

毛大奔在4.2中阐述了从业者在会展管理中应具备的知识以及管理技巧和能力。这为以培养具"就业能力"且能获得长久成功毕业生为己任的教育机构提供了充足的思考依据。

At the end of the last century, no professional higher education was available to those intending to embark on a career in the event industry. Ye Ding, H.-J. Gaida and H. Schwägermann compare the education systems for the event industry in Germany and China. The emergence of many programmes in China demonstrates interaction between the business and the educational sector (4.3).

在上世纪末，市场上还没有专业的会展高等教育可供打算在会展业从业的人进修或学习。丁烨、盖达和史怀格曼比较了中德会展教育的体系。许多在中国涌现的教育项目体现了企业与教育系统之间的互动（4.3）。

In their contribution (4.4), H. Schinnenburg, M. Walk and J. Qin shed light on the aspirations and expectations of business students. The empirical results of their survey in Shanghai confirm the need to establish close links between academia and the business sector. In this respect, internships might be an especially promising path.

文章4.4中，辛能博格，沃克和金泉聚焦于商科类学生的理想和期望的研究。他们在上海调查的实证结果验证了学校和企业建立紧密联系的必要性。基于此，实习可能是最理想的方法。

M. Louw, L. Louw and Y. Li reflect on their experience in teaching event management in Shanghai in Article 4.5. The theory-led discussion of learning styles is followed by empirical research using data from a survey with students at SUIBE in Shanghai. The results are important for educators in China.

文章4.5中，楼、楼和李艳霞对他们在上海有关会展管理的授课经历进行了思考。文章首先从理论角度探讨了学习风格，随后采用了上海对外经贸大学学生的调查数据进行了实证研究。研究结果对中国的会展教育具有重要意义。

C. Steinkuhl, C. Gray and A. Metz, who teach key competencies such as academic writing and intercultural communication in Germany and China, reflect on their experiences and the challenges they have encountered (Article 4.6). They state the reasons for the differences and specific phenomena experienced. Based on their observations, they present suggestions on how to develop event education in China.

在中德两国教授学术写作和文化沟通这些核心能力课程的史泰恩库尔，格蕾和麦茨，在文章4.6中对他们的经历和面临的挑战进行了思考。文章分析并解释了中德两国学生在学习上的差异和一些特殊现象，并对如何改进中国的会展教育提出了建议。

Introduction

The event market: An introduction

Schwägermann, Helmut

会展市场-引言/简介

Compared to other industries, the international event industry is relatively young. Most international event industry associations were founded only 50 or even 30 years ago. China embarked on its trade fair activities in the 1980s, and has experienced an unprecedented development of event-related activities ever since. The first university programmes in event management were launched a decade ago.

The event market is a highly fragmented market with many facets. The rate of labour division within the event value chain is high. Since the event market is so manifold, it is difficult to give this market a clear or even unified structure. Internationally accepted definitions within the event market are rare, and all languages give the term event their own special meaning. In China, in particular, there is no explicit translation for the word event. Consequently, a comprehensive concept of "the event market" does not yet exist in China.

This article introduces the event market from an international perspective, and comments on a number of special Chinese approaches.

与其他行业相比，国际会展业还相对年轻。大多数会展行业的协会组织都仅仅成立了50年，有的甚至只有30年。中国从上世纪80年代开始组办商品交易会，其会展相关经验也经历了史无前例的快速发展。国内第一个高校会展专业也在十年前成立。

会展市场是一个多面性的、高度碎片化的市场。在整个会展产业价值链中的劳动分工率也很高。由于市场的多样性，这使得市场结构很难形成统一清晰的划分。被国际普遍接受的会展市场定义很少，而且每种语言都给予"Event"特殊的定义。特别是在中国，对于"Event"一词并没有明确精准的翻译。因此，"The Event Market"（会展市场）这一综合概念在中国也还没有形成。

本文将从国际化的角度介绍会展市场，并对中国的一些特有做法进行评价

1 The development of the international event industry

The international event industry is – compared to other industries – a rather young one. One rather appropriate indicator of the growth and formation of an industry is the founding year of that industry's association. With the exception of AUMA, the German exhibition association, the founding of most international event-related associations dates back only 50, 40 or even 30 years. The first event programmes at universities date back only to the 1990s.

Taking into consideration that event management is a notably global industry, which occurs across different cultures, languages and countries, it is easy to understand that a set of united definitions is not yet available in our industry. The event market is a highly fragmented market with an extremely large number of aspects. The industry value chain is quite long and the rate of labour division is quite high. Therefore, a lot of industry associations for special event service suppliers exist in the event market; these associations filter their understandings of the market as a whole through the unique perspective of their particular members.

In addition, because the event market (especially the market for exhibitions and congresses) has its roots in Europe, many languages (German, French, Spanish, Italian, etc.) have been used to explain this market. While English has been the lingua franca for years, British English is rather different from the English used in Continental Europe, as well as from American English. Even the most basic terms may differ – in Europe, the term *congress* is used for major and complex meetings; similar events are called *conferences* in the UK, and *conventions* in the USA.

In addition, in almost all European countries, English terminology has been introduced parallel to national languages and partially replaced these "native" words. What happened in Europe and other parts of the world in the last century is now also taking place in China. Since the event market is so diverse, internationally accepted definitions within the event market are rare, and all languages give the term *event* their own special meaning. In China, in particular, there is no explicit translation for the word *event*. Consequently, a comprehensive concept of *the event market* does not yet exist in China. This article introduces the event market from an international perspective, and comments on a number of special Chinese approaches.

2 Definition of events

What characteristics do different events, from an IT exhibition, to a concert, to a congress or a corporate event, have in common? At first glance, probably not so very many. Although when you look a bit closer, they do share one common trait: at a specific time and place, people come together to form an "event." Events have certain characteristics in common. These common characteristics are: there is an event *initiator/organiser*, who created and initiated the event. Events take place at a special location (destination/venue) at a certain time and have a limited duration. There may or may not be an entrance fee, and entrance to the event may be regulated by the organiser or whoever owns the venue.

Events have special *topics and content* and are aimed at special *target groups*, who participate in the event. Both the organisers and participants want to achieve particular objectives during the event. Indeed, the word "event" itself implies two meanings: first, it can be a generic term for meetings and assemblies of all kind. This meaning will be used throughout this paper. Secondly, the term "event" can also describe a "sensation" or "experience". This second meaning has also become more important in the event business in recent decades, as marketing has shifted its focus from informational marketing to emotional marketing.

We define an *event* as an announced, planned and organised gathering or meeting of any kind held at a real as opposed to a virtual place with a certain time limit under the responsibility of an initiator/organiser. Events are usually delimited according to their topics, and serve one or several aims. Events are *services* with all the implications that result from that designation. Usually they are organised as *projects* with tools and methods of project management.

Event management can be defined as a particular management concept that aims to coordinate specific tasks and elements of an event to consciously influence the event results towards the required quality and at the required date. It comprises the creation, planning, organising and monitoring of the event in all phases and the coordination of all stakeholders involved.

3 Structure/typology of events

When looking at the structure of the event market, an abundance of segmentation criteria can be seen: the organiser, the target group, the size, regional reach, the topic or the industry of the event. In practice, events are quite often categorised according to their *target group* as well as to the type and motives of their *organisers*. Figure 1 uses both criteria at the same time, thus creating a *multi-dimensional matrix. The following section discusses these segmentation criteria in detail.*

3.1 Target groups: different motivations, different events

One of the most important criteria is the *target group*. Therefore it is crucial to know which target group (business clients or consumers) the event organiser is addressing.

This results in one first major distinction:

- *Business* events (B2B events) as opposed to
- *Consumer* events (B2C events).
- *Mixed events* may also take place if business clients as well as consumers are admitted.

Business events (B2B events)

Business events are events designed, planned and organised for participants who visit these events for professional reasons or for their professional relevance. Typical business events include meetings of non-profit organisations (associations as well as governmental), corporate events and trade fairs and exhibitions. Further segmentation of the target group results from the line of business in which the industry professionals operate. Other criteria include the participant's function, position, and authorisation to make decisions within the company. Often it is important to know if participants of small or medium-sized companies or participants of larger companies should be addressed. For this reason, the size of the company is another criterion for targeting events to specific customers.

Motivations to participate in an event include learning and discussing (at meetings and conventions), getting a market overview of the latest trends in their industry and preparing orders at trade fairs. In addition, business networking is always one of the key reasons to attend these platforms for communication.

Professionals from companies, non-profit organisations and government either choose to attend events by themselves or are asked or sent by their respective organisations. These professionals see their visit as a personal investment or an investment for the company, which over the long term is expected to yield both material and immaterial rewards. Professionals will define special goals that they hope to achieve over the course of the event, they evaluate the results of the event ("Return on Event, ROE"), and then they report these results to their organisation. Normally, all business-related expenses are covered by the company/organisation. Therefore, depending on their status and function in the company, they might travel business class and stay in a 3-star to 5-star hotel. They may also invite customers for a business meal.

Business events mainly take place during working days and working hours. Business events are often limited to business people from a special industry or profession. Whereas the majority of the participants will often be local, depending on the quality of the event, a certain proportion of the visitors will be from other areas of the country or even from overseas. They will also stay for a longer period of time in the area hosting the event. For these reasons, the regional effects from business events are much higher than those of consumer events. Destination managers mainly look for and focus on the marketing of business events.

In Asia as well as in other areas of the world, the term "MICE" describes what we call business events. *"MICE" stands for Meetings, Incentives, Conferences and Exhibitions*. As we can see from Figure 1, the term "business events" is more comprehensive than the term "MICE," which only highlights a few types of business events.

Consumer events (B2C events)

In contrast to business events, *consumer events* are targeted to the general public. Attendees are motivated by the entertainment value of the event, and motivations include elements of leisure, only sometimes including information or learning.

This target group can be segmented according to socio-demographic characteristics, such as age, sex, region, income, and so on. There are special events directed to the interests of men or women, children, adolescents or seniors. Often, however, special events targeting a specific age group are visited by persons of all ages.

As a consequence of increased fragmentation of the market and an incessant flood of emotional marketing campaigns, segmentation according to the "lifestyles" of consumers is becoming increasingly important. The spending pattern of participants at consumer events also differs vastly from business events: consumer events mostly take place in holiday seasons, at weekends and in the evening hours. Often these events are attended together with other members of the family and/or with friends in their leisure time. Compared to business events, the entrance fee is often quite low, but this fee must be paid and financed by the consumers/visitors themselves. The vast majority of the participants will be local people who spend their disposable income at events (see also the section on regional effects).

In real life, one can find all kinds of mixtures between B2B and B2C events. Many trade fairs or exhibitions take into account professional attendees as well as the general public. We call these events *mixed events*.

3.2 Event initiators/organisers: different motivations, different events

Every event needs somebody (a person or organisation) who takes the initiative to create, design and organise the event. This person/organisation is called the initiator (in German language: *Veranstalter*). Initiators are the creators and owners of events! In general, the *event initiator* is responsible for the content of the event, its financing, along with accepting legal liability. Initiators are also the *content providers*! They decide about topics, speakers, locations, etc. The so-called *event industry* or *event service industry* consists of particular service providers for these initiators. Initiators buy services from the event service industry (see Section 4). Initiators are therefore sometimes also called "buyers" by the event service industry.

Quite often, the initiator also organises the event himself and is therefore often also referred to as the *event organiser*. The organiser is the one who plans, organises and carries out an event. Sometimes the term *producer* or *host* is used instead of organiser.

There are different methods of "producing" an event. As events are quite complex and require specific expertise from different fields, it is normal for event initiators to cooperate with other specialists and to outsource some of their organisational tasks. A number of event agencies, congress and fair agencies and other service providers (catering, event technique, security, etc.) have specialised in taking on these more routine tasks. Some agencies, like professional congress organisers (PCOs), offer either partial service or full-service; full-service means that the PCO assumes the role of the event organiser and reports to the initiator.

Who are the initiators of an event? The main initiators for business events are:

- *Governmental and non-governmental organisations* (associations) organise events according to their general orientation, the industry of their membership (in the case of NGOs), and target groups. National and international *governmental organisations* are also initiators of events. In socialist countries like China, this market segment is very much dominated by governmental organisations at the national, provincial or city level (the role of China's government in the event industry will be further discussed in several articles in this handbook).
- *Exhibition companies* are special initiators and organisers of trade fairs and exhibitions. At the same time, in some countries, like Germany, most of these companies own and manage their own exhibition centre.
- *Companies/enterprises,* as producers of products and services, organise marketing events to promote their company and/or their product to a special target group; they also may organise internal events with and for their staff. These events are called "corporate events".

Consumer-oriented events have a wide variety of different types of initiators: various organisations and exhibition companies of course can be initiators, but municipal institutions, like multipurpose halls, congress centres and theatres, also may initiate events, and privately owned venues like hotels may organise consumer events. Clubs and private persons also initiate events.

These organisations all have different reasons or motivations to initiate and organise their events, and one has to understand these in order to understand the event market. Business events will be discussed later in the article (see Sections 6–8).

The following diagram classifies six types of events.

Business events are included in the first three columns, and consist of:

1) events by non-profit organisations, 2) trade fairs and exhibitions, and 3) corporate events. Consumer events are located in columns 4 to 6, with 4) social events and parties, 5) cultural events and 6) sporting events.

As has been said before, in the real world we can see a great deal of overlapping, such as when a trade fair (type 2) is accompanied by meetings and seminars (type 1), or when conventions (type 1) coincide with opening events/parties (type 4). However, in principle it can be stated that columns (types) on the left side of this chart tend to have the characteristics of business events, whereas those on the right tend to be consumer events.

Types of Events

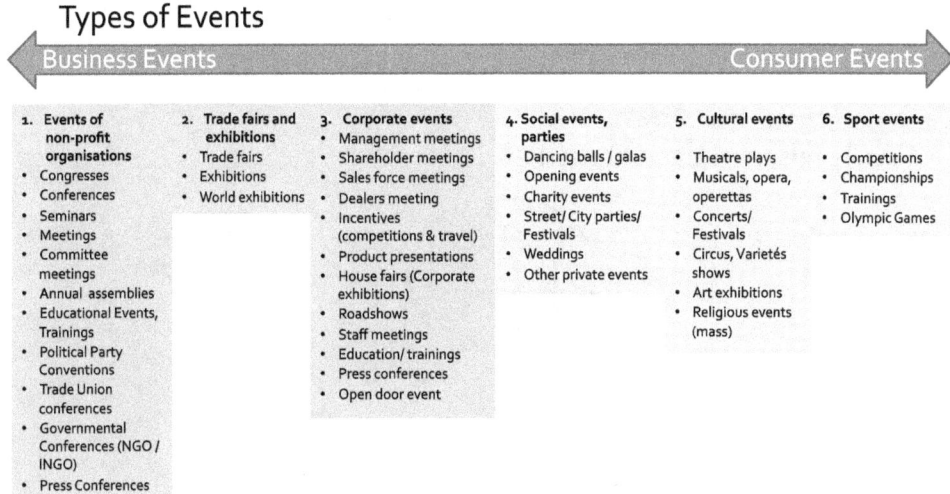

Figure 1: Types of events

4 The two levels/spheres of the event market

When talking about the event market, we obviously assume that there is a market for events. However, what exactly is produced and exchanged on the event market? What is offered and who are the producers and marketers, and who defines the demand? Who are the customers? Is it a homogenous or a diverse market?

According to a common definition, markets are gatherings of buyers and sellers of certain products/services at a third place (e. g. marketplaces, fairs, exhibitions). This means that both parties have to go to a third place in order to come into contact. This fact is also very important for the event market. It is because of this fact that people who want to participate in an event need to travel. This causes inconveniences and additional costs. This also means that the event must be worth going to.

From an economic point of view, the market equals the totality of buyers and sellers who participate in trade. The economist tries to describe the market using structures and processes. It is then necessary to know which companies and persons participate temporarily, permanently, partly, or exclusively in the market. Furthermore, it is good to know the number and distribution of buyers and sellers according to their field/industry, scale, and origin or region.

For this reason, we must acquaint ourselves with the structures and participants of the market in order to understand how it functions.

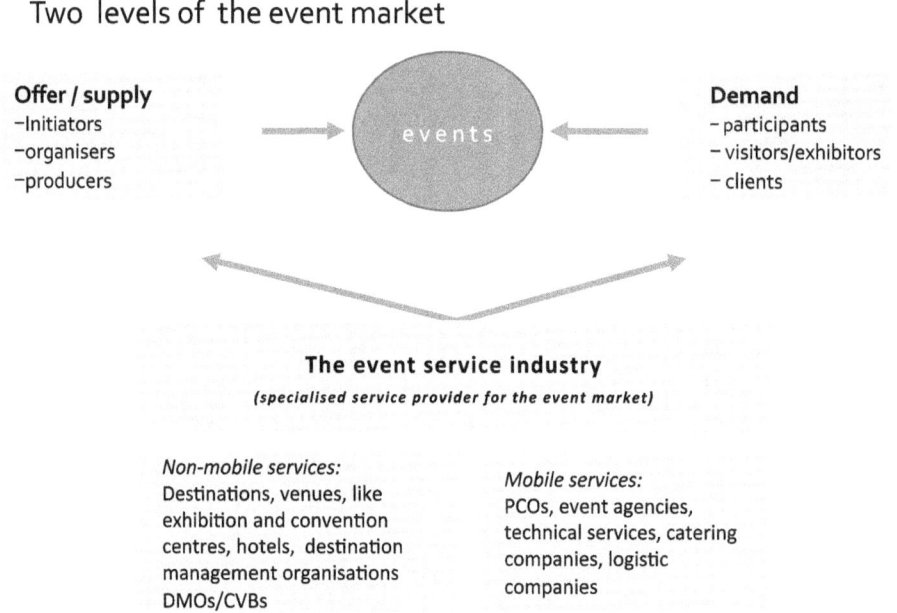

Figure 2: Two levels of the event market

In our understanding, the event market is divided into two levels. This is further explained in the following section.

The event market includes supply and demand factors for events of all kinds. Initiators of events, like trade fairs, meetings or concerts, develop an event as a product/project, and offer this to potential participants (Level One).

This part of the event market can thus be called the *first level of the event market*.

Moreover, the event market is also a *market for goods and services*, which are necessary for planning, organising and producing the event. Different event-related service providers offer their services directly to the organiser and/or to the participant. Without these service providers, which are sometimes called *the Event Industry* (and sometimes also the *MICE Industry*), a professional event cannot take place.

Therefore, at the *second level* of the event market, special event service companies offer their services to the event organiser and the event organiser has to decide if he wants to produce these services on his own (e. g. plan a meeting with an *in-house meeting planner*) or if he wants to *outsource a specific service* to a specialist.

The event market is a *service market and e*vents are services: organisers promise their clients the successful operation of an event, even though it might take place in a year or even later! Participants such as attendees or exhibitors *do not buy an event,* but they pay a certain fee to *use the event* for their purposes. They do this under uncertainty, because events are "experience goods", in the sense that customers can evaluate the quality of the service only during the production process, its completion or even after the event.

4.1   The event service industry: mobile and non-mobile services

The event service industry consists of companies that have more or less specialised in offering services for event organisers.

As Figure 1 shows, these include both *non-mobile* and *mobile* services. Why is this differentiation useful? Obviously, non-mobile services, like exhibition centres, event destinations (such as cities interested in hosting events) or hotels, offer their services only at a particular location. They produce and offer *"location-based services"*, which can only be *consumed by event organisers and their participants at this specific location!* In other words, they have to convince/attract customers to come to their city in order to use their service.

This location-based marketing is called *"incoming marketing"*. In normal product or service marketing, marketing experts develop a distribution chain in order to reach their customers at every place, wherever they want to buy the product. But since events – by definition – take place at a definite place, the organisers of events always have to attract/convince their customers to come to this special place. Therefore, for organisers, the choice of an event location as the *Point of Production and Consumption* for the event is critical to the success of an event. Moreover, destination or venue managers have to make sure that their location can offer convincing arguments for the organisers.

On the other hand, mobile event service providers, such as PCOs, and event agencies, are more flexible: though most of them started out at a "home" location, due to their customers' international mobility they have had to develop internationalisation strategies and must be able to work at the national level or even worldwide.

4.2   The relationship between events and tourism

Events and tourism have a close relationship: according to several tourism-related publications, events are seen as an integral element of tourism. From the viewpoint of an event organiser, however, events are organised for reasons of *communication*. Medical doctors have to meet to discuss new treatments of diseases, just as marketing directors of multinational companies meet in order to decide on new marketing strategies. For this reason, event participants inevitably have to travel to the event location. Therefore, events are *generators of tourism*, which is of course relevant for tourism managers, who are in charge of the *city marketing*. On the other hand, national and international events need a comprehensive tourism infrastructure for their participants at the destination. The expenses for tourism (travel, cost for overnight stays and meals, etc.) are of great economic importance for the surrounding regional tourism industry, not to mention indirect benefits for the city or region which is hosting the event. These regional effects of events are further discussed in the following section.

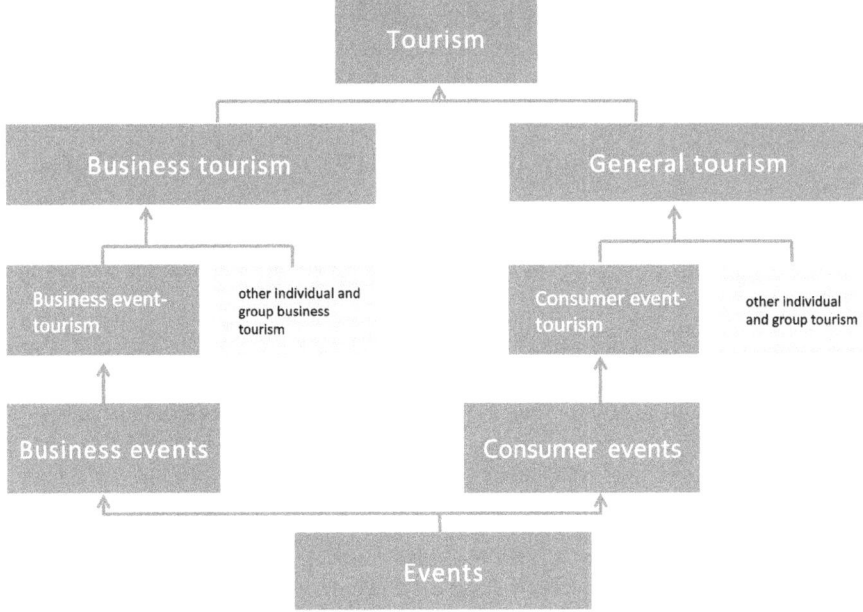

Figure 3: Events are generators of additional tourism

5 Regional effects of events

Events have a large number of different effects on the economy, the region and the society as a whole. "*Export effects*" of events result from the fact that, by definition, events take place at a particular location and bring together persons from other cities and countries. For this reason, the *region exports various services* to organisers and participants of the event. In particular, the hotel and restaurant sector, transport companies and other event service and tourism-related companies are the beneficiaries. However, these effects go even beyond the event- or tourism-related industries. Events create jobs on a considerable scale in the region, especially in small and medium-sized companies. In addition, substantial additional tax revenues are created for cities, regions and central governments. Nevertheless, we can differentiate between "*monetary regional effects*" and "*non-monetary* regional effects".

Monetary regional effects

The *direct expenditures* of persons travelling from outside to the event, also described as "*inflow of purchasing power*", have stimulating effects on *production and employment* of the directly affected event-related services companies in the region or city. These effects, also often described as "*primary effects*", only show a proportion of the aggregate economic effects.

Regional productivity effects are generated by the additional demand for regional products. These effects lead to further demand for input factors, which has an impact on the upstream production chain. This chain of consequential effects concerning all economic sectors is also described as an *indirect effect* and will be illustrated by the following example: the demand for more catering services stimulated by events leads to the additional production of food in the region (considering the case that the products are not regionally or nationally imported). This additional production again leads to a generation of agricultural goods: more fertilizers and (in the long run) even machines from the (local) mechanical engineering industry are again needed. These effects are obvious if a major or mega-event takes place in a city. The effects will also occur if a number of smaller or medium-sized events regularly choose the city or region as their location.

An additional effect results from the *additional income* that is created either due to direct demand, or by the indirect effects of income from work resulting from the event. These incomes are partly spent or reinvested in the community (less tax, social security contributions, savings, etc.). These effects have also been described as the "*income effect*".

An *input-output analysis* allows us to quantify the productivity effects (direct and conditional effects on the upstream of the production process).

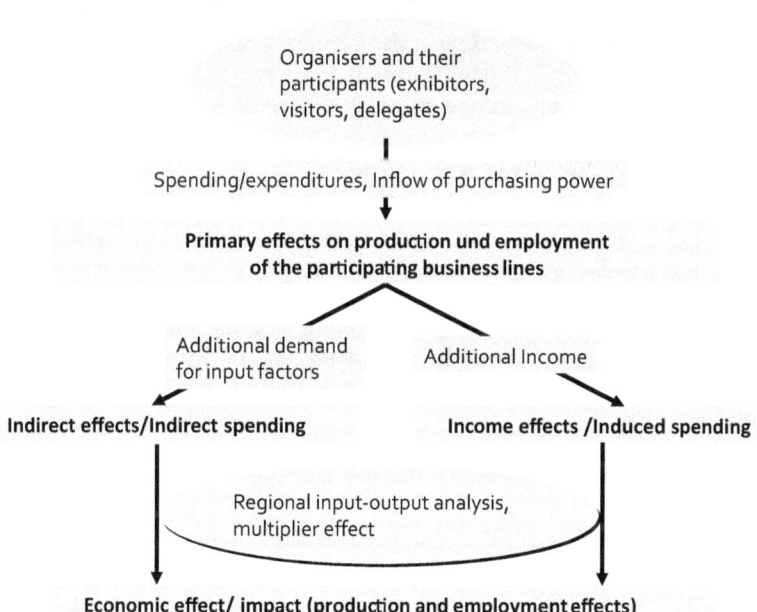

Figure 4: Regional monetary effects of events

The level of additional production and income can be calculated with the help of a so-called *"multiplier"*. Employment effects can be quantified with the help of what are known as *"sectoral labour coefficients"*. Figure 4 below gives an overview of the different effects.

International and national business events have a higher impact

It is important to note that not all events bring about the same regional economic effects. Monetary effects are *exclusively* created by organisers and participants of *supra-regional events*! The effects are positively correlated with the ratio of non-local participants.

The reason for this is that it can be assumed that *local* participants/attendees shift their disposable income from other local activities; moreover, surveys indicate that *daily regional* participants/visitors spend significantly less money (no overnight stay, no expensive catering, etc.).

As a consequence, the majority of cultural events directed at the inhabitants of a city or region rarely achieve any regional economic effects. Therefore, the discussion about regional economic effects is almost completely limited to business events, such as conventions, trade fairs and marketing events, but also includes other events of national and international significance.

Another important question leads to the discussion of how much of these effects will actually stay in the region, and conversely how much of the additional goods and services have to be imported from other regions. This facet is described by what is known as the *"regional import ratio"*. Only that part of the expenditure which is actually spent at the event location leads to regional economic effects at the event location. The level of this effect depends considerably on the capacities and quality of the event service industry in the region. If the complete event production chain is not present at the location, organisers and participants have to import services from other regions. This means that the regional import ratio of event services is paramount for the real and lasting effects in the region.

Overestimated monetary effects of events in China?

In Chinese publications, regional monetary effects are mostly referred to as the "economic pull factor of events", estimated to be 1:9, and authorities explain that "One yuan invested into the event market yields 9 yuan for the region/country."

On the other hand, in studies on the German exhibition industry, the multiplier, which seems to be a similar theoretical construct to the pull factor, amounts to 2 rather than 9 (AUMA, 2009); this leads to the question of why the multiplier/pull effect should be 4.5 times higher in China than in Germany.

There are several possible explanations of this phenomenon:

1. *The definition of the relation* of the input factor and the output factor (1/9).

Here, the question is how the input factor is defined. Is it a) the income of the event venue, or b) the spending of the event organisers, or c) the total direct spending of all organisers and visitors/participants, as was shown in Figure 4? Obviously version c) has a smaller "pull effect" than the versions a) or b).

2. The selection of the events

If the study includes only events with high spending patterns, like international business events for certain industries, such as automobiles or pharmaceuticals, the 1:9 ratio would not be an average value for all events, but a maximum.

To summarise, there is obviously a need for further research on international standardised surveys for multipliers and/or pull factors. Venue managers, cities and other governmental institutions quite often exaggerate the economic impact in order to justify the deficit of an event venue. Therefore, careful and differentiated argumentation is needed.

Non-monetary effects

In addition to economic or monetary effects, events have additional non-monetary or qualitative effects on the region or city where they take place. Not only do mega-events, like the Olympic Games, the FIFA World Cup or World Exhibitions, lead to increased media attention of the city or region. Cultural events, such as festivals and concerts, and even other events, such as trade fairs and conventions also have the same effect. In addition, events add quality of life for the inhabitants of a city! All in all, these qualitative effects can also be described as the *"indirect profitability"* of an event city or of an event centre.

For all these reasons, it is hardly surprising that cities, regions and countries set up appropriate event infrastructure (exhibition and convention centres, etc.) and compete for particularly lucrative and image-promoting events. Events can also be understood as an *instrument of city/destination marketing* due to the increased news coverage of the city in the media.

6 Events of non-profit organisations: the meetings market

While in the Western world the market for events of non-profit organisations is dominated by events of, by and for non-governmental organisations, such as international association meetings, in China, the direct and indirect influence of government is still very high. China's government and the industry organisations under its control still dominate this area of the market, which is also sometimes called the "congress market". One indicator of changing terminology in a globalised world is the fact that one of the leading industry associations in this field, ICCA, has unofficially changed its name from the "International Congress and Convention Association" to "The Meetings Association".

Congresses can be defined as events of organisations of all kinds for the purpose of gaining and exchanging new knowledge or of making decisions. Congresses will have from several hundred to several thousand participants attending, and are often accompanied by an exhibition. During the congress, several parallel sessions take place. Congresses are hosted in rotating destinations and in some instances require years of advanced planning. Congresses are often held on the occasion of the general assembly of the organisation.

International and national non-governmental organisations (NGOs) are the main focus of the meeting market. These NGOs are generally organised as associations. Associations are groups of persons or companies who voluntarily enter into an agreement to accomplish a purpose. Associations can be formed at the local, national or international level.

It is important to know what types of associations exist. These include:

- groups of individuals/persons with similar interests, such as a *professional* organisation
- or an association of companies, such as an *industry* association,
- or an academic or *scientific* organisation.

Knowing these facts, service suppliers such as destination managers will have a better understanding of the position, influence and interests of presidents, executive directors, secretaries, etc., as well as of likely patterns of action of these organisations.

Events of Non-Profit Organisations/Associations

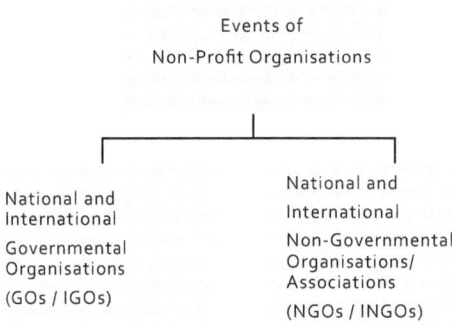

Figure 5: Events of non-profit organisations

The organisational structure of smaller associations depends completely on a voluntary executive committee and administration, whereas major associations, which are sometimes supported by firms from their related industry, have a professional administration, though the executive committee is also still made up of elected volunteers.

Compared to the trade fair market (see next section), the *meeting market is characterised* by:

- more events
- more initiators
- smaller events
- more and smaller venues
- more destinations which are able to host a meeting successfully.

Therefore, in the last decade, the meeting segment has increasingly come into the focus of second- and third-tier cities in China, which cannot offer the venue capacities and hotel rooms of big exhibition cities. Nevertheless, these cities can offer many other success factors, convincing organisers to take their meeting to such places. This segment, together with the corporate segment, will presumably show the strongest growth rate in China's event market.

7 Trade fairs and exhibitions

Trade fairs and exhibitions were the first type of events to be successfully implemented after the policy of opening and reform in China. There are many understandings and definitions of trade fairs and exhibitions. However, the following are generally and widely used:

– *Trade Fairs* are market events, which predominantly attract *trade and business visitors*. Trade fairs are business events.
– *Exhibitions* are market events, which predominantly attract the *general public*. Exhibitions are consumer events (cf. UFI, AUMA).

In addition, American phrases such as "trade show" are also in use and are mostly used for trade fair. In international practice, however, often both terms overlap, as many events are a mix between business events and consumer events. Therefore, it is advisable to have a closer look at the trade fair statistics that organisers provide.

7.1 Functions of trade fairs and exhibitions

The core functions of every trade fair or exhibition is to connect supply with demand, provide information, and show technical trends and developments of the industry, all in one time and at one place, using face-to-face communication. Trade fair companies in their role as initiator and organiser have to create a temporary market or a communication platform for the respective industry, where supply and demand can interact with each other. In other words, trade fair companies have two different target groups or clients: the companies, ("exhibitors") offering their products and services, and the potential customers/buyers of the products and services the exhibitors supply. These are the *trade fair visitors*.

Only if the trade fair organiser is in a position to attract enough potential visitors (the target group/clients of the exhibitors) will the exhibitors be satisfied. And only if enough leading companies from the expected industries exhibit their products will the visitors be satisfied. If both target groups are satisfied, the trade fair will be a success. In general, trade fairs can fulfil specific *business* functions, *economic* functions and *social* functions (cf. AUMA).

7.2 Location factors of trade fair cities

As mentioned before, the location of a trade fair is one of extreme importance when it comes to the success of trade fairs, as this is the place where exhibitors and visitors have to get together to exchange goods and information. Especially when offering non-mobile services such as hotels, congress centres and exhibition grounds are important factors of the marketing mix of these events. The full meaning of these factors become obvious when investors plan a new centre, or when organisers select a location for their next trade fair, or when exhibitors decide to participate in a trade fair. Moreover, trade fair locations (cities) are in competition among each other. Therefore they must offer their clients special benefits that other locations cannot offer.

In principle, there are three natural types of trade fair locations:

- *Locations where producers of one or more industries are located, as p*roducers can be potential exhibitors
- *Locations where customers are located* (trade, commercial users, private consumers). This applies to big agglomerations, such as Shanghai, Beijing, or Germany
- *Locations where exhibitions are easy to reach by exhibitors and visitors, and are well organised.*

Successful trade fair locations

trade fair locations
├── Place of production (exhibitors)
├── Place of demand (visitors)
└── Place of organisation

© Prof.Helmut Schwägermann, HS Osnabrück

Figure 6: Successful trade fair locations

Of course any combination of these three factors will be favourable.

All German trade fair cities, but also many major Chinese trade fair cities, can boast these combined advantages. Many (not only in China) newly established trade fair centres, however, have to analyse if they can really offer at least one of these advantages over their competitors. If not, they will have to be subsidised for the rest of their existence!

7.3 Trade fair companies: different tasks, different business models

In general, trade fair grounds are financed and built by the government or the municipality in order to generate the desired commercial, economic and social regional effects as described before. In most countries, a publicly owned, but privately operated company (Ltd, GmbH or similar) is set up as a management company in order to run this particular property and to rent it out to organisers.

Trade fair companies fulfil two different tasks:

– They own and/or manage exhibition grounds and rent the halls to exhibition organisers. Usually these companies are owned and controlled by the government or the municipality.
– They plan and organise trade fairs. In this case, they are called trade fair organisers, or exhibition producers.

Two different business models among trade fair companies can be found around the world. We call these the Anglo-American Business Model and the German Business Model.

7.3.1 The Anglo-American Business Model

The Anglo-American Business Model is characterised by the above-mentioned two types of companies: the management companies of the exhibition halls rent halls and services to independent organisers, be it private companies or associations or, like in China, to other government-controlled organisations.

This model is widely used in Great Britain, the USA and Australia, as well as in China and other Asian countries.

Anglo-American Business Model

Figure 7: The Anglo-American Business Model of trade fair companies

The advantage for the owner is that they can concentrate on their core business and require fewer personnel. The disadvantage for the owner is that they have only limited influence on the topics, the quality and the quantity of the trade fairs and exhibitions which take place on their exhibition grounds. The advantage for the organisers is that they can choose the best possible location for their trade fair.

7.3.2 The German Business Model

In contrast to the Anglo-American Business Model, trade fair companies in Germany normally have a "double role": on the one hand, they are owners and management companies of the exhibition grounds. Generally they are organised in the form of a private or publicly traded limited-liability company (GmbH or AG). The owner of the majority of the shares is the respective city or the federal state in which they are located. This also expresses the strong interest of regional politicians in trade fairs and exhibitions as a tool of regional economic development.

German exhibition ground owners not only rent out the exhibition space to other "independent" organisers, but they themselves are also initiators/producers of trade fairs and organise their own events on their own exhibition grounds. German trade fair companies see their role not only as a supplier of space, but also as special communication consultants for the exhibiting industry and their exhibitors.

This differentiation is of course very important to understand the goals and strategies of different trade fair companies: the trade fair company owning the grounds behaves as a real estate company *and* as a communication company.

The advantage of this model is that German trade fair companies can exert more influence on the industries and topics of the exhibition portfolio on their own grounds, because they are also creator and initiator of trade fairs and exhibitions. The disadvantage is that some of their own events might be more appropriately located elsewhere, but they cannot be flexible in changing the location to somewhere else in the country. Nevertheless, for more than two decades, German trade fair companies have also exported their trade fair concepts to locations in other countries (see internationalisation strategies).

The German Business Model

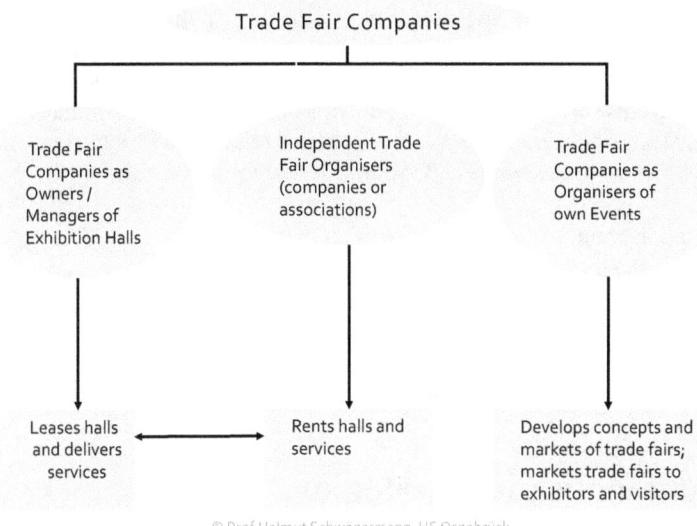

Figure 8: The German Business Model of trade fair companies

While Germany's exhibition industry is often referred to as the "Kingdom of Exhibitions", in China, the Anglo-American Business Model is the rule nonetheless, and venue management companies restrict themselves to managing the venue. Until recently, only the CIEC in Beijing (China International Exhibition Center), which is operated by CCPIT, adopted the German Business Model. All other exhibition centres in China were operated along the lines of the Anglo-American Business Model. The management of the recently opened National Exhibition and Convention Center in Shanghai Hongqiao as well as the one in Tianjin, which is still under construction seem to apply however the German Business Model.

7.4   Trade fair associations and statistics

The world's leading trade show organisers and exhibition grounds owners, as well as major national and international exhibition associations, and selected partners of the exhibition industry, are organised in the UFI (*Union des Foires Internationales*, or "Union of International Fairs" in English). The UFI represents 670 members from 83 countries, and the association has awarded its quality label on 930 trade fairs and exhibitions organised by its members. As one of its tasks, UFI publishes several studies and statistics on the international exhibition industry (cf. www.ufi.org). The AUMA (*Ausstellungs- und Messe-Ausschuss der Deutschen Wirtschaft e. V.*), the Association of the German Trade Fair Industry, represents the interests of exhibitors, organisers and visitors to trade fairs. The association was founded in 1907 in Berlin. The AUMA offers several studies and statistics on the German and the international exhibition market (see also article in this handbook).

The increasing number of events have led to complex problems for exhibitors in the selection of the right trade fair and the monitoring of trade fair success. A more systematic approach to trade fair planning and monitoring their success is necessary, rather than making decisions based on intuition. Comparability and reliability of trade fair statistics is needed in many nations, including in China. In Germany, the FKM, the Society for the Voluntary Control of Trade Fair and Exhibition Statistics, was established in 1965. The FKM is closely linked to AUMA. It has established uniform rules for the collection of exhibitor, space and visitor statistics as well as for visitor structures and makes sure that a certified public accountant audits compliance with rules. As a result, comparisons of different events are simple and reliable. With statistical material on the numbers and structure of exhibitors and visitors, the exhibitor can:

- obtain basic information about the topic and size of an event
- find out to what extent the target groups will be present at the trade fair
- gather comparative data for individual trade fair success monitoring (cf. FKM).

Together with the discussion about the need of a national trade fair association in China, this topic seems to be one of the hottest in China today.

7.5 Internationalisation strategies

Germany is one of the leading countries in international trade worldwide. The trade fair sector accordingly reflects this situation and has developed different strategies to foster the global impact of their activities. In general, one can differentiate between "incoming" and "outgoing" strategies.

"Incoming" strategies
An incoming strategy is applied if the trade fair company tries to attract international exhibitors and visitors to their leading trade fairs in Germany (*Leitmessen*) in order to make them truly international marketplaces for communication and trade. This has been the dominating strategy of German trade fair companies for at least the last 50 years, if not before. For these purposes, all German trade fair companies have established information offices or representatives abroad, and some have even established subsidiaries. The main task of these has been to research, contact and convince local government and associations to organise national stands at German trade fairs and to convince exhibitors and visitors to take part in these trade fairs.

"Outgoing" strategies
As one type of an outgoing strategy, German trade fair companies organise *"National Stands"* at foreign trade fairs that have some connection, such as some particular market competence, to their own trade fairs in Germany. Alternatively, trade fair companies sometimes organise their own events abroad. In these cases, they implement and organise exhibitions, most often

as satellite events to their own exhibitions. Different trade fair companies also use different branding strategies. Last but not least, trade fair companies sometimes build and manage their own exhibition centre abroad, for example the Shanghai New International Expo Center (SNIEC). German trade fair companies in AUMA organise around 220 of their *own events each year i*n key foreign growth regions, especially in Asia, North America and South America, as well as in Eastern Europe (see also Koetter, Spinger in this handbook). The Chinese exhibition and meeting industry is now starting to apply similar strategies.

8 Corporate events

Companies have also increasingly used events for internal and external communication. Events that are initiated and organised by companies are often called "corporate events". We can differentiate between internal and external corporate events (Figure 9).

Internal and external corporate events

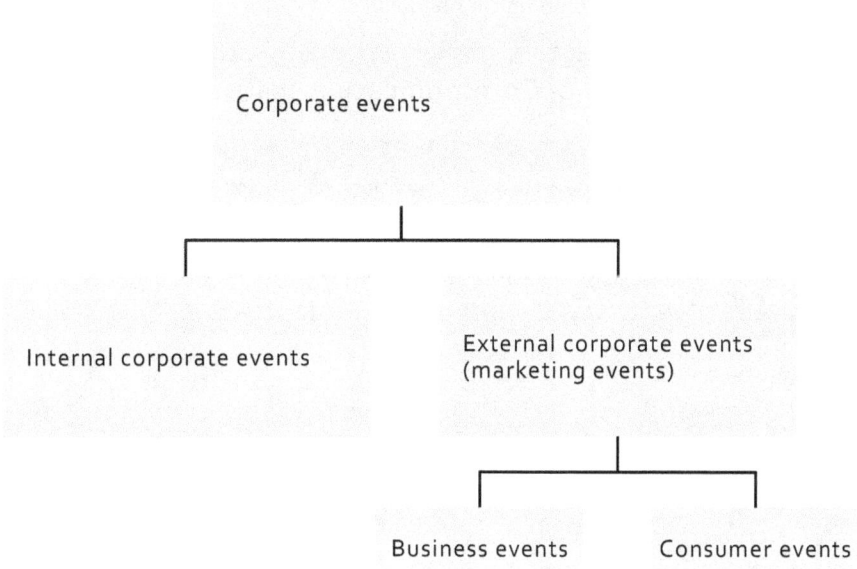

Figure 9: Corporate events

8.1 Internal corporate events

At internal corporate events, employees of the company are the participants. These events are mainly used for the dissemination of information, education, team-building and motivation. Internal problems are discussed face-to-face, new technical solutions are introduced, and employees are trained for specific skills or motivated to take on new tasks. Examples include board meetings, staff meetings, sales and marketing events, technical meetings, training/educational events, and incentive meetings and travel.

8.2 External corporate events, or marketing events

Corporate events also play an increasing role in the marketing strategy of companies. External corporate events aim at the market in which the company operates. They are therefore often called *"marketing events"*. These events are used as special *target group-focused* communication tools, Participants include the external target groups of the company, such as customers (private or professional), dealers, the press and other stakeholders, as well as investment companies, banks, government or other financiers. Examples include product presentations, dealer events, sales events, open house events, corporate exhibitions, user meetings, roadshows, shareholder meetings, dealer/customer trainings, press conferences and incentive events and travel. Companies use these unique face-to-face communication tools to position their company as well as their products or services in the market, building up trust and customer relations.

The following chart classifies events as communication tools, like advertising, PR or face-to-face sales. We have to acknowledge that companies and organisation have many ways of communicating with their market. Figure 10 shows the advantages and disadvantages of events in comparison to other communication tools.

Characteristics of Communication Instruments

Media	Traditional Communication	Live Communication	Web-based Communication
Communication Instruments	TV, Radio, Newspaper	Trade Fairs, Events	Websites, E-Mails, Chats, Forum, Blogs, Social Media, etc.
Reach	•••	•	•••
Fixed to location	•	•••	-
Fixed to time	•	•••	•
Intensity of contact	•	•••	•
Personal contact	•	•••	••
Control of environment	•	••	•
Cost of contacts	••	•••	•
Interaction	•	•••	•••
Experience	•	•••	•
Emotionality	••	•••	•
Multisensuality	•	•••	-

Source: Kirchgeorg et al., Live Communication Management, 2009, p .22, weak (•) strong (••) very strong (•••)

Figure 10: Characteristics of communication tools (cf. Kirchgeorg et al.: 22)

Traditional communication tools, like TV and print advertising, as well as web-based communication tools can easily reach millions of potential buyers! TV as well as print advertising both try to get more interaction with the viewer via televoting and social media. Web-based communication can also establish interaction and some sort of personal contact. Therefore, event initiators have to concentrate on the strengths of this special tool of live communication.

The strength of live communication is its *uniqueness,* which sometimes also seems to be a disadvantage (limited time, fixed to location). In addition, initiators/organisers have to take full advantage of direct personal contact, offering the guest/visitor an emotionally based unique experience by utilising all aspects of a multi-sensual approach (i. e. hearing, seeing, touching, tasting, smelling).

Social media of all kinds, like facebook, twitter and LinkedIn in the Western world, or Wechat, weibo and renren in China as well as programmes for mobile marketing are becoming increasingly relevant when marketing services, products and events. This occurs by building up a community of interest very quickly. Therefore event managers have to be aware how these media work and what the advantages and disadvantages are. They have to be able to use and to integrate them into live events, thus creating a new type of *hybrid event.*

9 Summary

The event market is a quite recent, but complex and ever-changing market. This article has attempted to suggest some useful segmentation criteria and has given a general overview of various aspects of events as communication tools and creators of economic and non-economic regional effects.

The article has concentrated on aspects for business events and their respective organisers. It pointed to some special developments in the Chinese event industry and has given some suggestion for further research.

10 Literature

AUMA. www.auma.de

AUMA (2009). Die gesamtwirtschaftliche Bedeutung von Messen und Ausstellungen in Deutschland.

Convention Industry. www.glossary.conventionindustry.org

FKM (Society for the Voluntary Control of Trade Fair and Exhibition Statistics). www.fkm.de.

Kirchgeorg et al. (2009). Live Communication Management.

UFI, Union des Foires Internationales. www.ufinet.org.

The event market China: A global view

The development of Asia-Pacific's meetings industry

Hamid, Noor Ahmad,
Lu, Margaret Kwai Ting

亚太地区会议产业的发展

The global meetings industry has become one of the key segments on which to concentrate for destinations throughout the world. This article provides an overview of the international association meetings market and a statistical profile of the Asia-Pacific region by drawing on data from the International Congress and Convention Association (ICCA), explaining destination attractiveness in the context of hosting meetings in cities. It examines the origin of the term "M.I.C.E.", which is ubiquitously adopted today, and explores its links with the wider tourism industry in various Asia-Pacific cities. From the development of meetings and trends to the wide-ranging nature of the subject of meetings, this article analyses the growth of the industry in the Asia-Pacific region over the past 20 years (and beyond), framing the recent and ever-changing meetings landscape.

全球会议产业已经成为世界目的地极力发展的最为重要的产业之一。本文通过对ICCA有关会议数据的分析，概述了亚太地区国际协会会议市场及统计数据特征，并以此体现了各个城市在主办会议方面的吸引力。本文同时考证了被广泛使用的术语"M.I.C.E"的起源，探讨了在亚太地区的几个城市中该术语与更为广泛的旅游产业之间的关系。文章还分析了亚太地区会议产业在过去20年甚至更久的成长历程，从会议的发展、趋势到会议主题的广泛性，并勾勒出了当前日新月异的会展产业的结构与特征。

1 Introduction

This paper aims to give an overview of the meetings industry with a specific focus on the Asia Pacific region. The content of the paper is mainly based on the source of ICCA statistics, to capture a snapshot of the international association meetings market from the past 20 years, from 1993 to 2014. Divided into four parts, we will look at the MICE industry in this region as a whole, the meetings industry performance, the trends for Asia Pacific and the top convention destinations, and close with information about the destinations' competitiveness.

According to the Convention Industry Council (CIC), the acronym "MICE" stands for "Meeting, Incentive, Conference/Congress, & Exhibition (CIC 2011)". It is probably one of the most widely used terms in Asia and other parts of the world, such as Africa, Latin America and the Middle East. It encompasses the business-oriented segment that involves obligatory (or non-discretionary) travel. The first usage of the term was non-attributable, but it is believed that this jargon was probably adopted as formal terminology by the tourism organisation back in late 1970s or early 1980s. All along, the leisure tourism-oriented market was the key activity managed by tourism organisations until the MICE industry emerged as one of the largest and high-yield sectors with positive economic multiplier effects to the community. In response to this, there has been a first big shift in strategic planning in many tourism organisations to set up a specific division to manage promotional activity for this market segment, as well as to formulate new growth strategies for the long-term success of this industry. However, there has been an industry-driven initiative recently to drop the "MICE Market" label and use "The Meetings Industry" instead. Hence, this market segment is commonly known as "Business Events" in Australia and New Zealand, and the "Meetings Industry" in Europe and the United States.

The importance of hosting a convention to a city has emerged as a crucial strategic decision for stakeholders of a destination since the number of meetings and attendees as well as spending have a tremendous economic impact on the destination. For this reason, most tourism organisations in Asia have set up a specific entity to cater to the broader MICE market. Below are a number of examples of entities in Asia that handle the MICE market:

- Chinese Taipei
  MeetTaiwan is an organisation established by the Bureau of Foreign Trade (Ministry of Economic Affairs) and implemented by Taiwan External Trade Development Council

- Hong Kong
  Meetings & Exhibitions Hong Kong is a division of the Hong Kong Tourism Board

- Japan
  Japan Convention Bureau is a division of Japan National Tourism Organisation

- Malaysia
  Malaysia Convention & Exhibition Bureau is a fully-fledged entity established by the Ministry of Tourism

- Singapore
  Singapore Exhibition & Convention Bureau is a group of Singapore Tourism Board

- Sri Lanka
  Sri Lanka Convention Bureau is a division of Sri Lanka Tourism

- Thailand
  Thailand Convention & Exhibition Bureau is a public organisation established by Royal Decree

Likewise, other destinations have a division within their organisation to manage MICE activities, such as:

- Australia, under Tourism Australia
- India, under the Ministry of Tourism, Government of India
- Indonesia, under the Ministry of Tourism & Creative Economy
- China P.R., under the China National Tourism Administration
- Macau, under Macau Government Tourist Office (MGTO) and Macau Trade & Investment Promotion Institute (IPIM)
- New Zealand, under Tourism New Zealand (TNZ) and Convention & Incentive New Zealand (CINZ)
- The Philippines, under Tourism Promotions Board (TPB)
- Republic of Korea, under the Korea Tourism Organisation

To further illustrate the point made in Section 1.1, we can look at the history of the establishment of the Asian Association of Convention and Visitors Bureau (AACVB). AACVB was formed in 1983 to enhance regional cooperation by developing Asia's convention capabilities. This leads to the concerted promotion of the region as an attractive destination (AACVB n. d.).

The seven founding members of AACVB are as follows:

- Hong Kong Tourist Association
- Directorate General of Tourism Indonesia
- Korea National Tourism Organisation
- Tourist Development Corporation Malaysia
- Ministry of Tourism, Philippines
- Singapore Tourist Promotion Board
- Tourism Authority of Thailand

As "co-opetition" (an industry term for cooperation + competition) among Asian cities increased, we saw how the MICE market gained prominence in this region and how, eventually these tourism offices in Asia, with a division catering exclusively to the needs and requirements of various travel segments that include MICE later evolved into fully-fledged entities. This integral part of segmentation within the tourism office may well explain why the term MICE has been commonly used in Asia since the 1970s or 1980s.

In China, the main thrust to develop, manage and supervise tourism activity comes under the ambit of the China National Tourism Administration (CNTA). The China National Tourism Administration, founded in 1949, is China's national tourism agency responsible for worldwide tourism marketing and promotion for China. Its mandate was to promote China as a premier tourist destination, as well as a hub for MICE segment. However, like other destinations in the Asia Pacific region, China never lags behind in this global race between convention visitor bureaux; Haikou Municipal Convention & Exhibition Bureau was the first convention & exhibition bureau in the nation, set up in 2012 (Haikoutour n. d.). The most prominent city convention bureaux in China are Beijing Municipal Commission of Tourism Development and Shanghai Municipal Tourism Administration. The MICE segment gained prominence with the establishment of the China MICE Cities Alliance in 2012, which consists of eight key Chinese cities, notably Beijing, Shanghai, Tianjin, Chengdu, Hangzhou, Kunming, Sanya and Xi'an (Donovan 2012). They all joined forces to increase China's share in the international MICE market.

"What's in a name?" Clearly, this Shakespearean quote echoed in today's industry, the names of things do not matter. The fact that our industry is either called MICE, Business Events or the Meetings Industry is neither wrong nor right. All that matters is how each city or country prioritises this business segment and promotes their destination positioning strategy. Against this background, we will gain a better understanding of the overview of the meetings industry in this Asia Pacific region.

In order to avoid confusion, the "meetings industry" in this paper will be referred to as the international association meetings market in particular. Generally, two global bodies are dedicated to collating data on the international association meetings field, namely the International Congress and Convention Association (ICCA) and the Union of International Associations (UIA). The distinct difference between these two associations lies in the fact that both organisations adopt different parameters for "international association meetings". As such, this paper will focus on the meetings industry from the perspective of ICCA, because references will be made based on information provided by this association.

2 The meetings industry

The international meetings market can be segmented in many different ways – by the size of the meetings, the kind of people who visit the meetings, the purpose of the meetings, and so on. However, the main criterion a supplier uses to segment the market is by the initiator of the meeting; in other words, the meeting planners. When segmenting the international meetings market by initiator, two primary markets can be defined:

– Corporate meetings
– Non-corporate meetings

Non-corporate meetings are subdivided into international governmental organisations and international non-governmental organisations.

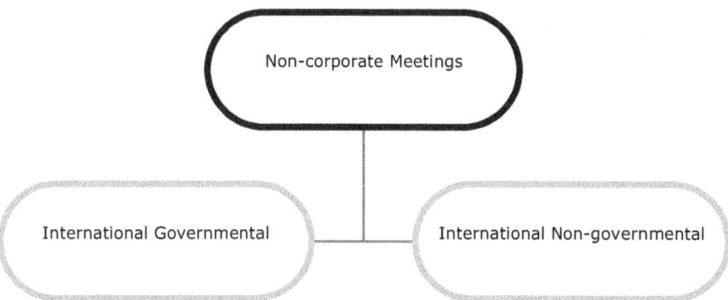

Figure 1: Segmentation of non-corporate meetings.

The latter are referred to as associations. Association meetings are categorised by the areas where meetings are held, for instance, those held at the national, regional or international level. Thus, in this paper, the term "meeting" is used primarily to examine regularly occurring, regionally or internationally rotating association meetings, which is under the area of expertise of the International Congress and Convention Association (ICCA). The foundation and comparison of the meetings industry in the Asia Pacific region will therefore be based on ICCA's statistics, the exclusive information of which is generated from its association statistics.

In this regard, it is important to note that ICCA has stipulated specific criteria concerning what they refer to as international association meetings, which are defined as meetings organised as international associations with the following characteristics:

- Attendance : A minimum of 50 delegates
- Rotation : Rotation between at least three countries and
- Frequency : Regular occurrence

The overview of the meetings market presented in this paper is based on a fifty-year span, from 1963 and 2013, in order to gain a big picture of the region's overall performance. The figures mentioned below were provided by ICCA.

3 The trend for Asia Pacific

The trend for the meetings industry will be examined through four key determinant areas, namely:

- The number of meetings recorded over the last 20 years
- The number of participants recorded over the last 20 years
- Top subject matters addressed by international association meetings
- Professionalism through global membership

3.1 The number of meetings recorded over the last 20 years

One of the pragmatic ways to evaluate a region's performance is to compare the number of meetings held in a region to its global counterparts – Asia Pacific, Europe, North America, Latin America and Africa. This figure explains the region's meeting attractiveness within the context of hosting a larger/smaller number of meetings. The number of meetings held globally has skyrocketed from 7,513 meetings in 1994 to 11,685 meetings in 2013. For the Asia Pacific region (including Asia, the Middle East and Oceania), the number of meetings increased gradually over the last 20 years, from 20.13 per cent in 1994 to 21.07 per cent in 2013. Despite a paltry 0.94 percentage of growth, this is significant in terms of the actual number of meetings. In 1994, the Asia Pacific region hosted a total of 1,513 meetings. However, the number of meetings held jumped to 2,463 in 2013, an increase of 950. This surge in the number of meetings indicates strong performance in two areas: regional rotation meetings and international/world rotation meetings. Interestingly, this positive increase correlates with the rapid economic growth experienced in the Asia Pacific region, driven by economic giants such as China, the Middle East and South-East Asian countries, as well as Australia.

Tab. 1: Comparison of the number of meetings over the last 20 years. (ICCA 2014a)

Region	# 1994	1994 (in percentage)	# 2013	2013 (in percentage)
Asia Pacific*	1,513	20.13 per cent	2,463	21.07 per cent
Europe	4,124	54.89 per cent	6,313	54.02 per cent
North America	1,036	13.78 per cent	1,291	11.04 per cent
Latin America	638	8.49 per cent	1,243	10.63 per cent
Africa	202	2.68 per cent	375	3.20 per cent
Total	*7,513*	*100 per cent*	*11,685*	*100 per cent*

Note: *Asia Pacific includes Asia, the Middle East and Oceania

It is important to note that there has also been a trend towards a healthy increase between 1994 and 2013 in other regions such as Latin America (from 8.49 to 10.63 per cent) and Africa (from 2.68 to 3.20 per cent).

However, the regions of Europe (from 54.89 to 54.02 per cent) and North America (from 13.78 to 11.04 per cent) have experienced a slight drop since the financial crisis hit the world economy in 2008.

3.2 The number of participants recorded over the last 20 years

The number of registered delegates for international association meetings held in the Asia Pacific region (which includes Asia, the Middle East and Oceania) increased from 721,382 to 1,074,752 delegates between 1994 and 2013, or from 22.51 to 23.37 per cent, a small increase of 0.86 per cent. Similarly, other regions such as Europe, Latin America and Africa also experienced a similar growth rate at a 0.95, 2.36 and 0.97 per cent, respectively. The only region that experienced a fall in delegate attendance is North America (−5.41 per cent).

Tab. 2: Comparison in terms of numbers of participants over the last 20 years. (ICCA 2014a)

Region	# 1994	1994 (in percentage)	# 2013	2013 in percentage
Asia Pacific*	721,382	22.51 per cent	1,074,752	23.37 per cent
Europe	1,577,722	49.24 per cent	2,307,784	50.19 per cent
North America	546,375	17.05 per cent	547,619	11.91 per cent
Latin America	287,123	8.96 per cent	520,711	11.32 per cent
Africa	71,018	2.21 per cent	146,414	3.18 per cent
Total	*3,203,620*	*100 per cent*	*4,597,280*	*100 per cent*

Note: *Asia Pacific includes Asia, the Middle East and Oceania

The fact that the Asia Pacific region received 353,370 more delegates in 2013 than it did 20 years earlier should come as no surprise. After all, the increase in delegates corresponds to the above-mentioned fact (Section 3.1) that the number of international association conventions held there has grown significantly every single year.

3.3 Subjects matters addressed by international association meetings

The association market covers a wide range of meeting types and categories: medical meetings (the largest segment); scientific; other academic; trade organisations; professional bodies; social groupings. In terms of size, budget, duration and complexity, there are massive variations between and also within categories. In this context, it is essential to identify which meetings were the key contributors for academic growth. In 2013, the top meeting subject dominating the Asia Pacific region was Technology, followed by Science, Medical Sciences, Industry, Education, Economics, Transport & Communications, Management, Social Sciences and Commerce. This simply illustrates that the region's growth is very much driven by its dominant economic activities, and advancement and development of intellectual capital in these subject matters.

Tab. 3: Subject matters for international association meetings in the Asia Pacific region in 2013. (ICCA 2013)

No.	Subject	Number of meetings in 2013	In percentage
1	Technology	574	18.62 per cent
2	Science	473	15.34 per cent
3	Medical Sciences	459	14.89 per cent
4	Industry	234	7.59 per cent
5	Education	158	5.12 per cent
6	Economics	128	4.15 per cent
7	Transport and Communications	124	4.02 per cent
8	Management	122	3.95 per cent
9	Social Sciences	106	3.43 per cent
10	Commerce	105	3.40 per cent
11	Others	599	19.43 per cent
	Total	**3,082**	**100 per cent**

3.4 Professionalism through global membership

Apart from data analysis, one of the ways to identify the trend for the meetings industry in the Asia Pacific region is to involve the supply chain or suppliers. Without a doubt, it is of paramount importance to have the active participation of key suppliers in the meetings industry or the "push factor", to further promote the region, and to encourage international meeting planners to bring their meetings to this part of the world. A number of global associations have recorded growth in terms of membership; again, we will use the International Congress and Convention Association (ICCA) as the benchmark. As seen from the table below, ICCA's membership recruitment in the Asia Pacific region grew from 95 members in 1998 to 208 members in 2014 (1 September 2014). With a remarkable growth rate of 119 per cent, the Asia Pacific Chapter outstrips both the Central European and Mediterranean Chapters, making it the largest of the 11 chapters worldwide.

Tab. 4: Number of ICCA members in the Asia Pacific Chapter in 1998 and 2014. (ICCA 2014b)

No.	Country	1998	2014 (Sep)	+/−
1	Australia	14	30	+16
2	China PR	1	42	+41
3	Chinese Taipei	3	11	+8
4	Hong Kong, China PR	7	6	−1
5	India	9	18	+9
6	Indonesia	11	7	−4
7	Japan	24	27	+3
8	Macao, China PR	1	6	+5
9	Malaysia	7	11	+4
10	New Zealand	1	7	+6
11	Philippines	4	4	–
12	Republic of Korea	4	21	+17
13	Singapore	3	9	+6
14	Sri Lanka	1	1	–
15	Thailand	5	9	+4
	Total	95	208	+113

According to the chart below, ICCA membership in the Asia Pacific region is dominated by the Destination Marketing Sector (34 per cent), represented by national and city convention bureaux. The remaining breakdown of members is as follows (ICCA 2014b):

− Destination Marketing Sector 34 per cent
− Venue Sector 31 per cent
− Meetings Management Sector 26 per cent
− Meetings Support Sector 7 per cent
− Honorary members 1 per cent
− Transport Sector 1 per cent

The other two membership sectors that have gained experienced a similar rate of growth are the Venue Sector and the Meetings Management Sector. The former comprises convention centres and hotels with meetings facilities; the latter represents the group of Professional Congress Organisers (PCO) and Destination Management Companies (DMC). We also identified a gradual increase in the Meetings Support sector, which includes research institutes, media practitioners, consultant firms, exhibition companies, meeting app developers and audiovisual companies.

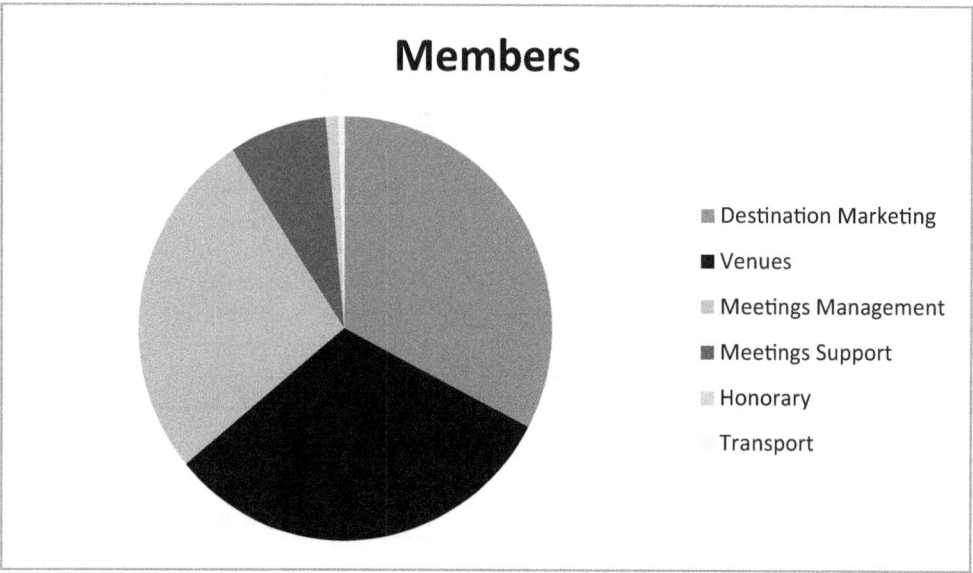

Figure 2: ICCA Asia Pacific Membership Distribution by sectors of membership, as of 1 September 2014. (ICCA 2014b)

In 1998, the ICCA Asia Pacific membership base represented just 37 cities within the region, with Japan and India forming the boundaries to the east and west, and China and New Zealand representing the northernmost and southernmost boundaries. However, there has been a steady growth in membership over the years, with the total number of members rising to 208 in 2014, covering 80 cities in the region. This vast distribution explains how smaller, second and third-level cities with unlimited potential have risen in profile, waiting to tap into this emerging business segment. As smaller cities increasingly value the importance and benefits of international association meetings, they start to develop their supplier chain, including new convention centres and hotels. They also set up city convention bureaux as part of their efforts to penetrate the market due to their awareness of the need for competitive infrastructure and a sophisticated business environment.

4 The top convention destinations

The issue of convention destination attributes has recently received considerable attention in academic literature. This section of the paper therefore looks at the top convention destinations in the Asia Pacific region. The content is based on ICCA statistics on the international association meetings market.

Tab. 5: The top ten countries in the Asia Pacific region in 2013. (ICCA 2013)

No.	Rank in the world	Country	Number of meetings in 2013
1	# 7	Japan	342
2	# 8	China PR	340
3	# 12	Republic of Korea	260
4	# 16	Australia	231
5	# 21	Singapore	175
6	# 27	India	142
7	# 29	Thailand	136
8	# 33	Chinese Taipei	122
9	# 35	Malaysia	117
10	# 37	Indonesia	108

Tab. 6: The top ten cities in the Asia Pacific region in 2013. (ICCA 2013)

No	Rank in the world	City	Number of meetings in 2013
1	# 6	Singapore	175
2	# 9	Seoul	125
3	# 18	Beijing	105
4	# 20	Sydney	93
5	# 20	Bangkok	93
6	# 23	Hong Kong, China PR	89
7	# 26	Tokyo	79
8	# 28	Taipei	78
9	# 29	Shanghai	72
10	# 33	Kuala Lumpur	68

We can see from the destination ranking that north Asian countries take the lead, with Japan, China and the Republic of Korea as the top three premier business destinations, all celebrated for their distinct culture and flavours of the Orient. In terms of the ranking for cities, the city state of Singapore scooped the top position as Asia Pacific's leading convention city. Seoul was runner-up with 85 meetings, followed by Beijing with 65. Notable performers in the 2014 rankings include Sydney, Bangkok, Hong Kong, Tokyo, Taipei, Shanghai and Kuala Lumpur. Since ranking levels rise and fall, the statistics should be read in the light of the types of meetings that took place in the respective countries/cities.

5 Closing – competitiveness of destinations

Each destination differs with regard to what makes it competitive. Destinations can emerge and participate in the international meetings market if they are capable of innovation and have the ability to be different. Although the meetings industry has evolved and progressed tremendously in the past, opportunities lie ahead for the Asia Pacific region. With the emergence of exciting new destinations every year, the industry should be perceived as being in its infancy, with so many destinations, countries or cities, all learning and sharpening their convention capabilities on how best to win in their quest for a bigger piece of the international MICE business pie. This is particularly the case when it comes to the international association meetings market segment, since we are able to examine the growth and identify the level of activity in this market based on reliable statistics and information provided by ICCA. Without a doubt, the outlook for the Asia Pacific region remains rosy, bearing in mind that so many other cities are expected to join force in developing their convention potential. We anticipate that the biggest soon-to-be players will be from the Pearl River Delta, which is also known as "magnate of megalopolis", Indian new cities and also emerging destinations within the Indochina region including Cambodia, Laos, Vietnam and Myanmar. This alone sets the bar high to pave the way for continued growth in the Asia Pacific region, the like of which we have never seen before.

6 Literature

AACVB (n. d.), *The Asian Association of Convention and Visitor Bureaus: Background and History*. Online: http://www.aacvb.org/background.html (accessed on 22 Sep. 2014)

CIC (2011), *Convention Industry Council: APEX Industry Glossary – 2011 Edition*. Online: http://www.conventionindustry.org/StandardsPractices/APEX/glossary.aspx (accessed on 23 Sep. 2014)

Donovan, Martin (15 Nov. 2012), *CEI Asia Talks to the City's Vice Chairman of Tourism Development*. Online: http://www.cei.asia/Article/323053,beijing-to-head-up-china-mice-alliance.aspx (accessed on 23 Sep. 2014)

Haikoutour (n. d.), *China's First Convention & Exhibition Bureau Set up in Haikou*. Online: http://en.haikoutour.gov.cn/view.asp?ArticleID=274 (accessed on 22 Oct. 2014)

ICCA (2013), *2013 ICCA Statistics Report*. Online: http://www.iccaworld.com/npps/story.cfm?nppage=3537 (accessed on 06 Oct. 2014)

ICCA (2014a), *ICCA 50-year statistics: International association meetings market shows exponential growth*. Online: http://www.iccaworld.com/npps/story.cfm?nppage=3823 (accessed on 06 Oct. 2014)

ICCA (2014b), *Membership Directory*. Online: http://members.iccaworld.com (accessed on 06 Oct. 2014)

China's MICE industry: Advancement through reform and opening

Chen, Zeyan

中国会展业在改革开放中前行

The continuous fast growth of China's MICE industry has promoted an interest to the international society since the Chinese reform starting in 1980s. The article aims to give an introduction on the development of China's MICE industry, covering the four aspects: understanding the MICE industry from the perspectives of government, enterprises and academia, the development of the MICE industry in the 21 century, the current situation of the industry, and the cooperation with overseas countries in the industry.

Firstly, the article explains the overall strategy of the Chinese government to develop the MICE industry, defines the three business categories, and discusses the common view on MICE concepts held by Chinese MICE academies. Secondly, the article lists the most important and representative events in the past 15 years. Thirdly, the article describes the current situation of the MICE industry through a series of data including the distribution of MICE cities in China, the number and size of exhibitions, branded exhibitions, venue construction, festivals and MICE educational institutions. Finally, the article introduces the investment, mergers and acquisitions in the Chinese MICE industry conducted by the overseas MICE companies, and their involvement into the MICE education is also discussed. Furthermore, the article describes the governmental administration of the overseas MICE enterprises and projects. Then, the article introduces the Chinese MICE enterprises doing the business overseas.

中国会展业从上世纪 80 年代改革开放以来持续高速的发展引起了国际社会的兴趣。本文从政企学界对会展的认识、21 世纪会展业的发展历程、会展业的实力以及会展业对外合作四个部分介绍了中国会展业的发展情况。

首先，文章介绍了中国政府对会展业发展的总体思路，划分了中国的三种会展企业类型，并探讨了学术界对会展概念的认识。第二部分，文章列举出过去 15 年间中国会展业发生的最重要和具有代表性的事件。第三部分，文章通过会展城市的分布、展览会的数量和面积、品牌展览会、场馆建设、会议节庆以及会展院校等一系列数据描述了会展业的发展现状。最后一部分，文章描述了海外会展公司在中国的投资、兼并与融合，在会展教育上的投入以及中国政府对涉外会展企业和会展项目的管理。文章还介绍了中国展览企业走出国门的情况。

1 Understanding the MICE industry from the perspectives of government, enterprises and academia

China's MICE industry is closely related to the operation of government administration, event companies and colleges. Their understanding of the MICE industry is reflected in their work.

1.1 Government regulations

The Chinese government publishes many regulations and policies on the MICE industry. The overall management method can be comprehended easily by considering the following four statements published by the related ministry.

Two national five-year plans

In March 2006, the National People's Congress (NPC) and the Communist Party of China (CPC) passed 'The outline of the 11th five-year plan' (Xinhuanet 2006). It states that the goal of the MICE industry is to plan the venue layout reasonably and to develop the MICE industry. Five years later, in March 2011, the NPC and CPC passed 'The outline of the 12th five-year plan' (MOFCOM.gov 2011a), which states that the goal of the MICE industry is to make healthy progress.

The national economy classification code

In November 2011, the General Administration of Quality Supervision, Inspection and Quarantine of the People's Republic of China (PRC) published the latest version of 'The national economy classification code' (National Standard No. GB/T 4754-2011) (CNIS.gov 2011). The MICE industry is one of around 900 small industries of the national economy with the code L7292. 'The national economy classification code' classifies the MICE industry as 'exhibitions and meetings which aim to improve the circulation of commodities, promotion, exhibition, trade talk, people-to-people communication, inter-corporate communication and international communication.' (STATS.gov 2013)

Documents from the National Bureau of Statistics of the PRC

In June 2012, the National Bureau of Statistics of the PRC published a 'Notice about the classification of culture and related industry (2012) by the National Bureau of Statistics' (code [2012] 63), which states that the 'organisation and service of events' includes 'the planning and organisation of theatrical performances, ceremonies, art and model shows, arts festivals, film festivals, non-governmental activities, commonwealth shows, exhibitions, and other kinds of large events' (WEHDZ.gov 2012). These kinds of events all belong to the culture industry and related industries.

Ministry of Commerce Guideline

In November 2011, the Ministry of Commerce published its 'Guideline for improving the MICE industry during the 12th five-year plan'. This document states that "The MICE industry is a crucial part of modern service industries". The MICE industry makes a large impact, related to many other industries, and has great potential. The level of its development reflects a country's comprehensive level of development concerning culture, economics and society. Developing the MICE industry will gather the stream of human capital, goods, capital and technology. It will also directly or indirectly improve the development of related and supporting industries. At the same time, improving the MICE industry will guide industrial upgrading and shifting, improve employment, stimulate consumption, optimise the allocation of resources and promote the development of innovation (MOFCOM.gov 2011a).

1.2 Business categories of the MICE industry

MICE companies in China are basically divided into three categories, which make up the MICE industry.

Organisation and planning of events

Some event companies in the cultural event field simply plan events. In other words, they offer plans only, whereas other companies execute event activities or undertake both planning and execution.

Venue offering and leasing

Various kinds of exhibition centres and meeting centres hire out exhibition halls and offer special services. They mainly manage their own venues, but sometimes also plan and organise events. A number of small-scale events are held in multi-purpose halls in hotels or stadiums.

Supporting services in the MICE industry

These companies represent many segments of the MICE chain. Supporting services include agents for inviting exhibitors, designing and building, transportation, media publicity, network communication, reception, field statistics, data audition, equipment leasing, the etiquette service, catering, traffic, travel, training, research and development and manufacturing exhibition models.

1.3 The common view held by MICE academies

MICE academies are responsible for teaching and conducting research on MICE. With regard to the subject of MICE, MICE academies currently hold the following basic common view:

MICE in a narrow and broad sense

In the past, the term 'MICE' in China only referred to the meeting and exhibition service industry in a narrow sense. Recently, academics have come to agree that the MICE industry also includes festivals, race competitions, incentive travels shows, and other events. In order to distinguish it from the narrow definition, academics also name it 'Great MICE'.

Generalisation as 'event'
The academic world and industry basically currently agree that the term 'event' can be used to generally describe 'Great MICE', i. e. all kinds of events.

The knowledge system of 'event'
According to the requirements of major tourism management (including event management) set by the teaching and guiding committee of the Ministry of Education, the 'state quality standard of teaching major Event Management' currently specifies the 'event knowledge system' as the following five parts: 'management, design, marketing, operation, risk'.

2 Development of China's MICE industry in the 21st century

China's MICE industry has so far undergone a distinct development in the 21st century. This article lists the most important and representative events of the past 15 years. These events show how the sequence and outline of China's MICE industry have developed.

2000: China developed the concept of the MICE economy
In October 2000, in a meeting held in Zhejiang Province, the Development and Research Centre under the State Council pointed out for the first time that 'China should greatly develop the MICE economy.' (She 2000) The background at that time was that China had proposed the direction of 'Readjusting industrial structure and developing greatly the third industry', after the Asian economic crisis. In fact, the MICE economy is the most promising and strongly growing third sector industry.

2001: the MICE industry opened fully when China joined the WTO
In November 2001, China successfully negotiated its entry to the WTO. China promised to fully open the MICE industry to foreign countries in the agreement, Appendix 9 (Xinhuanet 2004). Since then, the significant development of China's MICE industry has gathered pace.

2002: China confirmed the MICE code
In April 2002, the State Quality Supervision Bureau confirmed the position of the MICE industry for the first time in 'The national economy classification code' (National Standard Number: GB/T 4754–2001). The industry code at the time was L7491, which changed to L7292 at the end of 2011.

2003: the concept of MICE was introduced to the conference and exhibition industry

In the first China Conference and Exhibition Economy Forum organised by the Ministry of Commerce, China Council for the Promotion of International Trade and 'Economic Daily', the concept of MICE was first introduced to China's conference and exhibition industry in December 2003 (people.com 2003).

2004: approval of the first batch of establishing Event Management as a major subject

In June 2004, the content of major subjects in universities and colleges published by the Ministry of Education established the major subject of Event Management for the first time. The first two universities to establish Event Management as a major subject were Shanghai Normal University and Shanghai University of International Business and Economics.

2005: four goals proposed by the MICE industry

In January 2005, the international MICE organisations CCPIT (China Council for the Promotion of International Trade), UFI, IAEA and SISO organised the first CEFCO (China EXPO Forum for International Cooperation). At the opening ceremony, former Vice Premier of the State Council China, Mrs. Wu Yi, proposed the goals of China's MICE industry for the first time, namely industrialisation, marketisation, institutionalisation and internationalisation (MY.gov 2005).

2006: establishment of the China Convention Exhibition and Event Society (CCES)

In February 2006, the China Convention Exhibition and Event Society (CCES), permitted by the State Council, was established in Beijing. The CCES, managed by the Ministry of Commerce, was the first national research organisation that focused on the MICE industry in China. The establishment of CCES plays an important role in developing China's MICE industry (Liu 2006).

2007: UFI annual congress held in China for the first time

In November 2007, the Union of International Fairs (UFI) annual congress was held in China for the first time. This choice reflects UFI's great appreciation of the development of China's MICE industry. Before the congress began, a Chinese person was appointed to be in charge of the Asia-Pacific region.

2008: success of the Summer Olympic Games in Beijing

The Olympic Games is the most important sports event in the world. In August 2008, during the 29th Summer Olympic Games, other sports-related events were also held in Beijing. After a number of modifications, the news centre and fencing field are now being used as an International Convention Centre. It is one of the main venues for meetings and exhibitions in China.

2009: MICE had to be developed in order to overcome the financial crisis

2009 was the worst year of the financial crisis. A series of regulations published by the government, aimed at overcoming the crisis, pointed out that the 'increase in the consumption of vacations and events' was important for development (Wen and Zhang 2010). For this reason, considerable support was provided to various trade shows, general events and festival events. In order to counteract the sharp decline in demand, the government of Guangdong Province organised the 'Trade fair of export goods transfer into the domestic market' and the 'Guangdong products national tour trade show' (Xinhuanet 2009). Both of these trade fairs had a positive impact.

2010: China successfully hosted the World Expo

Between May and October 2010, China successfully hosted the World Expo in Shanghai. It attracted more than 70 million visitors, the largest number of visitors ever. In addition, Expo Shanghai was also record-breaking in many other aspects. The success of Expo Shanghai strongly supported the development of the MICE industry. Since then, China's event programme has improved considerably with regard to the level of novelties and plans, the design of stands, the management of venues, as well as the understanding and recognition of the Expo and events.

2011: the Ministry of Commerce strengthened the management of the MICE industry

The Ministry of Commerce is in charge of the national service industry, where the MICE industry also belongs. In June 2011, the Ministry of Commerce specially established a MICE Administration Office to strengthen the management of the national MICE industry. Following this, a number of policies were issued, such as 'Suggestions and advice for accelerating the development of the MICE industry during the 12th five-year-plan by the Ministry of Commerce' (MOFCOM.gov 2011b). These policies and regulations have been of paramount importance to accelerate the development of the MICE industry.

2012: important events before and after the 18th CPC National Congress

The 18th CPC National Congress was a very important congress. Event activities related to the 18th CPC National Congress were also important. Before the 18th CPC National Congress was held in November 2012, a photo exhibition entitled 'A glorious life through scientific development' was held at Beijing Exhibition Centre. Former General Secretary Hu Jintao and other state leaders visited the exhibition. General Secretary Xi Jinping and other state leaders mentioned the famous 'Chinese Dream' at the exhibition 'Towards recovery' in the National Museum of China after the 18th CPC National Congress.

2013: contract and regulation of the government's event programmes

After publishing 'The new state eight regulations' in December 2012, the State Council published a series of regulations which aim to compress and normalise the government's event programmes (You 2013). These regulations established by five departments of central government requested departments in all districts to put a stop to extravagance and waste, and encouraged frugal celebrations of national holidays and performances (Xinhuanet 2013). The Ministry of Finance, Government Offices Administration of the State Council, Government Offices Administration of the Central Committee of CPC jointly published 'The central government and state organs conference fees management approach' (MOF.gov 2013a). The Ministry of Commerce published 'Provision of implementing eight regulations and standard events' (MOF.gov 2013b).

2014: the development of the MICE industry enters a new stage

The number of government-organised events has fallen since 2014. At the same time, the interval of government-organised events has become shorter and the process of marketisation has also been accelerated. Interaction between competition and cooperation is increasing between different kinds of ownership systems such as state-owned business, private business and foreign business. The number of mergers of event programmes and event companies that aim to be listed on the stock market is growing. The development of the MICE industry is entering a new stage.

3 Current strength and level of China's MICE industry

The present status of China's MICE industry can be explained in the following five aspects.

3.1 Numerous MICE destinations throughout the country

The information collected by CCES indicates that various exhibitions were held in 124 cities in 2013. According to additional research by ACCH (the Alliance of China Conference Hotels), a total of 111 cities organised a variety of exhibitions, including international conferences, in 2012 (ACCH 2013).

With regard to the classification status, in all cities of mainland China, four municipalities, 11 sub-provincial cities, five cities listed independently in the state plan, 11 provincial capital cities and five capital cities from autonomous regions are MICE destinations. Hundreds of prefecture-level cities and dozens of county-level cities are also listed as MICE destinations. Based on these figures, China probably ranks top with such a large number of MICE destinations.

3.2 Data analysis for China's MICE industry in 2013

According to the CCES, all kinds of events and exhibitions were held in 124 cities in 2013, a 21.6 per cent increase over the previous year. The total number of events and exhibitions was 7,283, a rise of 2.8 per cent compared to the previous year. There was also a 16.5 per cent year-on-year increase in venue area, totalling 98.63 million square metres. In terms of the figures above, China ranks number 2, second only to the United States. Series of branding events and exhibitions projects

If we consider only UFI certification, there are 69 certified projects in mainland China (ranked third place in the UFI organisation), which can be recognised as branded projects (SCBEA.org 2015). There are also a number of renowned MICE projects that have not yet applied for UFI certification, e. g. China Import and Export Fair (aka Canton Trade Fair) and Beijing International Automotive Exhibition.

3.3 Globally remarkable venue construction

According to UFI statistics, within the six years from 2006 to 2011, 13 countries experienced a growth in venue area of over 50,000 square metres, totalling an approximate increase of 3.5 million square metres. China's increase of 1.6 million square metres accounts for 70 per cent of the total, which puts it in first place. Altogether, 1.12 million square metres, or 70 per cent, of this new venue space was created by building new venues. Enlargements of existing venues made up the remaining 30 per cent.

Based on UFI statistics for the world's 20 largest venues, venues from Guangzhou, Shanghai and Wuhan ranked fourth, 15th and 18th, respectively at the end of 2011. However, once a group of venues which are under construction is completed by 2015, seven or eight Chinese venues will be listed among the UFI's 20 world largest venues.

3.4 Development of conference and festival events

According to ICCA statistics, the number of international conferences hosted in China ranked 10th in the world and second in Asia in 2013.

In China, approximately 8,000 festival events are held every year. Some of these festivals, such as Beijing International Film Festival and Shanghai International Film Festival, have been gaining increasing influence world-wide; others with strong regional features, such as Shandong Weifang International Kite Festival and Jiangsu Xuyi Crayfish Festival, have also been certified by the International Festival and Events Association (IFEA).

3.5 Universities and colleges providing MICE education all over the country

By the end of 2013, there were a total of 220 MICE education institutions in mainland China, 57 of which were universities and 163 colleges. Over the past ten years, the number of MICE graduates hit the 50,000 mark; 13,000 students are still at college. In addition, nearly 500 textbooks have been published on the MICE industry. All the aforementioned figures suggest that China's strength in MICE education takes a leading position (ZCOM.gov 2014).

The development of China's MICE institutions also clearly illustrates the adequacy of Chinese human resources for the MICE industry.

4 The opening and cooperation of MICE

It has been 35 years since China adopted its opening-up policy. China has also been a member of the WTO for 13 years. The MICE industry has always been a pioneer industry in the opening-up process.

4.1 How foreign MICE companies have expanded in China

Back in the 1970s, Hong Kong exhibition companies began to operate small exhibitions involving mainly Hong Kong companies. Later, exhibition companies from Singapore started hosting exhibitions in Guangzhou. At this time, events held by foreign companies were mainly supplementary to the Guangzhou Export Commodities Fair.

In the 1980s, Hong Kong exhibition companies went to Beijing and started seeking cooperation with professional national associations and organisations. These companies aimed to host professional, international exhibitions. They also planned to develop their business from Beijing to Shanghai.

After the 1990s, led by Deutsche Messe, German companies began holding professional fairs in Beijing. Reed Exhibitions set up a branch office in Shanghai, and British Montgomery Exhibitions started holding international fairs. CMP Asia acquired the privately owned Shanghai Hua Zhan Exhibition Company. At that time, American MICE companies also started entering the Chinese market.

Since the turn of the century, Germany's top three event companies have invested jointly in building a new venue in Pudong District, Shanghai. This opportunity encouraged many other large and medium-sized German exhibition companies and those from other countries to enter the Chinese market. Every major exhibition company in the world now has business connections in China.

4.2 Main forms of external cooperation in the MICE industry

Generally, foreign MICE companies started entering China's MICE industry by cooperating in MICE projects. Companies then gradually expanded their branch offices in China. The next step was to establish MICE companies in sole proprietorship or as joint ventures. In recent years, however, entering the Chinese exhibition market was frequently conducted in the form of capital operating, such as fair acquisition, setting up proprietary companies and buying out franchises.

Cooperation fairs rely mainly on foreign brand exhibitions; hence the cooperation process is also the process of transplanting and expanding foreign MICE brands.

In the overview, foreign capital starts with Exhibitions/Exposition, including the related Conference/Convention; then continues into the meeting field, holding global meetings, including related exhibitions.

Based on the organisation of events, foreign capital is also penetrating the media industry and MICE services, such as the design and construction of stands and the transportation and manufacture of products.

Over the years, Australia's Info Salon and BPA of the United States have been actively expanding in the statistics and auditing of MICE information in China. In the field of education, British Reed Exhibitions has established a scholarship system for MICE majors at universities and colleges. In addition, the International Association of Exhibitions and Events (IAEE) started training for the Certification in Exhibition Management. In 2014, the Thailand Convention and Exhibition Bureau set up a scholarship system at the Institute of Economic and Trade and Exhibition of Beijing International Studies University.

4.3 Administration of foreign MICE companies in China

In February 2011, the Ministry of Finance and the Ministry of Foreign Affairs implemented a 'Notice on strictly controlling international conferences held in China' (GOV.cn 2011) to regulate international conferences. In January 2012, the Ministry of Finance also implemented a 'Notice on standards of the expenses of international conferences held in China and rules of financial management' (MOF.gov 2012).

If a company plans to hold international exhibitions with the word 'China' in the title, it is required to report to the Ministry of Commerce for approval. Other exhibitions without the word 'China' in their title need to report to offices where the event will be held.

Foreign investment can be used to establish a MICE company in sole proprietorship or as a joint venture, which must also be reported to the local government for approval.

The merger and acquisition of MICE projects in China involving foreign capital can be managed according to general trade and cooperation projects without specific approval.

4.4 China's MICE industry is gradually going global

The globalisation of China's MICE industry is progressing strongly. The route taken is, first: participate in overseas exhibitions, then: hold Chinese exhibitions within foreign exhibitions. The next step is to become guest of honour at foreign exhibitions; then to hold exclusive exhibitions on China in foreign countries and to co-organise international trade fairs overseas. The final step is to host overseas international trade fairs independently.

In 2013, nearly 20,000 Chinese companies went outside China to participate in over 1,500 overseas exhibitions. The net exhibition area was approximately 670,000 square metres. The main exhibits were Mechanical & Electrical Products (where automotive parts and metal tools grew fastest), Textiles & Garments, Household Products and Craft Gifts. The largest space used by Chinese exhibitors was in Russia, Brazil, the United Arab Emirates, India, South Africa, Turkey, Mexico and Germany.

Shanghai Meorient Exhibitions managed to hold International Exhibitions of Household Goods and Machinery Products several times in Jordan, Poland and Brazil (Meorient 2014). All of these successfully implemented projects were hosted and organised by this Chinese event company. The exhibitors came both from China and overseas countries, and the management was based on an international standard. Three such projects gained UFI certification, becoming the first group of overseas China exhibitions to earn UFI certification.

Moreover, Shanghai International Exhibition Company also managed to host the International Dye Exhibition twice.

5 Literature

China National Institute of Standardization/CNIS.gov (2011), *National economy classification code GB/T 4754-2011* [国民经济行业分类 GB/T 4754-2011]. Online: http://www.cnis.gov.cn/zyfw/bzsc/bzjd/201112/t20111202_11451.shtml (accessed on 20 Mar. 2015)

GOV.cn (2011), *Notice on strictly controlling international conferences held in China* [关于严格控制在华举办国际会议的通知]. Online: http://www.gov.cn/zwgk/2011-02/14/content_1803242.htm (accessed on 25 Mar. 2015)

Liu, B. (2006), *The China Convention Exhibition and Event Society / CCES is established officially.* [中国会展经济研究会高调成立]. Online: http://finance.sina.com.cn/chanjing/b/20060225/17562372809.shtml (accessed on 19 Mar. 2015)

Meorient (2014), *Homepage-History of Meorient.* Online: http://www.meorient.com/item.php?id=3 (accessed on 26 Mar. 2015)

Ministry of Commerce of the People's Republic China/MOFCOM.gov (2011a), *Guideline for improving the MICE industry during the 12th five-year plan by the Ministry of Commerce* [关于"十二五"期间促进会展业发展的指导意见]. Online: http://www.mofcom.gov.cn/aarticle/b/xxfb/201112/20111207895784.html (accessed on 29 Mar. 2015)

Ministry of Commerce of the People's Republic China/MOFCOM.gov (2011b), *MOF announced 'Guideline for improving the MICE industry during the 12th five-year plan by the Ministry of Commerce'* [商务部发布《关于"十二五"期间促进会展业发展的指导意见》]. Online: http://www.mofcom.gov.cn/aarticle/ae/ai/201112/20111207894272.html (accessed on 26 Jun. 2015)

Ministry of Finance of the People's Republic China/MOF.gov (2012), *Notice on standards of the expenses of international conferences held in China and rules of financial management* [在华举办国际会议费用开支标准和财务管理办法的通知]. Online: http://www.mof.gov.cn/zhengwuxinxi/caizhengwengao/2012wg/wg201203/201207/t20120717_667069.html (accessed on 26 Mar. 2015)

Ministry of Finance of the People's Republic China/MOF.gov (2013a), *Notification: the central government and state organs conference fees management approach* [中央和国家机关会议费管理办法的通知]. Online: http://www.mof.gov.cn/mofhome/shenzhen/lanmudaohang/zhengcefagui/201408/t20140812_1125715.htmln (accessed on 20 Mar. 2015)

Ministry of Finance of the People's Republic China/MOF.gov (2013b), *Provision of implementing eight regulations and standards in event management* [商务部落实八项规定规范展会管理]. Online: http://www.mofcom.gov.cn/article/jiguanzx/201307/20130700211863.shtml (accessed 21 Mar. 2015)

Government of MianYang/MY.gov (2005), *Vice Premier Wu Yi gave key speech on the first China Conference and Exhibition Economy Forum* [吴仪副总理在首届中国会展经济国际合作论坛上发表主旨演讲]. Online: http://www.my.gov.cn/bmwz/937046711619026944/20050829/47044.html (accessed on 20 Mar. 2015)

people.com (2003), *2003 the first China Conference and Exhibition Economy Forum in Beijing took place* [2003 中国会展经济论坛在京举办]. Online: http://www.people.com.cn/GB/paper53/10931/992000.html (accessed on 20 Mar. 2015)

She, P. (2000), *The exhibition industry will impulse economic development* [会展经济引发强大冲击波]. Online: http://www.people.com.cn/GB/paper53/1811/291614.html (accessed on 28 Mar. 2015)

Sichuan Bureau of Expo Affairs/SCBEA.org (2015), *Provision of implementing eight regulations and standard events* [2015 年我国会展业发展显现新趋势]. Online: http://www.scbea.org.cn/11498/11770/11515/2015/03/27/10221067.shtml (accessed 20 Mar. 2015)

National Bureau of Statistics of the People's Republic of China/STATS.gov (2013), *National economy classification code* [国民经济行业分类]. Online: http://www.stats.gov.cn/tjsj/tjbz/hyflbz/201310/P020131023307350246672.pdf (accessed on 27 Jun. 2015)

The Alliance of China Conference Hotels/ACCH (2013), *Blue book of Chinese Meeting 2013* [2013 年中国会议蓝皮书发布]. Online: http://www.confhotel.cn/OfficialWebsite/Twos2?id=14 (accessed 20 Mar. 2015)

Wuhan East Lake High-tech Development Zone/WEHDZ.gov (2012), *Notice about the classification of culture and related industry (2012) by the National Bureau of Statistics* [国家统计局关于印发文化及相关产业分类（2012）的通知]. Online: http://www.wehdz.gov.cn/upload/2012-08/201208020407201.doc (accessed on 26 Jun. 2015)

Wen, J. and Zhang, D. (2010), *The negative effect of financial crisis to domestic exhibition industry is weakening.* [中国贸促会：金融危机对我国会展业影响正在减弱]. Online: http://jjckb.xinhuanet.com/gnyw/2010-05/26/content_223053.htm (accessed on 20 Mar. 2015)

Xinhuanet (2004), *Future trend of Chinese Exhibition going overseas* [中国会展业对外开放大势所趋]. Online: http://news.xinhuanet.com/expo/2004-01/18/content_1283001.htm (accessed on 27 Mar. 2015)

Xinhuanet (2013), *Five departments of central government announced requirements to stop wasteful consumption and promote holding festival frugally.* [中宣部等五部门发出通知 要求制止豪华铺张 提倡节俭办晚会]. Online: http://news.xinhuanet.com/politics/2013-08/13/c_116929510.htm (accessed on 28 Mar. 2015)

Xinhuanet (2006), *Outline of the 11th five-year plan* [中国国民经济和社会发展十一五规划纲要]. Online: http://news.xinhuanet.com/politics/2006-03/16/content_4312362.htm (accessed on 21 Mar. 2015)

Xinhuanet (2009), *The first Guangdong Trade Fair of Export Goods explores the domestic market for export companies.* [广东首开"外博会"为外销企业开拓内销市场破局]. Online: http://news.xinhuanet.com/fortune/2009-06/15/content_11546367.htm (accessed on 23 Mar. 2015)

You, S. (2013), *The new state eight regulations* [八项规定]. Online: http://wfxy.fafu.edu.cn/s/31/t/6/b7/77/info46967.htm (accessed on 27 Jun. 2015)

Department of Commerce of Zhejiang Province/ZCOM.gov (2014), *2013 Industry analysis and future trend report based on statistical data of Chinese exhibition industry* [2013 年中国会展业统计数据分析报告]. Online: http://www.zcom.gov.cn/art/2014/9/18/art_1127_119084.html (accessed on19 Mar. 2015)

Raising the level of market-orientation in the Chinese exhibition industry – based on international experience

Chen, Xianjin

借鉴国际经验, 努力提高我国展览业市场化水平

The Chinese Exhibition Industry was rooted from a planned economy, this has caused an imbalanced relationship between the government and the market, which has become an obstacle for a further development of the Chinese Exhibition Industry.

In order to solve the problem, the report has analysed and contrasted the global practices regarding the investments in exhibition halls and their management, the organisation and operation of exhibition projects, and the role played by government and the position it takes. Furthermore, the report has generalised and summarised the characteristics and trends of the marketisation in the global event industry.

Finally, the report has put forward some suggestions. China should respect the basic principles of the market economy, allowing the market to play a decisive role in the allocation of resources. The government should pay attention to establish a open, fair, tolerant, non-discriminatory exhibition market system and an exhibition market mechanism without industry protection, area protection and a government monopoly. By doing so, the influence of the government will not be weakened; instead, it will play a greater role in maintaining social equity and justice.

中国展览业的发展起源于计划经济体制，这导致了行业中政府职责与市场规律两者之间关系不平衡的矛盾，并将阻碍中国展览业的进一步发展。

为了解决这个矛盾，文章首先从展览场馆投资与管理、展览项目组织与运营、政府作用与定位三个方面分析与对比了全球展览业的基本操作模式。随后，文章又对国际展览业市场化的特点与趋势做了概括和总结。

最后，文章对提高中国展览业市场化水平提出了一些建议。中国应该尊重市场经济的基本规律，让市场在资源配置中起到决定性的作用。政府则应该专注于建立一个公开、公平、宽容、无歧视的展览市场体系，设立一个无行业保护、地区保护、行政垄断的展览市场机制。政府的作用并非在弱化，而是在维护社会公平正义方面发挥更大的作用。

1 Introduction

In March of 2015, Chinese State Council issued a document named, 'Some Suggestions on Further Promoting the Reform and Development of the Exhibition Industry' (Chinese State Council). This is the first time that the Chinese government put forward the strategic goals and major tasks of the development of the exhibition industry in a thorough and systematic way. The document clearly pointed out that the governmental functions should be transformed, administrative procedures should be simplified and powers should be delegated to lower levels in a more expeditious way. The relationship between the government and the market should be clarified; government-organised exhibitions should be regulated and the numbers reduced. The market should play a decisive role in the distribution of resources, at the same time, the government should function in a better way.

This report will illustrate the practices and experience of other governments and exhibitions in assessing this issue, enabling these problems to be resolved successfully in China. The article is divided into three parts. The first part is about global practice concerning three aspects: investments in exhibition halls and their management; the organisation and operation of exhibition projects; and the role played by government and the position it takes. In the second part, the characteristics and trends concerning marketisation in the global event industry will be summarised and conclusions drawn. Finally, the third part will provide suggestions on how to boost the marketisation process of China's event industry.

2 The marketisation conditions of the global event industry

In order to make the examples more representative for analysis and comparison, this article takes the United States of America as the example from North America; Germany, France, Italy, Spain and the UK as examples from Europe; and Japan, South Korea, Thailand, Singapore, Taiwan region and Hong Kong region as examples from Asia.

2.1 Investments in exhibition venues and their management

Each country invests in exhibition halls and manages them based on its practical situation. In the USA, local governments invest in and operate almost all exhibition venues and meeting centres. In Europe, investment and management models vary from country to country. In countries such as Germany, France, Italy and Spain, where the event industry is quite developed, exhibition halls are invested in by the governmental institutions and managed by enterprises. In the UK, however, some halls are funded and managed by private companies, and others by the local government. In Asia, the models are diverse: in places like Japan, South Korea, Taiwan region and Hong Kong region, the government or its representatives such as quasi-official trade promotion associations assume the role of investor and manager of exhibitions halls, whereas the first and second largest venues in Thailand are funded by private enterprises. The model in Singapore is mixed – two of the three largest halls are funded by private enterprises, the other by the government. In other words, there is a wide range of investment models in countries around the world.

2.2 Organising and operating exhibition projects

In this article, exhibition organisers are divided into three types. The first type is exhibition venues. If the venues are funded by the government, they belong to state-owned enterprises. The second type is industry associations. The last type is the exclusive exhibition organisers, either private enterprises or listed companies. In countries where the market economy is developed, there are no exclusive state-owned exhibition organisers.

The organiser classification of US exhibitions is quite clear. Namely, 70 per cent of trade fairs are held by industry associations and the remaining 30 per cent by private enterprises (there have been a number of changes in recent years, which will be mentioned below).

Nearly half of all exhibitions held in Germany, France, Italy and Spain are organised by the exhibition hall owners. Not only do they own the venue, they are also the lessor and organiser. This dual role makes them the leader of the market, while industry associations also support and help organise these exhibitions. Historical factors of the German model are worth mentioning: above all, many German cities were badly destroyed in WWII, which meant that also exhibition halls needed to be rebuilt. Another factor is the historical tradition of holding exhibitions. It is well acknowledged globally that the German model cannot be copied or imitated.

2.3 The role played by government and the position it takes

In order to show the characteristics of the role played by the government in different countries, the table below illustrates the activities in which certain levels of government are involved.

Tab. 1: The role played by government and the position it takes.

Role & position / Level of government	Venue investment	Organise exhitibion projects	Facilitate the industry	Governing the market
Central government	rare	rare	common	infrequent
Provincial government	common	rare	common	rare
City government	common	rare	common	common
Government-controlled entities	not often	common	not often	never seen

The USA has a typical market economy, which means that the government never participates in the organisation of events, only in the investment process. In the past, some local governments have collected hotel taxes, which are invested in operating and extending exhibition halls. Hence the exhibition company and the industry association obtain greater indirect discounts on the rental fee.

Exhibition halls in Germany, France, Italy, Spain and other countries are funded by the regional government and the local CCI (Chamber of Commerce and Industry). However, there are now also numerous private exhibition companies. Since the paramount task for government is to regulate the market to ensure fair competition, the governments of these countries have formulated a series of systems and measures or passing laws and regulations in order to achieve this objective.

As the exhibition industry in Asia started developing much later than in the USA and Europe, the Asian governments are still at the first phase of developing the event industry. For example, South Korea and Singapore have adopted laws, and Thailand has laid down a number of regulations, aiming at advancing the exhibition industry and encouraging more projects to be held in the destinations. On the other hand, very few rules have been issued to truly ensure fair competition.

3 Characteristics and tendencies of international exhibition marketisation

3.1 One model

There is no unified developing model in the event industry all over the world. This is a model in itself. Due to the existence of different backgrounds, different stages of economic growth and different market entities, there are various systems and mechanisms in exhibition marketisation. Countries started designing and practicing the marketisation of the exhibition industry according to their conditions and characteristics. Since there is no unified model in the process of marketisation, we cannot say decisively that we have the only successful model, at the same time, we cannot say our model is not adequate.

3.2 Two weakening tendencies

The first weakening tendency is a reduction in government participation in domestic trade fairs and other commercial exhibitions. In countries with a market-oriented system, the government will not usually participate in such exhibitions. Neither will do they review or approve such exhibitions, nor may they use administrative resources to help attract investments in the exhibition or – more importantly – use government funds to support such shows. Last but not least, concerning naming – the names of certain provinces and city's governments are rarely mentioned as the organiser.

The other weakening tendency is a reduction in government investment in exhibition halls, and in the operation and management of financial support. As mentioned above, local governments in the USA invest in and operate nearly all exhibition halls and meeting centres. A number of local governments have collected hotel tax to support, operate and construct these pavilions. In the past two years, the government began gradually decreasing its support, which meant that a large number of exhibition halls had to consider how to generate a profit. The following two issues create a fierce conflict with organisers: first, rental rates have to be increased and, second, hall owners are starting to organise exhibitions and hold exhibitions themselves. It is a well-known fact that a number of associations have held negotiations with the government about this problem.

3.3 Three important issues

There are three types of stakeholder or key interest groups: exhibition centres, organisers and exhibition service suppliers. Since there are two types of main investor – the government and private investors – they are unavoidably inseparable. Three hot issues currently surround the development of the market in the international exhibition industry.

3.3.1 Imbalance between venue supply and demand

Competition between exhibition venues is fierce if there are several venues in one city or an oversupply of venues. On the one hand, organisers have a greater choice of venues and may be able to negotiate favourable terms. On the other hand, it poses a great challenge for market order stability. Hong Kong has two venues – the Hong Kong Convention and Exhibition Centre, and Asia World Expo. Since the establishment of Asia World Expo, conflicts have frequently erupted between them concerning similar titles of exhibitions and their content. When there are two similar trade shows organized by different organizers and taken place in different venues, one of the organizers sort dozens of volunteers to another venue to lobby and register visitors, they even provided free shuttle buses and transported away many professional visitors. The other organiser was very confused, but was unable to tackle the problem. Now, Shanghai has two mega venues: The National Exhibition and Convention Center (NECC) and Shanghai New International Exhibition Center (SNIEC). In Sep. 2015, both venues held similar trade fairs with four days overlapping. The two organisers all declared that their show was a great success. However, people argue that it is a healthy competition or it is competed excessively.

3.3.2 Challenge of venue operators becoming exhibition organisers

Most exhibition organisers hope that venue operators will not also become exhibition organisers. They hope that lessors and lessees will continue to do their respective jobs and not interfere with each other. However, these fears are unfounded. It is common practice for venue operators to also be exhibition organisers. This trend is visible not only in Europe, but also in the USA. We therefore believe that it is unreasonable to expect venue operators and exhibition organisers to concentrate solely on their own respective business, refraining from entering the other side of the business. However, a problem needs to be discussed. Namely, if venue operators become exhibition organisers, should they establish public, fair and transparent renting policies and treat their clients' and their own exhibitions equally? In addition, should the government make progress and monitor this aspect?

3.3.3 Theme protection

Over the years, in order to protect certain branded exhibitions, a number of local governments have applied 'theme protection' when reviewing and approving exhibitions. As a result, even good-quality exhibitions with a similar subject or topic may not be held at these venues for a certain length of time (usually one to three months) before and after the date of the branded exhibition.

This leads to a controversy. The market economy encourages competition because it leads to advances from which consumers benefit. However, it is obvious that such a competition is not welcomed by companies, that occupy the market. 'theme protection' measures objectively exclude companies that wish to participate in the competition at a later stage.

In the past, we advocated being 'against imitated exhibitions'. Later, we acknowledged being wrong, because this slogan limits the entry of new competitors; it was later amended to 'against a low level of imitated exhibitions'. We should therefore consider cancelling 'theme protection' measures, as long as new competitors comply with conditions and have a more advanced exhibition concept. The government should therefore welcome their entry. We should also consider forcing low-efficiency and ineffective companies to withdraw from the market by way of competition. After all, the exhibitors and visitors will ultimately benefit most from this.

4 Suggestions on how to improve the market level of China's exhibition industry

As we can clearly see from the content of 'one model, two weakening tendencies and three important issues', the key to improving the marketisation level of the exhibition industry is to deal with the relationship between an efficient market and the government.

We are familiar with the exhibition market economy, and yet the 30-year development of China's exhibition industry, especially the events of the past 20 years, cannot be explained by any planned economy. In the past, there was one state-owned exhibition company; now there are different kinds of ownership systems. In the past, the use of foreign currency was depended on planned distribution; now we can trade freely. In the past, there was almost no service company involved in exhibitions; today, the exhibition industry chain is complete. All these changes are due to the 'miracle' of the market economy.

However, what we should also bear in mind is that China started the reform from a command economy rather than a market economy, where the government intervention was dominant.

The core of today's exhibition industry marketisation is clarifying the government governance and the boundaries of market functioning, resolving the problem of the government's malpractice, absence and interference in exhibition marketisation. There are three proposals.

4.1 Respect the basic rules of the market economy

The pattern of government-led trade shows should end as quickly as possible. We know that whether a trade fair should be held, where it should be held, who should hold it and how it should be held should depend on market demand, and not on forecasts and assumptions by the relevant head of department. General trading activities should be handed over to the market. The government should transform its function of organising specific projects and participating in the exhibition business, and should not mix the roles. For example, the government should concentrate on the role of being a referee, rather than being an athlete.

4.2 Reform of the licencing system

Since the reforms and opening up of the economy, it is incumbent upon the relevant government department to issue a licence to international economic and technological trade fairs in advance. From a historical perspective, this licence system had a positive effect on the promotion of the international outlook of the exhibition industry in China, introducing advanced technology and equipment, accelerating the speed of opening up to the outside world, and other aspects. However, we also know that the actual effect of the licencing system resolved the problem of various kinds of mechanisms and systems caused by the control of foreign exchange, import control and a single regulation mode of temporary entry exhibits under historical conditions.

Today, with China's three decades of experience in opening up, these problems no longer exist. For this reason, a reasonable conclusion is that it is unfair to require prior approval for international exhibitions in China. Because doing so will enhance the government's power, restrict market efficiency and gives the government the potential power of rent-seeking. As mentioned above, licencing systems do not exist in countries with a mature market economy. We should immediately reform these licencing systems. Initially, the licencing system can be changed into a checking system based on governmental rules, providing replies to applicants as to whether or not the application can be checked within a certain period. If this is not the case, reasons should be specified. Alternatively, it could be developed into a filing-system, turning prior approval into ex-post supervision. This would mean that applicants could hold exhibitions without government approval, but if problems occurred, the government would have to investigate the issue.

4.3 Establish a fair, open and transparent exhibition market

What does the government need to do most for China's rapidly developing event industry? Should it lead exhibitions? Of course not, because it is not within it's remit. Should it manage the industry in order to limit the number of exhibitions, ensure programme compliance, optimise structures, and ensure rational layouts and results? I think here, too, the answer is no because these tasks are not directly linked to the government's remit. What should the government do instead? It ought to make up for the current absence of its functions. This means enforcing market supervision and establishing a fair, open and transparent event market system. The main content of such a system is having event market entities formed by various forms of ownerships that are on equal terms, sharing the same rights, obeying the same rules, taking on the same level of responsibility, operating on a level playing field and interacting with each other.

The following two examples are given as an aside.
Example 1: In 2007, the French government asked France's biggest private exhibition company, Exposium, to manage the largest exhibition centre in Paris. To avoid unfair competition caused by private companies using venue resources, under the leadership of the French Finance Ministry, the venue investor and Paris Chamber of Commerce signed an agreement containing detailed provisions, three rules of which are worth noting by our venue management companies.

1. Promote the principle of non-discrimination concerning the hiring of venues.

The key to this principle can be summarised into three pieces of advice: (1) Big exhibitions should take priority over small exhibitions. (2) Old exhibitions should take priority over new exhibitions. (3) Guest exhibitions should take priority over host exhibitions.

2. Promote the principle of transparent venue pricing mechanisms
3. Promote the compulsory competitive principle for venue supporting services.

Example 2: In April 2014, CCI (Competition Commission of India) decided the case concerning India exhibition association's appeal against India's largest venue investor, manager and organiser – India Trade Promotion Organisation (ITPO). ITPO lost the case and was fined 67.5 million rupees, which equated to about 1.12 million dollars. ITPO lost because it scheduled two exhibitions to be held simultaneously on the same theme, meaning that the schedule was not conducive to existing exhibitions in the market, but beneficial to exhibitions held by ITPO. It is worth noting in this case that ITPO is a subordinate department of the Indian government. However, CCI still ruled against it.

These two cases demonstrate that the management function of government is very important and efficient concerning market supervision and ensuring fair competition in the market.

5 Conclusion

What the government should do, needs to do and can do well is establish a fair, tolerant, non-discriminatory, exhibition market system and an exhibition market mechanism without industry protection, area protection and a government monopoly. The market plays a decisive but not all-encompassing role in the allocation of resources. A market economy is an economy governed simultaneously by law. And the economic behaviour of market entities is not only constrained by self-motivation and competitive stress, but also by laws and regulations. Accordingly, the function of government is not weakened; instead, it should seek to play a greater role in maintaining social equity and justice.

As the Chinese saying goes, the water in the canal is always clear when the fresh water from the upstream continuously flows into it. If our government can concentrate all its attention on dealing with problems of unclear supervision and the imperfect system in two or three years, the marketisation level of our exhibition industry is bound to grow quickly, and the dream of creating a nation that hosts great exhibitions will come true soon.

6 Literature

Chinese State Council, http://www.gov.cn/zhengce/content/2015-04/19/content_9621.htm

The role of China in Germany's exhibition industry

Koetter, Harald,
Spinger, Marco

中国对于德国会展行业的意义

China has advanced to being one of the German trade fair industry's most important partners in recent years. This is visible in the growing participation of Chinese exhibitors and visitors to German fairs, as well as in the significant presence of German exhibitors in China. The reason why Chinese exporters' presence at German fairs is growing so quickly is that trade fairs in Germany are international leaders in terms of both quality and visitors from around the world. The Association of the German Trade Fair Industry (AUMA) plays an important role in maintaining this dynamic by offering information to interested individuals and organisations from all over the world and, moreover, by supporting the development of the industry. In particular, it coordinates German associations' interests in establishing the federal ministries' foreign trade fair programme, which also supports the participation of German exhibitors in trade fairs in China. China is without doubt the most important target region for German organisers involved in trade fairs abroad. It is the country where the most and the biggest German trade fairs abroad are organised.

近年来中国已发展成德国展览业中最重要的合作伙伴之一。这体现在日益增加的中国参展商和观众参与了德国的展览会，同时德国参展商也大量地出现于在中国举办的展览会中。中国参展商发展如此迅速的原因在于德国的展览会在质量和观众的全球性上具有世界领先的地位。德国展览业协会（AUMA）为保持这种地位发挥了举足轻重的作用。它不但为来自世界各地对展览会感兴趣的个人或团体提供信息，而且还为行业的发展提供支持。尤其值得一提的是，它还通过建立联邦政府的海外展览会项目来协调德国各协会之间的利益，而该项目本身也支持德国参展商参加中国的展览会。毋庸置疑，中国是德国海外展览主办商最为重要的目标区域，它拥有德国在海外举办的最多和最大的德国展览会。

1 Introduction

Trade fair involvement plays a central role in trade relationships between China and Germany. More than 10,000 exhibitors and 50,000 visitors come from China to Germany each year to present their companies at trade fairs or to gather information. These Chinese companies benefit greatly from the quality and international reputation of German trade fairs; likewise, German trade fair organisers and companies have a strong presence in China. A total of 303 trade fairs were held abroad by German organisers in 2014, 90 of which were in China. This makes China the most important target market for German organisers.

German exhibitors participate in around 50 trade fairs in China every year within the exhibitor support programme run by the German Federal Ministry for Economic Affairs and Energy (BMWi). This means that Chinese trade fairs take the leading role in this programme, together with Russia.

AUMA, the association of the German trade fair industry, supports this programme. Furthermore, AUMA offers numerous services to exhibitors and visitors from both countries, promoting German-Sino trade fair relations.

2 Trade fair relations between Germany and China: a success for both countries

2.1 The German trade fair industry

Over the past few decades, trade fairs in Germany have developed into meeting points for exhibitors and visitors from around the world. More than half of the exhibitors come from abroad; one third of these are from countries outside Europe. One quarter of all visitors come from abroad; this figure exceeds 30 per cent for industry professionals.

Foreign suppliers therefore participate in trade fairs in order to acquire customers from other European countries or continents; importers find a wide range of products from around the world, allowing them to compare quality and prices at one single event.

As a trade fair venue, Germany functions as a hub for international trade, utilised intensively by Chinese companies. In the last ten years alone, the number of visitors from China increased nearly threefold to around 50,000 per year (see Figure 1).

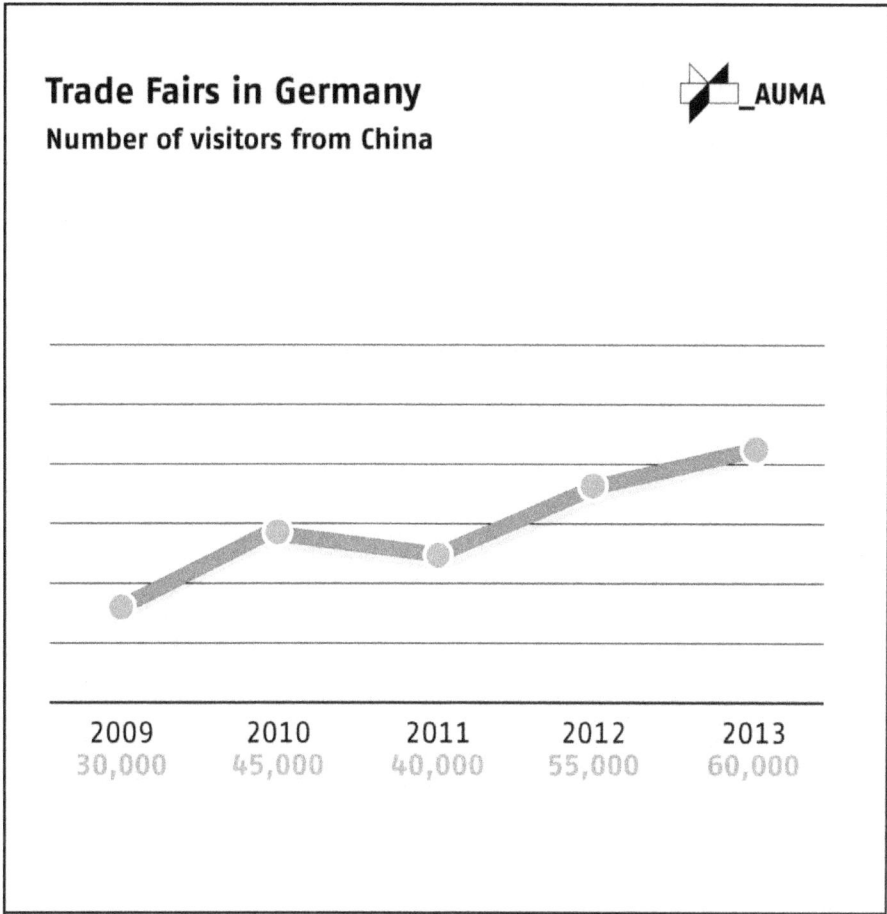

Figure 1: Number of visitors from China.

The number of exhibitors has also increased greatly; this figure increased by around 100 per cent between 2003 and 2013 to over 10,000 per year. China became the largest foreign exhibitor for the first time in 2012. In the future, China will alternate with Italy to top the exhibitor statistics, depending on which trade fair programmes are held in the respective year. Chinese companies are present at around 120 trade fairs held each year in Germany (see Figure 2).

In addition to the ideal opportunities for establishing international business contacts, there are numerous other reasons for becoming involved in trade fairs in Germany.

German trade fairs are organised professionally: organisers have considerable experience in implementing international trade fairs. They organise more than just one or two globally leading trade fairs per year. Some organise more than 20, employing highly specialised, internationally experienced experts for every aspect of the trade fair industry, whether for marketing, distribution, services or technology.

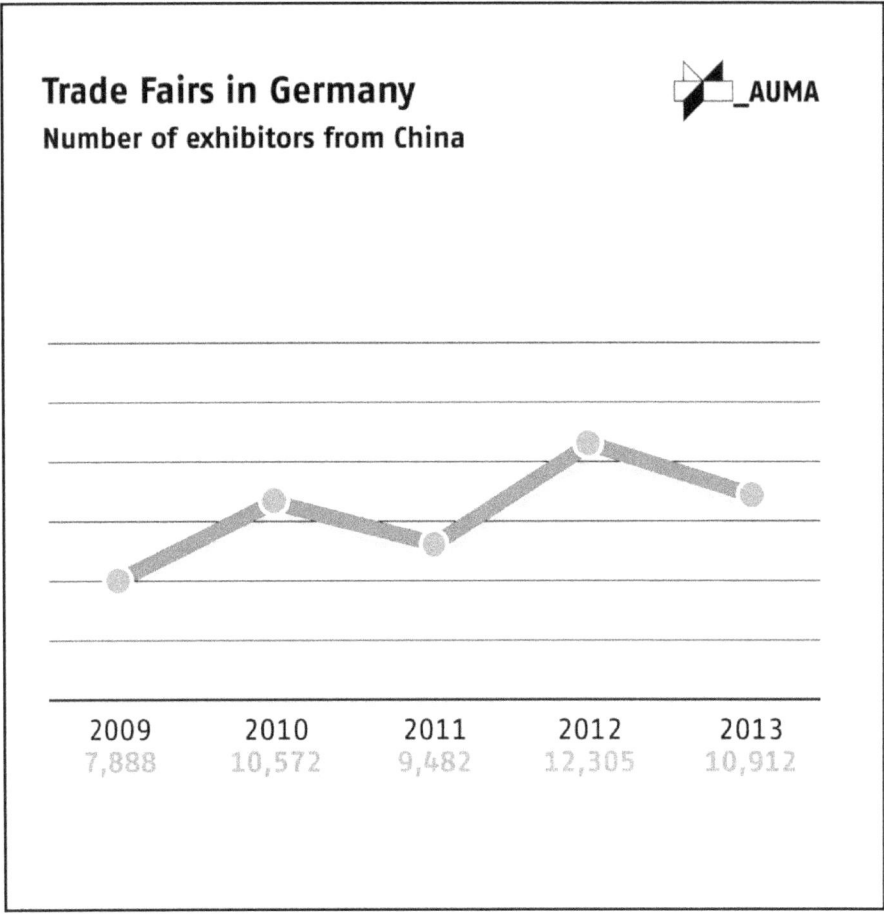

Figure 2: Number of exhibitors from China.

The organisers undertake global exhibitor and visitor marketing. The large trade fair companies have an extremely tightly knit network of foreign representatives who can provide exhibitors and visitors with information locally. There are around 600 information agents around the world that establish contacts between potentially interested parties and German trade fair organisers. Individual trade fair companies have representatives in up to 150 countries.

Exhibitors, visitors and organisers cooperate in the long term: a particularly important factor in the success of the German trade fair industry is that all of the parties involved cooperate closely. Most trade fairs have an advisory committee in which, together with organisers and representatives from the exhibiting and visiting industries, the development of trade fairs is regularly discussed. This ensures the ideal scheduling of trade fair dates and the development of market-oriented concepts that are successful in the long term.

The trade fair service leads the way internationally: German trade fair companies are constantly expanding their range of services. They offer support in constructing exhibitor stands, in the search for additional, multilingual personnel, booking trips, in PR and marketing campaigns, and in realising online presence for exhibitors on the organisers' websites.

The quality of exhibition sites and infrastructure is also at the forefront of international standards: the well-recognised quality of Germany's transportation infrastructure represents an important requirement for efficient travel to and from trade fairs in Germany. German exhibition venues meet the latest architectural, logistical and technical demands made by exhibitors and visitors. This also applies to congress and conference centres.

More than 2.8 million square metres of hall space in 22 German exhibition venues is available for national and international trade fairs. Ten sites have over 100,000 square metres of hall space; five have more than 50,000 square metres.

Trade fairs are excellent value for money. Stand rental prices at German trade fairs are moderate compared to other international trade fairs, and offer a very high quality and quantity of visitors. German trade fairs therefore offer a low price per visitor contact in comparison with foreign trade fairs, also compared to other media.

3 AUMA – Association of the German Trade Fair Industry

As the German trade fair association, AUMA represents the interests of exhibitors, organisers and visitors of trade fairs alike. Founded in Berlin in 1907 as the "Permanent Exhibition Commission of German Industry", it is one of the oldest German associations in the services sector. It is independent of government institutions, and is financed exclusively by contributions from members and companies that exhibit in Germany.

AUMA has 78 members, including exhibition organisers, leading associations of the retail, wholesale, foreign trade, craft and agricultural industries, as well as the association of German Chambers of Commerce and Industry. In addition, all significant specialist industry associations interested in trade fairs are involved with AUMA; organisers of foreign trade fair involvements are also members. Additional members include the organisers' associations GDG (Association of Major German Exhibition Organisers), IDFA (Association of German Trade Fair Organisers and Exhibition Venues) and FAMA (Special Association for Fairs and Exhibitions).

Service provider organisations, headed by FAMAB (German Association of Direct Business Communications) as the lobby for stand construction companies, designers and event agencies and the Association of Trade Fair Forwarders, are also members of AUMA. In line with the strong integration of the trade fair and event industries, the EVVC (European Association of Event Centres) is also a member.

Representing interests
AUMA represents the interests of the trade fair industry vis-à-vis legislative and executive authorities at federal and state levels, especially concerning sales and export promotion, sustainability and even fiscal, building and employment regulations. It maintains contact with foreign and international trade fair organisations. AUMA is a member of The Global Associa-

tion of the Exhibition Industry (UFI). AUMA collaborates with committees from other organisations in the trade fair industry, including IDFA and FAMA organisers' associations. AUMA occupies a permanent seat at meetings of the Federal/State Committee for trade fairs and exhibitions, which is where trade fair experts from the German Federal States' economic ministries and the Federal Ministry for Economic Affairs and Energy (BMWi) meet.

Providing information and advice on trade fairs

AUMA provides information on dates, services, exhibitor and visitor figures at trade fairs in Germany and abroad, assisting exhibitors and visitors from around the world with their decision-making with regard to trade fair participation. AUMA provides data on more than 5,000 events in its global online database at www.auma.de, which is available in four languages. It publicises suggestions for planning and carrying out trade fair participations. Furthermore, AUMA offers individual consultation regarding trade fairs, participation and supporting programmes. AUMA manages the German Society for Voluntary Control of Fair and Exhibition Statistics (FKM).

Coordinating German industry's involvement in trade fairs abroad

AUMA coordinates the interests of German industry when BMWi and the Federal Ministry of Food and Agriculture (BMEL) choose their foreign trade fair representations. It also assists the ministries in communicating their trade fair programmes abroad. In particular, these programmes support small- and medium-sized enterprises in their efforts to access foreign markets by organising joint company representations at trade fairs abroad. AUMA helps its members to market their trade fairs abroad by publicising event dates in the brochure entitled "German Trade Fair Quality Abroad" and in its trade fair database.

Umbrella marketing of Germany as a trade fair venue and trade fairs as a medium

AUMA publishes a trade fair calendar for interested parties in other countries in up to ten languages as well as posters and advertising carrying the slogan "Trade fairs made in Germany". It advertises the benefits of trade fairs as a corporate communication tool and provides information to assist in the decision-making process.

The Institute of the German Trade Fair Industry

The Institute of the German Trade Fair Industry represents AUMA's commitment towards trade fair research, training and development. AUMA awards research assignments and conducts its own surveys, while also helping to formulate occupational profiles for the trade fair and events industries and running training courses for vocational instructors. The institute supports universities and other institutions by holding guest lectures and providing information on the trade fair industry. The institute is also home to the German Trade Fair Library, which lists 8,000 items from the trade fair, congress and events industries.

PR and events

AUMA publishes newsletters for the media and the community dealing with topics concerning the trade fair industry, research, lobbying and the EU. AUMA's annual review entitled "The German Trade Fair Industry" provides a general overview. As the main organisation representing the trade fair industry, AUMA hosts "AUMA-MesseTreff", a major annual event that brings together the entire industry and promotes dialogue between the trade fair

industry, politicians, associations and the media. AUMA organises expert forums on a range of different topics for its members several times a year.

FKM

The German Society for Voluntary Control of Fair and Exhibition Statistics (FKM) is the German certification organisation for trade fair data. From the very beginning in 1965, FKM's basic principles included establishing comparable and reliable exhibition statistics. FKM set up uniform rules for obtaining exhibitor numbers, visitor attendance, exhibition space data and visitor breakdown statistics, ensuring that independent auditors check adherence to the rules. After all, exhibitors and visitors can only plan properly if they can be certain that the data available for the period in question, compared with other trade fairs, is based on uniform criteria.

FKM data provides exhibitors with access to visitor breakdowns, enabling them to judge whether a trade fair is suitably appealing to its target groups. By having their trade fairs certified, organisers show that they are prepared to adhere to customary standards of the industry and to publish all significant facts about their trade fairs.

Every year, more than 50 organisers from Germany and two foreign guest members from Verona, Italy, and Hong Kong have over 200 exhibitions and trade fairs audited by FKM. The statistics they obtain are published as preliminary figures on the website fkm.de. After completion of the auditing, the statistics are compiled in the FKM annual report, entitled "Certified exhibition data". In addition, together with other European auditing companies, FKM publishes an annual brochure called Euro Fair Statistics, containing audited data on some 2,500 trade fairs in 23 countries. The brochure is produced by the UFI.

4 Coordinating German industry trade fair activities abroad and the role of associations

4.1 The foreign trade fair programme

AUMA prepares Germany's foreign trade fair programme in close cooperation with the Federal Ministry for Economic Affairs and Energy (BMWi).

As part of this programme, around 6,000 to 7,000 predominantly medium-sized companies are supported at approximately 250 trade fairs abroad each year. About one-fifth of these trade fairs are located in China, involving a total of some 1,400 companies.

With an annual budget of more than € 40 million, the German Federal Government provides export platforms that German companies can use on favourable terms. In addition to the financial component, this support is based particularly on technical and organisational support by German trade fair companies and specialised agencies. It is also based on improving a company's image provided by the umbrella brand "Made in Germany", which is used for all German Pavilions in the programme. The foreign trade fair programme is part of Germany's foreign trade promotion to ensure that German products continue to be exported at high rates.

Economic and political interests in this sector are coordinated in a working group for foreign trade fair participations moderated by AUMA. Representatives from 40 export-oriented associations regularly meet representatives from the ministries for discussions. Meeting demand is a defining factor in determining and implementing involvements in trade fairs throughout all of the phases of BMWi's foreign trade fair programme. The associations evaluate trade fair priorities for the relevant industry in their trade fair working boards and other boards, and, according to this preselection, apply directly to AUMA for the so-called German Pavilions. AUMA then examines these applications according to specialist trade fair criteria. Here, emphasis is placed on questions concerning the definition of valid event types (congresses, roadshows and garden shows, for example, are not valid), international trade fair relevance (export-related) and avoidance of overlapping topics with trade fairs that have already been applied for or that have already been admitted to the programme. When selecting trade fairs, an economically rational emphasis is placed on markets that could not be exploited properly without the support for trade fair involvement, due to the difficulty that small- and medium-sized companies have in accessing them.

The demand-oriented approach taken enables a positive impact to be made on the global trade fair industry, by setting priorities within the foreign trade fair programme. This is also one of the main reasons why associations contribute considerably to the configuration of the programme. German Pavilions enhance the image of trade fairs abroad, which leads to a concentration on crucial trade fairs, promoting more straightforward event calendars. In this respect, the foreign trade fair programme concentrates on the most important industry events in the country/region. In turn, German export-oriented companies are supported by their associations, when choosing trade fairs.

The exhibiting industry is integrated in the project support during the implementation phase. AUMA is a joint organiser of all German Pavilions, contributing its trade fair expertise to the projects. The associations that have applied support exhibitor acquisition and provide industry experts who offer specialist advice at the German Pavilion. Associations can also contribute industry-specific designs for German Pavilions. The intrinsic planning role of the industry ensures the programme's company orientation.

Participation in universal and multi-branch trade fairs has become an exception. The industry-specific support of representations at trade fairs by relevant industry associations is, therefore, an important requirement for successfully participating in a trade fair and for creating a competent appearance of the German Pavilion at the trade fair location. In addition, special country associations support German companies with their specific regional expertise in implementing the foreign trade fair programme, especially in Africa and the Middle East.

The foreign trade fair programme generally has a strong orientation towards medium-sized companies, but reserves the opportunity to include market leaders from the relevant branch in order to demonstrate Germany's economic leadership in quality and technology, and to fully reach important visitor target groups. Visitors drawn by the market leaders are also beneficial to small companies and new entrants to the market. This is supported by the export-oriented associations.

In order to promote the export of technology in the renewable energy/energy efficiency sector, BMWi has been helping companies to participate in trade fairs in this sector since 2003. AUMA has also been contributing to the choice of trade fairs for this programme since 2007.

In addition, the Federal Ministry of Food and Agriculture (BMEL) supports German companies in the agricultural sector and food industries that exhibit German products at trade fairs abroad. BMEL has an annual budget of more than € 5 million. AUMA is also a joint organiser at this trade fair programme of German Pavilions, and supports the ministry in implementing participation. The Federal Ministry determines the programme in cooperation with the specialist associations of this industry. AUMA has been involved more intensively in the determination procedure since 2014.

Furthermore, trade fair activities abroad organised by the German Federal States are coordinated in a special committee comprising the Federal Government and the Federal States, and assisted by AUMA. Here AUMA represents the common interests of the associations contributing towards the Federal Government's foreign trade fair programme.

4.2 German organisers' trade fairs abroad

German trade fair organisers have been progressively increasing their foreign activities over the past few years. A total of 277 trade fairs were held abroad in 2013, the concepts of which revolved around the standards of leading international trade fairs in Germany. This is a new record. In comparison: 153 trade fairs were held in 2004.

In order to emphasise the quality standards of German trade fairs abroad, AUMA has developed the label "German Trade Fair Quality Abroad (GTQ)" in coordination with its members involved abroad. AUMA has also been distributing the GTQ label to foreign trade fairs held by organisers that are members of FAMA (Special Association for Fairs and Exhibitions The Association for Trade Fairs and Exhibitions) since 2011. An AUMA working committee including these members ensures that the organisers hold regular discussions about experiences and opinions.

Around 3 million square metres of stand space was rented at trade fairs abroad in 2013. More than 108,000 companies exhibited their products. In comparison, this figure was 45,500 in 2004. The number of visitors rose to 7.4 million (2004: 2.8 million).

In 2013, all of the five trade fairs with the most exhibitors were in China. More than 4,000 exhibitors attended the Automechanika Shanghai (4,618); Intertextile Shanghai Apparel Fabrics and CHINAPLAS had more than 3,000 exhibitors (3,751 and 3,186, respectively). More than 2,000 exhibitors registered for two other trade fairs: Guangzhou International Lighting Exhibition (2,588) and China International Hardware Show Powered by PRACTICAL WORLD (2,500).

The events that attracted the most visitors were the public exhibitions in the automobile sector: Seoul Motor Show, which attracted more than 1 million visitors, Auto Shanghai with 813,000, Chengdu Motor Show with 620,000 and Wuhan Motor Show with 413,000.

China asserted its position at the top of the league table in 2013, when German trade fair companies once again rented over 1.6 million square metres of stand space there. More than 51,000 exhibitors and 3.8 million visitors at 79 trade fairs signified a 2 and 5 per cent increase, respectively, compared to the previous year (see Figures 3 and 4).

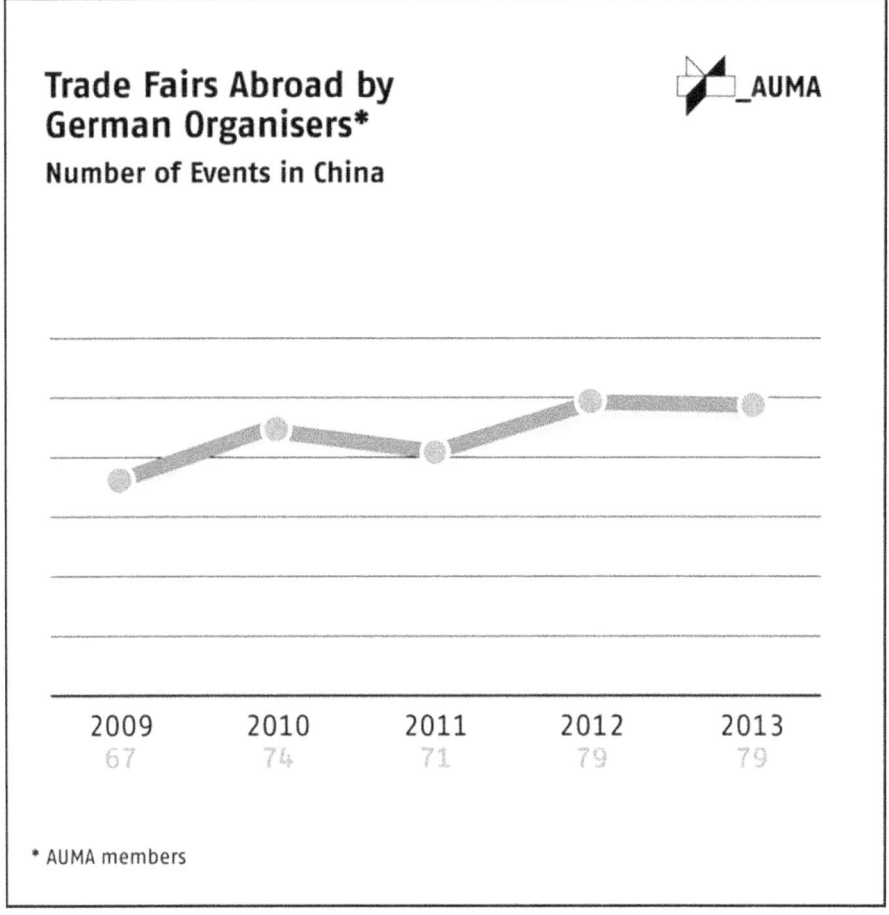

Figure 3: Number of events in China by German organisers.

In comparison: German organisers organised 39 trade fairs in Russia in 2013. Although the number of trade fairs stagnated, the overall figures developed positively: featuring more than 17,500 exhibitors and 580,000 visitors. The stand space remained stable at 500,000 square metres. The positive development visible in previous years continued in India, too. Around 120,000 square metres of space was rented to more than 4,800 exhibitors across 32 trade fairs visited by around 170,000 individuals.

Figure 4: Number of exhibitors in China at events by German Organisers.

Turkey managed to take fourth place among the most important GTQ target countries, with 20 trade fairs. Over 6,400 exhibitors occupied 258,000 square metres of exhibition space, visited by 470,000 people. Brazil was in the top six for the first time, with 16 trade fairs. Approximately 3,000 exhibitors rented over 90,000 square metres of space here; more than 170,000 visitors attended these trade fairs.

In 2014, 21 members of AUMA and FAMA intended to hold more than 300 trade fairs on all continents. The most important market for German organisers is China, with 88 trade fairs, followed by Russia (41) and India (37). 19 trade fairs will be held in the USA, while 17 are to be held in Turkey, and 14 in Brazil. Shanghai (44) and Moscow (34) are the two cities with the most GTQ trade fairs. Other important cities include Mumbai (19), Beijing (15), Istanbul (13), New Delhi (11) and Dubai (10).

China's meetings industry: A future market for Germany

Schultze, Matthias

中国会议产业：德国未来的市场

Germany has been one of the world's leading destinations for meetings and congresses for many years. It is the role of the GCB German Convention Bureau to secure this position for the future by marketing German meeting and congress facilities and products in source markets, but also by stimulating new ideas in order to prepare the sector for important future developments. As the globalisation megatrend continues, the GCB supports the event sector in adapting its services to the needs of international customers.

As a future market with outstanding potential, China is a major focus of the GCB's marketing activities, which primarily highlight the expertise of German cities and regions in areas of business and science that are important for international trade between the two countries. These cities and regions offer an ideal framework for events run by Chinese companies and organisations. Germany's expertise in the automobile industry, chemicals and pharmaceuticals and other technological sectors is of particular interest to Chinese meeting planners.

多年来，德国一直是世界领先的会议及大型会议举办地之一。德国会议促进局（GCB）把德国在将来仍拥有这样的地位当成主要任务，它不仅在各个客源市场推广德国的会议设施和产品，而且促进创新以保证会展产业积极应对未来的发展。随着全球化趋势不断深入，德国会议促进局倡导和支持会展产业改善其服务以满足世界各地顾客的需求。

作为有杰出发展潜力的未来市场，中国是德国会议促进局的市场推广重点。德国会议促进局强调了德国的城市和地区在商业与科学方面的优势与专长，这也正是两国贸易关系的关键所在。这些城市和地区为中国企业和机构举办会展活动提供了理想的架构。德国在汽车工业、化工和制药以及其他技术领域的专长正是中国会议策划者们的兴趣所在。

1 Event destination Germany

A leader in Europe and around the world

Germany is one of the world's leading destinations for meetings and congresses. In the rankings published by the International Congress & Convention Association (ICCA), which include international association events with at least 50 participants, Germany has been the No. 1 in the European comparison and No. 2 worldwide after the USA for the past 11 years. In 2014, the ICCA statistics for Germany registered 659 international association meetings. (Source: ICCA statistics "International Association Meetings" ICCA, April 2014).

Figure 1: International significance of event destinations

The "Meeting- & EventBarometer Deutschland 2014/15" published in May 2015 includes events and smaller meetings. In 2014, this survey recorded 3.04 million events in Germany. These were attended by a total of 383 million participants, 3.3 per cent more than in the previous year.

China's meetings industry: A future market for Germany 79

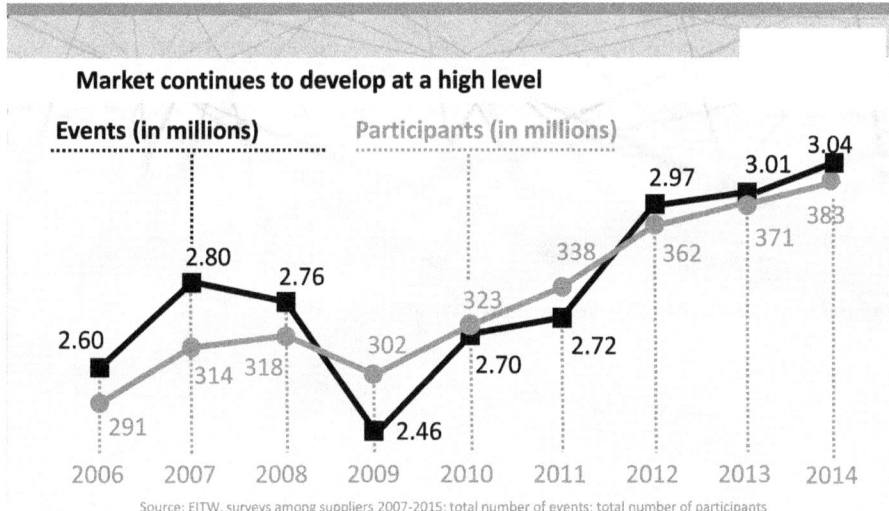

Figure 2: Market development 2006–2014

Greater demand has also stimulated growth on the supply side: 7,152 meeting and event locations were available in 2014, an increase of 1.7 per cent compared to the previous year.

Figure 3: Event locations in Germany

At the same time, the number of international participants has grown constantly over recent years – from 14.3 million in 2006 to 25.6 million in 2014. Moreover, the sector expects this trend to continue. 58 per cent of the suppliers who participated in the study and 51,7 per cent of German event organisers believe that international events will continue to grow in importance over the coming years.

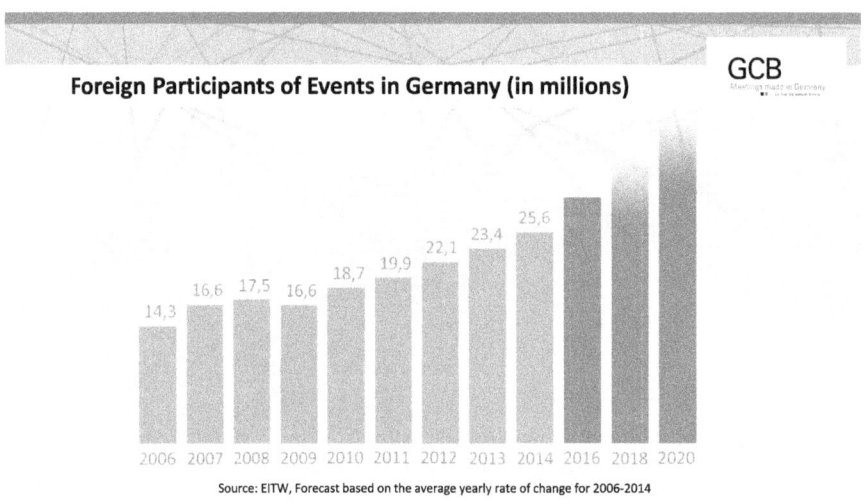

Figure 4: Foreign participants of events in Germany

Good reasons for events in Germany

For an event location to be internationally competitive, it must satisfy three important needs. As well as excellent value for money, it must also offer outstanding infrastructure. The quality of Germany's infrastructure is ranked No. 3 in the world (Global Competitiveness Report of the World Economic Forum, 2013). Event planners profit not only from outstanding transport connections with more than 40 airports, a dense railway network and excellent highways but also from the country's many first-class conference hotels, convention centres and event locations.

Germany also scores highly due to its expertise in important areas of science and commerce that offers meeting and event organisers useful synergy effects and enables them to link conferences with topical and related events – such as factory tours or accompanying programmes.

German convention organisers have also been quick to tap into the innovative power of business and science, for example Germany is an international leader in the growing area of "green meetings".

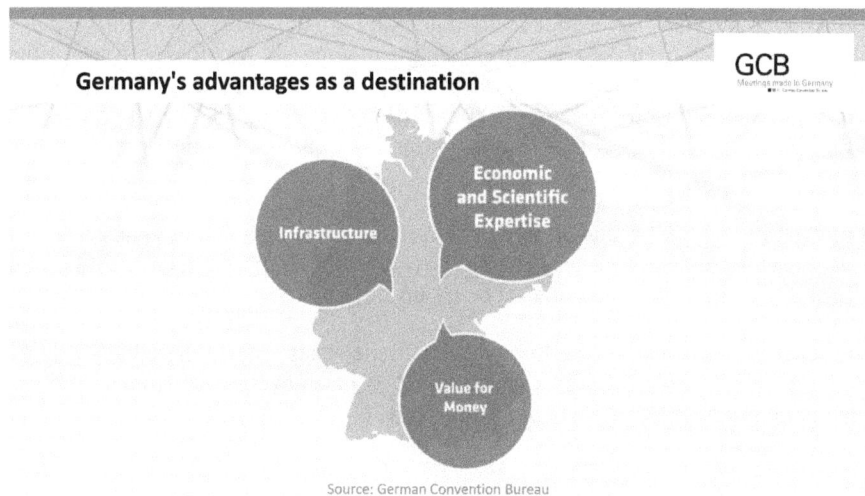

Figure 5: Germany's advantage as a destination

GCB German Convention Bureau e. V.

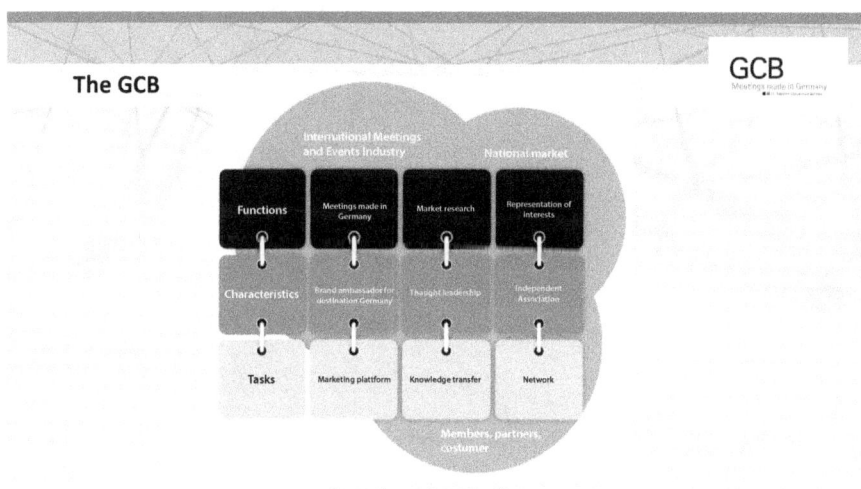

Figure 6: The GCB

The GCB German Convention Bureau is the marketing organisation that represents the German meeting and congress sector. It supports its members and partners in marketing their products and services both nationally and internationally while also stimulating new ideas in the sector. The GCB has around 200 members representing over 450 businesses including leading hotels, convention centres, locations, city marketing organisations and event agencies as well as service providers from the German meeting and congress sector. The roles of the GCB are clearly defined: representation, marketing and promotion of sales, creation of platforms, monitoring the market and collecting data as well as consulting and taking care of the interests of the sector in dealings with international and national authorities, organisations and media.

The GCB's marketing activities focus on three major themes: Germany's key industries as a powerhouse of business and science, sustainable development in the German meeting and congress sector and the innovative potential of Germany.

Industrial and scientific expertise, mutually beneficial trade relations and shared key sectors are becoming ever more important factors in the selection of an event destination – and the GCB's key industries strategy takes account of this trend.

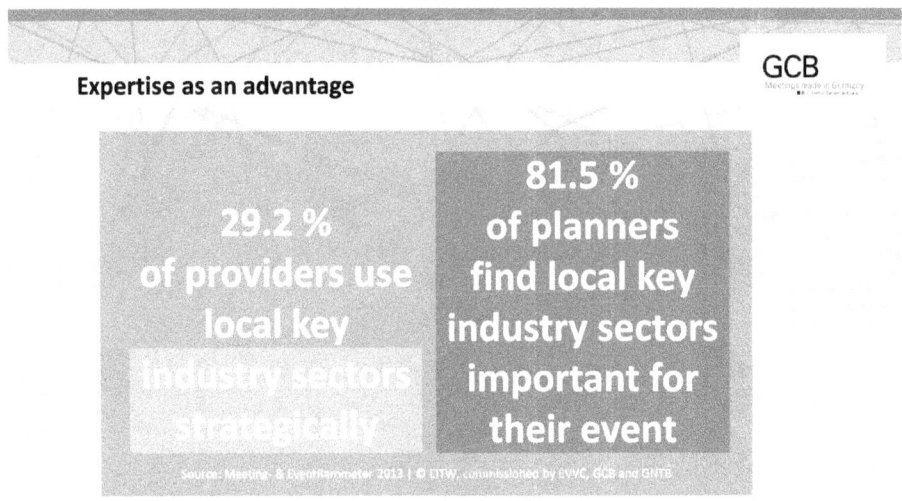

Figure 7: Expertise as an advantage

In the area of sustainability, the GCB takes its responsibilities seriously – not only for the benefit of the environment and society as a whole but also in order to create a competitive advantage for the German meeting and congress sector. As sustainability grows in importance as a mark of quality and as a criterion in the selection process for event destinations around the world, Germany's commitment as a pioneer in the area of "green meetings" will also pay financial dividends in the future.

The GCB began addressing the topic of innovation in 2013 with the study published in cooperation with its partners "Meetings and conventions 2030: A study of megatrends shaping our industry". It is no longer sufficient for companies to keep pace with developments. They must forge ahead and proactively shape the future. In doing so, the GCB also implements its own innovative ideas helping the event sector to prepare for the megatrends and challenges identified in the study.

2 The future of the event sector

The study "Meetings and conventions 2030" sheds light on current megatrends, their future development and the ways in which they will affect the meeting and congress sector. Megatrends are an important concept in futurology. They are used to describe transformations, which take place over a number of decades and impact every area of life and society – politics, leisure, working lives and value creation structures. They are frequently global in nature. This study identified five megatrends, which are of particular relevance to the meeting and congress sector:

- Technology in work and life
- globalisation and internationalisation
- mobility of the future
- sustainable development
- demographic change.

These megatrends offer opportunities for events in Germany but also create significant challenges for those involved in the meeting and congress sector.

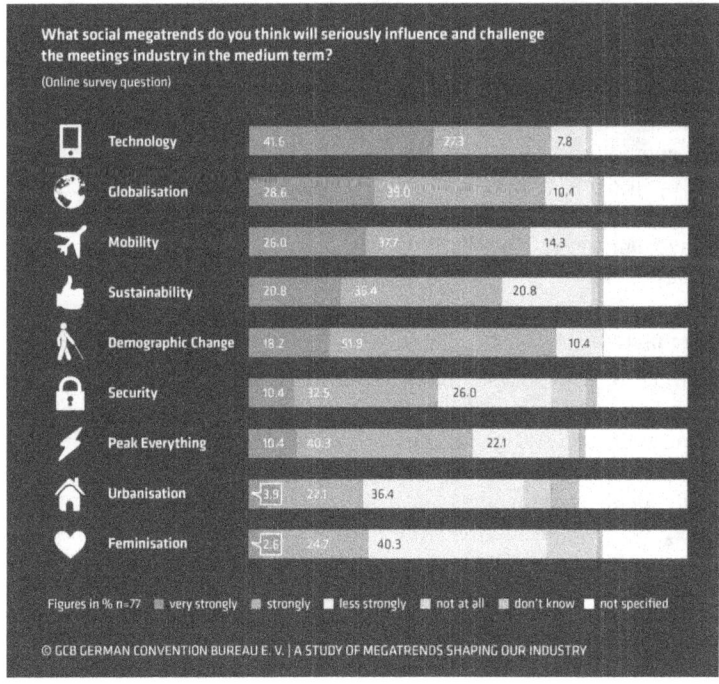

Figure 8: Megatrends

Megatrend: Globalisation and internationalisation

Observers have been monitoring the phenomenon of globalisation for a number of decades. It directly affects an ever-growing number of population groups on every continent. For example, thriving global networks are being observed in areas such as business, science, politics, social structures, culture, communication and the environment. Global relationships are becoming more densely interconnected and can be seen on every level: from individuals and institutions to states, companies and associations as well as supranational organisations, such as the EU.

Virtually every indicator of globalisation, such as mobility of persons, the volume of global trade or communication and Internet access, is rising. The same applies in the areas of culture, language and politics. The international legal business is expanding, the number of organisations likewise.

Cultural diversity

The continuing trend of globalisation means that an ever growing number of international participants are attending an ever growing number of international events. The result is greater cultural difference and diversity. Despite the homogenisation of many product areas, it means that global companies have to take better account of the needs of local customers and markets.

This has special implications for the meeting and congress sector. As conditions change more and more rapidly, the importance of globally distributed meetings and conferences across many locations is growing. It is therefore vital to understand and study the backgrounds of different markets, countries and participants in order to be able to plan and respond appropriately. Patterns of expected behaviour, languages and cultural norms as well as forms of communication and interaction must become even greater priorities in the organisation of successful meetings and congresses. This affects areas such as formal greetings, religious rituals, provision of breaks and places for prayer, rules regarding physical contact, taboos, holidays and food cultures. In Germany, it is standard practice for employees in the event sector to speak foreign languages. Intercultural understanding and competences are also being promoted enthusiastically.

New competitors and new markets

With the advance of globalisation, new competitors such as the BRIC nations (Brazil, Russia, India and China) are emerging and claiming a growing proportion of the international meeting and congress business. In order to gain an early foothold in the markets of tomorrow, the GCB continuously evaluates the markets it monitors and observes. It tests market development concepts for its members as well as for its own presence in these markets and develops market entry strategies. Globalisation is an important trend of the future and therefore also offers excellent opportunities for German suppliers to grow in existing and future markets.

The growth of worldwide networking

As the internationalisation and globalisation of markets and social structures continues, the meeting and congress sector is taking on fresh importance. Well-equipped meeting places and events are essential as the foundation for more widespread and wide-ranging clarification and networking processes. International organisations, in particular, are highly dependent on the ability to exchange information and ideas effectively as their market positions and services are based primarily on the development and commercial exploitation of intellectual resources.

Accessibility and mobility

Greater internationalisation with growing numbers of international guests attending events also means that Germany, as an international event destination with an outstanding position, must continue to be highly accessible in the future. The rising cost of energy around the world and the need for greater investment in security systems are two of the challenges in this area. Moreover, participants at these events have ever higher expectations regarding the flexibility and individuality of mobility services. Consequently, it will be necessary to make transportation more multimodal, cooperative and efficient and also incorporate input from event providers and planners.

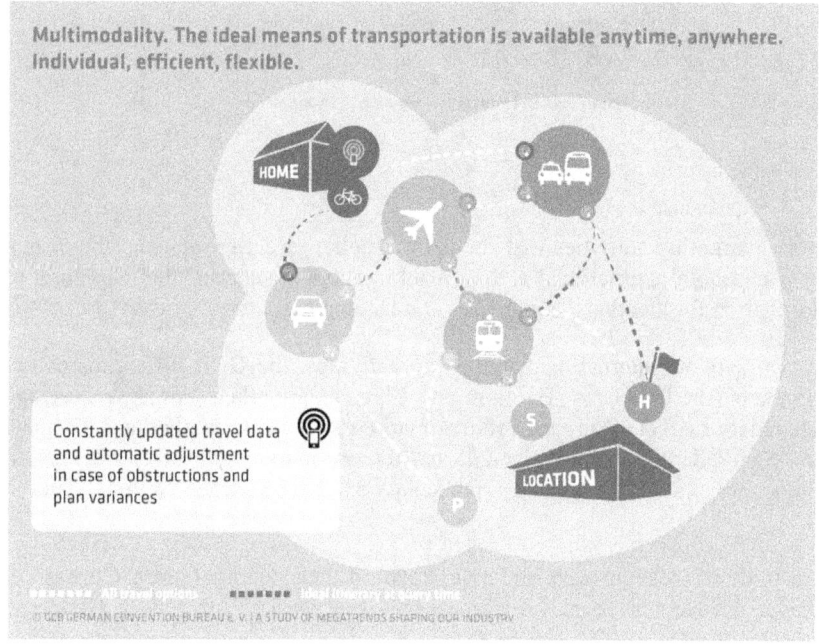

Figure 9: Accessibility and mobility

3   The GCB market development strategy

Source markets with potential

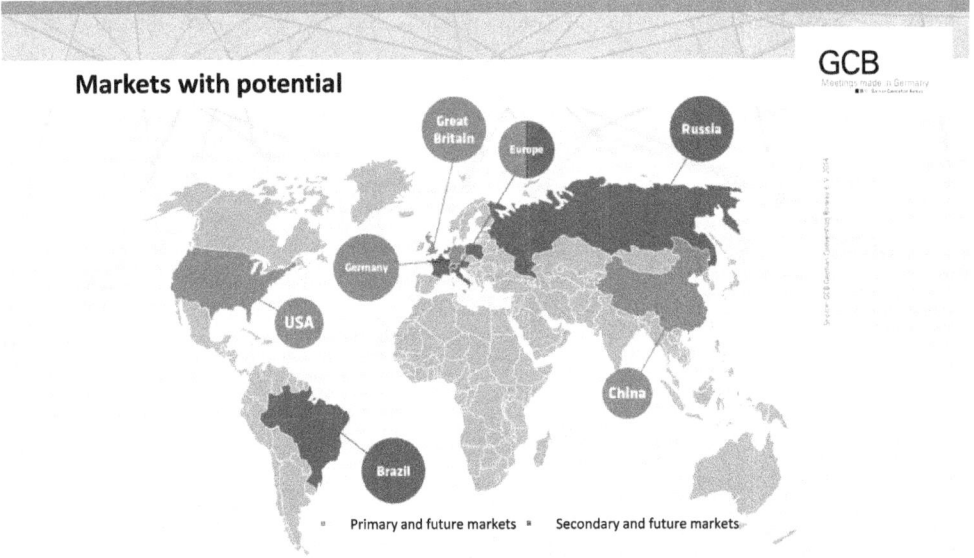

Figure 10: Markets with potential

The GCB develops marketing activities that focus on specific target groups and thus has a widespread presence in both international and national markets. It supports the marketing of Germany as a destination for meetings, congresses and incentives.

Within the framework of its international marketing activities, the GCB differentiates between primary markets (the UK, USA, Belgium and China as a market with above-average growth rates), secondary markets (European source markets such as the Netherlands, France, Italy, Austria and Switzerland as well as Brazil) and tertiary markets (all other markets, in which the GCB cooperates with the foreign representations of the German National Tourist Board (GNTB)).

After an in-depth study of these markets and assessment of their potential, the GCB has decided to focus, over the coming years, on China as well as the key markets of Germany, Europe and the USA.

The importance of the Chinese market

The Chinese market has emerged as an important future market for the German meeting and congress sector. According to the "Meeting- & EventBarometer 2012/2013", China has already risen to become the 11th most important source market for suppliers to the German meeting and congress industry and stands alongside the USA as the only non-European country to feature in the upper regions of the rankings.

The GCB's marketing activities primarily highlight the expertise of German cities and regions in areas of business and science, which are important for international trade between the two countries. These cities and regions offer an ideal framework for events from China. This was confirmed, among other things, by a survey of predominantly Chinese MICE buyers in the "China and Asia Meetings Industry Research Report 2011", which identified important factors influencing the selection of an event destination as being not only price, location and quality of accommodation and service but also the strength of the trade relationships with China.

China is Germany's largest trading partner after France and the Netherlands. The German Chambers of Commerce and Industry forecast that China will become the country's number one trading partner in approximately 10 years. Germany is already China's top trading partner in terms of export volumes.

German joint ventures have taken on a central role in the world's largest automobile market and the boom in the Chinese chemicals and pharmaceuticals sector has benefited Germany as well through rising exports. Moreover, China is an important market for German engineering companies in the rapidly expanding area of laboratory, measurement and control technology as well as in medical-technical systems.

China: Economic partner
In 2013, Germany and China traded goods with a total value of more than €140 billion.
- Exports: In 2013, Germany' exports to China were worth around €67 billion, primarily machinery, vehicles and chemical products.
- Imports: Chinese companies exported goods worth over €73 billion to Germany in 2013 – a fourfold increase compared to 2000. The most important products were computers, mobile phones and electronics as well as clothing and electrical equipment.
- Investment: So far, German companies have invested more than €26.5 billion in China. Some 4,000 companies are currently active in the country. In 2012 alone, German investment in China rose by 28.5 per cent to US$ 1.45 billion. Conversely, 98 new Chinese companies settled in Germany in 2012. There are now a total of 2,000 Chinese businesses operating in the Federal Republic making China the third largest foreign investor in Germany after the USA and Switzerland.

Source: Handelsblatt Online, 31.03.2014

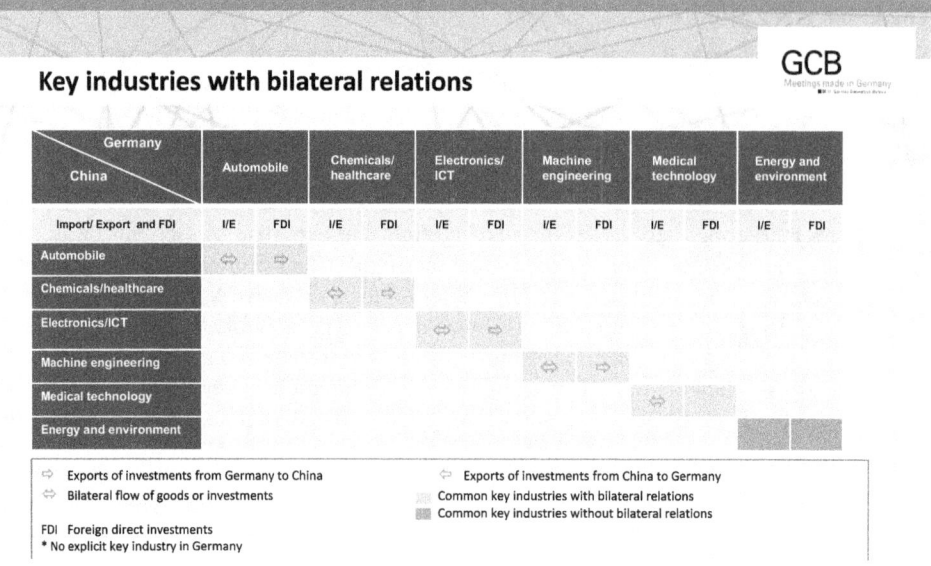

Figure 11: Key industries

GCB marketing in China

The GCB's activities in China are based on intensive market research and evaluation. Of these, a study the GCB commissioned from TNS Infratest with a special focus on bilateral German-Chinese key industry sectors and the development of business travel statistics are worthy of special mention. Other sources, surveys and studies have also been taken into account.

For entering the Chinese market, the GCB has implemented the following strategy and formulated objectives for the near future:

- August 2013: Opening event in the "Audi City Digital Showroom" in Beijing as part of the GNTB theme of the year "Germany: open for business – trade fairs and conventions" – the theme and selection of the event location were closely related to the GCB's key industry strategy
- 2014: Market development in cooperation with GNTB representatives in Beijing. As well as media relations and sales calls, the focus was on a multi-month online training programme for Chinese event planners in order to inform them about Germany as a meeting and congress destination
- 2015: Opening of GCB representative office in Beijing, expansion of marketing activities, step-by-step development of further opportunities for participation by GCB members.

Outlook

Germany's success as a destination for events from the Chinese market depends heavily on the mutual trade relationships between Germany and China, which is expected to continue its positive trend and indeed intensify over the coming years.

Furthermore, the GCB together with many partners in the German events sector supports German market participants – such as hotels, convention centres, locations and mobility service providers – in presenting their products. These have been adjusted to the needs of an increasingly international market and the expectations of Chinese customers in particular. To ensure that employees working in the sector in Germany meet these expectations it is crucial that companies and institutions in the event sector invest in effective training and professional development programmes. The globalisation megatrend will make competence in foreign languages and intercultural skills a key criterion in the selection process for event locations.

Mobility services capable of handling the challenges of the future are equally important – multimodal concepts, which not only ensure that international guests are able to find their way around easily and comfortably using the latest technology but also integrate services from a wide range of transport systems that are both flexible and conserve resources.

The study "Meetings and conventions 2030: A study of megatrends shaping our industry" has supplied the foundation for vital initiatives in the sector. The activities implemented by the GCB together with its partners in the wake of this study continue to sharpen awareness of the significance of these areas among providers of events products and services in Germany. The aim is to secure Germany's top position as a destination for international event planners – including and especially those in China – for the future.

4 Literature

Global Competitiveness Report of the World Economic Forum, 2013

Handelsblatt Online, 31.03.2014

ICCA statistics "International Association Meetings" ICCA, April 2015

Externalities, market potential and tourism development: Empirical evidence from China

Zhao, Lei,
Quan, Hua,
Xie, Jia

外部性，市场潜力和旅游发展：来自中国的实证研究

Externalities are important in explaining the development path of whole industries. The same is true for the development of tourism. This article analyses empirically which externalities have been most important in explaining the agglomeration of tourism in China. The findings of the regression analysis provide for food for thought for policy makers and researchers.

外部性对解释产业的发展路径至关重要。它同样适用于解析旅游产业的发展。本文以实证研究的方式分析了哪些外部性在剖析中国旅游业集聚现象时最为重要。通过回归计算得出的研究结果为政策制定者和研究人员提供了思考依据。

1 Introduction

According to the economic growth theory, higher efficiency can improve the state of development. Therefore, it follows that tourism efficiency can basically increase the quality of tourism development. However, in the final analysis, it also depends on whether the internal structure of the tourism is reasonable or not (Baoping Ren, 2010). From this perspective, the tourism sectors' structure is one of the important variables that influences the development of tourism.

Relying on a macro perspective, one of the external features of the tourism structure's1 dynamic changes is the tourism industry agglomeration2 phenomenon. It is also the same when specifying to the internal tourism industry. Externalities and increasing returns to scale can enhance the technology innovation capability of tourism enterprises through the skilled labour market, professional service of intermediate input and technology spill-overs. These effects have become important for achieving adjustment, optimization, transformation and upgrading of tourism's structure. As a result of the tourism structure's dynamic evolution, the tourism industry agglomeration phenomenon includes both historical causal factors and other factors. For the former, neoclassical location theory gives the answer. Regarding the latter, spatial economy and the new economic geography provide a more precise explanation and the latter is the focus of our concern. Ultimately, the dynamic adjustment of the tourism structure is just the result of the specialization within the tourism industry. In fact, the specialization of tourism industry segmentation in the process of structure adjustment is the internal sources of tourism industry agglomeration; the tourism industry agglomeration is the form of the spatial organization of the structural adjustment performance.

Referring to the agglomeration in the tourism industry agglomeration, the main reason is that industrial agglomeration not only represents the dynamics of the economic structure. More importantly, it highlights the space factors missing in the neoclassic growth theory, namely the tourism market potential. Moreover, it also subverts the assumptions about perfect competition and constant returns to scale, which were key elements in the neoclassical growth theory. The contribution of the new economic geography school is remarkable. It integrates the industrial spatial agglomeration, market potential and economic growth into a unified analytical framework for dynamic investigation. According to this theory, the tourism industry's agglomeration accompanies tourism scale expansion. Tourism industry agglomeration promotes tourism scale expansion mainly by expanding market breadth and depth: for the former, the tourism industry's agglomeration can expand internal product markets through the accumulative cycle effects of the self-reinforcing demand which is released by the market potential. A typical example is what Krugman called the "Home Market Effect". For the latter, the tourism industry's agglomeration cannot only reduce tourists' search costs, but can also reduce tourism enterprises transaction costs. In short, tourism industry agglomeration can promote tourism development by expanding the market potential and releasing agglomeration economy.

2 Theoretical exploration

As mentioned above, tourism industry agglomeration mainly comes from the tourism structure's dynamic adjustment under the market allocation, and it affects the tourism industry scale through the generalized form of agglomeration economy. In detail, the logical starting point lies in the differences between the level of sophistication and rationalization of interregional tourism structure. Dynamic mechanism performances as the externalities of overall tourism industry's development dominated by the tourism structure, because relying on tourism resources endowment, tourism development model driven by traditional factors is no longer suitable for industry requirements of shifting to the modern service industry, the externalities of tourism industry agglomeration becomes an important potential power for the development of tourism industry. As mention above, the externalities of tourism industry agglomeration not only refers to labour market share and the home market effect, but also includes the industry correlation effect. In a narrow sense, tourism industry correlation effect usually refers to the backward correlation or linkage, which mainly manifests in demand-pull effect between tourism industry and related industries. While tourism productive service function is targeted at tourism industry forward correlation problem, forward correlation can reflect more importance that the tourism industry contributes to the development of the other national economy industries. The interpretation of the relationship between tourism industry agglomeration and the financial externalities and the theoretical notion of it is relatively clear.

Based on the existing theoretical research, the interaction relationship principle of tourism structure, agglomeration and development is provided with universality3. In terms of tourism, the static configuration and dynamic adjustment of tourism industry structure have the same important influence on it. Nevertheless, it is also noted that the existence of technical externalities is indisputable as the general industrial economic theory suggested. But for this issue, there have been for a long time two arguments: specialization and monopoly are more conducive to industrial development or diversification and competition are more conducive to industrial development. This refers to the so-called MAR externalities (Marshall, 1890; Arrow, 1962; Romer, 1986) and Jacobs externalities (Jacobs1969) (Qi Liang and Xuefeng Qian, 2007). For the development of tourism, the externalities of different industrial sectors take effect in the same way. The MAR externalities theory states that, in a particular space, a large number of agglomerations or monopoly can promote technology and knowledge spill-over among the enterprises in the industry. This allows for the internalization of technology externalities, which is conducive to the development of an industry. The Jacobs externalities theory suggests that knowledge can spill-over among the enterprise belonging to different and complementary industries. Thus the higher the degree of diversification of local industries, the more conducive to externalities generated, and promoted the development of the industry. The phenomenon is important to explain urbanization. In comparison, MAR externalities theory emphasizes that monopoly is more conducive to innovation, while Jacobs externalities theory emphasizes competition is more conducive to innovation. In addition, different from these two externalities theories, Porter externalities identifies with Jacobs externalities viewpoints about competition conducive to spill-over of knowledge innovation, but that knowledge spill-over mainly occurs in the same industry. The three theoretical reflections on externalities can help addressing the question what kind of tourism industry market structure is more conducive to innovation. Exactly, which kind of externalities promoted the industry growth? The research conclusion is not given by the empirical evidence (Glaeser, etc., 1992; Feldman and Audretsch, 1999; Blien etc., 2006). Moreover, for the literatures of industry agglomeration mainly focusing on the externalities between industries, few literatures explore the externalities of subdivision in a particular industry. Therefore, based on the current status of Chinese tourism industry statistics, this paper goes deep into the interior of single tourism sector: it constructs the index of specialization and diversification of tourism subdivision. Furthermore, based on the perspective of market potential generated in the process of tourism industry agglomeration, the paper tries to reveal and empirically verify the influence mechanism between tourism industry agglomeration and development.

3 Model specification and variable definitions

3.1 Model specification

In order to analyse the relationship between tourism industry scale and static configuration and dynamic adjustment of tourism sector structure, we adopt a two-factor (capital and labour) Cobb-Douglas production function:

$$Y_{it} = A_{it} K_{it}^{\alpha} L_{it}^{\beta} \quad (1)$$

Where Y is total output of tourism industry, A is technical level, K is capital and L is labour input, i is region and t is time.

Lag type (1) for one period and take the logarithmic on both sides, we can derive the model of growth rate:

$$\ln(Y_{it}/Y_{i,t-1}) = \ln(A_{it}/A_{i,t-1}) + \alpha \ln(K_{it}/K_{i,t-1}) + \beta \ln(L_{it}/L_{i,t-1}) \quad (2)$$

We assume that in region i, tourism sector subdivision's growth of the technical level A in period t depends on the static and dynamic adjustment of tourism sector structure, namely it depends on the ratio of tourism sector structure static configuration and the various dynamic externalities of tourism industry agglomeration. Therefore, type (2) can be further converted to:

$$\ln(A_{it}/A_{i,t-1}) = g(H、S、D、C)_{it} + e_t \quad (3)$$

Where H is concentration ratio, S is specialization, D is diversification and C is competition.

Plug type (3) into type (2) and get:

$$\ln(Y_{it}/Y_{i,t-1}) = \ln H_{it} + \ln S_{it} + \ln D_{it} + \ln C_{it} \quad (4)$$

3.2 Variable Definitions

Explained variable is tourism total output4, namely the revenue of five kind of tourism industry segment is adopted to measure the output.

Explanatory variables include the ratio of static configuration and externalities of dynamic agglomeration of tourism industry structure: five basic segments' fixed assets and employment were selected to represent the inputs of capital and labour. Other explanatory variables are defined as follows:

3.3 Concentration of tourism

Considering the current situation of Chinese tourism industry statistics and the difference between the annual statistics indicators, the paper uses the ratio of two kinds of tourism subdivision output except star hotels, travel agencies and scenic spots (points) to the tourism industry total output to measure the concentration of the tourism industry in order to keep the consistency and comparability of the statistical data. The lower proportion indicates that the leading position of three kinds of tourism subdivisions in tourism development is more obvious and the concentration of tourism industry is higher. Basically two aspects are considered: first, in the annual China Tourism Statistics Yearbook, the existing statistical index about the star hotels, travel agencies and tourist scenic spots (points) is relatively intact, furthermore,

Externalities, market potential and tourism development

the proportion of three tourism basic subdivision output is higher. Second, due to the borderless nature of tourism industry development, new formats originating from industry convergence emerge constantly. The existing official tourism statistics did not give a specific statistical classification standard, only generally merged it into the tourism subdivision of other tourism enterprises.

3.4   Specialization of tourism

The formula is:

$$S_{i,j} = \frac{Y_{i,j}/Y_i}{Y_{n,j}/Y_n} \quad (5)$$

Where n is whole country, $Y_{n,j}$ is national output of j industry (respectively represents star hotels, travel agencies and scenic spots (points)), Y_i is tourism total output of i province, Y_n is national tourism total output. Obviously, this index measures specialization degree of j industry relative to the national level in region i.

3.5   Diversification of tourism

A feasible and intuitive method is adopting the ratio of other tourism enterprises belonging to five basic tourism industry subdivisions to measure the diversification of tourism. This method can reflect the diversified trend of tourism sector to a certain extent, but it also ignores the diversified competition of four kinds of most important tourism subdivisions namely star hotels, travel agencies, scenic spots (points) and tourism transport companies. In addition, for the other tourism companies, the China Tourism Statistics Yearbook did not give a clear definition of content and statistical standards varied. Furthermore, there was a serious lack of other tourism enterprises' statistical indicators in some years. For example, China Tourism Statistics Yearbook (Copy 2000) missing all statistical indicators of the other tourism enterprises'; China Tourism Statistics Yearbook (Copy 2003) classified the rest enterprises as the other tourism enterprises excepted star hotels and travel agencies; China Tourism Statistics Yearbook (Copy 2005) classified the rest enterprises as the other tourism enterprises excepted star hotels, travel agencies and scenic spots (points). Therefore, if we only use the other enterprises as the proxy index of tourism diversification, the problem of divestiture will emerge.

$$D_{i,j} = \frac{1/\sum_{j \neq j}^{M}[\frac{Y_{i,j'}}{Y_i - Y_{i,j}}]^2}{1/\sum_{j \neq j}^{M}[\frac{Y_{n,j'}}{Y_n - Y_{n,j}}]^2} \quad (6)$$

Where M is the total number of tourism sectors $Y_{i,j'}$ is the sum of all other tourism sectors output excepted sector j in i province. $Y_{n,j'}$ is the sum of all the other tourism sectors output excepted sector j in whole country. The indicator reflects the diversified environment possessed by sector j in i.

3.6 Competition of tourism

The indicator is designed to measure the intensity of competition facing the tourism sector in a certain region, namely, $C_{i,j}$ is the intensity of competition facing sector j in i province, which is defined as the quotient of two ratios: one ratio is generated from the enterprises number of sector j in i province divided by the output of these enterprises while the other ratio accounted these two numbers on the national level.

$$C_{i,j} = \frac{q_{i,j}/Y_{i,j}}{q_{n,j}/Y_{n,j}} \quad (7)$$

Where $q_{i,j}$ is the enterprises number of sector j in i province, $q_{n,j}$ is the enterprises number of sector j in whole country. Obviously, the ratio is larger indicates that in this region, the enterprises' competition of the certain sector is more intensive.

In addition to these variables, we also introduce the variable of tourism market potential. This variable not only can be used to measure the degree of a regional tourism market closed to the external market, but also reflect the financial externalities generated in the process of tourism industry agglomeration. The empirical literatures of the new economic geography commonly adopted Harris (1954) market potential function. According to the calculation method, construction of tourism market potential function as follows:

$$MP_i = \sum_j Y_j/d_{ij} = \sum_{j \neq i} Y_j/d_{ij} + Y_i/d_{ii} \quad (8)$$

Where MP_i is the region's tourism market potential; Y_i is the national tourism total output in i region; d_{ij} is the distance between i and j; d_{ii} is the internal distance in region i, its calculating formula is $d_{ii} = 2/3\sqrt{area_i/\pi}$; $area_i$ is the land area of region i.

Tourism market potential can also reflects the output of tourism industry on the level of province, namely the spatial agglomeration structure of tourism economy development. Specifically, a regional tourism market potential is greater, meaning that the tourism industry structure adjustment is more helpful to optimize the environment; the ability for output of tourism industry is stronger. Moreover, if the accessible tourism market scale of certain region is larger, the agglomeration economy caused by financial externalities and technical externalities of tourism industry development can effectively enhance the tourism industry productive efficiency.

Except using growth rate to represent tourism productive element, all other variables in this paper take the logarithmic. Plug type (8) into type (4) and get:

$$\ln(Y_{it}/Y_{i,t-1}) = \alpha \ln(K_{it}/K_{i,t-1}) + \beta \ln(L_{it}/L_{i,t-1}) + \phi \ln H_{it}$$
$$+ \varphi \ln S_{it} + \psi \ln D_{it} + \delta \ln C_{it} + \vartheta \ln MP_{it} + \mu_{it} \qquad (9)$$

4 The analysis of the empirical results

The study sample in this paper is the panel data (excluding Tibet) of 30 provinces and autonomous region in China from 2000 to 2009. Respectively, the original data comes from China Tourism Yearbook and China Tourism Statistics Yearbook over the years.

4.1 The preliminary regression of national data

Table 1 reports the preliminary regression results of the tourism sector structure static configuration and dynamic adjustment, namely the concentration of tourism sector structure and agglomeration externalities to the scale of tourism industry at the national level. Table 1 shows that the coefficient of tourism sector capital input is positive. Nevertheless, the coefficient of the tourism sector labour input is positive, but basically not significant. Comparing above two regression coefficients, the former is bigger than the latter, which indicates that the expansion of Chinese tourism industry scale is basically driven by capital input. The input of capital has a significant role in promoting the tourism industry's development. In addition, tourism regression coefficient on the initial condition is significantly negative at 1 % level, which shows there is a catch-up effect at the beginning of tourism development in backward areas compared with developed areas. The result indicates that these backward areas show relatively higher growth and the differences in the level of regional tourism development are gradually reduced.

In Table 1, model 2 to model 9, the relevant variables reflecting the tourism industry structure static and dynamic characteristics are plugged into the regression model. Because of a collinearity problem between the tourism competition and tourism market potential, these two variables will be regressed respectively in model 6 and model 7. Excluding model 2, model 3 and model 8, the regression coefficient of the tourism specialization is significantly negative and significant at the 1 % level, which shows that tourism specialization affected the tourism development in a negative way. In the province, the higher specialization level of tourism sector, or the tourism sector in the geographic location becomes more concentrated and its position in the geographical pattern becomes the more prominent, the further development of this tourism sector is slower, which means MAR externalities do not exist. In contrast, the regression coefficient of tourism diversification is significantly positive at the 1 % level, which shows the diversified development environment is conducive to the development of overall tourism industry. In the process of tourism industry agglomeration, the externalities originated from the symbiotic effect benefit the development of tourism industry. The result verifies the existence of Jacobs's externalities. This is especially important in the reality of tourism development. From the perspective of demand, the demand of tourists are various and diverse. This requires the product function in the tourism market to be comprehensive. Specific to the realities, only the diverse and symbiosis environment created by the extension of tourism industry chain can achieve the equilibrium of tourism market at the most extent. From supply perspective, due to the low entry barriers of tourism market and less standardized of tourism Market economic order at this stage, it is highly possible to incur the phenomenon that a certain tourism sector specificities at a high level within the same geographical area. The endogenous mismatch risk of tourism industry structure caused by contradiction of supply and demand not only reduces the efficiency of tourism industry, but also against the development of tourism industry. The above two research conclusions are consistent with the research result about the relationship of specialization, diversification and tourism development (Yong Yang, 2011). In addition, in other industries, such as manufacturing industry of China, the existence of MAR externalities effect was not found while the existence of Jacobs externalities remains controversial (WenGuangBo, 2007; Sanmang Wu and Shantong Li, 2011).

In model 4 and model 5, the coefficient of tourism competition is significantly negative at 1 % level and the coefficient of tourism concentration is significantly positive at 1 % level is. The two regression results are obviously consistent. The former shows that the tourism industry internal competition and tourism development is a negative relationship, namely, higher degree of internal competition in certain tourism sector not conducive to the development of tourism industry, which proves that Porter externalities does not exist; The latter further reveals only by reducing the degree of tourism sectors monopoly or concentration, implementing the balanced development between tourism sectors, the development of all over tourism industry can be promoted. The model 5 shows that as long as the other two types of tourism sectors output accounted for 1 % increase, the speed rate of promoting tourism scale expansion will increase 0.1121 %. The possible reason for the former is existence of monopoly enterprises in the tourism industry. These monopoly enterprises dominate in resource acquisition, technology innovation, or product pricing, while other small and medium-sized tourism enterprises are in a weak position in the competition. Therefore, a temporary phenomenon is that if the monopoly price of monopoly enterprises in tourism industry is higher than marginal cost, a low utilization rate of resources will appear easily in the long-term market equilibrium. On the other hand, the small and medium-sized tourism enterprises gradually withdraw from the market due to a lack of competitiveness. For the current competition variables, it is difficult to distinguish between the competition effect and the scale effect. More attention should be paid to explain this variable. In order to describe the influence mechanism of this variable to the development of the tourism industry, we plugged tourism competition lagged on period into type (9) and regress. Model 6 reports the result. As showed in model 6, the coefficient of current tourism competition is still significantly negative, while this coefficient lagged one period is significantly positive at 5 % level. Another possible explanation is that with the deepening of the tourism industry competition degree, the competition effect stimulates tourism enterprises to reform technology, promote

The Basic Regression Results of the Externalities and Tourism Development

Table 1

Independent Variables	Model 1	Model 2	Model 3	Model 4	Model 5	Model 6	Model 7	Model 8	Model 9
Capital (K)	0.2327** (0.097)	0.2297*** (0.061)	0.2091*** (0.088)	0.1474*** (0.052)	0.1730*** (0.053)	0.1362** (0.052)	0.0568* (0.033)	0.1188** (0.052)	0.0664** (0.032)
Labour (L)	0.0219 (0.018)	0.0217 (0.069)	0.0709** (0.029)	0.0214 (0.060)	0.0236 (0.061)	0.0116 (0.060)	0.0229 (0.038)	0.0571 (0.053)	0.0177 (0.037)
Specialization (S)		0.0606 (0.172)	−0.1921 (0.441)	−0.4759*** (0.158)	−0.5067*** (0.163)	−0.4792*** (0.157)	−0.3208*** (0.010)	−0.3130 (0.214)	−0.3809*** (0.097)
Diversification (D)			0.2617*** (0.042)	0.3210*** (0.049)	0.2921*** (0.049)	0.3268*** (0.049)	0.3591*** (0.031)	0.2906*** (0.065)	0.3370*** (0.029)
Competition (C)				−0.1691*** (0.022)		−0.1889*** (0.024)	−0.1252*** (0.014)	−0.1722*** (0.026)	
Lag one Period of Competition (L.C)						0.0481** (0.024)		0.0991*** (0.024)	
Concentration (H)					0.1121*** (0.016)				
Market potential (MP)							1.1469*** (0.061)	0.1472*** (0.037)	1.1952*** (0.058)
Initial Condition (Y)	−0.2457*** (0.060)	−0.2483 (0.041)	−0.2333 (0.075)	−0.2941*** (0.036)	−0.2836*** (0.037)	−0.2571*** (0.040)	−0.8687*** (0.038)	−0.1408*** (0.022)	−0.8925*** (0.0367)
R2	0.0831	0.2080	0.2807	0.4275	0.4054	0.4370	0.7740	0.7744	0.7903
F	0.96	0.96	1.09	1.82***	1.87***	25.84***	15.82***	99.53***	18.29***
Hausman Value	24.40***	24.43***	29.34***	57.55***	67.55***	33.90***	484.13***	427.67***	639.31***
Remark	FE	FE	FE	FE	FE	FE	FE	FE	FE
Observation	270	270	270	270	270	270	270	270	270

Remark: ***, **and * respectively represents significant at 1 %, 5 % 10 % level, the numbers in brackets are standard deviation.

technological progress and realize the tourism development. In short, the current phenomenon is caused by a negative effect of the enterprise scale; the lag process is caused by the positive effect of enterprise competition.

The regression results of model 7 and model 8 respectively generated from model 4 and model 6 plugged in the variable of tourism market potential. It can be seen that the tourism competition coefficients of the current item and lag is still robust. Studies have pointed out that the regional market potential and space agglomeration of manufacturing existed positive correlation (Xiuyan Liu etc., 2007). The theoretical basis lays in the greater the market potential of a region, the region, the more net profit the representative enterprises will obtain, which prompts the enterprises with profit maximization orientation to cluster in this region. In this process, the potential demand of the market gradually expanded and eventually leads the degree of industry concentration to increase. According to general principle of the new economic geography, tourism market potential also improves tourism industry agglomeration. What we care about is whether the development of tourism industry will be promoted when this process happens. There are two sides on the analysis of the problem: for one side, tourism industry agglomeration economy can promote the tourism industry development through the core – edge structure; for the other side, tourism industry agglomeration economy can lead to unbalanced in regional economic development, which may postpone tourism development. Obviously, the empirical study results of model 7, model 8 and model 9 support the positive theoretical analysis and prognosis, namely the bigger the tourism market potential is, the more greater the tourism scale will expand, which demonstrates the existence of financial externalities and consistent with the theoretical expectations. Model 7, as an example, every 1 % increase in tourism market potential, can significantly improve the tourism scale expansion rate of 1.1469 %. The numerical changes are very significant. This number is also similar with the coefficient of tourism market potential reported by model 9.

4.2   The nonlinear regression results of national data

In addition, in order to explore the possible nonlinear relationship between tourism specialization, diversification and explained variable, this paper plugged square items of tourism specialization and diversification into equation (9) and executed variable inspection. In table 2, model 1 and model 2 report the first degree coefficient of tourism specialization is significant negative, square coefficient is significant positive, namely the relationship between tourism specialization and interpreted variable is nonlinear U-shaped which indicates the situation became worsen before it improve. There are threshold-effect between tourism specialization and the explained variables. From the perspective of the numbers, the critical value of U-shape curve, which indicates the relationship of tourism diversification and tourism industry development is 1.1296 while during sample period, the mean value of tourism specialization is 1.0921. It is obvious that most of the provinces are still in the left half of the U-shaped curve. In other words, tourism specialization level can promote the expansion of tourism industry scale only after crossing the threshold value. To test the pre-set conditions, we respectively plugged the product item of tourism specialization lag one period and tourism diversification into model 1 and model 2. The regression results of model 3 and model 4 show that the coefficient of product item is significant positive. The economic meaning of the results indicate that tourism diversification possess the adjusting effects on the process of tourism specialization lag one period influencing tourism industry

The Nonlinear Regression Results of the Externalities and Tourism Development

Table 2

Independent Variables	Model 1	Model 2	Model 3	Model 4	Model 5	Model 6	Model 7	Model 8
Capital (K)	0.1284***	0.0557*	0.0579=	0.0675**	0.0620*	0.0699**	0.0506*	0.0608**
	(0.054)	(0.031)	(0.033)	(0.029)	(0.033)	(0.032)	(0.030)	(0.030)
Labour (L)	0.0847	0.0081	0.0362	0.0274***	0.0187	0.0146	-0.0002	0.0011
	(0.052)	(0.035)	(0.038)	(0.009)	(0.038)	(0.037)	(0.035)	(0.034)
Specialization (S)	-1.7003***	-1.4156***	-0.3414***	-0.3928**	-0.2918***	-0.3563***	-1.6785***	-1.5027***
	(0.669)	(0.226)	(0.101)	(0.184)	(0.101)	(0.099)	(0.222)	(0.225)
Specialization Square (S2)	0.7526**	0.6461***					0.8607***	0.7286***
	(0.306)	(0.129)					(0.125)	(0.130)
Diversification (D)	0.2486***	0.2906***	0.1977***	0.2239**	0.1728	0.1956*	-0.0041	0.0247
	(0.068)	(0.029)	(0.083)	(0.094)	(0.105)	(0.101)	(0.099)	(0.099)
Diversification Square (D2)					0.0399*	0.0305	0.0642***	0.0561***
					(0.021)	(0.021)	(0.020)	(0.020)
Product Item of Lag one Period of Specialization and Diversification (L.S× D)			0.1409**	0.0986*				
			(0.067)	(0.055)				
Competition (C)	-0.1122***		-0.1249***		-0.1176***		-0.0946***	
	(0.019)		(0.014)		(0.015)		(0.014)	
Concentration (H)		0.0825***		0.0968***		0.0934***		0.0724***
		(0.010)		(0.009)		(0.010)		(0.010)
Market potential (MP)	0.1319***	1.1579***	1.1536***	1.2002***	1.1430***	1.1899***	1.0953***	1.1434***
	(0.036)	(0.056)	(0.060)	(0.082)	(0.060)	(0.058)	(0.056)	(0.055)
Initial Condition (Y)	-0.1727***	-0.8946***	-0.8771***	-0.8981***	-0.8667***	-0.8899***	-0.8732***	-0.8901***
	(0.022)	(0.035)	(0.038)	(0.057)	(0.038)	(0.037)	(0.035)	(0.034)
R2	0.3974	0.8109	0.7781	0.7924	0.7773	0.7923	0.8151	0.8171
F	17.98***	20.37***	16.14***	18.47***	15.94***	18.34***	18.71***	20.88***
Hausman Value	578.75****	717.15****	501.43****	648.46****	489.25***	637.85****	610.15***	736.75****
Remark	FE	FE	FE	FE	FE	FE	FE	FE
Observation	270	270	270	270	270	270	270	270

Remark: ***, **and * respectively represents significant at 1 %, 5 % 10 % level, the numbers in brackets are standard deviation scale. In the diversified environment of tourism industry development, tourism specialization will show its positive effect on tourism industry development only after desirable structural adjustment. It also proved that the claim about tourism specialization effected tourism industry development negatively is too arbitrary. Model 5 shows the first degree coefficient of tourism diversification is not significant while square coefficient is significant positive. The result of model 6 is just opposite. Both two regression-results indicate that tourism diversification and interpreted variables does not exist nonlinear relationships. The positive effects of tourism diversification and tourism industry development have continuity. Model 7 and model 8 respectively carries out the regression with the first-degree item and the square item of tourism specialization and diversification. The result proved the robustness of research conclusion.

The Externalities Mechanism of Tourism Industry Agglomeration

Table 3

Independent Variables	Model 1	Model 2	Model 3	Model 4	Model 5	Model 6
Capital (K)	0.0525 (0.035)	0.0603* (0.031)	0.1117*** (0.042)	0.1326*** (0.044)	0.1445*** (0.055)	0.1647*** (0.057)
Labour (L)	0.0378* (0.020)	0.0325** (0.015)	0.0876* (0.049)	0.0899*** (0.021)	0.0970* (0.054)	0.0969* (0.053)
Specialization (S)	−2.0756*** (0.319)	−2.2331*** (0.257)	−0.4300*** (0.127)	−0.4606** (0.207)	−0.3604* (0.211)	−0.5351** (0.237)
Product Item of Specialization and market potential (S× MP)	1.0283*** (0.070)	1.0827*** (0.066)				
Product Item of Lag one Period of Specialization and Diversification (L.S× MP)			0.5825*** (0.051)	0.5936*** (0.161)		
Diversification (D)	0.3861*** (0.045)	0.3662*** (0.041)	0.3228*** (0.039)	0.2902*** (0.025)	0.1967** (0.077)	0.1569** (0.078)
Product Item of Diversification and Market Potential (D*MP)					0.0871*** (0.027)	0.1034*** (0.028)
Competition (C)	−0.1265*** (0.015)		−0.1471*** (0.018)		−0.1207*** (0.020)	
Concentration (H)		0.1006*** (0.010)		0.0988*** (0.019)		0.0853*** (0.018)
Initial Condition (Y)	−0.8355*** (0.057)	−0.8648*** (0.051)	−0.6245*** (0.041)	−0.6226*** (0.115)	−0.1657*** (0.022)	−0.1275*** (0.020)
R2	0.7375	0.7580	0.6339	0.6205	0.3506	0.3308
F	12.65***	14.97***	6.55***	6.56***	6.62***	7.16***
Hausman Value	331.60***	477.03***	19.44***	175.97***	51.97***	194.46***
Remark	FE	FE	FE	FE	FE	FE
Observation	270	270	270	270	270	270

Remark: ***、**and * respectively represents significant at 1%, 5% 10% level, the numbers in brackets are standard deviation.

4.3 A discovery: mechanism of tourism industry agglomeration externalities

As proved above, financial externalities effect offered by tourism market potential in the process of tourism industry agglomerations remarkable. In order to improve the construction of tourism products' integrated system, externalities and IRS originated from the labour division of tourism sectors improved spatial agglomeration of tourism economic activities. The above content focuses on the influence of technical externalities on tourism industry development, in particular, determining the existence of different technical externalities and its impact on tourism development, the secondary geographic role should not be ignored in the development of the tourism industry. Furthermore, the specific mechanism of the interaction between financial externalities and technical externalities generated by tourism economic activities and tourism development remains to be revealed. In order to facilitate research, there are two hypothesis needed to be empirically tested under the framework of new economic geography.

Hypothesis 1: when tourism market potential represented the profit space of tourism enterprises, two kinds of decision-making behaviour of tourism operators will appear: one is that the tourism industry specialization of blindness, the overcapacity of tourism industry have a negative impact to the development of tourism; Another is that the tourism industry coordinating specialization, which essentially has the characteristics of tourism diversification. Therefore, the symbol of product item coefficient about tourism market potential and tourism specialization is uncertain.

Hypothesis 2: tourism market potential to some extent can represent the demand of tourism market or the supply of tourism product, which provides the necessary environment for the development of tourism industry the diversification. During the interactive process in certain space, tourism sectors with higher market potential can enhance the Jacobs externalities and more likely form agglomeration economy by additional financial externalities which originated from the elements flow effect, industry correlation effect and capital creation effect. The product item coefficient of tourism market potential and tourism diversification is positive.

In table 3, model 1 and model 2 regression results shows: tourism specialization coefficient is significantly negative, the product item coefficient of tourism specialization and tourism market potential is significantly positive. Therefore, the uncertainty of hypothesis 1 is clearly. Tourism industry agglomeration originated from the process of financial externalities is actually conducive to MAR externalities effect of tourism and tourism industry development. In other words, the tourism market potential can induce the technology and knowledge spill overs between different scale enterprises of tourism industry subdivision. As tourism market potential expanding, regional agglomeration of tourism industry subdivision can improve tourism industry development in certain degree. Model 3 and model 4 is a supplementary analysis on hypothesis 1, which respectively focuses on the regression results of the product item containing tourism specialization lag one period and tourism market potential lag issue.

The result shows that the product item coefficient is significantly positive. Although tourism specialization coefficient remains significantly negative, the absolute value of product item coefficient is still bigger than that of tourism specialization coefficient. This finding primarily based on two aspects: on the one hand, the expansion of tourism market potential provides release space for productive capacity of tourism specialization development; On the other hand, the entities of tourism industry subdivision operates the tourism industry agglomeration in the Rational standard target-oriented after identified the time lag existing in the process of interaction between the increasing of tourism market potential and the development of tourism industry. Model 5 and model 6 are empirical tests of the hypothesis 2. The coefficients of tourism diversification and tourism market potential are significantly positive which supports the prejudge of hypothesis 2.

4.4 Further discussion

The further research on why there is tourism diversification rather than tourism specialization can promote the development of tourism in China. At this stage it is meaningful even we obtained the empirical evidence that Jacobs externalities could promote the development of tourism industry. On the one hand, from the producers' point of view, the diversified environment of tourism industry development provides market choices for more non-traditional tourism enterprises, which can stimulate these enterprises to provide multi-level and multi-form tourism product system. It is naturally to form two endogenous situations in this process: for one case, different types of complementary enterprises in the upstream or downstream tourism industry can obtain the financial externalities through elements flow effect and industry correlation effect. For the other case, due to the optimized adjustment of tourism industry structure, technology and knowledge are liable to produce spill-overs between the enterprises belonging different tourism sectors, which will reduce the cost of tourism enterprises innovation. From a consumers' point of view, the differential preference of tourism consumption demand is liable to be satisfied in diversified tourism industry environment, which can effectively reduce the search and transaction costs in the tourism market. On the other hand, travel experience is at the core of the tourism industry existence. The complexity of tourism motivation dominants the differentiations of tourism demand. Compared with the single specialization supply of tourism products, tourists will be more inclined to complicated and diversified tourism products system if they can obtain the psychological and emotional cognition. In the literatures of new economic geography, producers and consumers agglomeration a positive cycle mechanism of cumulative causation (Krugman, 1991). This kind of agglomeration effect can contribute to the path lock of tourism industry in certain region and expand the tourism market potential further. The preference of the tourism producers who operated basing on the technology or market choice is diversified tourism industry development environment while the preference of the tourists who choose from the perspective of differentiation demand is diversified tourism industry development environment. The coupling relationship between the supply and demand completely originated from the tourism market regulation will further enhance the effectiveness of intensive effect of diversified tourism production system in the development of the tourism industry.

5 Conclusion and Policy Implications

This article's main conclusions are the following: (1) On a national scale, the diversification of tourism has a significant positive influence on the tourism scale expansion rate. In other words, the diversification of the development environment for tourism industry is conducive to promoting tourism development, that is to say there is the externalities mentioned by Jacobs. At the same time, the MAR externalities and Porter externalities hypothesis are rejected. (2) Referring to the tourism competition degree and concentration coefficient of regression, it shows both the tourism industry monopoly, and subdivision tourism industry monopoly enterprises, have a significant negative impact on tourism development. (3) The expansion of the tourism market potential can significantly promote the development of the tourism industry, which mainly provides profitable outcome for tourism producers, which fits the framework of new economic geography theory. (4) There is a significant u-shaped nonlinear relationship between tourism professionalism and tourism development, when the tourism specialized level is low, it is not good for the tourism development; when the tourism professionalism cross threshold value, it will promote the development of tourism. The basic reason why this happens is that tourism specialized specification development not only has a certain time lag, but also need to have interaction with other factors such as the diversification of tourism, the tourism market potential and so on. (5) The potential of the tourism market is helpful to improve tourism specialization and diversification of the positive effect for the tourism development.

The research conclusion of this paper has a certain theoretical reference value when making the policy of the tourism industry. (1) The agglomeration and the tourism industry is the necessary carrier for adjusting and optimizing the tourism industry structure and promoting the development of the tourism industry, which is not only reflected that the tourism industry cluster can effectively raise the productivity of the tourism industry, can also directly promote the economic development of the tourism industry by releasing the agglomeration economy. Therefore, local governments shall formulate policies, which promote the development of tourism industry agglomeration and in this way, it can realize the tourism industrial structure optimization and upgrading through the tourist market spontaneous adjustment mechanism. (2) Encouraging the diversified tourism industry development environment, in order to create positive conditions for tourism industry integration, which not only can expand unconventional "other travel companies" content of the tourism industry from two aspects: depth and breadth, also can promote the development of traditional basic tourism industry. (3) Professional development needs to be based on the tourism industry situation, in order to avoid blind expansion, on the one hand, we need to consider how much degree that the development of regional tourism market potential and diversification of tourism to tourism industry specialization combined, considering the tourism market information, then strengthen the mutual exchanges and relate tourism industry sectors collaboration; on the other hand, at the same time we need to reduce the concentration of tourism, to further improve proportion extensibility consumer spending of tourism industry in the tourism department, to promote and regulate tourism industry or business segment to establish positive interaction between competition mechanism. (4) From the regional development, the tourism industry cluster have two positive meaning to regional economic growth from both inside and outside, mainly for two reasons: on one hand, tourism producer and consumer preference have a self-reinforcing agglomeration mechanism to diversification of tourism industry development environment, it promotes regional economic growth by the direct economic benefit of tourism industry development; On the other hand, the strength of tourism industry agglomeration, or agglomeration forwards to expand, can be turned into a regional development pole by the industry associations depth fusion indirectly effecting on regional economic growth, which a diversified growth pole will make the region economy development more vitality.

Notes:

1 In view of the similarity, we define the tourism sector structure and tourism industry structure as tourism structure in theoretical research in order to avoid confusion.

2 In general, tourism industry agglomeration comes from the dynamic change of tourism industry structure. Nevertheless, this paper focuses on tourism sector structure. In fact, tourism industry agglomeration in this paper is strictly called core tourism industry agglomeration. The connotation of tourism industry agglomeration is richer than core tourism industry agglomeration. Considering that tourism industry agglomeration is the conventional appellation in tourism research, so this paper still uses this term.

3 The reason of universality is that the interactive relationship among tourism structure, agglomeration and tourism development is mainly explanted on the level of industry. Accounting existing theoretical foundation is mainly related to the features of industry, few literatures discussed the relationship of subdivision structure and agglomeration in a single industry. According to the dialectical deduction principle, the paper attempts to provide theoretical evidence for interactive relationship among tourism industry structure, agglomeration and development by researching deeply in a single industrial boundary. In fact, the industry classification of tourism sector structure and tourism industry structure are similar, the mechanism of structure, agglomeration and development is basically identical, no matter in tourism sector or in tourism industry, and the difference only lies in the extension of tourism economy strength.

4 Explained variable in this paper is the degree of tourism development, which represented by economic scale of tourism industry; the latter is measured by tourism industry total output rather than tourism industry total revenue. There are four reasons to explain it: first, two indexes including fixed assets and employment of tourism industry are no longer recorded in tourism statistics after 2004, instead of this, these two indexes were replaced by fixed assets and employment of tourism sector. Second, the subdivision revenue of "non-tourism enterprises" accounts for a larger proportion in tourism total revenue; For example, the proportion reached 85.6 % in 2009. However, unfortunately, official tourism statistics did not carry on the detailed classification, in particular, the ambiguity of the tourism industry boundaries brought difficulties to this part of the statistics. The result is that the "non-tourism enterprises" of tourism sector unable to record in statistical number of tourism enterprises and couldn't verify the existence of tourism Porter externalities. Third, if we view "non-tourism enterprises" of tourism industry as single sector, estimate the diversification and specialization index, the relationship between partial and whole contained by "non-tourism enterprises" will be fragmented.

6 Literature

Arrow K., The Economic Implications of Learning by Doing. Review of Economic Studies, Vol. 12, No. 6, 1962, pp. 155–173.

Baoping Ren, To the Quality View of Growth: Evaluation and Reflection on the Quality of China Economic Growth. Beijing: China Economic Publishing House, 2010

Blien U., Suedekum J., Wolf K., Local Employment Growth in West Germany: A Dynamic Approach, in: Labor Economics, Vol. 13, No. 4, 2006, pp. 445–458.

China Economic Publishing House

Feldman M., Audretsch D., Innovation in Cities: Science-based Diversity, Specialization and Localized Competition, in: European Economic Review, Vol. 43, No. 2, 1999, pp. 409–429.

Glaeser E., Kallal H., Scheinkman J., Growth in Cities, in: Journal of Political Economy, Vol. 100, No. 6, 1992, pp. 1126–1153.

Harris C., The market as a Factor in the localization of Industry in the United States. Vol. 44, No. 4, 1954, pp. 315–348.

Jacobs J., The Economy of Cities. New York: Vintage, 1962.

Krugman P., Increasing Returns and Economic Geography, in: The Journal of Political Economy, Vol. 99, No. 3, 1991, pp. 483–499.

Marshall A., Principles of Economics, London: Macmillan, 1920.

Qi Liang, Xuefeng Qian, Externalities and Agglomeration: A Literature Review. Word Economy. No 2, 2007, pp. 84–96

Romer P., Increasing Returns and Long-run Growth, in: Journal of Political Economy, Vol. 94, No. 5, 1986,

Sanmang Wu, Shantong Li, Specialization, Diversity and Industrial Growth. An Empirical Research Based on Manufacturing Data of Chinese Provinces, in: The Journal of Quantitative & Technical Economics No. 8, 2011, pp. 21–34

Wenguang Bo. Externalities and Industrial Economic Growth – Evidences From Chinese

Provincial Panel Data, in: China Industrial Economy, No. 1,2007, pp. 37–44

Xiuyan Liu, Xingmin Yin, Xiaohai He. Market potential and Manufacturing Space Agglomeration: the Empirical Study Based on Panel Data of China Cities. Management Word. No. 11,2007, pp. 56–63

Yong Yang, Specialization, Diversification and Tourism Development – An Empirical Research Based on Chinese Current Statistical Data, in: Economy Review. No. 2, 2011, pp. 120–128

Internationalisation of trade fair organisers – Theoretical considerations and practical implications

Kaur-Lahrmann, Ravinder,
Mayer, Peter

展览会主办商的国际化 – 理论考量及实际操作

International perspectives have always played an important role in the organisation of trade fairs, bearing in mind that the international dimension has evolved in nature. One particularly interesting feature of internationalisation is that trade fair organisers now offer their services abroad. Three considerations are of fundamental importance for enterprises seeking to go abroad: 1. Why do trade fair organisers go abroad, and why should they do so? 2. Which types of market entry are available and suitable? 3. Which criteria are applied in the selection of markets on which to focus? The theory on internationalisation may provide useful information on how to approach internationalisation.

This paper reflects on these issues by initially presenting the theoretical approach, and then applying it to the case of event organisers shifting towards internationalisation.

国际化的视角对筹备展览会非常重要，然而值得关注的是国际化的内容在不断演变。一个相当有趣的特征是现在展览会主办商已把他们的服务推向了海外。对打算进入海外的主办商来说有三个最为关键的考量因素：1. 企业为什么要进入海外市场？为什么必须去呢？2. 哪些市场进入模式是可获得并且合适的？3. 在市场选择中他们应该重点根据哪些选择标准？通过研究国际化相关理论也许可以得到实用的信息来实现这一目标。

本文将基于这些话题进行探讨，先从陈述理论方法开始，再而将理论运用于会展主办商进入国际市场的案例，并从中得出结论。

1 Introduction

Event organizers do consider internationalization as one of their options for being profitable at a sustainable level. The following article reflects first on theoretical considerations with respect to rationales of internationalization, and then applies the theories presented to trade fair organizers from Germany. It is followed by a reflection on activities of German trade fair organizers in China. It ends with a conclusion.

2 Theory of internationalisation – a brief summary

Internationalization can be broadly described and understood as a process of successively integrating an international and intercultural dimension in the delivery of goods and services of an institution: there is generally a growing importance of international aspects in the reality of firms. This might reflect in various forms, including among others companies selling an increasing share of their output to foreigners, companies employing factors of production such as labour or capital from abroad and/or companies using production possibilities abroad to produce goods or services.

The transnationality index, an indicator used by UNCTAD, gauges trends in terms of internationalization. It measures the percentage of sales abroad of total sales, the percentage of employees abroad of the total, and the ratio of foreign assets to total assets. It is calculated by computing the arithmetic mean of these three ratios and has been used for ranking multinational corporations. In some cases the indicator reaches levels above 90: As of 2013 Nestle, a food, beverages and tobacco producer has a TNI of 97, Vodafone, a telecommunication provider has a TNI of 90,4 Arcelor-Mittal, a metal producer has a TNI of 92,8. German companies like Siemens, Volkswagen, Daimler and Deutsche Telekom all have TNIs over 50 (UNCTAD 2014).

2.1 Reasons for going abroad

A common form of classifying the reasons for companies moving into foreign markets distinguishes three such categories: Resources, markets, efficiency. The resource motive refers to taking advantage of access to inputs such as labour, material and electricity. The market objective refers to having access to large markets, to growing and / or potentially dynamic markets. The efficiency motive refers to such issues like tax optimization and diversification of risks. Which of these objectives is most relevant depends on the specific enterprise, product and market. And it can change over time, when the strategy changes or markets develop.

2.2 Forms of internationalising production

2.2.1 The framework

A common form of describing the forms of international activities of firms is shown in figure 1. It describes alternative modes of expansion into foreign markets, and distinguishes basically between equity arrangements and non-equity arrangements on the one hand, and producing at home versus producing abroad on the other.

Tab. 1: Forms of internationalization.

Production ownership	Production location	
	Home country	Foreign country
Equity arrangements	Exporting	Wholly owned operations
		Partially owned with remainder widely held
		Joint ventures
		Equity alliances
Non-equity arrangements		Licensing
		Franchising
		Management contracts
		Turnkey operations

Companies can internationalize by producing at and exporting from the home country. Alternatively companies can decide to make use of country-specific advantages abroad and produce in a foreign country. Here they have a variety of options to do this. A typical way of describing the options is by separating between equity and non-equity arrangements. In the case that the producers own part of the equity of a company which operates abroad, we can distinguish four kinds of approaches: wholly owned operations, where the investor is the sole owner; partially owned operations where part of the equity is widely held; a joint venture, an arrangement where a small number of firms cooperate; another option is the forming of an equity alliance.

Collaborative agreements can have many advantages: they help to spread and reduce costs, companies can specialize in core competencies, they gain knowledge, and they can minimize exposure in high risk environments. In some cases, however, they are the result of legal constraints where governments require local collaboration.

When the company from the home country does not invest in the other countries, but likes to take advantage of attractive conditions for production abroad, licensing or franchising are options which have gained importance in the past. Two other forms of internationalization without being the owner of production facilities abroad are management contracts and turnkey operations, where firms build or operate a facility on behalf of another company.

2.2.2 Ownership, location and internalisation – the eclectic theory

The theoretical framework most commonly used to explain why companies choose a specific approach of entering a foreign market has been proposed by Dunning: A basic requirement for being successful internationally is the existence of a firm-specific advantage, be it the ownership of a technology, the existence of a recognized brand or the ability to produce more efficiently than other competitors. Without having a clear and specific advantage over other producers, production with competitive products would not take place. This advantage can be called "ownership advantage" (or "firm-specific advantage"). Another important consideration is the relative attractiveness of the location abroad as compared to producing at home: If the location abroad does not offer advantages over producing at home, exporting would be the preferred option. If however the location abroad is attractive because of low wages, low taxes, better infrastructure or other reasons, this location is said to offer a "location advantage". A third element of the decision to produce at home or abroad refers to the ability to use the specific know-how within the company or alternatively sell or lease the technology to companies abroad. If the use of the know-how within the firm is preferable, it is said that "internalization" is advantageous (Rugman 2009: 69). Dunning argued that for investment in other countries to take place all three conditions have to be met: There needs to be an ownership advantage, a location advantage and an internalization advantage. If only the first and second conditions are met, then selling a license or franchising might be preferred. If there is no location advantage but an ownership and an internalization advantage, then exporting is the preferred option. Dunning's theoretical reflection has become known as "ownership-location-internalization"-theory, in short OLI, also referred to as "eclectic theory". It has been widely recognized as a powerful tool to understand decisions to go abroad and to explain the form chosen.

2.2.3 Dynamic aspects of internationalisation

The decision to produce at home or abroad is not a static one. Building on Dunning or other theoretical tools, a number of theories shed light on the decision making process and the relative attractiveness of various strategies over time. Johanson's and Vahlne's theory, which has become known as Uppsala model, reflects on the learning process: Companies typically start with producing for the home market, then start to export, and with some experience with exporting they learn about production conditions, about strengths and weaknesses of other places and consider investing abroad. They tend to focus first on markets which are close and/or similar, and later move into markets which differ even more from their home environment. Attention is paid to the building up and emergence of know-how about other markets and the growing confidence in doing business abroad. The Uppsala-model explicitly emphasizes the evolutionary character of going abroad. Investing abroad is not only the result of abstract reasoning and comparisons of rate of returns; it has to be seen as a result of growing experience and confidence.

Another approach of looking at decisions to go abroad from a dynamic perspective is the product-life-cycle theory advanced by Raymond Vernon. He argued in his seminal work that production at the beginning takes place where the innovation is developed and introduced into the market. After some time exports are chosen in order to expand the market, and after another period production would move to foreign markets. This last phase is in response to rising cost pressure and the interest to extend the life cycle of the product or service.

2.3 Deciding on market attractiveness

Many reasons for being active in certain markets can be identified. Three issues will be emphasized here: the size of the market, the regional location and the role it plays with respect to the product life cycle of a product.

Companies have an interest to be active in markets where demand is large. Some markets are attractive because the growth potential is such that large sales can be expected after some time. A related argument which, however, focuses on the cost of production, is the existence of economies of scale. When such cost advantages can be exploited large markets gain in attractiveness.

The Triade-concept proposed by K. Ohmae was influential in explaining (and recommending) the choice of markets. Ohmae argued that international firms need to be present in three markets: the US-market, the European market and the Japanese market. When he conceptualized his approach, these were the largest and most dynamic markets. A more contemporary interpretation would emphasize the North American, the European and the Asian market in general or the Chinese market specifically.

Other authors adapted the portfolio-concept which is widely used and well accepted in financial management. It is argued that firms should diversify the markets they operate in. Diversification can maximize expected return on investment when the risk is given, or minimizes risk with a certain expected return on investment.

All these theoretical considerations are useful for a reflection about international activities of trade fair organizers.

3 Internationalisation of trade fair organisers – the case of German organisers

The most important and traditional form of internationalization of trade fair organizers is the participation of foreign visitors and foreign exhibitors at trade fairs hosted at home. German trade fairs have been seen as particularly attractive for foreign participants. The number of foreign visitors is high and further increased over the years. Between 2009 and 2013 the number of visitors to international trade fairs hosted in Germany increased to 2,6 million, an increase of 24 per cent over this period. This constituted 26 per cent of the total of all visitors in 2013.

Tab. 2: International participation in trade fairs in Germany.

	2009	2010	2011	2012	2013
Number of foreign visitors to German international trade fairs	2,1 million	2,55 million	2,5 million	2,65 million	2,6 million
Number of foreign exhibitors at German international trade fairs	81870	92254	88608	98926	94881

Source: Auma 2014

A similar trend can be seen for the exhibitors. The number of foreign exhibitors increased and reached about 95,000 in 2013, an increase of 16 per cent since 2009.

In total the percentage of foreign exhibitors of all exhibitors increased from 53 to 57 per cent. International trade fairs have always required the participation of international exhibitors, but the extent of foreign involvement has increased substantially and reflects an important element of the internationalization of trade fair business.

Trade fair organizers from Germany increasingly organize trade fairs abroad. This is in line with a general trend in the trade fair world: More than 1000 exhibitions organised by UFI-members were organised by a company whose headquarters is outside the country where the exhibition was held. This was about one-third of all UFI-exhibitions.

According to AUMA-statistics, the number of trade shows organized abroad by German trade fair organizers increased from 220 in 2008 to 266 in 2012, an increase of 21 per cent. The number of visitors, in 2012 of more than six million, increased in the same period by more than 30 per cent.

Tab. 3: Trade fairs abroad by German organizers.

	2008	2009	2010	2011	2012	2013
Trade fairs abroad	220	211	226	263	266	277
Number of visitors	4,9 million	5,6 million	5,3 million	6,4 million	6,4 million	7,4 million

Source: Auma 2014

In line with their increasing activities abroad, there has been a substantial share of foreign sales of total sales. This ratio is largest for Messe Frankfurt with over 30 per cent, followed by Messe Düsseldorf with 23 per cent and Messe München with around 15 per cent (SZ 2014).

In order to organize their substantial activities abroad, German trade fair organizers increased their presence abroad. This can be quantitatively measured by observing the number of employees abroad or the ratio of foreign employees to all employees.

> Messe Frankfurt's activities show how significant the changes are: according to their company yearly report, this leading German trade fair organizer had in 2002 – 208 employees abroad. The number of employees abroad grew to 629 in 2012. The percentage of the total of all employees grew from 18 per cent to 34 per cent (Messe Frankfurt 2012).

Other interesting indicators which shed light on internationalization might be the number of representative offices abroad, the participation in international bodies, the role of international investors, the total of investments abroad or the ratio of such investments to total investments. Most indicators show a trend towards internationalization.

A dimension where trade fair organizers in Germany are still at the beginning of internationalization is both the capital and governance structure. Because of the peculiar nature of their ownership by state and cities, there is no foreign capital invested in German trade fair organizers. Supervisory boards of German trade fair organizers are equally national at least in terms of the citizenship of members.

The transnationality index for Frankfurt, calculated using the ratios of foreign capital, foreign employees and foreign sales was 6,6 in 2002, and stands at 44,8 in 2012 (Messe Frankfurt 2002 and Messe Frankfurt 2012). The respective transnationality index for Deutsche Messe in Hannover was substantially lower at 13.1.(Deutsche Messe 2013).

While there has not been a major study detailing the internationalization of German trade fair organizers, the data presented show a clear picture: The level of internationalization is substantial and growing.

3.1 Reasons for going abroad

The dominating reason for going abroad is the interest to be active in growing and potentially large markets. Fundamental changes in economic policies have unleashed the power of markets in countries in Asia and Latin America and Africa. Growth rates especially in Asia have consistently been much higher than in the developed Western world. A similar trend can be observed for major market places in Latin America and Africa. Thus, emerging markets are interesting because of their size, and they are interesting because of their enormous growth and their still existing growth potential. Given the average growth rate of China, the GDP per capita is doubling after seven years. With an average growth rate in Europe of two per cent a doubling can be expected only after 35 years. Given that there is some positive correlation between the demand for trade fairs and GDP, investing in growing markets is promising.

When market entry does not involve crowding out well-established competitors and cut-throat competition, investing in unsaturated but promising markets is attractive. And serving markets from home by inviting foreigners to participate in trade fairs in Germany has clear limits in terms of size: After reaching a certain size, trade fairs become unattractive and difficult to manage. Since participation in trade fairs from the visitors' and exhibitors' perspective involves high costs including travel, offering fairs where such costs are much lower increases the potential market.

An important reason which falls under the category of "efficiency" is the diversification of markets and the resulting reduction of risk. Economic trends in general and event market trends in particular are not synchronous. Activities in markets where developments are not perfectly correlated can reduce the overall business risk, a clear lesson from financial market theory. A perfect example of implications of a lack of diversification is the fate of organizers who have specialized and focused on markets in Russia where the current political and economic developments have an enormously negative influence on the profitability of investments. For those organizers whose activities are more diversified, results are less severe. It is not possible to "keep risks at a minimum", foreign activities are risky, but theory predicts that a diversified portfolio can generate a certain rate of return with lower risk than concentrating on only very few investments.

Going abroad and offering services at home are, however, not mutually exclusive alternatives. Offering a trade fair in another country has important externalities. It potentially enhances the brand value of the trade fair organizer and the exhibition itself It can lead to more attractive trade fairs at home because of exhibitors finding it more engaging to work with an organizer and discovering the appeal of going to the fair in the home country, which in turn can extend the networks which make trade fair organizers unique, arguments frequently brought up in discussions of internationalization strategies of event companies (Wutzlhofer 2005).

3.2 Forms of internationalisation of trade fair organisers – choosing the strategy

3.2.1 Variety of options

The trade fair organizers need to decide on the appropriate and suitable mode of market entry.

Offering trade fairs at home

The framework depicted in table 1 shows a key option for internationalization, which offers the product and service without moving production abroad and hence exporting the good. The equivalent to producing at home and selling goods to foreigners in the event market is the hosting of trade fairs in the home country of the trade fair organizer and having foreign exhibitors and more so foreign visitors attending the function. Foreign visitors have become essential for all international fairs and for the event organizers. This has always been important, but has increased in importance. The number of visitors and the percentage increased (see table 2 and 3) remains – for the time being – the main form of internationalization of German trade fair organizers. It corresponds with the mission, the ownership structure, the strength of the German market and its export-orientation.

Offering services abroad

Offering fairs at home is important, but other forms of internationalization have gained importance.

– **Equity arrangements**

Wholly owned operations and joint ventures are the two main alternatives of investing abroad. The analysis of ownership arrangements of German trade fair organizers' foreign investments shows a clear preference for 100 per cent-ownership.

According to their yearly reports, Messe Frankfurt holds 100 per cent of the equity of ten trade fair offices abroad, and only for three they hold less. Messe Köln lists seven trade fair organizers where they hold 100 per cent, and only two with equity less than 100. The same figures apply to Messe Düsseldorf.

In China, however, all German trade fair organizers chose joint ventures as market entry mode, following legal requirements to have a local partner. China is special in another way as well, in that there is a unique arrangement where three German trade fair organizers and a Chinese state-owned company have formed a joint venture, collaborating with each other while they are competitors in other markets.

- **Non-equity arrangements**

In terms of non-equity arrangements there is some relevance of licensing. Trade fair organizers do experiment with this approach. A key problem of using licensing for a service is control of quality, and it might bring risks for the original brand (Raue 2005). Clear contractual arrangements and precise definitions of rights and responsibilities are required when taking this route.

Trade fair organizers can as well offer a service of managing trade fair sites on behalf of others. Such management contracts can have multiple advantages like exposing the trade fair organizers to a new environment and let them develop networks. There have been a few examples where trade fair organizers from Germany took this direction.

3.2.2 Eclectic theory and German trade fair organisers

The key ownership advantage of German trade fair organizers is their reputation of being able to organize internationally recognized events, of hosting carefully planned trade fairs where renowned exhibitors and influential visitors would meet and promising networking opportunities exist. Many companies have confidence in suggestions and recommendations by representatives of German trade fair organizers, a phenomenon most prevalent in small and medium sized enterprises. Furthermore, international trade fairs hosted by German organizers are typically UFI-approved. For some fairs there is a clear locational advantage when fairs are organized in Germany. Space is available, supporting networks are functional, costs are reasonable. And at home the question of internalization does not arise.

For a considerable number of trade fairs, there is a locational advantage with the country abroad. Due to the cost of participation at a fair in Germany being rather high for local firms, hosting a trade fair abroad is the only way to reach otherwise unreachable target-groups.

Selling the license to foreign trade fair organizers to offer a trade fair remains an option, but has rarely been used, due to the difficulties of controlling the quality of German trade fairs.

The OLI-theory does apply and has the potential to explain the phenomenon of internationalization of German trade fair organizers.

3.2.3 Dynamic considerations

A thorough analysis of German trade fair organizer's global activities shows a clear path: Participants, both exhibitors and visitors, from the Triade country dominated in the distant past. Experience with trade fairs hosted abroad developed only step by step: Representative offices were offered abroad. Bigger investments abroad were made after exhibitors and visitors from foreign countries signaled the attractiveness and reachability of foreign markets. Instead of going abroad on many markets all at the same time, activities developed step-by-step, reflecting the waterfall-approach discussed in the internationalization theory and it corresponds well with Johanson and Vahlne's Uppsala-model.

Successful hosting of flagship fairs quite often leads to similar offers at other places. This logic reflects the idea of an expansion of markets. The product life cycle theory, quite suitable in manufacturing, would not be applicable, because the theory would suggest that the production moves completely to places where production costs are lower.

3.3 Which markets are the markets to go

With fairs hosted at home, both in terms of visitors and exhibitors, a domination by the Trade-countries has been substituted by a more balanced mix, including now the emerging markets in Asia, Latin America and Africa.

However, when German trade fair organizers offer their services abroad, the Asian market clearly dominates. The following pie chart shows this orientation.

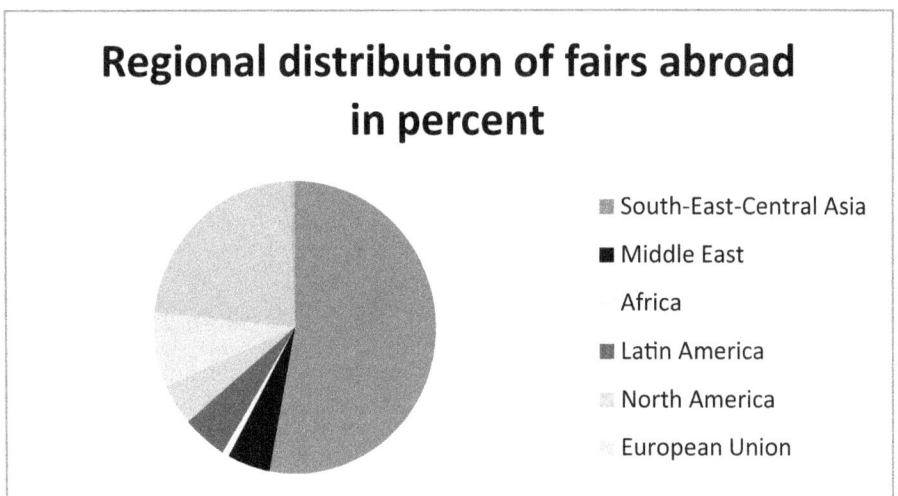

Figure 1: Trade fairs abroad by German Organizers 2012.
Source: AUMA 2013: Key indicators of the exhibition industry, p. 70.

The key markets for Messe Frankfurt are all in Asia. Messe Düsseldorf and Messe München have as well a clear pivot to Asia, with China and India being the most important investment destinations. In terms of number of potential exhibitors, visitors, industry structure and growth dynamics it is reasonable to have a strong presence in these markets.

Given the current assumptions about the long-term growth, the per-capita income in the long run and the size of population in Asia, this seems to be a rational choice. And the European market can be easily served by trade fairs in Germany, having the advantage of requiring participants to travel only short distances. However, the absence of a strong presence in North and South America is striking. The absence of a strong position in North America is typically explained by the nature of the market, being highly diversified and characterized by high competitive pressure, not allowing for substantial profits. The weak position in Latin America might be in response to the sluggish growth for decades. However, diversification and long-term growth might suggest to develop activities in the Western hemisphere. After all, the US accounts for more than 20 per cent of the global in-door exhibition space (UFI 2014). And the regional venue capacity in Latin America has increased between 2006 and 2011 by seven per cent (UFI 2014).

Some specific markets might have considerable potential to be attractive in the future, in terms of the general economic potential of the country and because of being a location for regional fairs. Brazil, Indonesia and Nigeria are countries with a large population and a growing industry. Chile, Myanmar, Kenya and Ghana are countries where substantial potential exist, both in terms of national activities and of being a regional hub. Investments in such places might prove interesting in the long-run.

Diversification arguments would suggest having more activities in the Western hemisphere, both North and South America and Africa. The long-term implication of diversification can be substantial. There is little reason to believe that risks of markets are perfectly correlated.

4 Implications for activities in China

Because of the huge market potential, the focus of German trade fair organizers on China seems to be appropriate. A more diversified approach within China might be advisable, i. e. not focusing on fairs at the East Coast only, but moving into larger cities in China where the number of exhibitors and participants is substantial and German trade fair organizers can use their expertise and experience for developing the trade fair market.

Options to internationalize are not only hosting international fairs at home and entering joint ventures abroad, but also offering management services for trade fair sites. Following the analysis presented in this article, German trade fair organizers might be able to use their special competitive advantage to run trade fair sites on behalf of others.

While China has a huge potential as a market for successful trade fairs, German trade fair organizers must bear in mind that risk diversification remains an essential element of prudent business strategy. Other markets in Europe, North America, Latin America and Africa need to be addressed too. Their long-term market potential is non-negligible as well, and investment in such markets can reduce the overall risk of investing abroad.

While the collaborative agreement in China has been a unique approach for German organizers, it might be advisable for German trade fair organizers to explore such forms of cooperation in other circumstances as well.

5 Conclusion

Even more internationalization can be expected as there are growing markets which cannot be reached by staying in Germany: Many target groups in Asia, Latin America or Africa are powerful and important in the long run, but unreachable by offering services only in Germany or Europe. Being a major player on such new markets will open new opportunities, and will stabilize as well the reputation and attractiveness of fairs at home. Looked at it from this perspective, internationalization is not really an option but a must.

New forms of cooperation internationally should be considered. While trade fair organizers are in competition in Germany, cooperation abroad can be advantageous. "Co-opetition" might be the right description of what is needed, at least in some locations. Furthermore, exploring possibilities to be more active in terms of offering to manage trade fair sites for foreign owners seems to be an option where German firms can bring in their firm-specific advantage and not water-down their competitive lead.

While foreign experts play a role in various advisory functions, it might be important to involve foreign expertise more formally in decision making processes, for example at the executive or supervisory boards. Internationalization will require as well new governance models.

6 Literature

AUMA (2012): Auma Review 2012, German Trade Fair Industry – Review 2013, Berlin.

Erwin, Joachim (2005): Messe Düsseldorf as a pioneer in China's growth market, in: : Kirchgeorg, Manfred et. al: (eds): Trade show management – Planning, implementing and Controlling of trade shows, conventions and events, Gabler Verlag, Wiesbaden, p. 607–614.

Giese, Wilhelm (2005): "The exportation of premium trade show brands", in: Kirchgeorg, Manfred et. al: (eds): Trade show management – Planning, implementing and Controlling of trade shows, conventions and events, Gabler Verlag, Wiesbaden, p. 543–554.

Kay, L. (2007): International Exhibition Organizers in China and their performance. Doctoral thesis, The Hong Kong Polytechnic University, Hong Kong, Internet:www.cpexhibition.com/introd/Kay%20DBA.pdf

Messe Frankfurt (2013): Geschäftsbericht 2012, Frankfurt, online: https://www.messefrankfurt.com/frankfurt/de/messe/publikationen/geschaeftsberichte.html, retrieved on 23.7.2014.

Raue, Ernst (2005): "The exportation of premium trade show brands", in: Kirchgeorg, Manfred et. al: (eds): Trade show management – Planning, implementing and Controlling of trade shows, conventions and events, Gabler Verlag, Wiesbaden, p. 555–562.

Rugman, Alan M. / Simon Collinson (2009): International Business, 5th edition, New York.

Ufi (2014): Global exhibition industry statistics – March 2014, internet: ... accessed on 1st September 2014.

Von Grega, Felix (2013): Internationalisierung des Messewesens: Auswirkungen auf öffentliche Veranstaltungsgesellschaften, Leipzig.

Wutzlhofer (2005): Success factors for internationalization trade fair organisations, in: Kirchgeorg, Manfred et. al: (eds): Trade show management – Planning, implementing and Controlling of trade shows, conventions and events, Gabler Verlag, Wiesbaden, p. 563–574.

The role of the state in the exhibition industry in Germany and China – A reflection based on the varieties of capitalism-approach

Mayer, Peter,
Ding, Yi

德中两国会展业中的政府角色—基于资本主义多样性理论的分析

The role of the state with respect to economic development differs in many ways when comparing countries around the world. The "varieties of capitalism-approach" provides for a conceptual framework to identify the state's role in different spheres of the economy. Using this approach to reflect on the role of the state in China's and Germany's exhibition industry helps to recognise how important – though different – the state is in both countries' exhibition industry.

在世界范围内进行比较，各国政府在经济发展中的角色各不相同。资本主义多样性理论为确认政府在经济活动的不同层面上的角色提供了理论框架。基于该理论的分析，我们发现中德两国政府在会展业的发展中都起着相当重要然而各不相同的作用。

1 Introduction

The exhibition industry is increasingly recognized as an economically important and attractive pillar of modern economies. Exhibitions with a global reach, national exhibitions, regional and local exhibitions are all said to bestow substantial tangible and intangible benefits to the economy and society: The linkages of the exhibition industry with other sectors of the economy can bring growth and employment and can substantially accelerate economic development, both in the short-run and the long-run. The exhibition industry is claimed to be a seedbed for creativity and innovation.

Based on the perception of the exhibition industry as being economically attractive, many national, state and local governments around the world are interested to boost the development of the exhibition industry. The question needs to be answered whether governments can and need to nurture the exhibition industry in a particular way, whether specific government actions are required to develop a strong exhibition industry, and whether there is any best practice which would guide countries, regions, cities in fostering an emerging exhibition industry.

The specific role of the state in providing conditions for economic activities and developing competitive advantages in certain industries cannot be seen independently from the overall political and economic system. The "variety of capitalism approach" highlights substantial systematic differences of the political economies of nations. Differences between nations are not seen as deviation from any benchmark; rather they are interpreted as expression of the choice countries have and opted for, their decisions to have unique political economy models: there are many paths to economic success. What matters is the internal consistency of the institutional arrangements. And when reforms of the political economy of countries are considered, the peculiar institutional arrangements and how they interrelate need to be borne in mind. This theoretical framework can be used to draw lessons for governments trying to develop new industries and seeking to have a competitive edge. Furthermore, economic theory can help in identifying areas where market mechanisms would typically fail to produce a social welfare enhancing outcome.

This article reflects first on the concept of "variety of capitalism" and shows that the role of the state, the firms, the educational institutions and the associations depend on the kind of capitalist system adopted. Based on this and drawing on theoretical work, the case of Germany is discussed, showing the role of the state in Germany's exhibition industry. A chapter on the role of the state in China's exhibition industry follows. For both Germany and China the status quo and the discussion for a need to change is presented. The article ends with concluding remarks.

2 "Varieties of capitalism" – a reflection on Germany and China

The role of the state in a market economy has been thoroughly discussed in social sciences. However, quite often economic analysis tends to downplay the virtues of differences between economic and political institutions. It seems that nations should pursue very similar governmental policies: market failures such as the existence of public goods, externalities and the like should be considered when designing policies, but little or no attention is paid to the institutional framework of economies, to the existence of organizations articulating the interests of firms, to the culture of cooperation which can take very different forms. The international discussion frequently observes and proposes convergence of such institutional arrangements, and seems to suggest that countries can easily pick single successful instruments from other countries. However, many social scientists observe important differences of the political economies and interpret these differences as neither accidental nor necessarily in need of being eliminated. Rather, it is argued that different systems have their distinct logic which makes them functioning, strong and attractive. There is no need for "uniformization".

A common dichotomy used in describing political-economic systems is the one between the Anglo-Saxon capitalism and the Rhine capitalism, where the former refers mainly to the political-economic systems in US, the UK and Australia, and the latter to the systems in continental Europe, mainly in Germany and France. Another dichotomy which recently gained ground in the intellectual discourse on political economies around the world distinguishes between coordinated market economies (CME) and liberal market economies (LME): According to the "variety of capitalism-school of thought", national political economies can be analysed by looking at how firms resolve their coordination problem with other actors in the economy or society. Hall and Soskice propose to use a relational view of the firm, distinguishing five spheres in which firms need to solve coordination problems: industrial relations; vocational training and education; inter-firm relations; employees, and corporate governance (Hall and Soskice 2001: 6f). Coordinated market economies such as Germany and liberal market economies such as the US address the coordination needs in very different forms. In liberal market economies, the primary form of coordination by firms is via hierarchies and competitive market arrangements (Hall and Soskice 2001: 8). Deregulated labor markets and strong competition in product markets are characteristic of liberal market economies. In coordinated market economies, however, non-market relationships are more important avenues for coordination. Networks between firms are crucial, the state and industry association are recognized as playing an important role. The trajectory of national developments, the culture of cooperation developed within nations, the formal and informal rules developed within the economic realm influence heavily the coordination. Given the complementarities of institutional arrangements and organizations, it is difficult to switch from one regime to another (Ahrens and Jünemann 2010).

Germany's political economy represents the coordinated market economy type. Strong and intensive interaction between firms, with associations and the state characterize the political economy: Company needs are conveyed through strategic interaction with other players in the field: firms are represented in business associations and chambers of commerce. These organizations play an important role in influencing curricula at vocational schools and partly higher education institutions. Associations communicate industry's needs, interests and perspectives to state institutions. Associations influence companies to participate in developing the industry, to train staff and to open up for innovations. With respect to reaping the benefits from investing in modern skills for employees, associations are able to limit free riding by applying pressure to participate in respective investments. Participation in supervisory boards of related organizations allows for alleviating information asymmetry problems. The German corporate governance system with mandatory representation of employees and trade unions on supervisory boards of large public companies and the establishment of works councils in virtually all companies ensures that workers' interest are articulated, that management shares information with employees on strategically important developments.

Coordination processes take time, building consensus requires complex interactions, but they finally generate "ownership" of what is agreed upon. The need to network limits the capacity for managers to make unilateral decisions, and potentially slows down decision making, but it generally enhances the quality and the acceptance of decisions made. In summary, such non-market relationships are part and parcel of the German coordinated market economy-model and help solve the coordination problem.

China's political economy is in a rapid transition process. Markets mechanisms have been strengthened since opening up the economy in 1979, the role of the state changed substantially. Social institutions have been going through processes of transformation, new institutions emerged, and old disappeared. The culture of coordination has changed. China does not neatly fall into the categorization of CME versus LME. Differences as compared to the archetype of CME and LME are substantial. Some argue that market coordination is nowadays dominating and hence see China as LME (Witt 2010); others argue that it is clearly a coordinated economy, and hence see China rather as CME. Some authors see China's political economy as a hybrid form: capitalism with Chinese characteristics. Some see the Chinese model in an entirely different category, because of the one-party system and the completely different nature of decision making (Halper 2010). Or maybe China must be seen as a country where dualistic structures exist: in some regions and sectors coordination might be through markets, while in other sectors networks dominate.

Whatever the categorization finally is, the structure provided by Hall and Soskice can be used to reflect on coordination of economic and social activities in China. The state at the national, the provincial and the local level and the political party play essential roles in the overall coordination of economic activities. Links between the state and the political party on the one side and large firms are strong, while links with small firms on the other side are less strong and less institutionalized. The influence of associations – where they exist at all – is limited, their impact is small. Links between the educational system and the firms are less developed, due to the rapid transformation of the industrial sector, the heterogeneity of firms and the lack of institutionalized representation.

3 Germany's exhibition industry and the state

Germany's exhibition industry provides a good case study of how the coexistence of market-based and non-competitive coordination mechanisms contributes towards sustainable solutions. Firms, business associations, the state, trade unions and educational institutions collaborate in various ways, elaborate systems of networking provide for strategic decisions which find support within the industry, and ensure that decisions taken are followed through.

The German exhibition industry

The German exhibition industry is recognized internationally as strong, innovative and international. 40 trade fair organizers stage international events. Five of the top 10 trade fair organizers worldwide are based in Germany. Because of the large number of exhibitions taking place in Germany, the number of companies participating in trade fairs as exhibitors is high: according to AUMA 59.000 German companies have been active as exhibitors, the majority of them belonging to the group of small and medium sized companies (AUMA 2014). A considerable number of service companies are doing stand construction, they focus on design, the provide services as freight forwarder etc. These companies are the key players who relate in numerous ways with each other. Such network activities are typically taking place in regional clusters: regional proximity matters for many services. One of the traditional features of the German institutional arrangement which is instrumental in exchange of information, networking etc. is the participation in associations.

The role of associations and inter-firm-relationships

Companies are member of the local chamber of commerce and industry or the chamber of handicraft respectively. These organizations articulate interests of the local business community, they communicate interests and perspectives, they work with state institutions, they collaborate with educational bodies in designing curricula or even testing skills, they provide important information for members, they help in standard setting. In addition, companies are typically member of their respective business association, which addresses issues of the specific sector. German trade fair organizers are members of the Association of the German Trade Fair Industry (AUMA). Many companies in the event industry are member of the "Federal German Association for the Promotors and Exhibition Business" (Bundesverband der Veranstaltungswirtschaft 2014).

With reference to the German CME, the varieties of capitalism-approach postulates that participation in associations allows for solving the problem of information asymmetry, associations are said to be instrumental in forging consensus for collective action. Membership in chambers of commerce and industry or handicraft respectively is mandatory: Government prescribes that businesses are members, based on the general conviction that some of the services, e. g. collecting and disseminating information or influencing vocational training curricula are services of a public good character and/or are services which generate substantial externalities, hence such services would not be offered in the market without such mandatory participation in the provision of these services. Membership in industry associations, however, is voluntary. But because associations are typically able to offer advantages for members of the club (they offer "club goods"), the vast majority of firms opts for membership.

Firms cooperate because and when cooperation brings economic benefits: this is the case when externalities exist and non-cooperation would be counterproductive. At the same time, firms are in competition and market shares have developed dynamically at virtually all segments of the exhibition industry. Cooperation and competition co-exist. The role of associations in the German institutional arrangement of the event industry can hardly be overestimated.

The Governmental level

Understanding how the exhibition industry in Germany works requires recognition of the federal structure of Germany: the federal system in Germany allocates specific rights and responsibilities to the various levels of state activities, i. e. the national (federal) level, the state level (sometimes in English called the provincial or regional level) and the local level. Federal structures imply that each level is explicitly responsible for tasks allocated to it, which is not only involving administrative responsibilities, but as well the overall responsibility to design policies.

The role of government at the federal level

The federal level of Germany is an important player for determining the framework conditions for the exhibition industry: the most important tax laws are decided upon at the federal level, employment laws and the legal framework for industrial relations are federal responsibilities, financial market policies are decided upon at the national level. All these are generally important for the overall attractiveness of the German economy and activities in the field of exhibitions. Some of the exhibition laws are federal laws. These policies have important repercussions for the exhibition industry, for the attractiveness to invest, to expand, and to innovate. Because many exhibitions have a global dimension, immigration rules have an impact on the positioning of the exhibition market in Germany as well.

The federal policy level has a major direct influence on the exhibition industry when it comes to mega events such as EXPO 2000. Here the federal government initiated, prepared and supported campaigns, provided funds and used its foreign policy leverage to strengthen campaigns. However, with very few and typically small exceptions, the federal government would not be host and would not be a major exhibitor or an initiator of exhibitions.

The role of government at the state and local level

The state level deals more specifically with the needs of the exhibition industry. Some states together with cities and other players own trade fair organizers, working towards attracting trade fairs which bring benefits to the regional and local economy. Some examples can show the approach chosen: The state of North-Rhine Westphalia holds substantial shares in Messe Düsseldorf and in Messe Köln, the state of Hessen is co-owner of Messe Frankfurt, the state of Bavaria has an equity stake in Messe München and Messe Nürnberg, the state of Lower Saxony is co-owner of Deutsche Messe AG DMAG in Hannover. The states consider their involvement in trade fair organizers as strategic investment, based on the conviction that this generates net benefits to society.

Cities reap the most direct benefits from having exhibitions: more employment, more growth, higher tax revenue, and a positive city image are some of the benefits expected from hosting exhibitions. Local governments can facilitate the development of exhibitions by building grounds where exhibitions can be held, by using their administrative policies to attract hotels to invest, by developing local transport in such a way as to have it conducive for investment.

A key avenue for influencing the exhibition industry is through having a direct influence on trade fair organizers by being one of the owners of trade fair organizers.

The following table shows the stakes of states and cities for four major trade fair organizers which play a pivotal role in the German trade fair industry.

Tab. 1: Ownership structures of selected trade fair organizers.

	State's share	City's share	Chamber of commerce, chamber of handicraft	others
Messe Köln	20	79, 075	0,775	
Messe Düsseldorf	20	56	3,5	20
Messe Frankfurt	40	60	–	–
Deutsche Messe AG Hannover	50	49,871	–	0,129

Source: various yearly reports of the respective organizations

Three of the four most powerful trade fair organizers in Germany are characterized by a dominating equity share held by city governments. When the share of local and state government is taken together, it is more than 99 per cent for Messe Köln, Messe Frankfurt and Deutsche Messe. As owners the state and the respective city can influence the management of the trade fair organizers. City representatives such as city mayors, members of city councils are typically members of the supervisory board and allow for a say in the strategies pursued. The day-to-day management, however, is left to the professional management of the organizations.

The role of trade unions and worker representatives

The German corporatist model seeks to foster mechanisms of consensus-building where civil society, industry and the state work on identifying suitable strategies. A key feature of the coordinated market philosophy is the strong role accorded to trade union and worker representatives. Companies have works councils which together with management identify solutions for shop-floor problems. The same is true for trade fair organizers in Germany. Such representation is said to help in providing stability by allowing the voice of workers to be heard, by creating an atmosphere of trust within the organization. Substantial challenges for the organization such as major reorganizations can be dealt with in a way that cooperation and not confrontation prevails. Because of the workers' unique perspective on the needs on the work place, the system allows as well for the identification of training needs, and so can contribute in the medium term to a highly qualified work force.

For large enterprises worker representatives are as well represented at the supervisory council. All large trade fair organisers have such representation of labour (see for example http://www.messefrankfurt.com/frankfurt/de/messe/unternehmensprofil/aufsichtsrat.html?nc for Messe Frankfurt).

While there are some critical voices of the German corporate governance model being not flexible enough, allowing labour too much influence, being not understood elsewhere etc., the corporatist model of giving voice to workers at the level of supervisory boards is widely accepted, and implemented in the German event industry.

Training, education and research

The vocational training system with its numerous apprenticeship schemes belongs to overall responsibility of the state. However, it represents a classic example of the corporatist nature of developing and implementing such schemes. Programs offered by vocational schools need to be seen as attractive by the business community, not only because of the general interest to have attractive programs, but as well because of a financial incentive. The German vocational training system is called "dual system" because of two places of learning: at a vocational school and at the site of a company. The apprenticeship typically takes two to three years before the apprentices graduate: While government pays for the running of the vocational schools, the firm pays salaries for their apprentices during the time of training and education: They invest in the building of human resources. Hence involvement of firms in designing curricula, in developing programs, in adopting new features in vocational training is crucial, for the firms, for the apprentices, and for the system at large. Numerous mechanisms allow for information sharing, coordination and collaboration. Firms are called to evaluate programs, they participate in testing skills. Most importantly: the very fact of deciding to have apprentices reflects a basic appreciation of the education as providing benefits.

There is as well cooperation at the level of higher education institutions, but this is typically less formalized. Practitioners are called to give lectures, and when curricula are designed practitioners are involved as well. Internship for students allow not only for students' learning, but as well for contacts between professors and experts on the practical side. Some trade fair institutions sponsor explicitly research and teaching. Messe Köln is financially supporting an institute for trade fairs at the University of Cologne, AUMA financially sponsors a research institute.

Summary

Successful exhibitions organized by trade fair organizers require participation by exhibitors, visitors and organizers. Before deciding to organize a fair, complex coordination mechanisms help in forging consensus on the most appropriate strategy. And such close coordination is equally true during implementation and afterwards.

The role of the state is strong. The state, mainly at the federal level, is creating the framework conditions for the exhibition industry and thus has a strong influence. By owning trade fairs at the state and the local level, the state has the ability to influence developments. The nature of the political economy in Germany guarantees that interests of firms, associations, workers and other stakeholders are articulated and heard. The power of each individual player is moderate, but collectively their voices become part of the decision making process. This characterization of the influence would most probably be accepted as well for and by the state: the state is part and parcel of a tightly-knit network of non-competitive mechanisms to identify the best strategy. Some observers would argue that herein lays the strength of the German system: forging consensus, making sure that strategies adopted are widely believed to be good, creating "ownership" of new developments.

Privatizing the states' stakes in public entities such as trade fair organizers has been repeatedly an issue in the public discourse on economic policy and public administration. In the 1980s and 1990s, there was in the Western world in general and in Germany in particular strong pressure to privatize and to sell state assets, it was what some call the age of "market triumphalism": it was emphasized that private ownership bestows greater benefits to society than public ownership. It was pointed out that private owners tend to be more efficient. And because many states experienced growing debt and deficit levels, states considered selling state assets as a revenue generating activity. This line of thought influenced the discussion about the event industry: The selling of the governments' stakes in trade fair organizations would have an important influence on the nature of coordination and later on the policy pursued. However, a discussion at the beginning of the 21. century in the state of Hessen to sell the state's share of Messe Frankfurt showed the complexity and the difficulties of such a transformative change. It seems that the relevant actors recognized the public good-character of the service provided, the externalities involved, and the low financial profitability of trade fair organizers when only the private benefits for investing companies are considered. There is currently no further debate on privatizing trade fair organizations in Germany.

4 China's exhibition industry and the state

The Current Situation of Chinese MICE Industry

Chinese MICE industry has been developing rapidly since the 1980s. According to UFI, the indoor exhibition space has reached 4,755,102 square meters, taking 15 per cent share of the whole world market, and is ranked No 2 in the international market. Since 2006, the indoor exhibition space has increased 48 per cent, which shows the fastest increase in the whole world. Moreover, the net space rented also has increased 64 per cent (UFI 2014). After the Chinese Reform in the 1980s, the international meetings held in China have been growing exponentially, from almost zero in 1980 to 340 in 2013, becoming the eighth largest destination worldwide (ICCA 2013).

In order to find the reasons for this fast development, the theoretical principles of the "varieties of capitalism approach" are applied to the Chinese MICE industry. China has been under the process of transformation from a command economy to a market economy since the 1980s. Presently, China is accepted as a country in transition and its economy is a mixture of command economy and market economy, which creates a dichotomy in the financial and manufacturing environment for companies. The framework of the varieties of capitalism approach is suitable for the analysis of Chinese MICE industry.

The financial institution for companies' management

Due to the special features of Chinese transition economy, the financial environment shows a dichotomy: large-scale state owned enterprises (SOEs) find it relatively easy to get funding from the government and government-owned banks and can invest in long-term projects. Chinese privately owned enterprises (POEs) and foreign owned enterprises (FOEs), however, have to rely on more market-driven funding approaches.

- **The Chinese government realizes its long-term developing goals via direct investment through SOEs**

Due to the historical circumstances, the relationship between SOEs and government is called an 'administrative subordinating relationship'; the government does not only fully own the enterprises but also frequently directly assigns managers to the enterprises. The SOEs should get the approval from the government at first when they intend to invest in any important project. Since most of the banks in China are also owned by the state, the approved projects can easily get funding from banks. Moreover, in some cases the intention to invest comes directly from the government rather than the enterprises themselves: the government finds a company to realize the plan. The advantage of the institution is that the companies do not need to worry about the short-term benefits and can pay attention to the long-term goal instead.

The construction of Chinese exhibition venues is evidence for the point made above. The exhibition venues are of large scale, with huge investment, long construction periods, substantial externalities and unrealizable short-term profits, which make it impossible or unattractive to POEs to invest. Instead, SOEs invest in such major projects. The construction of venues grew even faster when the government identified the MICE industry as a development priority. For example, there are almost 40 cities that are positioned as 'central MICE cities' in the city developing strategy of 'The 12th Five-Year Plan', which resulted in China becoming the second largest exhibition country of the world in 2011 with its indoor exhibition space expanding 48 per cent compared with 2006. Without the investment from the government, it would have been hard to expect and realize such a high-speed growth.

However, a disadvantage of this institutional arrangement is probably the lack of consideration of demand and supply, which contributed to the low performance of some investments. For example, currently the average occupancy rate in the venues of China is only 25 per cent, much lower than the international average level of 35 per cent (Guo 2012). This is mainly because of a lack of attention to market demands, the insufficient urban infrastructure, the incomplete supplier network and low level of MICE human resources. To some extent, the too-early investment has caused a waste of scarce resources.

– **Access to loans difficult for POEs**

The financial institutions for privately owned enterprises, both Chinese and foreign, in the MICE industry are closer to the one in liberal market economies. Companies need to raise funds without the help of government. Many of the foreign owned enterprises are multinational enterprises with solid financial support from their headquarters, whereas the Chinese privately owned enterprises are often small and lack such support. Even if there are some financial support policies, however, the outcome is typically not sufficient (Shen and Xiang 2013). On the other hand, like in liberal market economies, venture capital has provided access to risk capital for the industry. For example, some economy hotels which are important suppliers of the MICE industry have already got funds from these venture capital firms.

– **Other financial support from the government**

There are many other types of financial support from the government, whose purposes are usually to create an image of an "event city" through raising the scale and level of local event programs. For example, some cities claim that any exhibitions with more than 10,000 square meters qualify for funds from the government. Other cities promise to give funds to companies who hold forums and seminars. The budget of such financial support, to give some examples, in Wuxi, Jiangsu province is 8,000,000 RMB. Xiamen, Fujian Province offers up to 1,000,000 RMB to large-scale exhibitions (Guo 2012).

The industrial institutions for employment

– **The labour market shares the features of LMEs**

The professional education system is quite similar to the ones in liberal market economies. This is shown in two ways: first of all, the event management education is provided by universities or colleges which focus on formal and general skills rather than specialized ones. By 2011, there were 187 universities and colleges which set up MICE related majors. They had recruited 10,176 students (Guo 2012b). Although this number has shown a substantial increase which was four times as high as 2004, the human talents supplied by the educational institutions still do not meet the needs of the industry. There is very little input from the industry to the curricula and syllabi of the education institutions (Guo 2012a). Furthermore, the graduates of MICE majors have shown very low identification with the event industry, with a low percentage of graduates finally working in the MICE industry (Guo 2012a). The students pay more attention to acquire general rather than specialized skills.

The results mentioned above are due to a 'two way options' employment policy applied in China, under which students are free to choose their jobs and companies are free to choose the students. On the one hand, since the companies are not able to guarantee that the students who receive their training finally work for them, they are not interested in putting effort in the training program. On the other hand, students set the maximized economic returns as their first priorities, showing less interest in their major. Even worse, the income level for the newcomers in the MICE industry is relatively low in the first three years (Guo 2012a), which pushes the graduates to look for higher-paid jobs in other industries.

– **Small income, high work-load, low opportunity to give opinion**

There is also a dichotomy in terms of income level between state-owned and private enterprises. In SOEs, incomes are composed of class-related salary and performance-related salary. Due to its stability, employees feel that positions are attractive and hence show low mobility. In private enterprises, the salary is fully decided by the company itself. Most of the companies use the 'basic income plus commission' system. However, in the first three years, the new employees are unlikely to earn enough commissions, so the basic monthly income is not enough to cover their basic needs (Guo 2012a). Meanwhile, the nature of the job in the MICE industry is highly time-intensive. People even have to work through the night in order to meet the deadlines such as opening time; this heavy work-load also results in a higher labor turnover rate in the MICE industry as compared to other industries.

The ordinary employees have no chances to express their opinions at either the company level or the industry level. According to Guo's research, a large number of MICE companies are characterized by top-down decision making. Employees are hardly asked for their opinion (Guo 2012a). This also leads to a high turnover rate in the MICE industry.

The role of industrial associations

Under the system of coordinated market economies, industrial associations are important in defining the industrial standards, offering training and sharing relevant information (Hall and Soskice 2001). On the one hand, they negotiate and communicate with government and other industries on behalf of the MICE industry. On the other hand, they provide services, such as training, education and information and also stipulate the standards for the development of the industry. The MICE industrial association emerged in China late. Even now there is no industrial association at the national level. The well-accepted industrial association, Shanghai Conference and Exhibition Industry Association (SCEIA), so far has only existed for 12 years (SCEIA 2014), while AUMA in Germany was set up in 1907, lasting for more than 100 years (AUMA 2014). Furthermore, the industrial associations exist in China in an exclusive way, meaning that each industry is only allowed to set up one industrial association.

Industrial associations are working closely with the government, directly guided by its higher authorities when making strategies. For example, SCEIA introduces itself as an association which assists the government to manage the MICE industry under the guidance of the Shanghai municipality' (SCEIA 2014). Moreover, the Chinese government directly offered a good amount of support via the industrial associations. After the financial turmoil in 2008, many provincial governments provided tens of million RMB to run exhibitions for the sake of driving domestic demands and rescuing the export enterprises. Not only the booth rents were wiped out, but also the accommodation was free of charge to the exhibitors (Chen 2014).

The standard of the service from industrial associations should be improved. Currently, the main job of the industrial associations is to set up industrial standards and collect data of the industry (Guo 2012a). For example, Zhejiang Province has set up a MICE standardization commission. Shanghai, Hunan Province, Guangzhou Province has strengthened the MICE statistical job (Guo 2012c). Compared with AUMA, the Chinese indusial statistical data is inadequate. At AUMA's official website, the exhibition data does not only include domestic shows but also foreign ones. Exhibitors are given tips on how to take part in an exhibition in Germany. Moreover, organizers and visitors are also capable of getting information on how to run and visit an exhibition. However, the information listed at SCEIA's website is relatively rough and national in nature, with the data lagging behind and no English version of the website shown.

The relationship between the companies

- **State-owned enterprises communicate well and carry on the governmental strategies**

State-owned enterprises (SOEs) have their superiorities both in financial and administrative policies. The 'father and son' relationship between government and companies, and the siblings-like relationships between companies facilitate the sound communication among them. For instance, in 2011 National (Shanghai) Centre for Exhibition and Convention (CEC) was started to be built. It was at that time the largest single site exhibition hall with 530,000 square meters. In order to manage the project, a company, Shanghai Expo Company Ltd., with a registration capital of six billion RMB was set up, which was a joint-venture between China Foreign Trade Centre (60 per cent) and Shanghai Eastbest International (40 per cent) (CEC 2014). China Foreign Trade Centre is a state-run institution, the organizer of China Import and Export Fair (Canton Fair)(CFTC 2014), while Shanghai Eastbest is one of the organizers of Shanghai Expo(EASTBEST 2014). The co-operation exemplifies the good communication and negotiation between SOEs. Besides this, the project has also received support from other SOEs. For example, the designers of CEC are East China Architectural Design & Research Institute Co., Ltd and Architectural Design and Research Institute of Tsinghua University, and the builders are Shanghai Construction Group (SCG) and China Construction Eighth Engineering Division Corp. Ltd. All of them are SOEs.

According to the principles of varieties of capitalism, companies in CMEs pay more attention to the quality of the products (Hall and Soskice 2001). In China, it might be more precise that SOEs are playing a role to lead the market. Besides the leading function of the SOEs' investment in large venues, SOEs also set a model for other Chinese enterprises on how to do business overseas. For example, since 2000, the CCPIT TEX (China Council for the Promotion of International Trade) has been holding 'China Textile and Apparel Trade Show (New York)' at Javits Centre for 14 years (CCPITTEX 2014). This has served an important role in terms of demonstrating the feasibility of going abroad successfully.

- **Private enterprises, both domestic and foreign, are under a more competitive environment, bringing about innovation and fast growth**

POEs and FOEs in China operate in an environment similar to LMEs. According to the principles of varieties of capitalism, the institutional arrangement of LMEs are better for production innovation and upgrading (Hall and Soskice 2001), which can also be observed in China. For instances, the Show of Gifts and Home organized by Reed Exhibition has resulted in people being more interested in innovation and green issues, putting forward the theme of "innovative gifts, low-carbon life", which brought the company an outstanding success (Reeds 2014). Moreover, in order to raise its competitive capacity, foreign-owned enterprises have introduced more well-known exhibitions into the Chinese market, such as CeBITAsia, ElectronicChina of German companies and ComdexChina of British companies (Guo 2012a).

Furthermore, the acquisitions and mergers in the event industry are also progressing: Foreign owned enterprises acquire Chinese enterprises in the event industry. For instances, in June of 2007, Reed Exhibitions bought Shenzhen Huabo Exhibitions, a private enterprise in Shenzhen and set up a joint venture, Reed Huabo Exhibitions. In May of 2008, a British exhibition company, Tarsus, purchased an exhibition company, Haobo, in Hubei Province. The purchase of exhibition itself is another popular mode. For instance, in September of 2007, Koeln Messe (China) successfully purchased two shows called CME and SME of a British exhibition company, simply Group Ltd (Wang 2009). After several years, foreign-owned enterprises have a substantial share in the Chinese event industry. By 2012, six of 16 sized exhibition companies with more than 100 thousand square meters exhibitions in Shanghai are foreign-owned (Guo 2012a).

The high turnover of FOEs and POEs has also brought about spill over effects to the Chinese event industry. The effect is actualized via three different ways: the demonstration from the FOEs' advanced management helps POEs to improve their managerial capacity; the more competitive environment pushes the effectiveness of POEs, and also the technology transfers between companies through the inter-mobility of the employees. The spill over effect pushes a rapid growth in the Chinese event industry.

Summary

The speedy development of Chinese event industry and the current institutions are inseparably intertwined. The most important element is the economic transformation from the command economy to the market economy, which allows the 'invisible hand' to allocate the resources rationally, resulting in efficiency and prosperity. After the economic reform, the POEs and FOEs have been overlaid with a LME kind of environment, which shows that the financial supply usually depends on the quarterly balance sheets, the highly fluid labor market, the high level of authority in management, and the more competitive than cooperative relationship. FOEs and POEs pay more attention to the market demands and production innovation, raising the managerial skills in the industry.

However, China has not been fully transformed to a LME type of country. When introducing the market mechanism, the government still keeps substantial non-market power which is shown in governmental interference with the economy. The government achieves its goals through direct controls over the SOEs which are able to fully follow the government strategy, pay attention to long-term interests, assist the government for its strategic plotting, and this way lead the whole industry. Due to the 'father and son relationship' between government and SOEs, the financial and industrial regulations are more favourable to the SOEs. Meanwhile, the 'sibling's relationship' among SOEs facilitates their better communication and information-sharing. This way, the problem of information asymmetry is reduced. This non-competitive and non-market coordination is a stable foundation for Chinese economy, which allows the governmental industrial policy to operate smoothly.

Currently, Chinese associations have not reached a level of maturity. Therefore, the event industry is short of the support it deserves. The lack of industrial data is not good for industrial policy making, neither is the imperfection of the industrial service standard in favour of improving the service quality. Also, the incompleteness of the industrial training system can hardly satisfy the long-term development. Due to its quasi-governmental nature, the association is more accustomed to its supervision than its service function. It is probably a feasible solution to introduce the market mechanism into the operation of association just the same as what have been done for the enterprises since the 1980s, such as allowing the private capital to invest in operating associations.

5 Outlook

The varieties of capitalism-approach is an analytical framework to understand how systems work, how institutional mechanisms solve various problems and how political and economic paths have shaped the political economies of countries.

The state in Germany has substantial influence on the development of the trade fair industry. While the vast majority of employment in the trade fair industry is in private businesses, there is considerable influence by the state with respect to setting the framework conditions and by being co-owner of trade fair organizers. However, the specific coordination mechanisms which are typical for the German corporatist model by giving voice to firms via the role of associations and by having trade unions involved at various levels implies that each players' role is limited, unilateral (and quick) decision making is not common.

A substantial change of the overall institutional arrangement is unlikely, given the success of the model so far and the overall satisfaction with participatory mechanisms. The current discussion on the role of the state allows for an unbiased reflection on the relative merits of the state and markets, the phase of "market triumphalism" is over. Rather, changes can be expected at the level of detail, i. e. modernization of curricula, forms of transparency and competition rules with respect to subsidies.

The history and the present state of the Chinese event industry reflect the conviction that a nation's development cannot only rely on the 'invisible hand'; the government is also playing an active part. The non-market governmental power is more in favor of allocating the resources to the long-term projects to lead the development of the industry. The key issue probably is how to make the proportion of market and non-market power balanced. This is a topic deserving to be further discussed.

6 Literature

Ahrens, Joachim and Jünemann, Patrick (2010), *Transitional institutions, institutional complementarities and economic performance in China: A 'Varieties of Capitalism'-approach*, Ordnungspolitische Diskurse 2010/11

AUMA (2014), '*About us – AUMA*'. Online: www.auma.de (accessed on 1st July 2014)

CCPITTEX. (2014), '*China Textile & Apparel Trade Show (New York)*'

CEC. (2014), '*National (Shanghai) Centre for Exhibition and Convention*'

Chen, Jinbo (2014), '*Overview: China Convention Association*'

CFTC. (2014), '*CHINA FOREIGN TRADE CENTRE*'

Coase, Ronald and Ning Wang (2012), How China Became Capitalist, New York, Palgrave Macmillan.

EASTBEST (2014), '*Shanghai EastBest International (Group) Co., Ltd~Group Overview*'

Guo, Jurong ed. (2012a), *Under the complex environment of the global economy: the Chinese convention and exhibition industry continue to develop*, Beijing: Social Science Academic Press (in Chinese language)

Guo, Jurong ed. (2012b), *Overview: China convention and exhibition education development in 2011Beijing*: Social Science Academic Press (in Chinese language)

Guo, Jurong ed. (2012c), *Report on Shanghai's development in CEE-industry in 2011*, Beijing, Social Science Academic Press (in Chinese language)

Hall, Peter A. and Soskice, David (eds.) (2001): *Varieties of Capitalism – The Institutional Foundations of Comparative Advantage*, Oxford, Oxford University Press

Halper, Stefan (2010), T*he Beijing Consensus: How China's Authoritarian Model will Dominate The Twenty-First Century*, New York, Basic Books

ICCA (2013), '*2013 ICCA Statistics Report*' Amsterdam, the Netherlands

Reeds (2014), '*Shanghai International Houseware, Premium, Arts & Crafts Creative Design Exhibition 2014 at ShanghaiMart Exhibition Centre*'

SCEIA (2014), '*Shanghai Convention & Exhibition Industries Association*'

Shen, Chengjun and Xiang, Dewei. (2013), 'Study on Financial Support for the Development of SMEs in China', in: *Review of Economic Research*, Beijing

UFI (2014), '*Global Exhibition Industry Statistics*' Levallois-Perret France: UFI.

Wang, Fanghua ed. (2009), '*Research on Chinese Convention Merger and Acquisition during 2007–2008*', Social Science Academic Press, Beijing (in Chinese language)

Witt, Michael A. (2010), '*China: What Variety of Capitalism?*', INSEAD Working Paper 2010/88/EPS

Green economy and tourism

Frey, Andreas,
Gervers, Susanne

绿色经济及旅游业

This paper seeks to provide insight into the difficulty of adopting the concept of green tourism due to the conflicting interests of tourism and sustainability: tourism implies going beyond familiar boundaries, embarking on a wide range of travel and conspicuously consuming resources, whereas sustainability implies staying at home, limiting travel and conserving resources. Tourism means travelling to places outside the usual environment and staying there, crossing boundaries, and may be for either leisure or business purposes. The challenge is to find out how to make tourists respect local boundaries, and how to make tourism more compatible with sustainability goals. Recent international criteria for sustainability may guide tour operators, hotels and event managers, but marketing green tourism seems to be inconsistent with leisure travel. In contrast, business travel creates new opportunities for sustainability. We highlight this using two examples: green business travel in Germany and green leisure travel in China.

此义意在理解运用绿色旅游概念时产生的困难。由于旅游事业和可持续性两者之间存在利益冲突：一方面旅游意味着在熟悉的地域范围之外活动并显著地消耗资源，然而另一方面可持续性则意味着居家，保持有限的活动且节约资源。旅游意味着去别处旅行，居住在平时熟悉的环境以外的地方，并且跨越边界。因此不论是休闲型还是商务型的旅游，挑战在于如何使旅游业尊重当地地域，如何使旅游业与可持续性发展的目标相兼容。如今国际上的可持续性准则可以用于指导旅行运营方、旅馆和会展管理方，但推广绿色旅游概念似乎并不适用于休闲型旅游。与此相反的是，商务旅游创造了实现可持续性的新机遇。我们将通过两个例子证明这个观点：在德国的绿色商务旅游和在中国的绿色休闲旅游。

1 Introduction

Bridging theory and practice in green tourism is possible and necessary: in practice, tourism and sustainability call for intense multilevel cooperation and networking, whereas both need more theory in order to understand their complex references to nature, society and the economy. Furthermore, to be successful in adopting the concept of green tourism, meaning greening the economy and mitigating the negative impacts of economic progress, it is certainly important to know about its difficulty and to reflect on its challenges. Another reason pursue this approach is that professional cooperation requires shared views and common understandings.

First of all, to understand the concept of green tourism, it is essential to look back at its history: the idea of sustainability came up very early and in different cultures, but in 18th century Europe, the so-called Age of Enlightenment, it emerged as a topic in different disciplines reflecting the conditions of human progress, at first emerging in forest management. The 19th century industrial revolution with its pioneering successes did not leave space for these sorts of considerations and intellectual debates and only at the end of the 20th century, faced with the century's catastrophes and progresses, has the sustainability debate merged as a serious concern for the global community.

Sustainability has seemingly attained more and more predominance in various fields since the 1980s, but only when the Rio Conference in 1992 shaped its conceptual framework and the idea of sustainable development did it emerge as a leading term in the global vocabulary (Grober 2013: 13). Twenty years later, the UN Conference on Sustainable Development, known as Rio+20, reflected on events to date and confirmed that these steps were leading to a more sustainable future. At the same time different groups worked together to define useful sustainability criteria, as will be discussed in chapter three.

Since the Second World War, intensive growth of global tourism has occurred and it has become clear that there has to be control and mitigation of tourism's negative effects as there has been an increase worldwide from 25 million international tourists in 1950 to 1,087 million and, as estimated, five to six billion domestic tourists in 2013 (UNWTO 2014).

One forecast predicts that international tourism will further increase to 1.8 billion by 2030 (ibid.). Today, tourism already amounts to six per cent of the world's exports (ibid.), but in basically industrial countries such as Germany, it still is underestimated as an economic factor.

As the tourism industry reacted very slowly to embrace sustainability practices, it became obvious that political action had to be taken and social-political preconditions in Germany were due to change. Events developed to the point where it appeared rather difficult for the tourism industry to reconquer liberal spaces. A central question is: how the opinions about these developments align among tourism scientists and practitioners?

The scientists' point of view recently has been presented by Conrady (2014: 36), scientific director of the world leading ITB Berlin Congress and president of the German Society of Tourism Research. Conrady pointed out that tourists show opportunistic behaviors and no clear targets are set within the "magic triangle" of ecological, social and economic sustainability, but there is a prominent market segment of 22 per cent (ibid.: 5) for sustainable tourism. Working in this segment to start should avoid confusion and to provide orientation (ibid.) to the question of sustainable tourism.

Orientation has already been given by NGOs from different fields working together on transparency and comparability (see Naturfreunde Internationale et al. 2012), but tourism managers are hesitant to make clear commitments, preferring to say: "We want to sell after all the most beautiful weeks of the year and not the perfect handling of crises and problems" (Nuyken, cited by Hildebrandt 2014: 13, Author's translation). The statement sustainability "does not play a role" in booking decisions (Leitner-Rauchdobler, cited by Feyerherd 2014: 74; Author's translation) goes along with the ill-defined idea of implementing the "experience" of sustainability in the luxury niche (ibid.: 75).

What are the reasons and arguments behind these opinions from the tourism line? First of all, we need an understanding of tourist behavior in general; chapter two serves this purpose. We then look at the criteria for sustainable tourism and aspects of corporate responsibility in chapter three. Whether there are sectors in the tourism industry more amenable to green marketing is the subject of chapter four, where we take green business travel in Germany as an example. Green leisure travel will be studied by the example of China in chapter five.

Many challenges for research lie behind the question of green economics and tourism. Chapter six puts forth tentative conclusions regarding the difficulty of forming clear targets in tourism and further raises important questionings about recent trends in the shared economy. Attention is given to, first, the kind of academic research that has to be done to create liberal spaces, and, second, how these spaces could be occupied by entrepreneurial activity and creativity.

2 What is tourism?

For an understanding of tourist behaviour in general we need more theory: what characterizes tourist activity, what is important in creating new products and in understanding the touristic service chain? In fact, little academic research has been done on the preconditions of innovative tourism management as well as on the philosophy and theory of tourism. A theoretical understanding of the many facets of tourism could contribute to many efforts; it would allow us, for instance, to identify and compare the phenomenon in different cultures.

How can we define tourism? The World Tourism Organization defines tourist activity and tourism in its tourism statistics yearbook:

"A visitor is a traveler taking a trip to a main destination outside his/her usual environment, for less than a year, for any main purpose (business, leisure or other personal purpose) other than to be employed by a resident entity in the country or place visited. These trips taken by visitors qualify as tourism trips. Tourism refers to the activity of visitors." (UN/ UNWTO 2010: 10)

This definition comprises many forms of tourism, but not all of them. It refers to leisure travel as well as to business travel. Tourism appears as a complex phenomenon linked to spatial mobility, ranging from a weekend-trip by car to a long-distance flight, but it can also mean staying in well-known places, if only away from home and for less than a year. In seeking the factors that differentiate the forms of tourism, we come first of all to motivation as decisive, e. g. culture, health or nature as motivations for leisure travel in contrast to the MICE-segment in business travel. Abundant market research exists in the field of motivation, but not enough to show how the different types of tourism activity interact. Still, we can recognize in the definition of tourism four key elements:

- **The touristic motif** characterizes different sorts of travel and tourism, e. g. arts and culture for a study trip
    - Part-time employees of the destination are not regarded as tourists

- **The touristic space** denotes travel outside day-to-day life, away from the normal sphere and its boundaries
    - To reach distant places and to cross boundaries plays a preeminent role

- **The touristic mobility** in its different aspects, e. g. a bus trip, impacts the travel experience
    - Although there is an emotional effect, mobility is mostly seen as a necessity unlike e. g. staying in a hotel

- **The touristic duration** denotes the time spent away from home and is limited to a year, e. g. holiday travel of four overnight stays or short-term travel with one to three
    - Time is a structuring element in the travel experience, creating highly emotional moments such as "once in a lifetime"

Tourism comprises an activity that can be described as a circle moving away from home, staying in a place outside and returning home again. The Greek tornos, where the term tourism comes from, meant a kind of spacious circle. As tourism has become a cultural practice prevailing in contemporary advanced societies, its unrelenting search for new experiences has produced new conflicts, including the potential for overuse of resources, such as fresh water, beaches or mountain locales; the danger to protected wildlife or world heritage places; and the potential to disturb local communities. These conflicts undermine the achievements of the tourism industry and threaten the industry's prosperity. Numerous examples illustrate how the tourism industry has suffered because of pollution or political crises.

Greening the business is a difficult mission as tourism refers to strong individual motifs. More psychological research is needed to understand tourist behaviour, its inner conflicts and inter-connecting experiences. Various forms of tourism, so-called dark tourism, e. g. slum tourism, as well as extensive sports and other forms, e. g. intensive health care or even cultural events may illustrate what Picard and Di Giovine (2014: 23) describe as "Otherness" in tourism, namely that which can "satisfy desires that are hidden or otherwise repressed in tourists' everyday lives". The desire to consume "Otherness" may be associated with high costs for the environment and the hosting society.

How then could tourism be designed as green? What is needed for greening the tourism industry? What are the key factors of success, both from the business perspective and from the perspective of sustainability? To answer these questions, it is necessary to explain sustainable tourism and the problem of responsibility in the service chain.

3 Sustainable tourism

Since cultural and psychological knowledge is needed to understand the role of boundaries in tourism, it becomes clear that the importance of crossing these psychological borders, of breaking the rules of day-to-day life, at least once a year, creates a potential conflict with the idea of sustainability, since this idea is fundamentally linked to the awareness and respect for ecological, social and economic boundaries. There are deep intellectual roots behind this conflict, reaching back to the tradition of Judeo-Christian principles and those of modern capitalism. Traditional forms of Western thought stemming from the ethics of Aristotle also play into this conflict, as do, from another side, the strong focus on **balance** inspired by Eastern traditions.

Because of the multiple factors at play here, making sustainable tourism a reality requires more fundamental research in how to strengthen the idea of sustainability in the minds of all involved in the tourism industry, whether tourist or tour operators or support services. This goal raises the question of how best to educate these members of the industry. Another challenging strategic demand is to make the goal of sustainability quite clear and to achieve an unequivocal recognition of the standards that go along with it. To come to that point, green thinking requires first of all, as El Dief and Font (2010: 159) highlight, a "holistic view" covering all aspects of business activity instead of a view that seeks to preserve existing practices and uses business communication to "greenwash", i. e. to disseminate misleading information for the purpose of presenting an environmentally responsible public image. A holistic view is further essential if we are to understand the important cultural and psychological aspects of tourism.

Before developing criteria and performance indicators, the goal of sustainability needs to be operationalized. In 2005 the World Tourism Organization defined sustainable tourism as follows:

"Tourism that takes full account of its current and future economic, social and environmental impacts, addressing the needs of visitors, the industry, the environment and host communities" (UNEP/ UNWTO 2005: 12).

There are opinions in the tourism industry altering between uncertainty and avoidance, as have been cited above in chapter one. It is particularly not true that there is no orientation, because since 2012 respective 2013 (GSTC 2012; 2013a; 2013b) internationally accepted criteria have served as guidelines for sustainable tourism and have provided a clear code of conduct for hotels, tour operators and destinations.

Since 2007, 27 organizations, among them the World Tourism Organization and the German market-leader TUI AG, have participated in a cooperative process together with the public. They have worked together in the "Global Sustainable Tourism Council" and have created criteria as a global system of reference, representing "the minimum that any tourism business should aspire to reach"(GSTC 2012). These criteria give a quite clear orientation for any actor directly or indirectly involved in the touristic service chain, not only for business, but also for the tourist or the citizen:

The criteria describes how effective sustainable management can be demonstrated, how social and economic benefits to the local community can be maximized, and how negative impacts of tourism on cultural heritage and the environment can be minimized. The criteria for environmental protection explain conserving of resources (ibid.: D1) and of biodiversity, ecosystems and landscapes (ibid.: D3) and the reduction of pollution (ibid.: D2).

To take an example, reducing pollution refers to minimizing greenhouse gas emissions, wastewater, waste, harmful substances as well as pollution from noise, light, runoff, erosion, ozone-depleting compounds, and air, water and soil contaminants. Indicators for each criteria serve as a management guideline to show exemplary sustainability performance.

Tab. 1: Indicators for criteria D2 Reducing pollution/ 1. (GSTC 2013b: D2.1/ IN-D2.1)

Criteria	Indicators
D2.1 Greenhouse gas emissions from all sources controlled by the organization are measured, procedures are implemented to minimize them, and offsetting remaining emissions is encouraged.	IN-D2.1.a Total direct and indirect greenhouse gas emissions are calculated as far as practical. The Carbon Footprint (emissions less offsets) per tourist activity or guest-night is monitored and is not increasing year on year. IN-D2.1.b Carbon offset mechanisms are used where practical. GUIDANCE The rigour of the greenhouse/ carbon measurement and offset program should be commensurate with the level of energy used, e. g. a wilderness trekking tour operator may focus on the pre/ port trip transport aspects whereas a city hotel or a large resort should have detailed carbon measurement systems in place.

Before an implementation of these criteria can be considered, we have to first take into account the fact that the touristic service chain is highly complex and sensitive to multiple influences: the touristic product is generated in interaction with diverse tourists, consists of many support services, and is based on an intense collaboration among suppliers and on local networks. Local people play an important role in producing the touristic experience, but they are not directly involved. Sustainable tourism that respects these references can therefore convey an emotional benefit to the tourist seeking a convincing overall experience. If it is a package tour, e. g. a holiday trip, a tour operator designs, creates and controls the travel experience to fulfil the tourist's wishes. In Europe, due to consumer protection, the tour operator has to take the legal responsibility, e. g. in Germany according to §§ 651 a–m BGB.

Tour operators still play a dominant role in the touristic service chain, but more and more their role has declined as the digital tourist has gained prominence, interacting with service suppliers as well as in new networks where new services have recently emerged from the so-called share economy and now are challenging tour operators' business models. These commercial or voluntary services offer more opportunities. They give rise to the question, however, of how to get the tourist back into the professional commercial service chain, illustrated by the following:

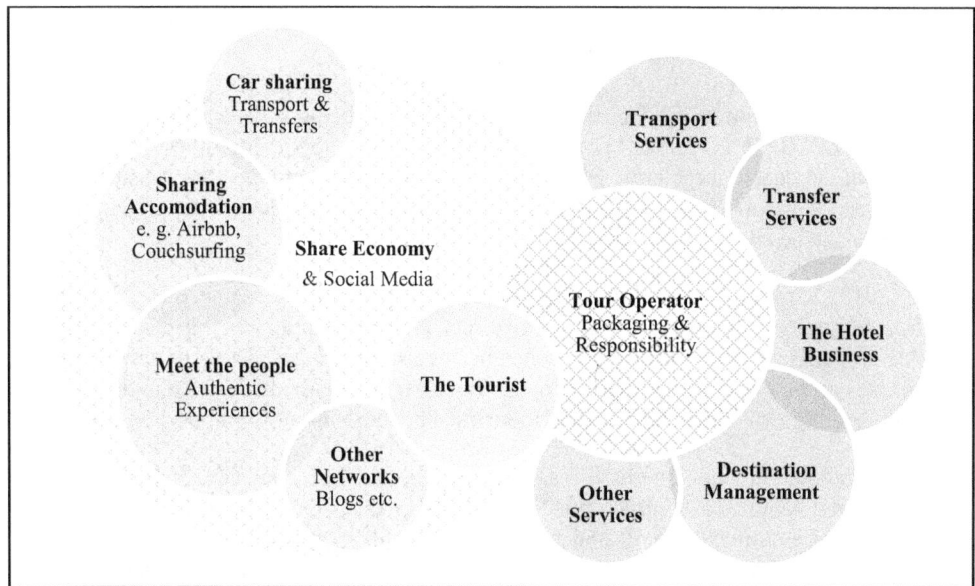

Figure 1: The Touristic Service Chain.

Another challenge to realizing sustainable tourism can arise from the support services that for many reasons do not go along with the tour operator's sustainable strategy. Consider two core services of a package tour, transportation and accommodation:

1. In the transportation sector, we find different preconditions for sustainable tourism. Whereas green positioning may appear as a sensible step for a rail company such as the Deutsche Bahn AG, or for the airline industry, it remains extremely difficult for these businesses to adopt green models. The Deutsche Lufthansa AG, by focusing on fuel efficiency, has played a pioneering role, but still has a long way to go before the paradigm change to green thinking fully matches business changes to green practices. The practice, for example, of asking the tourist for voluntary compensation of the greenhouse gas emissions produced by his or her flight has recently been criticized on several grounds. As Schmücker has argued (2011: 140) it is not only a well-established way to fight climate change, but it can also lead to "green-wash" and to unreasonably long distance flights.

2. Cost efficiency plays an important role in hotel management because of the typically high fixed costs in the accommodation business. Hence, hotel suppliers have taken on a pioneering role in greening the business. The market leader in Europe, TUI Hotels & Resorts, with 215,590 beds (Lettl-Schröder 2014: 9), serves as an example of sustainable strategy and responsibility, as evidenced by its membership in the Global Sustainable Tourism Council. Lund-Durlacher has pointed out the leading role of the international hotel chains in greening the business (2012: 561f.) and has described different measures to provide ecological sustainability (ibid.: 565f.), but social aspects such as stressful working conditions still remain a problem for the industry, underscoring the fact that sustainability requires a holistic approach. Baddeley and Font (2011: 211) also show for

Thomas Cook UK the challenge to address human aspects of behaviour change within the staff to change organizational habits.

Global institutions point to the fact that there is a growing demand for greening the tourism industry (UNEP/ UNWTO 2012: 419). This could convince suppliers to invest in sustainable products, but the question remains: what can be done to finally convince the consumer of the value of green tourism? If the tourist is to become responsible for closing the green gap, how should he or she be educated (see also Pomering et al. 2011: 964)?

Wehrli (2013: 26) found that cultural differences need to be taken into account. Whereas in the USA, consumers have appreciated a more direct, educative approach, this has not been the case in Europe. Here, as Wehrli notes, consumer decisions are based less on emotions and, when so based, the decisions so made carry a rather negative connotation. To understand the preconditions of green demand, therefore, there must be more interdisciplinary research.

This research could be done on emotions and happiness, as Ram et al. (2013: 1019) propose, or on emotional benefit-based green positioning, as Lee et al. (2010: 911) suggest. The conflicting goals of emotional benefit and rational sustainability could be merged, as Lee et al. describe, in "selfish altruism" (ibid.: 910). MacCannell, who has made important contributions to the field (1999), explains the difficulty of understanding the tourist's emotions, which could cause some disorientation (2011: 75). Robinson (2012: 23) refers to the specific methodological challenges of the field; another option could also be found following Khoo-Lattimore and Prideaux (2013) in their search for new psychological and even psychoanalytical methods.

It becomes obvious that only if the tourist attains an **emotional benefit** can tour operators or the service suppliers succeed. Anything that detracts from this benefit provokes either reluctance from the industry or withdrawal. McKercher (2014) demonstrated in the Hong Kong market that respondents of the travel trade avoided green topics not to question higher sales provisions, e. g. for long distance flights, but simply to turn over responsibility to the producer's side of the service chain, i. e. the tour operator or the airline industry. Another study in the UK (Burns 2014: 762) showed that airlines have behaved quite the same way and handed over their responsibility to the consumer's side.

From this perspective a central research question has emerged: how to provide a setting for tourism management that will motivate the decision makers to take over **responsibility** for sustainability. Recent contributions to this question have been made (Lovelock and Lovelock 2013; Goodwin 2011; Mundt 2011; Müller 2007) and to social justice as another aspect of the problem (Wearing et al. 2012: 48), but a stronger focus would necessarily emphasize the role of political governance and of corporate citizenship. Because for these considerations ethics are essential and go far behind the idea of compliance, an intellectual debate is needed to create awareness for sustainable criteria. The ethics of sustainable tourism have to be developed over a long period of civic activity as a positive experience.

There have been several attempts to shape the green values: the Global Code of Ethics for Tourism (see UNWTO 2001) gives a clear orientation for these values and the UN Global Compact (see UN 2000; 2004; 2013) with its ten essential principles enables business and civic groups to participate in the process of implementing green criteria. But, in fact, the tourism industry does not show much **commitment** here, either because there could be better communication of these UN-initiatives, or because the tourism industry does not yet see the importance of political activity and of professional lobbying as prerequisites for economic sustainability.

Consider the participants of the UN Global Compact: the tourism industry is almost absent. Among the 342 participants from Germany, only five come from the tourism industry; these include the Deutsche Lufthansa AG, which first joined in 2002 (UN n. d.). The UK has sent 322 participants, but only five from the tourism industry, those since 2007, but two of which do "not communicate" (ibid.). Among the 286 participants from China, three came from the tourism industry, among those the China National Travel Service (HK) Group Corporation which joined in 2012 (ibid.).

If the emotional benefit for the tourist comes under question, a strong commitment from the industry appears difficult. The sectors of the industry that are less dependent on the complex and highly variable dynamics of leisure travel, namely those serving business travellers, could then assume a pioneering role, as we will see in the next chapter.

4 Green business travel in Germany

Sustainable business travel has emerged as an important topic, but if we look, for example, at the business travel segment in Germany, we also find some incoherence. Sustainable criteria are still of little relevance for travel managers in the German source market (DRV 2014: 61); efficiency and cost savings are in the top ranks, while only 16 per cent prioritize ethical values (Pracht and Jürs 2014: 21) when planning a business trip.

On the other hand, Germany presents itself very successfully as a green business travel destination (GNTB 2014b; 2012): the traditional business travel, e. g. visiting partners, and the promotable business travel, e. g. trade fairs and conventions, have added up to 12.6 million business trips in 2014 (GNTB 2014a: 15). In many aspects, Germany is the first choice for business travel in Europe: it not only attracts most of the 61.0 million business trips, but it also is the first choice for a conference location in Europe, and the second one worldwide after the USA. As a destination for trade fairs, Germany ranks first (ibid.: 14).

Additionally, a strong national image could has developed since the reunification: the "lasting impact of the World Cup, plus sporting success define Germany's international image, just as much as museums, design and music" (ibid.: 6). Germany's leadership in green technology, e. g. renewable energies, may also play a decisive role in branding the country and its tourism industry.

Further growing, there are actually 4.5 per cent more, i. e. 31.5 million, international arrivals in Germany (ibid.: 8), and the segment of promotable business trips even adds to five per cent and now sums up to 6.9 million trips, or 55 per cent of all business trips (ibid.: 15). In 2012, business travel was highlighted as a special issue with a focus on green meetings and accessibility; sustainability was seen a competitive advantage (Tödter 2012: 61). Germany's green positioning strategy is strongly international. Its website www.germany.travel offers information in 26 languages and received the Gold Award from the Pacific Asia Travel Association (BMWi 2013: 32).

But this positioning is not yet finished. Große Ophoff (2012: 180) points out that the widely known Green Globe certification system works on a voluntary basis without full transparency. Green events are "designed, organized and implemented in a way that minimizes negative environmental impacts and leaves a positive legacy for the host community" (UNEP 2009: 9) and therefore need more transparency.

Although there is a potential for conflict in working toward sustainability, at least the goal appears clear to both sides. There is not a deep-seated psychological conflict at work within the motivations for business travel, as there is for leisure travel. The tourist's emotions only come up when making use of the free time on a business trip; for the most part, as the trip is for business, reasonable thinking is the only decisive factor, especially as it embraces efficiency and cost saving. Furthermore, green positioning helps managers to communicate with their stakeholders and to participate in public or political debates; it offers effective opportunities to influence these debates and to create good will.

The national framework for greening business travel as well as its individual setting could cut liberally into spaces of the tourism industry. In order to keep these spaces open for business activity, political action has to be taken.

5 Green leisure travel in China

On becoming the largest economy in the world, China became on the other hand the world-leader in CO2 emissions (Xue et al. 2013). The reasons behind this are manifold. The economy developed rapidly since China's reform in 1978, the environmental pollution has never been fundamentally controlled and hence, especially due to the high energy consumption, the carbon emissions increased dramatically.

Since the beginning of the 21st century, China set-up a number of laws and regulations related to low carbon economy. In the Copenhagen conference China proposed to reduce its carbon emissions/GDP by 40–50 per cent by 2020 relative to 2005 (see Xue et al. 2013). This can be seen in the 11th and 12th Five-Year Plan. In the 11th Five-Year Plan (starting from 2006) a reduction in energy and in the 12th Five-Year Plan the low carbon development was declared.

China's international tourism industry developed rapidly in the last thirty years due to the implementation of the economic reform and due to the openness to the outside of the world (Zhang et al. 2000). This can be also seen by the statistics of the World Tourism Organization (WTO) which ranked China on place seven worldwide in 1998 as for the number of international tourist arrivals and predicted China to be ranked first in 2020 with 137 millions of arrivals. Furthermore, the WTO predicted China to be ranked fourth in 2020 with respect to the number of outbound tourist departures.

The World Tourism Organization showed (UNWTO 2009) in 2009 that the tourism sector accounts for five per cent of the total greenhouse gas emission, with two per cent for aviation and three per cent for tourism excluding aviation. It is further estimated that the latter part will grow at 2.5 per cent per year until 2035. Furthermore, Gössling (Gössling 2002) showed that in 2001 the tourism sector accounts for 3.9 per cent of the global energy consumption. Wu and Shi (Wu et al. 2011) focused on China and showed the energy consumption and CO_2-emission of tourism-related transport in China in 2008. They calculated that the tourism sector in China contributed in 2008 to less than one per cent of the nationwide energy consumption and to less than one per cent of the nationwide carbon dioxide emissions. Having in mind that the tourism industry is rapidly growing and that China tops the world in CO_2 emissions, these numbers have to be reduced. This leads to the development of the Low-Carbon Tourism in China, in accordance with the 12th Five-Year Plan.

Due to the above-described effects, low-carbon tourism is growing in China and recently scientific papers can be found on this topic. In a first paper, (Zhibo 2012) described the current situation of green tourism in China. (Wang et al. 2012) then defined low-carbon tourism as a kind of low power consumption and low pollution tourism, which is an important and necessary contribution to the 12th Five-Year Plan. According to Wang et al., low-carbon tourism, which has brought new opportunities for today's tourism style transformation, is becoming the trend of the future development of tourism, since on the basis of the protection of the natural environment, low-carbon tourism is intended to ensure the sustainable development of health tourism.

How the low-carbon tourism system in China can work in practice can be recently seen in the papers from (Xiao et al. 2013) and (Xu et al. 2014), who analyse the effects of such a system in detail.

6 Conclusions

How can tourism be made part of the green economy? Tourism, by itself, is difficult to transform into an integral part of sustainable processes; only if the tourist's motivation can be steered into the direction of a more sustainable tourism can the tourism industry become a part of the green economy and benefit from this paradigm change. As political action has been taken to define useful criteria, it has become clear that the tourism industry is avoiding a clear commitment to sustainability, as only a small number of tour operators and service suppliers have been working together with NGOs to promote it. To understand this, the complexity of the touristic service chain has to be taken into account as well as the new challenges of having the sharing economy answer tourist's wishes in a completely different way.

As targets and responsibilities have not been clearly defined by the tourism industry, politics has moved into to occupy the space. In Germany, green business travel has been mutually reinforced by state, industry and destination management, as the underlying principles could have made clear. In China, the 11th and 12th Five-Year-Plans have significantly contributed to the development of the low-carbon tourism.

The growth of global tourism as a leading industry has positive and negative impacts; all forms of tourism could contribute to a green economy, but in different ways. First of all, clear targets are needed, and then a clear understanding of the tourist's wishes. New trends, as actually emerging from the share economy, could help identify **motivations** for travel and tourism, if these trends are not fought by the established line. More academic research, on the theory of tourism and travel and also on its psychological boundaries, could answer relevant questions, such as: how can supporters of a more sustainable tourism motivate and influence other stakeholders to show commitment? As the tourism industry is dominated by SMEs, the question of **free access** could be regarded as critical. There is also more **knowledge** needed, on theory and structures as well as on measurable targets: what are the ethics strengthening theses attempts, how to encourage innovation for sustainability?

In pluralistic consumer societies, it may cause some disturbances to insist on ethical values. As these, however, can serve as a foundation to make tourism more sustainable and governance implies defining such priorities, the question of social justice arises. Namely how can governance, either public or private, use liberal spaces to make education for sustainability more successful?

7 Literature

Baddeley, Joanne and X. Font (2011), 'Barriers to Tour Operator Sustainable Supply Chain Management', in: *Tourism Recreation Research*, 36 (3), pp. 205–214

Burns, Peter M. and Ch. Cowlishaw (2014), 'Climate change discourse: how UK airlines communicate their case to the public', in: *Journal of Sustainable Tourism*, 22 (5), pp. 750–767

[BMWi] Bundesministerium für Wirtschaft und Technologie (2013), *Tourismuspolitischer Bericht der Bundesregierung*, 17. Legislaturperiode. Online: http://www.bmwi.de/BMWi/Redaktion/PDF/S-T/tourismuspolitischer-bericht,property=pdf,bereich=bmwi2012,sprache=de,rwb=true.pdf (accessed on 19 July 2014)

Conrady, Roland (2014), 'Corporate Social Responsibility in der touristischen Wertschöpfungskette: Status Quo, Trends, Herausforderungen', keynote to *anniversary conference Chair of Tourism/ Center for Entrepreneurship Catholic University Eichstätt-Ingolstadt*, 15 May 2014. Online: http://www.ku.de/fileadmin/150306/css/Jubil%C3%A4umstagung/Conrady.pdf (accessed on 21 June 2014)

Deutscher ReiseVerband (DRV) (ed.) (2014), *Chefsache Business Travel. Studie 2014*. Online: http://www.chefsache-busi-nesstravel.de/fileadmin/user_upload/docs/Studie/DRV_Business_Travel_2014_HintergrundinformationWeb.pdf (accessed on 20 July 2014)

El Dief, Mohammed and X. Font (2010), 'The determinants of hotels' marketing managers' green marketing behavior', in: *Journal of Sustainable Tourism*, 18 (2), pp. 157–174

Feyerherd, Martina (2014), 'Luxusreisen. Anspruchsvolle Kunden von Nachhaltigkeit überzeugen', in: *fvw-magazin. touristic & business travel*, 06/ 2014, pp. 72–74

[GNTB] German National Tourist Board (ed.) (2012), *Sustainability for success. Conferences, conventions & events in Germany*, Frankfurt/ Main. Online: http://viewer.zmags.com/publication/cdb3ceef#/cdb3ceef/1 (accessed on 16 July 2014)

[GNTB] German National Tourist Board (ed.) (2014a), *Incoming-Tourism Germany. Facts and Figures 2013*. Online: http://www.germany.travel/media/pdf/dzt_marktforschung/GNTB-Incoming-Tourism-Germany-2014.pdf (accessed 13 July 2014)

[GNTB] German National Tourist Board (ed.) (n. d. [2014b]), *Naturally unique. Sustainable Travel in Germany*, Frankfurt/ Main. Online: http://viewer.zmags.com/publication/f5a29dae#/f5a29dae/40 (accessed on 16 July 2014)

Gössling, Stefan (2002), 'Global environmental consequences of tourism', in: *Global Environmental Change*, 12(4): 283–302.

Goodwin, Harold (2011), *Taking Responsibility for Tourism. Responsible Tourism Management*, Oxford: Goodfellow Publishers Ltd.

Grober, Ulrich (2013), 'Die Entdeckung der Nachhaltigkeit. Zur Genealogie eines Leitbegriffs', in: Judith C. Enders and Moritz Remig (eds), *Perspektiven nachhaltiger Entwicklung – Theorien am Scheideweg*, Marburg: Metropolis-Verlag, pp. 13–25

Große Ophoff, Markus (2012), 'Green Meetings & Events: Nachhaltiges Tagen in Deutschland', in: Michael-Thaddäus Schreiber (ed.), *Kongresse, Tagungen und Events. Potenziale, Strategien und Trends der Veranstaltungswirtschaft*, München: Oldenbourg Verlag, pp. 173–186

[GSTC] Global Sustainable Tourism Council Washington (ed.) (2012), *Global Sustainable Tourism Criteria for Hotels and Tour Operators*, Version 2, 23 February 2012. Online: http://www.gstcouncil.org/images/pdf/gstc-hto-indicators_v2.0_10dec13%20.pdf (accessed on 14 June 2014)

[GSTC] Global Sustainable Tourism Council Washington (ed.) (2013a), *Global Sustainable Tourism Council Criteria*, Version 1, 1 November 2013, and Suggested Performance Indicators, Version 1, 10 December 2013, for Destinations. Online: http://www.gstcouncil.org/images/Dest-_CRITERIA_and_INDICATORS_6-9-14.pdf (accessed on 12 July 2014)

[GSTC] Global Sustainable Tourism Council Washington (ed.) (2013b), *Global Sustainable Tourism Criteria for Hotels and Tour Operators – Suggested Performance Indicators*, Draft Version 2.0, 10 December 2013. Online: http://www.gstcouncil.org/images/pdf/ global%20sustainable%20tourism%20criteria%20h-to%20version%202_final.pdf. (accessed on 14 June 2014)

Hildebrandt, Klaus (2014), 'Thema der Woche. DRV legt Verhaltenskodex für Veranstalter auf', in: *fvw-magazin. touristic & business travel*, 05/ 2014, pp. 12 f.

Khoo-Lattimore, Catheryn and B. Prideaux (2013), 'ZMET: a psychological approach to understanding unsustainable tourism mobility', in: *Journal of Sustainable Tourism*, 21 (7), pp. 1036–1048

Lee, Jin-Soo et al. (2010), 'Understanding how consumers view green hotels: how a hotel's green image can influence behavioural intentions', in: *Journal of Sustainable Tourism*, 18 (7), pp. 901–914

Lettl-Schröder, Maria (2014), 'Deutsche Veranstalter. Hotelerlebnis nach Maß', in: *fvw-dossier. FerienHotellerie 2014*, 10/ 2014, pp. 4–9

Lovelock, Brent and K. M. Lovelock (2013), *The Ethics of Tourism. Critical and applied perspectives*, London and New York: Routledge

Lund-Durlacher, Dagmar (2012), 'CSR und nachhaltiger Tourismus', in: Schneider, Andreas and R. Schmidpeter (eds), *Corporate Social Resonsibility. Verantwortungsvolle Unternehmensführung in Theorie und Praxis*, Berlin and Heidelberg: Springer Gabler, pp. 559–570

MacCannell, Dean (1999 [1976]), *The Tourist. A new theory of the leisure class*, With a New Foreword by Lucy R. Lippard and a New Epilogue by the Author, Berkely, Los Angeles and London: University of California Press

McKercher, Bob et al. (2014): 'Does climate change matter to the travel trade?', in: *Journal of Sustainable Tourism*, 22 (5), pp. 685–704

Mundt, Jörn W. (2011), *Tourism and Sustainable Development. Reconsidering a Concept of Vague Policies*, Berlin: Erich Schmidt Verlag

Müller, Hansruedi (2007), *Tourismus und Ökologie. Wechselwirkungen und Handlungsfelder*, 3rd, rev. Edition, München and Wien: R. Oldenbourg Verlag

Naturfreunde Internationale/ arbeitskreis tourismus & entwcklung/ ECOTRANS e. V./ Evangelischer Entwicklungsdienst (eds) (2012), *Nachhaltigkeit im Tourismus. Wegweiser durch den Labeldschungel*, Online: http://tourism-watch.de/files/nfi_tourismus_labelguide_web.pdf (accessed on 09 July 2014)

Picard, David and M. Di Giovine (2014), 'Introduction: Through other Worlds', in: id. (eds): *Tourism and the Power of Otherness. Seductions of Difference*, Bristol, Buffalo and Toronto: Channel view publications

Pomering, Alan et al. (2011), 'Conceptualizing a contemporary marketing mix for sustainable tourism', in: *Journal of Sustainable Tourism*, 19 (8), pp. 953–969

Pracht, Sabine and M. Jürs (2014), 'Firmen-Reisebüros. Problemlösungen dringend gesucht', in: *fvw-magazin. touristik & business travel*, 08/ 2014, pp. 16–21

Ram, Yael et al. (2013), 'Happiness and limits to sustainable tourism mobility: a new conceptual model', in: *Journal of Sustainable Tourism*, 21 (7), pp. 1017–1035

Robinson, Mike (2012), 'The Emotional Tourist', in: Picard, David and M. Robinson (eds), *Emotion in Motion. Tourism, Affect and Transformation*, Farnham and Burlington: Ashgate, pp. 21–46

Schmücker, Dirk J. (2011), 'Freiwillige Kompensation von Flugreisenemissionen als nachfrageinduzierte Anpassungsstrategie – ein empirischer Anbietervergleich', in: *Zeitschrift für Tourismuswissenschaft*, 3 (2), pp. 139–149

Tödter, Norbert (2012), 'Internationale Bedeutung des Geschäftstourismus für das Reiseland Deutschland', in: Michael-Thaddäus Schreiber (ed.), *Kongresse, Tagungen und Events. Potenziale, Strategien und Trends der Veranstaltungswirtschaft*, München: Oldenbourg Verlag, pp. 49–63

[UN] United Nations Global Compact (ed.) (n. d. [2000; 24 June 2004]), *The Ten Principles*. Online: http://www.unglobalcompact.org/AboutTheGC/TheTenPrinciples/index.html (accessed on 16 July 2014)

[UN] United Nations Global Compact (ed.) (2013), *Overview of the UN Global Compact* (Last update 22 April 2013). Online: http://www.unglobalcompact.org/AboutTheGC/index.html (accessed on 16 July 2014)

[UN] United Nations Global Compact (ed.) (n. d.), *Participants & Stakeholders*. Online: http://www.unglobalcompact.org/participants/search?business_type=all&commit=Search&cop_status=all&country[]=38&joined_after=&joined_before=&keyword=&listing_status_id=all&organization_type_id=&page=10&sector_id=all&utf8=%E2%9C%93 (accessed 16 July 2014) [China]; http://www.unglobalcompact.org/participants/search?utf8=%E2%9C%93&commit=Search&keyword=&country[]=45&joined_after=&joined_before=&business_type=all&sector_id=all&listing_status_id=all&cop_status=all&organization_type_id=&commit=Search (accessed 16 July 2014) [Germany; UK]

[UN/ UNWTO] United Nations, Department of Economic and Social Affairs, Statistics Division and World Tourism Organization (eds) (2010), *International Recommendations for Tourism Statistics 2008*, Studies in Methods, Series M, No. 83/ Rev. 1, New York. Online: http://unstats.un.org/unsd/publication/Seriesm/SeriesM_83rev1e.pdf#page=21 (accessed on 14 June 2014)

[UNEP] United Nations Environment Programme (ed.) (2009), *Green Meeting Guide 2009. Roll out the Green Carpet for your Participants*, Nairobi. Online: http://www.unep.fr/shared/publications/pdf/DTIx1141xPA-GreenMeetingGuide.pdf (accessed on 16 July 2014)

[UNEP/ UNWTO] United Nations Environment Programme and World Tourism Organization (eds) (2005), *Making Tourism more sustainable. A Guide for Policy Makers, Paris and Madrid*. Online: http://www.unep.fr/shared/publications/pdf/DTIx0592xPA-TourismPolicyEN.pdf (accessed on 14 June 2014)

[UNEP/ UNWTO] United Nations Environment Programme and World Tourism Organization (eds) (2012), *Tourism in the Green Economy. Background Report*, Madrid. Online: http://www.unep.org/greeneconomy/Portals/88/documents/ger/ger_final_dec_2011/Tourism%20in%20the%20green_economy%20unwto_unep.pdf (accessed on 20 June 2014)

[UNWTO] World Tourism Organization (UNWTO) (ed.) (2001), *Global Code of Ethics for Tourism*. Online: http://dtxtq4w60xqpw.cloudfront.net/sites/all/files/docpdf/gcetbrochureglobalcodeen.pdf (accessed on 19 July 2014)

[UNWTO] World Tourism Organization (UNWTO) (ed.) (2009), *Towards a low carbon travel & tourism sector*. Report in World Economic Forum.

[UNWTO] World Tourism Organization (UNWTO) (ed.) (2014), *Tourism Highlights 2014 Edition*. Online: http://dtxtq4w60xqpw.cloudfront.net/sites/all/files/pdf/unwto_highlights14_en.pdf (accessed on 07 July 2014)

Wang, Xuefend and Zhang, Hui (2012), 'Discussion on Countermeasures of China's Low-Carbon Tourism Development', in: F.Chen et al (eds.), *LTLGB Proceedings of International Conference on Low-Carbon Transportation and Logistics and Green Buildings*, Springer, pp. 91–99.

Wearing, Stephen et al. (2012), 'Slow'n Down the Town to Let Nature Grow: Ecotourism, Social Justice and Sustainability', in: Simone Fullagar et al. (eds), *Slow Tourism. Experiences and Mobilities*, Bristol, Buffalo and Toronto: Channel View Publications

Wehrli, Roger (2013), *Advertising Sustainable Tourism Products: Research Findings for higher Sales*, Presentation at the 2013 ITB in Berlin. Online: http://www.itb-kongress.de/media/global/global_image/global_apps/ global_edb/ global_edb_ upload_2013/ global_ edb_ events_itbk_1/edb_261878.pdf. (accessed on 20 June 2014)

Wu, Pu and Shi, Peihua (2011), 'An estimation of energy consumption and CO2 emissions in tourism sector of China', in: *Journal of Geogr. Science*, 21(4): 733–745.

Xiao, Lan and Zhao Li-ming (2013), 'Low-Carbon Tourism Research Nased on System Dynamics', in: E. Qi et al. (eds.) *Proceedings of 20th International Conference on Industrial Engineering and Engineering Management*, Springer, pp. 335–345.

Xu, Jiuping and Yao, Liming and Lu, Yi (2014), 'Low Carbon Tourism', in: *Innovative Approaches Towards Low Carbon Economics*, Springer, berlin, pp. 395–422.

Xue, Jinjun and Xuan, Xiaowei (2013), 'China's Green Low-Carbon Development', in: *Green Low-Carbon Development in China*, Springer, Switzerland.

Zhang, Guangrui and Pine, Ray and Zhang, Hanqin Qiu (2000), 'China's international tourism development: present and future', in: *International Journal of Contemporary Hospitality Management*, 12(5): 282–290.

Zhibo, Diao (2012), 'The Current Situation of Green Tourism in China', in: 2012 International Conference on Affective Computing and Intelligent Interaction, *Lecture Notes in Information Technology*, Vol. 10, pp. 72–75.

China outbound: How China will affect the international meetings industry

Schwägermann, Helmut,
Zhang, Li

中国的出境游：中国会展市场将如何影响国际会展行业

This article focuses on the future influence of China on the meetings industry in all major countries and cities that are active in the meetings business.

In the first part, we discuss why, where and when Chinese delegates, exhibitors, visitors and event organisers play an important role, and attempt to determine suitable parameters that function as driving factors or predictors for this development. Next, we identify and discuss these driving factors and suggest a comprehensive qualitative forecast model for China's outbound meeting activities.

In the second part, we present the main results of an online study involving 196 ICCA members. The responses reflect the attitudes of ICCA members towards a new player on the international scene.

In addition, the article explores whether these foreign meeting service suppliers, such as destination management organisations, conference centres and professional congress organisers, have already established a special "China Strategy".

这篇文章关注中国在未来对世界各地会展行业的影响，尤其是在一些会议产业十分活跃的城市和地区。

在第一部分，我们将讨论中国参会代表、参展商、专业观众和会展主办商为何、何地、何时将在这个发展中发挥重要作用，并试图找到作为发展驱动因子或预测因子的合适参量。接着，我们将分析并讨论这些驱动因子，并为中国将来的出境会议活动提出一个综合性的定性预测模型。

在第二部分，我们将公布一份由 196 名 ICCA 成员参与的网络调查结果。它反映了 ICCA 成员对于这个世界舞台上新竞争者的态度。

此外，本文还提出了一个问题，包括目的地管理组织，会议中心和专业的会议组织者在内的海外会议服务供应商是否已经制定了特殊的"中国战略"？

1 Introduction

China's market for business events has grown and developed dramatically over the last twenty years. Until now, most researchers, scholars and event companies have concentrated on China's huge home market and focused on the inbound aspects.

In contrast, this article focuses on the future influence of China to the meetings business worldwide and, consequently, to the meetings industry in all major countries and cities that are active in the meetings business. We will discuss why, where and when Chinese delegates, exhibitors, visitors and event organisers will play an important role, and try to find suitable parameters that function as *driving factors* or *predictors* for this development.

The article has two main parts. In the first part, we will identify and discuss these driving factors for China's outbound event business and suggest a comprehensive qualitative forecast model for China's outbound meeting activities. In the second part, we will report on the main results of an online study involving members of the worldwide organisation International Congress and Convention Association (ICCA). It reflects the attitude of ICCA members towards a new player on the international scene.

The purpose of this article is therefore to determine whether there is evidence of a growth in those activities and whether foreign meeting service suppliers, such as destination management organisations (DMOs), conference centres and professional congress organisers (PCOs), have already established a special "China Strategy".

This article is based on two presentations that the author gave during the ICCA Congress 2012 in Puerto Rico and 2013 in Shanghai. ICCA is the world's leading association for the meetings industry.

2 Definitions and methodology

The term *meetings* is increasingly used as a generic term for all kinds of gatherings, like congresses, conventions and seminars. However, it is sometimes also used for business events as such, especially by ICCA, because its target group are professional persons from all kinds of organisations. By definition, business events are events that are designed, planned and organised for participants who visit these events for professional reasons. Business events are also sometimes described by the acronym MICE (meetings, incentives, conventions and exhibitions).

Although our focus is on the meetings market, we will use the broader concept of business events because, for several good reasons, a combination of meetings and exhibitions or trade fairs is increasingly taking place. Moreover, most ICCA members are not only interested in association meetings, which are their core business, but also in international business events of all kinds!

Our overall research questions were:

1. *How will China affect the international meetings industry?*
2. *How do ICCA members react to this challenge? Do they have a "China Strategy"?*

Our research statements were:

- Chinese exhibitors are already one of the biggest national groups at many exhibitions worldwide
- More Chinese individuals or group of delegates/visitors will take part in international meetings/business events worldwide
- China will soon be one of the biggest national delegations, also at international meetings
- China's meetings business is different due to strong governmental influence
- An increasing number of Chinese decision-makers (e. g. board members in international associations or companies) will influence international meetings and the selection of destinations
- China's outgoing event business will start with incentive travel to Asian countries
- Direction (countries and cities) and volume (number of delegates and/or meetings) will be influenced by several factors which determine the general relationship between China as the "source market" and the "target country"
- Countries that are generally attractive and/or specifically competitive for business events will gain most from this development
- ICCA members who already have experience with Chinese delegates and/or events are more aware of the potential of this market
- Few ICCA members/destination already have a "China Strategy"

In the first part of our study, we endeavour to identify the factors that may influence the growing involvement of Chinese individuals, companies and organisations in the international meetings industry, whether as participants, speakers and moderators or even as organisers of their own events abroad.

3 Driving factors for China's outbound meeting activities. Volume and direction

Finally, we identified *ten driving factors*, i. e. factors that may influence the volume and direction of China's outbound event activities (see also Figure 1).

The term *driving factor* is used in this article to describe the relation between two variables, where the driving factors are the *causing* factors (which can also be called *predictors*) and the meetings activities are the *effects* of altering these driving factors. Most of these parameters have exhibited an upward swing in recent years, suggesting an interrelationship with the growing business events sector.

However, since only few Chinese business events have taken place abroad so far, we were unable to find any reliable statistics for a quantitative model with characteristics such as correlation and factor analysis. We will need further years of observation to gather appropriate statistics. Our model can therefore be classified as a *qualitative model*, which explains the reasons and direction of the forces behind the outgoing activities. The task of this initial model is to suggest *cause-and-effects relations* between these factors and the meetings activities of China outside the country.

The long-term aim of this research is, however, to set up a quantitative forecast model on the basis of time series of valid statistical data, which can be analysed in various ways.

Some of these factors are visible and easy to quantify because official or semi-official statistical data is available. Other factors, which can also be assumed to have a direct or indirect influence, are hard to quantify as yet. In the following sections, we will discuss these driving factors individually. Some of these factors are part of the macro-environment, and cannot be influenced by Chinese or foreign event managers. Other factors can be actively and strategically managed by the event service industry, in order to boost the attractiveness of destinations and other event services for the Chinese market.

Fig. 1: Ten driving factors for China's outbound meetings business

3.1 Business events in China

Assumption:

A growing and experienced event industry in China enhances the chance for acting outside of China.

As the first factor, we analyse the volume, structure and development of the market for business events in China. The *assumption* is: The stronger China's home market for meetings and other business events is, the more successful and experienced Chinese companies and organisations are. In addition: the more international companies and organisations either organise or participate in international trade fairs and meetings in China, the more experienced and professional Chinese companies and organisations will get. Once they have gained experience with international partners at home, they will be more ready and able to attend business events and meetings in their international target markets.

When it comes to the Chinese *meetings market*, ICCA statistics exhibit a 125 per cent growth over the last ten years (ICCA2014). The China Meeting Statistical Analysis Report specifies 8,270 meetings in 2008 and 14,350 in 2013, including 69 per cent corporate meetings, 12 per cent meetings of institutions, 10 per cent government meetings and 9 per cent association meetings (CMSAR 2014, calculated by the authors).

As the meetings industry in China is a completely new service industry, where no hardware (infrastructure) or software (a special meeting professionalism) existed ten years ago, we expect a further two-digit growth in national and international events.

China's *exhibition market*, however, developed much earlier than the meetings market, namely already in the 1980s in a response to the opening policy of Deng Xiaoping. Nowadays, all international trade fair companies have subsidiaries in China, some of which already organise more important exhibitions in China than at home. According to UFI, the indoor exhibition space offered by Chinese exhibition venues in 2011 grew by 45 per cent compared to 2006, and now ranks second (behind the USA, but in front of Germany). UFI also puts China in second place behind the USA and in front of Germany, with 13.7 million sqm net space rented (UFI 2014). As China continues to experience remarkable growth rates compared to its competitors, many experts already consider China to be the most important exhibition place worldwide.

The market for *corporate events* is less transparent than the markets for meetings and exhibitions, also in China, where leading associations such as UFI and ICCA report on development. However, multinational companies have been operating in China for more than 20 years, relying on face-to-face communication with their dealers or customers in China, too. As Chinese companies like Lenovo, Haier and Hisense first shaped their brands and profiles in their home market and only later emerged as global players, they increasingly used marketing events like product presentations and dealer events in their communication mix. We will see more *Hidden Chinese Champions* in the years to come. International communication and event agencies entered the Chinese market ten or more years ago and added to the professionalism of this communication tool. Incentive travel as a special corporate event was successfully introduced to China's leading companies.

Conclusion:

China's market for business events is one of the fastest growing markets worldwide with a modern infrastructure and increasing specialist know-how for business events of all kinds. Many Chinese organisers and agencies have acquired global professional standards that enable them to go abroad with some of their activities.

3.2 Economy and trade

Assumption:

A growing Chinese economy and trade is the basis for a flourishing event market. The structure and volume of the trade will reveal relevant industry sectors and the regional direction for China's outgoing event business.

According to the Worldbank statistics, China's gross domestic product (GDP), which measures the growth of the national economy, rose at a two-digit rate for years, and stagnated at 7.7 per cent over the last three years, which is still far higher than that of all industrialised countries (The Worldbank 2014).

According to statistics from the National Bureau of Statistics of the People's Republic of China, the following countries were the ten leading trade countries (areas) for China in 2013.

Export: 1. Hong Kong 2. United States 3. Japan 4. North Korea 5. Germany 6. Netherlands 7. United Kingdom 8. Vietnam 9. Russia 10. India

Import: 1. South Korea 2. Japan 3. Taiwan 4. United States 5. Australia 6. Germany 7. Malaysia 8. Switzerland 9. Brazil 10. Saudi Arabia (NBSPRC 2014).

Not surprisingly, five (four) out of ten countries are Asian countries. In addition, the leading industries involved in trade must be investigated more closely. Obviously, many companies in these countries have strong business relations to Chinese partners, which lead to a number of individual business travel and meetings as well as participation in national and international meetings and conferences from their respective industries.

Conclusion:

China's economy has developed into one of the world's leading economic powers. The stronger the commercial ties between countries are, the greater the chance for meetings and other events to be held with a strong Chinese participation in other countries. Most of China's important trade partners are, naturally, situated in Asia. A number of other countries, such as the USA, Germany and the Netherlands, have special trade relations, which also form the basis for special business as well as trade-related meetings and events. It goes without saying that these commercial relations with China focus on different industries, which have to be determined individually by each country.

3.3 Currency exchange rate

Assumption:

As a result of China's exchange rate development, events outside China are becoming financially more favourable and even gaining a cost advantage

Some years ago, even experts believed that events in China could be produced a low cost. However, the Chinese government floated the currency RMB more than a decade ago. Since then, the RMB has continuously been revaluated against the US dollar, the euro and the Japanese yen and other currencies. According to the China National Bureau of Statistics, the exchange rate against the US dollar rose from RMB 8.20 in 2005 to 6.31 in 2013 (CNBS, 2014). As a consequence, expenditures for goods and services, including event-related services from abroad, fell by about 25 per cent. Nonetheless, many scholars consider the RMB to be systematically undervalued, i. e. there is an inherent tendency for the RMB to rise further in value against other currencies. In addition, the continuously growing income and modest inflation rate in China will lead to the higher purchasing power of Chinese organisers and delegates for foreign event services.

Conclusion:

Due to the strong revaluation of the RMB in the past as well as to expected similar tendencies in the future, the purchasing power of Chinese event managers for foreign goods and services has permanently risen in the last decade and will presumably do so in the years to come. Combined with the noticeable inflation rate in the Chinese metropolises, events held in China will lose their comparative cost advantage. It is becoming increasingly attractive to organise events and buy event services outside China.

3.4 Government policy

Assumption:

The Chinese government's influence on international meetings will be eased, but is still more important/decisive than many western observers believe.

Many western observers continue to overlook the importance of China's government at all regional levels concerning the Chinese event market. Although on the surface, especially in metropolises like Shanghai, China may show a "capitalist face", the country has a one-party system and is led by the Communist Party of China (CPC), which has a firm control over the government and the army.

China's economic model is that of a socialistic market economy with a dominating state sector, which is sometimes referred to as "state capitalism" or a "command economy". Since 1953, the country has been "managed" by central five-year plans, which are consequently deployed "top-down". The 12th plan, now called a "guideline", is currently in effect (2011–2015). Before Deng Xiaoping's opening policy, when the first elements of a market economy were introduced, all activities were planned and operated by state organisations under their respective ministries.

Especially in the field of exhibitions and foreign trade, both foreign exhibition organisers and foreign exhibitors had to deal with one institution: the China Council of the Promotion of International Trade (CCPIT) and its respective regional sub-councils, founded in 1952. In 1988, CCPIT also adopted the name and functions of China's Chamber of International Commerce (CCOIC). CCPIT is an organisation under the Chinese Ministry of Commerce (MOFCOM). In the course of decentralisation, CCPIT was reorganised and generated several affiliated companies, like the Shanghai World Expo Group which, after some reorganisation and renaming, has now emerged as the developer and owner of the new National Exhibition and Convention Center (Shanghai), as well as the organiser of its own exhibitions, not only in that venue. Most experts who worked in China's exhibition industry prior to 2000 worked at CCPIT in one way or the other.

CIEC, the China International Exhibition Center Group Corporation, a subsidiary of CCPIT, is not only the management company of the Beijing China International Exhibition Center, but also the central organiser of China's participations at exhibitions and trade fairs abroad. At the same time, industry organisations, sometimes with the English translation of "associations", which are in fact branches of the respective ministries, are also heavily involved in organising exhibitions and congresses in China (see also Section 3.5). As demonstrated using these examples, so-called State Owned Enterprises (SOE) and other governmental organisations act as organisers of trade fairs as well as organisers of meetings, congresses and conferences in this country.

For years, academics and other experts have been discussing the role of government in the event market in China. Most agree that the government should withdraw from the function of event organiser, and restrict itself to developing and monitoring the legal frame of the event market concerning quality, safety and competition, and stop organising its own events. After all, due to several business practices, this would lead to unfair competition. We can therefore expect government influence in the event industry to be gradually restricted; state organisations will be transferred to public-private partnerships (PPP) of all kinds, and new partners will appear in the international event business.

On the other hand, China's government already recognised the role of meetings and exhibitions as driving factors for the development of the service industries of cities and regions at the turn of the century. As such, it invested in the infrastructure, and issued special "preferential policies", such as tax exemptions, for the event industry in certain cities. In addition, for years, China's central and provincial government as well as industry associations have been organising joint Chinese stands at international trade fairs worldwide, supporting individual companies in their efforts to be present on international markets.

Other governmental issues, such as visa procedures, have not improved much over the years. On the contrary, some have become even more complicated. Although a 72-hour visa-free transit has been introduced for 11 Chinese cities and for citizens from 51 countries, the visa for both inbound and outbound travel remains a contentious issue.

Last but not least, it is obviously easier for Chinese event organisers to do international business with partners from nations that have had a stable and reliable relationship with China over time.

Conclusion:

The direct and indirect influence of the CPC and China's government is still very strong. The government's direct influence on the organisation of events, by transforming organisations and adapting certain laws, is expected to diminish gradually. However, China will remain a centrally led country for a long time with a stronger governmental influence than most western countries. Western companies and organisations that want to deal with China's event industry must understand this special Chinese model.

3.5 Non-governmental organisations in China

Assumption:

Non-governmental organisations (NGO), the main organisers of meetings worldwide, will gradually emerge as more or less state-independent bodies in the time to come, although this will not be an easy path. The meetings market, where NGOs and associations are the organisers, will be the most dynamic sector in China's event market. We also expect a strongly growing Chinese influence on international associations.

As in other countries, there are associations in China that are involved in organising their own meetings and events, most of which hold annual conferences, particularly in the field of science, medicine, technology and engineering (Salsbury 2010:14*)*. However, due to China's political system, it is not easy to understand the structure, volume and development of this important sector.

Civil society and its accompanying legal framework have become considerably more complex in China in recent decades (ICNL 2015). NGOs, sometimes also called *civil society organisations* (CSO), *civil organisations, social organisations* or *public welfare organisations,* are moving gradually from the margins of society into the mainstream. Management of the emerging civil society sector by the CPC and state agencies remained restrictive, but is at the same time unable to keep up with the growth of NGOs (Shieh, Knutson 2012:3).

In China, the Nongovernmental Organisations Administrative Bureau of the Ministry of Civil Affairs (MOCA) is responsible for overseeing and administering NGOs that operate in China. MOCA itself considers "trade associations, fraternities, business associations, foundations, advocacy associations, academic associations, research associations, and friendship associations" to be NGOs (FCTACC).

According to Lau, there were 4,544 registered social organisations in 1989; this figure rose to more than 354,000 NGOs registered with the Ministry in 2006. It is also reported by Lau that 90 per cent of NGOs operating in China are not registered (Lau, 2009:2). In 2004, the Worldbank estimated that there were more than one million "unregistered" or "unofficial" grassroots or community-based organisations operating in China (The Worldbank 2004).

Edele (2005:12ff) classified four types of NGOs with respect to their legal status and degree of autonomy:

1. Government-organised NGOs (GONGOs)
In the early 1980s, the government and party departments started establishing non-profit organisations called "government-organised NGOs" (GONGOs). Like some NGOs, GONGOs are registered as social organisations with the Ministry of Civil Affairs and sponsored by a government agency. GONGOs tend to have close ties with the government, because many are led by retired high-ranking government officials. Some of their employees are even on the government payroll (Cf. Lau, 2009: 4). Due to this relationship, GONGOs are considered to be the least independent organisations.

2. Registered NGOs
Even individually founded NGOs that manage to register with the Ministry of Civil Affairs either have strong governmental backing or some link to the government or the party. As already mentioned, this is the reason why several experts argue that there are no "real" Chinese NGOs.

3. Non-Registered NGOs
One of the most popular strategies of evasion for NGOs was to found a company and register with the Bureau of Industry and Commerce as business enterprises, which was far easier. Other association-like NGOs, also called *grassroots organisations,* receive little or no funding from the government. Since they are self-supporting and do not depend on government funds, they tend to be more independent in their operations.

4. International NGOs (INGOs)
The work of international NGOs in China is also subject to several limitations. There are still no laws governing the activities of international NGOs in China. Chinese authorities are very insecure about how to deal with international NGOs. The Chinese government's attitude and policy toward international NGOs has been to tolerate them, and to avoid issuing a clear set of policies and regulations that would legitimise their presence. Their status can be described by the slogan "no recognition, yet no prohibition" (Edele 2005). It is difficult to say exactly how many INGOs are now operating in China because the number of unregistered INGOs is quite large, due to the absence of clear regulations for the registration and management of INGOs. Estimates of the number of INGOs in China range widely from 1,000 to 6,000, and should be viewed with caution, given that it is unclear how these estimates were made (Shieh, Knutson, 2012:9). The government is also suspicious of the role played by INGOs due to the values they represent, particularly INGOs engaged in the promotion of democracy and "Western values" (Lau, 2009).

Until 2012, any NGO that wanted to register with the MOCA in order to be legal also had to have a sponsoring official organisation, typically a government agency working in the area of the NGO's interest. This procedure was called *dual registration.* The dual regulation system was a unique regulation system that is used in the supervision of NGOs in China. All NGOs in China had two regulators: one was called the "registration administration", generally the department of civil administration, where the NGO must register in its name list; another is called the "competent business unit", generally a government department related in some way to the field of the NGO's practice that administrates it and is responsible for the NGO's daily happenings. These units are sometimes also called "mother-in-law agencies".

As an important member of NGO groups, trade associations in China have to have two regulators, as is the case for all other NGOs (cf. FTACC 2013).

However, registration regulations were eased in 2013: some NGOs can register directly with the MOCA and no longer need a sponsoring official organisation. Dual administration was abolished for trade associations and chambers of commerce, and NGOs working for technology, public welfare and community service. These four categories of NGOs are allowed to register directly with the MOCA without requiring approval by professional supervision units (Yang et al., 2015). At the same time, however, the degree of scrutinisation concerning personnel, projects, Chinese partners and financing was intensified (FAZ 2014).

The growth of NGOs has not always been a smooth one. In 2005, after the so-called colour revolution in neighbouring countries such as Ukraine, Georgia and Kyrgisistan, Chinese leaders clamped down on NGOs, especially in their more activist manifestations. A big boost to China's growth in NGOs came with the huge earthquake in Sichuan in 2008. Thousands of volunteers came to Sichuan to lend a hand. Ordinary people found out what it was like to get organised and join in. The government drew similar conclusions, and allowed more NGOs to register through state organisations (The Economist 2014). Recent protests, however, which broke out in Hong Kong in August 2014 and peaked in September with tens of thousands of protestors congregating, have led again to closer scrutiny and restrictions on civil society activity in mainland China (New York Times 2014).

Conclusion:

Although NGOs in China are not easy to understand and so-called "associations" can also be "GONGOS", there are several hundred thousands of registered NGOs in China and even more unregistered ones, while the growth rate is still unbroken. These NGOs have similar goals and duties as NGOs across the world. Their goals include providing education and information. Whatever the concrete political situation may be, it seems obvious that these NGOs will increasingly assume their role as organisers of all kinds of conferences. They will also increasingly integrate into their respective world organisations and play a more important role in the future.

Chinese membership can easily outweigh or even dominate international membership in these organisations in terms of numbers. Leaders of Chinese NGOs will be elected onto the international boards of the pan-Pacific and/or world organisations of their respective field. They will assert more influence not only on the leadership but also on the selection of the future destination of meetings and conventions held by these organisations.

3.6 Sino-foreign cooperation in science, R&D and education

Assumption:

More international cooperation projects between Chinese and foreign universities and other research institutions will generate more meetings to be held in the respective cooperating countries. Innovation, Research and Development (R&D), joint education and research pro-

jects between universities and other research institutions will lead to more meetings and conventions and also to a larger number of delegates from China and the cooperation country.

As an indicator of cooperation between universities, we can take the number of Chinese students enrolled in foreign countries. The chances are quite high that these former students will prefer to cooperate with their former host country, once they are in a position to decide. The leading countries in 2009 were: 1. USA 2. Australia 3. Japan 4. UK 5. South Korea 6. Canada 7. Germany 8. France 9. New Zealand 10. Russia. It is easy to understand that, for reasons of convenience, Asian-Pacific and/or English-speaking countries lead this list. The position of Germany and France is therefore especially remarkable (DAAD 2012: 52,53).

Conclusion:

There are many Sino-foreign research or education projects. International Event Management Shanghai (IEMS) is just one example of the latter. Chinese graduates or researchers with international experience, who have often stayed in the host country for one semester or longer, will tend to prefer to attend meetings and other business events in their former host country, when given the choice.

3.7 Participation in foreign trade fairs and exhibitions

Assumption:

The more Chinese companies are involved in trade fairs abroad, the more likely it is that their meetings activities will be held at these trade fair places and countries.

In the course of integrating international production and trade, international trade fairs traditionally play a dominant role to open new regional markets for cooperation and export. Germany, the former "export champion", was also the market leader for international trade fairs in recent decades, and is still in a leading position when it comes to international participation in their trade fairs. AUMA states in this handbook that foreign exhibitors make up more than half of all exhibitors, while Chinese exhibitors are the biggest national group at German exhibitions, which underlines China's position as the world's new export champion (Koetter, Spinger, 2015). Chinese companies that exhibit at international trade fairs abroad are obviously among the most advanced companies in their respective industries. As Chinese companies can no longer be regarded as the world's "elongated workbench" or contract manufacturer, since innovation is one of the keywords of China's economic policy, these companies also go to exhibitions to communicate and learn. The consequence of this is that some may also be interested in taking part in international seminars, workshops or congresses, organised by the respective international associations of the industry or the trade fair organiser in combination with trade fairs. While this could be the first contact to the international meetings world, leading Chinese companies will be eager to meet other leading companies, and may also join international associations for further meeting activities worldwide.

Conclusion:

The large number of Chinese companies participating in international trade fairs also represents a huge potential for the international meetings market. They should be regarded as a special target group by the respective meetings industry.

3.8 China's outbound business tourism

Assumption:

China has surpassed Germany as the international travel champion. Some of the destination selection criteria of general outbound tourism will also be paramount for travel generated by business events.

In 2014, China's yearly outbound tourists numbered 109 million, an 11 per cent increase over 2013 (Travelchinaguide, 2015). In 2013, Chinese tourists spent 128.7 billion dollars abroad, an 26.8 per cent increase over 2012. In 2013, the Chinese surpassed the Germans as "travel champions" for the first time. From the perspective of geographical convenience, cities like Seoul, Busan and Sapporo in Japan and South Korea were the most visited foreign cities by Chinese tourists in 2013. For long-distance travelling, cities such as Paris, London, Rome, Berlin, Washington and Los Angeles appeal more to Chinese tourists because they can enjoy sightseeing, shopping and leisure time in the same location. Special worries of Chinese tourists before leaving include: language barriers, personal and property safety, cultural differences, quality of services and products, signs (not in Chinese characters) and Medical Aid (WTCF: 6, 9,14,15).

GBTA, the Global Business Travel Association, reports that business travel spending in China grew at an average of 16.2 per cent per year from USD 32 billion in 2000 to USD 225 billion in 2013. By comparison, growth in business travel spending from the US has grown at an annual rate of just 1.1 per cent since 2000 (GBTA, 2013). In October 2014, it predicted that China's total business travel spending would grow by 15.9 per cent in 2014 to USD 262 billion and another 18 per cent in 2015 (GBTA, 2014).

On its website, CITS International M.I.C.E., a leading Chinese agency for incentives travel and business events, provides information about groups of several thousand participants of outbound incentive travel, starting in 2005 with a group of 7,000 to Thailand. China Daily reported about a group of 7,000 incentive travellers from a direct marketing company, which broke the record for a trip to the USA (China Daily, 2014). Germany's DZT reported 870,748 arrivals and 1,734,693 overnight stays by Chinese tourists with an average growth rate of 12.5 per cent over the last ten years. 36 per cent of these were declared as business travel. Obviously, the figures of exhibitors at German trade fairs (see Section 3.3) are included in this data.

Conclusion:

China's general tourism, including outbound tourism, is well researched. China is already the leading country for outbound tourism. There are only incomplete sources, however, for Chinese business tourism, including tourism for meetings and exhibitions. The findings of the direction and motives of general Chinese tourism cannot be transferred directly to business tourism. However, the behaviour and motives of business people overlap with those of "normal" Chinese travellers, and should be taken into account by service suppliers of the international meetings industry.

3.9 Meeting destination selection criteria

Assumption:

In addition to the various factors quoted above, not all destinations are suitable for the Chinese potential. The destination selection is a multi-stage process with many influencing factors. General destination selection criteria, such as convenience of travel (ease of access), price and the general attractiveness of the country and the city, play a more important role than in other countries, as Chinese business people still have less travel experience than their international peers.

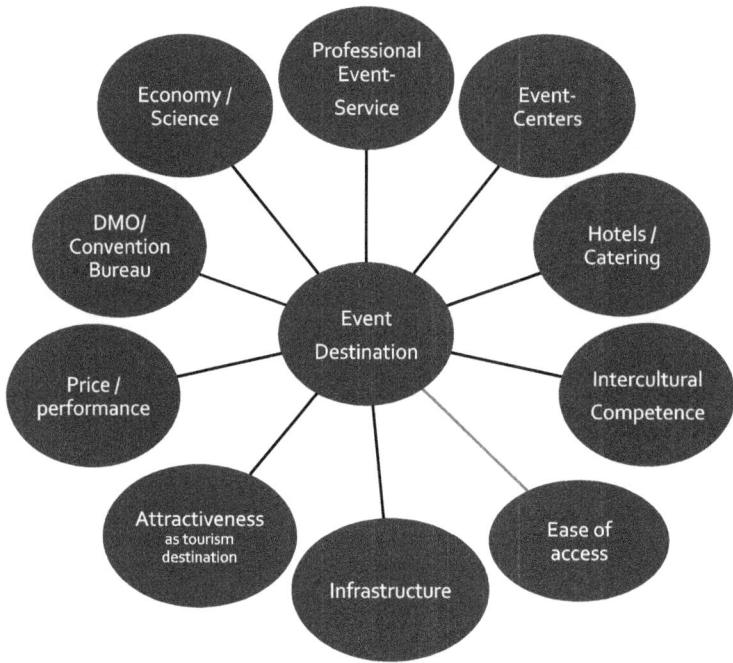

Fig. 2: Destination selection criteria for meeting organisers (cf. Schwägermann, 2013)

Figure 2 provides an overview of the typical decision criteria of meeting planners when it comes to selecting a destination for their next meeting. Of course, the importance (weight) of these factors varies between decision makers and industries. It is obvious that these selection factors are, in turn, the success factors of the destinations!

However, there are some knock-out criteria, such as a hostile relationship between countries or an unstable political or health situation in specific countries. Other no-go criteria are a lack of an appropriate meetings and accommodation infrastructure or a certain minimum level of professionalism in this country/city. Having eliminated those countries/regions, meeting organisers will look for a destination that best fits the specific needs of the industries or members of the organisations involved.

If, however, we concentrate on the likelihood of being a first-choice destination, elements such as a *positive nation brand* provide a crucial competitive advantage. The Anholt-GfK Nation Brands Index measures global perceptions of each country, based on 23 different attributes that make up the six overall dimensions on which a national image is based: *exports, governance, culture, people, tourism and immigration/investment.* For the 2014 study, a total of 20,125 interviews were conducted across 20 countries. For the first time ever, Germany passed the USA, whereas the UK, France and Canada came next in this survey (GfK, 2015). Recent China MICE Buyers Reports which, among other things, investigate the decision factors for outbound meeting destinations, seem to be biased by opinions of incentive travel agents, as climate, economic stability and visa requirements rank before "classic" decision criteria such as professionals and ease of access. Price ranks second last in this study, a finding that contradicts most of the foregoing evaluations of Chinese decision-makers and should, according to the author of the study, be examined further (Davidson, 2013). It is to be expected that, in the course of the increasing professionalism of China's meetings industry, the decision criteria of Chinese meetings organisers and agencies will sooner or later be quite similar to those of the international meetings industry.

However, before China-based meetings and events move abroad, single delegates as well as delegations or major groups of Chinese participants will take part in international meetings worldwide! They will be attracted not only by the destinations, but also by the topic and quality of the international meeting they wish to attend. They have to follow the meeting organiser's decisions. If the meeting is organised by an international organising committee, the above-mentioned selection criteria will more or less apply.

Conclusion:

Destinations with a high brand index will be first choice for Chinese meetings. In the long run, Chinese decision-makers in the meetings industry will take decisions in a similar fashion to other professionals worldwide.

3.10 Intercultural competence and a welcoming culture

Assumption:

Most western business people prefer destinations, venues and hotels in Asia for their business travel and conferences where English-speaking services are available and where – in general – they can enjoy some western amenities such as food, newspapers and television channels. Chinese congress delegates and meeting organisers will do the same – only in reverse!

As we well know, Chinese traditions, values, language and habits differ to those in most western countries.

Only a few Chinese delegates speak excellent English, even fewer speak other languages, like Japanese, German or French. And yet they, too, want to feel welcomed and understood when they are abroad. Much has been said and written about so-called intercultural competencies as a success factor for internationally operating organisations, and it should also be included in the list of success factors for meeting destinations (see Section 3.9), as it is truly a selection factor of growing importance.

Event service suppliers should therefore learn about the (changing) values and behaviour of the Chinese in order to understand them better and to be able to offer them more appropriate services. The meetings market is a *buyers' market* in the sense that international meeting organisers have a big choice between destinations. So why not establish something like a 'Welcoming Culture' in the destination? Although this term is usually used by nations or companies that want to attract and integrate the brightest and best employees from the international labour market, in our view this philosophy is also appropriate for the internationalisation strategy of event destinations and other service suppliers. So what if destinations and venues offer information in Chinese characters on websites, brochures, signs at hotspots of the city, and at the venues and hotels? What if event service suppliers ensure that Mandarin-speaking experts and/or translators are at hand? And why not teach everybody at least a few simple Chinese words to ensure a friendly greeting? Or why not try to offer "real" Chinese food to delegates rather than the kind of Chinese food that has little in common with its original name, having been (over)adapted to local tastes.

Conclusion:

Destinations that actively demonstrate that they are not only interested in the Chinese market, but also make attractive offers to meet the wishes and needs of Chinese delegates and organisations will be able to attract more business and get a bigger share of this new market.

4 Does the international meetings industry have a "China Strategy"?

4.1 ICCA – the International Congress and Convention Association

ICCA describes itself as 'the global community for the meetings industry, enabling its members to generate and maintain significant competitive advantage'. ICCA is now one of the most prominent organisations in the world of international meetings. It is the only association that comprises a membership representing the main specialists in handling, transporting and accommodating international events. ICCA's network of almost 1,000 suppliers to the international meetings industry spans the globe, with members in more than 90 countries (ICCA, website; see also the article by Hamid/Lu in this handbook). It can be claimed that all of the world's main players in the meetings industry are ICCA members.

4.2 Online survey of ICCA members

Osnabrück University of Applied Sciences, which has ICCA membership, was asked by ICCA to conduct a survey among ICCA members to find answers to the question: *How will the development of China's Market for Business Events affect the international Event Industry and especially ICCA members?*

The first aim of this survey was therefore to ascertain the attitude and assessments of ICCA members towards the development of the meetings market in China. The second aim was to evaluate how well prepared ICCA members are for China's meeting market or, in other words: *"Do ICCA members have a China strategy?"*

After consulting ICCA headquarters, we sent an online questionnaire containing nine questions to all ICCA members in October 2013. A total of 196 questionnaires were completed and returned, representing a return rate of more than 20 per cent. ICCA is structured in so-called sectors, such as: destinations, venues and event agencies, as well as in regional chapters. It is relevant to point out that this survey was completed weeks *before* the ICCA Congress November 2013 in Shanghai, where many ICCA members came to China for the first time and were impressed by the infrastructure and services of their host destination!

Our sample was representative according to both ICCA Sectors and Chapters, i. e. the *sample* had a very similar distribution as the *population* (total ICCA membership). The following results do not include answers by Chinese ICCA members!

4.3 Main results

4.3.1 Majority already has experience with China

- 67 per cent of the respondents already had experience with participants from China.
- 41 per cent of the respondents already had experience with events organised in China, including participants from China. (Not only meetings, but all kinds of events, like incentives.)
- Nearly 30 per cent of the respondents had experienced a Chinese delegation as the biggest foreign *delegation* in at least one event

We found that these answers by no means stemmed mainly from Asian ICCA members, but from all regional chapters. Respondents who agreed to at least one of these answers will be classified later in this text as "experienced ICCA members", which does NOT necessarily mean that they have already been to China.

4.3.2 ICCA members need a China Strategy

In the second part of the questionnaire, we put forward a number of statements to ICCA members and asked them to answer using a seven-point Likert scale, where 1= I strongly disagree and 7 = I strongly agree. The results are displayed in order according to the degree of acceptance.

International destinations need special China strategies	5.8
China's multinational companies will play an important role	5.6
China's trade will influence China's outbound event activities.	5.5
China's FDI will influence China's outbound event activities.	5.4
CEB will still be mainly driven by the government in ten years.*	5.4
CEB still has to learn how to organise international events.	5.2
China is the strongest Asian event market.	5.0
China will be in ICCA's top five country ranking within ten years.	5.0
Chinese decision-makers assert more influence on the destination selection.	5.0
Chinese multinational companies are already relevant for us.	4.6
China has taken over from Japan as the source market for leisure tourism.	4.4
China will be in ICCA's top five country ranking within five years.	4.2
China will be the strongest Asian source market.	4.1
Chinese decision-makers do not need any special treatment.	3.7

*CEB= China's Event Business

As we can see, ICCA members strongly believe that international destinations should have a special strategy for the "newcomer" China. They also agree that China's multinational companies, such as Lenovo, Haier and Hisense, will play an important role in the international event market. Trade and Chinese FDI (Foreign Direct Investment of Chinese Investors as well as mergers and acquisitions of international companies) will also influence the international meetings business. They do not believe very strongly that China will be the strongest Asian source market since Asian respondents' home market is believed to remain their strongest market. For non-Asian respondents, this value is certainly much higher! Most respondents are of the opinion that Chinese decision-makers (maybe compared to "ordinary" participants from China) do not need any special treatment. ICCA members who have experience with China express greater agreement throughout all of the statements.

4.3.3 Many already offer China-specific services

By asking the following question, we intended to evaluate the kind of special services that were already offered to Chinese delegates and/or event organisers by ICCA members.

Question:

Which of the following measures for Chinese events and/or delegates do you already apply or do you think are relevant for your future business?

The response options were as follows: A) Have/offer already. B) In planning. C) Relevant, but not planned yet. D) Not relevant to us. E) No answer. The following table summarises *options A and B*.

1. Chinese food	55 %
2. Travel agent specialised in China	46 %
3. Train our staff in special cross-cultural competence	43 %
4. Chinese delegations/site inspections	41 %
5. Participating in Chinese trade shows	41 %
6. Special touristic pre- and post-convention tours	38 %
7. Chinese-speaking contact person in our office	37 %
8. Interpretation services	36 %
9. Visits to local enterprises and organisations	35 %
10. Chinese contact person in our office	32 %
11. Special market surveys on the Chinese event market	31 %
12. Special representative in China for meetings and events	30 %
13. Chinese/Mandarin version of our website	29 %
14. Complete travel services including visa issues	21 %

It came as no surprise that Chinese food ranked No. 1, as it is common in many international metropolises. Also, considering the development of China's general tourism, there are many travel agents worldwide that specialised in China. Cross-cultural competence has been a popular topic for years, hence many ICCA members had already trained their staff, but not necessarily with regard to China.

4.3.4 Vast majority sees relevance for additional China-specific services

However, if you add the third response option C: *"relevant, but not planned yet"*, a number of substantial differences become apparent. First, the approval rate rose to 83 per cent for the first items, compared to 55 per cent in list before. This means that we have obviously identified a "latent problem" for the international meetings industry, where only a few ICCA members have already taken concrete steps, although the vast majority understands that they have to do something:

1. Chinese delegations/site inspections	83 %
2. Special market surveys on the Chinese event market	82 %
3. Train our staff in special cross-cultural competence	81 %
4. Chinese food	80 %
5. Travel agent specialised in China	78 %
6. Participating in Chinese trade shows	77 %
7. Visits to local enterprises and organisations	75 %
8. Special touristic pre- and post-convention tours	68 %
9. Chinese/Mandarin version of our website	67 %
10. Chinese-speaking contact person in our office	67 %
11. Interpretation services	65 %
12. Special representative in China for meetings and events	63 %
13. Chinese contact person in our office	61 %
14. Complete travel services including visa issues	59 %

Maybe the issue ranked second (special market surveys) says at lot about the respondents' sentiments: they have understood that they need to know more about this market before being able to assess and invest in it.

4.4 Summary of ICCA survey on China

As early as October 2013, most ICCA members were aware of the potential of the Chinese event market, and some members offered special China-related services. The ICCA Congress 2013 in Shanghai, where the first results of this study were presented, had a further impact on many ICCA members, prompting them to research and invest more in this future market.

5 Conclusion

This article focused on the future of China's outbound meetings business. In the first part, a qualitative cause-effect model was developed, which suggested that China will very soon have a strong and visible influence on the international meetings market. This qualitative model should be the basis for a quantitative forecasting model that predicts the volume and direction of China's outbound event business, once the relevant statistics are available. For this reason, several global and specific indicators have to be observed.

Whereas the first part concentrated on the *source market* (China) and its relation to other countries as potential destinations for these meeting activities, the second part of this article concentrated on the *destinations* of this business, i. e. the international suppliers of meeting services, which were represented by ICCA members. The ICCA survey was conducted among managers of international destinations, venues and other services, which compete for this new and large potential market. The study successfully showed that the international meetings industry is increasingly aware of this new market, but only pioneers have already developed a kind of *China Strategy*. According to the results of this study, it is predictable that we will see a shift in marketing strategies, budgets and activities towards the Chinese outbound meeting market very soon.

6 Literature

AUMA, Ausstellungs- und Messeausschuss der Deutschen Wirtschaft, www.auma.de

CCTV News (2015), 15 January 2015

China Daily (2014) 24 May 2014, p. 4

CITS International M.I.C.E. http://www.citsmice.net/our-service/outbound/

CMSA, China Meeting Statistical Analysis Report (2014)

CNBS, China National Bureau of Statistics, (2014)
http://data.stats.gov.cn/workspace/index?m=hgnd

DAAD, Deutscher Akademischer Austauschdienst (2012) www.wissenschaft-weltoffen.de

Davidson, R. (2013) CIBTM China MICE Buyers Report

DZT, Deutsche Zentral für Tourismus, Kurz-Marktinformationen China 2015

Edele, Andreas (2005) Non-Governmental Organizations in China, Geneva

FAZ (2014), Westliche Werte als trojanische Pferde, 6 July 2014

FCTACC (2013) Federation of China Trade Associations & Chamber of Commerce, (2013), About Dual Regulation System in China, http://english.fctacc.org/aboutmore.aspx, retreived on 20 October 2013

GCB (2013) German Convention Bureau 2013, www.gcb.de

GBTA, Global Business Travel Chambers Association, http://www.gbta.org/PressReleases/Pages/rls_102413.aspx?Source=http%3A%2F%2Fwww%2Egbta%2Eorg%2 FLists%2FNews%2FAllItems%5Ffoundation%2Easpx

GfK (2014), Anholt-GfK Nation Brands Index 2014, http://www.gfk.com/documents/press-releases/2014/2014-11-2_anholt_gfk%20nation%20brand%20index%202014.pdf

ICCA, International Congress and Convention Association, www.iccaworld.com

ICCA (2013) International Congress and Convention Association, ICCA STATISTICS 2013

ICNL (2015) NGO Law Monitor: China, International Center for Not-for-Profit Law (ICNL), http://www.icnl.org/research/monitor/china.html, retrieved on 20 January 2015

Koetter, Harald, Spinger, Marco (2015) The Role of China for Germany's Exhibition Industry in: Handbook Event Market China, 2015

Lau, C.C.S. (2009), The Role of NGOs in China, Quarterly Journal of Ideology, Volume 31, 2009

NBSPRC (2014) National Bureau of Statistics of the People's Republic of China (2014), http://data.stats.gov.cn/workspace/index?m=hgnd

New York Times (2014), New Signs that China is Scrutinising Foreign NGOs, 27 June 2014

Salsbury, Jennifer (2010), An Overview of the Association Community in China, in: Headquarters Asia-Pacific, 8.2010, p. 14–15

Shieh, Shawn., Brown-Inz, Amanda (2013) Mapping China' Public Interest NGOs, in: Chinese NGO Directory: A Civil Society in the Making

Shieh, Shawn, Knutson, Signe, (2012) The Roles and Challenges of International NGOS in China's Development, 2012

The Economist (2014) Enter the Chinese NGO, 12 April 2014

The Worldbank (2004) The World Bank and NGOs in China

The Worldbank (2007) http://web.worldbank.org/WBSITE/EXTERNAL/COUNTRIES/EASTASIAPACIFICEXT/CHINAEXTN/0,,con tent-MDK:20600359~menuPK:1460599~pagePK:1497618~piPK:217854~theSitePK:318950,00.html (retrieved in 2007)

The Worldbank (2014) http://data.worldbank.org/indicator/NY.GDP.MKTP.KD.ZG

Travelchinaguide (2014) http://www.travelchinaguide.com/tourism/2014statistics/outbound.htm

UFI (2014) Union des Foires Internationales, 2014_exhibiton_industry_statistics_b.pdf

Wang, Yong (2013) Prospect for China's transition, in: Agora Asia-Europe, No. 14. March 2013

WTCF (2014) World Tourism Cities Federation, Market Research Report on Chinese Outbound Tourist (City) Consumption, 2014, http://en.wtcf.travel/download/report201409en.pdf

Yang, Yongjiao, Zhang Xiongxiong, Tang Delong, Wilkinson, Mick (2015) The Abolition of Dual Administration of NGOs in China: Imperatives and Challenges, International Journal of Social Science and Humanity, Vol. 5, No. 6, 2015

Management aspects in China's event industry

Green meeting standards: A conceptual review

Cai, Meng,
Griese, Kai-Michael,
Große Ophoff, Markus,
Tang, Jiani

绿色会议标准：基于概念上的评论

The challenge of a negative environmental impact caused by economic growth is increasingly accounted for in the organisation of green events. However, planners and organisers are confused by the wide range of Green Meeting Standards. This article provides an overview of existing green meeting standards that are considered useful for organizing green meetings; these are evaluated with regard to their practical use. The central point of reference for the overview of existing studies on explaining green meetings is the reflection on the role of a Green Meetings officer and to explore how those who lead green meetings can gain the support of individuals. The standards analysed show that most of the operating figures used to manage green meetings were environmental figures. Especially when considering the Triple Bottom Line (TBL) of Elkington, it becomes apparent that not many social and economic operating figures were available.

经济增长带来了负面环境冲击的挑战，这日益影响着绿色会展的组织。但多种多样的绿色会议标准却让策划者和组织者感到无所适从。这篇文章从实践运用价值的视角出发，概括总结了当今被认可的一些绿色会议标准。并从一位绿色会议官的角度反映了已有绿色会议文献的主旨，并探讨了绿色会议的组织者如何可以从个人那里获得支持。在分析这些标准时发现，用于衡量绿色会议的操作数据大多是环境方面的数据。这尤其体现在 Elkington 的三重底线标准（TBL）上，显然，这个标准并没有使用太多社会及经济相关的运营数据。

1 Introduction

In the last 40 years, a large number of studies that address the environmental impact caused by economic growth have emerged (e. g. Meadows, Meadows, Randers, & Behrens, 1972). This demonstrates the need for economic activities to orientate themselves more towards the planetary boundaries of our earth. Some global breaking points, with regard to biodiversity, the carbon dioxide concentration in the atmosphere and the strain on the nitrogen cycle, have already been exceeded. Further dimensions, for example, the use of fresh water or land-use patterns are currently critically developing and will require changes in the short run (Rockström et al. 2009). The need for short-term essential adjustments to the economic process can be seen in the example of the increase in carbon dioxide in the atmosphere. The results of a research project by English, German and Swiss academics indicates that the time corridor for adjustments should take place within the next 10–20 years in order to limit global warming to maximum 2 °C (Meinshausen et al. 2009). The formulation of the millennium goals of the UN shows that these current undesirable, environmental developments are globally recognized problems and that almost all countries in the world are confronted with these challenges (UN 2013).

These challenges are more frequently considered when it comes to organizing green events. In order to reduce the negative impact that meetings have on the environment, the concept of 'green meetings' was born and some practices have been developed accordingly based on environmental aspects. Associations such as the Oceans Blue Foundation (EPA 2010), the Convention Industry Council (CIC 2004) and the United Nations (UN 2009) have developed Green meeting standards. Destination management departments, such as the German Convention Bureau (GCB 2013), have made green meetings one of its key objectives. Meeting organizers such as the 2012 Women in Green Forum (WIGF) for the small and medium category (Three Squares 2013) and the Danish Presidency of the Council of the European Union (DPEU 2013) have designed some green meeting practices for on-site management and marketing. However, an intact and integrated theory about green meetings has not yet been formulated and there are still public misconceptions regarding the concept of Green Meetings. Planners and organizers also confuse different Green Meeting Standards. Furthermore, there is not currently a recognized definition in literature.

The aim of this article is to give an overview of existing green meeting standards about the explanation of green meetings and to evaluate these in regard to their practical use. The article ends with a forecast for future developments and the need for further research. Due to the space available, the following thoughts will be concentrated on the environmental dimension of green meetings, as well as the economic and social dimensions.

The central point of reference for the following overview of existing studies about the explanation of green meetings is hiring an individual to plan a Green Meeting and the question of how leadership of a green meeting can gain support for the green meeting from individuals. We propose that the theory of planned behavior (Ajzen 1991) offers valuable guidance.

2 Theory of planned behavior

Each individual tends to view a green meeting through his or her own filter and each individual approaches a green meeting with different motivations (Merrilees et al. 2012; Hankinson 2001). We propose that green meetings can be best understood by appreciating the attitudes and beliefs that make up each individual's filter of green meetings. Our proposition and suggestions for influencing individuals to support a green meeting are based upon the theory of planned behavior (Ajzen 1991). The theory of planned behavior (Ajzen 1991), an extension of the theory of reasoned action (Ajzen and Fishbein 1980), integrates social and behavioral concepts to explain what motivates an individual's intentions and behavior.

Its purpose is to clarify "the unique factors that induce one person to engage in the behavior of interest and to prompt another to follow a different course of action," (Ajzen 1991, 206–207). While we focus on the theory's application in the context of behavioral support for a green meeting, we also hope this review spurs greater interest in applying this perspective to green meetings and practices in other contexts. We encourage those interested to also consider more extensive deliberations of this theory (Ajzen and Fishbein 1980; Ajzen 1991; Manning 2009; Ajzen 2011; Armitage and Conner 2001) and extensions to the theory to models of goal-directed behavior (Bagozzi et al. 2003; Xie et al. 2013). In its simplest form, the theory of planned behavior (TPB) states that behavior is driven by behavioral intentions and perceived behavioral control (Ajzen 1991). Behavioral intentions are influenced by perceived behavioral control, subjective norms, and attitudes. Individual behavioral beliefs influence their attitudes, while normative beliefs influence subjective norms and control beliefs influence perceptions of behavioral control (Ajzen 1991).

Behavioral intentions represent an individual's motivation and planned effort to behave in a certain way (Ajzen 1991). The higher an individual's intention to behave in a certain way, the more likely the individual is to enact the respective behavior. Behavioral intentions are generally relevant indicators of behavior when the individual has volitional control over their behavior and when the behavior is not habitual in nature (Ajzen 1991; 2011). Regarding individuals behavioral support for a green meeting, the behavior is not likely to be habitual, at least upon each individual's initial decision to actively support the green meeting. However, an individual may lack complete volitional control in that an individual may not be able to independently decide to implement a particular element of green meeting because of the communal nature of green meetings (Hanna and Rowley 2011; Baker 2007; Cai 2002; 2009). We assume the theory remains relevant in this context because individuals can plausibly have volitional control over behaviors related to actively participating in a green meeting process. For example, individuals can contribute money to support the green meeting, custodians of public goods can adapt their promotions in support of the green meetings, or individual residents can agree to encourage neighbors and friends to buy into the strategy.

Subjective norms, defined as "directly felt expectations from other people, which are largely based on the need for approval" (Bagozzi et al. 2003, p. 279), are theorized to have a direct positive influence on behavioral intentions (Bagozzi et al. 2003; Ajzen 1991). These norms are derived from an individual's normative beliefs. Normative beliefs refer to an individual's perception that key individuals or groups approve or disapprove of a behavior (Ajzen 1991). For example, consider an individual member of the business community who believes that the residents in a city may think a particular green meeting is beneficial for a city while believing others in the business community generally think the same green meeting will not be beneficial to them. The TPB assumes that the individual will weigh up the beliefs about the expectations of residents, who may be family, friends, and customers, with the beliefs about the business community's expectations to establish an overall sense of whether he or she is expected to support the green meeting. This global subjective norm will influence the individual's behavioral intentions to actively support the green meeting, and in turn these intentions will influence actual behavioral support.

Attitudes are summary evaluations in regards to a particular object (Ajzen 2001). These evaluations are influenced by the individual's behavioral beliefs (Ajzen 1991). Behavioral beliefs link the behavior to a specific attribute of the behavior, such as an anticipated outcome or cost (Ajzen 1991; 2001). The theoretical nature of the attitude construction is complex (Ajzen 2001; Bagozzi et al, 2003). However, for our purposes it will suffice to note that attitudes represent personal evaluations of behavior and subject norms represent social expectations of behavior (Ajzen 1991; 2011). An individual may personally believe that actively supporting a particular green meeting will have positive outcomes and subsequently have a positive attitude about the supportive the green meeting. The same individual can simultaneously perceive other members of an important reference group as seeing the same approach as unbeneficial, thus leading to a perceived subjective norm that the person should not support the proposed green meeting. In this way, the TPB provides a perspective that compliments existing understandings of the social nature of green meetings (Hanna and Rowley 2011; Baker 2007; 2008; Cai 2002; 2009).

Perceived behavioral control is a cognitive determinate of behavioral intentions that "reflects the decision maker's sense of control over performing the chosen actions," (Bagozzi et al. 2003, p. 279). Perceived behavioral control enables individuals to overcome the anticipation of obstacles and fears of personal limitations that may hinder intentions towards a certain behavior (Bagozzi et al. 2003; Ajzen 1991). The TPB also states that perceived behavioral control can directly influence behaviors (Ajzen 1991; 2011). A person's control beliefs determine their level of perceived behavioral control and these beliefs are based upon the "presence or absence of requisite resources and opportunities" to carry out the behavior (Ajzen 1991, 196). In green meeting contexts, individuals need not necessarily perceive control over the entire process. Instead, individuals need to perceive control over their role in behaviorally supporting the green meeting. In a green meeting context, this means it is important to clarify the role that individuals have in supporting the green meeting's implementation. Failing to clearly establish a role or establishing a role that is perceived as unrealistic can lead the individual to believe that they lack the necessary resources or opportunities to carry out the behavior. These beliefs can reduce the individual's perceived behavioral control regarding the behavior. Because perceptions about behavioral control tend to positively influence intentions and behavior (Ajzen 1991), green marketing leadership should seek to clarify and enhance each individual's sense of control over performing the actions expected of them. To do this, it will help to first understand each individual's perception of their role in actively supporting a green meeting. For example, is their role to encourage employees to deliver a green meeting to tourists or is it to support promotional activities by providing monetary or creative support?

In regard to green meetings standards, these findings in the context of the TPB and green meetings can be variously interpreted. For example, it is conceivable that the selection of a standard for an event is influenced by the existing attitudes of an actor who is involved. It is possible that a person had positive experience towards a special green meeting standard and is therefore less open to other standards. Also, an organizer of an event could make a conscious decision for a voluntary standard because the possibility exists to be more flexible within the operational implementation. In essence, green meeting standards offer different settings by concrete indicators for the operational implementation. Also, the individual belief that one or the other indicator is more or less important within green meetings standards is neutralized by cross-validity of a standard.

3 Green meeting standards

Many green meeting standards have been developed, especially in the last 10 years, for business common practice. These serve primarily as a guideline towards which businesses can orientate themselves while organizing events. Furthermore, some of these standards have been introduced internationally, although only limitedly. The following overview describes the chosen standards based on their content concentration (see table 1). Generally speaking it becomes obvious, that the vast majority of the standards are concentrated on the environmental aspect of events and that the basic understanding of green meetings varies widely (see above). A full description of some of these standards follows.

Tab. 1: Chosen standards for the organisation of green meetings.

Standard	Focus			Source
	Economic aspects	Environmental aspects	Social aspects	
APEX/ASTM		X		http://www.conventionindustry.org/standardspractices/apexastm.aspx (accessed on: 25 June 2014)
BMU Leitfaden		X		http://www.bmub.bund.de/themen/wirtschaft-produkte-ressourcen/produkte-und-umwelt/umweltfreundliche-beschaffung/leitfaden-fuer-die-nachhaltige-organisation-von-veranstaltungen/ (accessed on: 25 June 2014)
BS 8901		X		http://sustainable-event-alliance.org/how-to-guides/projects/bs-8901/ (accessed on: 25 June 2014)
EcoLogo		X		http://industries.ul.com/environment/ (accessed on: 25 June 2014)
EMAS		X		http://www.emas.de/ (accessed on: 25 June 2014)
Fairpflichtet	X	X	X	http://www.fairpflichtet.de/ (accessed on: 25 June 2014)
Global Reporting Initiative	X	X	X	https://www.globalreporting.org/Pages/default.aspx (accessed on: 25 June 2014)
Green Globe	X	X	X	http://greenglobe.com/germany/ (Accessed on: 25 June 2014)
Green Note		X		http://www.my-green-meeting.de/de/wir-ueber-uns/greennote.html (accessed on: 25 June 2014)
ISO 14001		X		http://www.tuev-sued.de/management_systeme/umwelt/iso_140012004 (accessed on: 25 June 2014)
ISO 20121		X		http://www.mci-germany.de/ISO_20121/ (accessed on: 25 June 2014)
ISO 26000	X	X	X	http://www.iso.org/iso/iso26000 (accessed on: 08 July 2014)
MPI		X		http://www.mpiweb.org/ (accessed on: 25 June 2014)
OACC Green Star		X		http://www.iacconline.org/education/index.cfm?fuseaction=environmental (accessed on: 25 June 2014)
Ökoprofit	X	X		http://www.oekoprofit-nrw.de/ (accessed on: 25 June 2014)
Österreichisches Umweltzeichen		X		http://www.umweltzeichen.at/cms/home233/content.html (accessed on: 25 June 2014)
The Green Key		X		http://www.umwelterziehung.de/projekte/GreenKey/ (accessed on: 25 June 2014)

3.1 Sustainable Event Management System

British Standard (BS) 8901:2009, Sustainable Event Management System, was the first voluntary standard for event sustainable management systems. It was developed by the British Standards Institution in 2009 together with various professionals from the event and meeting industry, and used for the event management system in the UK's event industry. It focuses on the management system of the events and provides standards for strategic approaches to the events and the processes of planning and managing the events rather than a checklist for the event itself (GMIC 2011). It requires the identification of several sustainable issues such as supply chain management, procurement, operations, communications, transportation etc. and can be applied to large event management processes which contain event organizers, venues, destinations, organizations or individuals throughout the whole supply chain. If the event management system meets all of the established criteria and the entire process is well documented, the entity can be eligible to apply for the certification that shows its compliance with the BS 8901 standards. It is important to be note that only the event management system can be certified, not the event itself. Also, this standard only applies for large events (GMIC 2011).

3.2 Event Sustainability Management Systems

As a result, an improved sustainable event management system, the international ISO 2012, was developed. Based on the BSI standards, the International Standards Organization (ISO), the world's largest publisher and developer of more than 159 international standards organisation, developed internationally sustainable standards for managing events in 2012. Over 26 countries and several leading associations in the event industry are participating in the process of the standard's establishment (GMIC 2011), which provides guidance for the event management system as well as controlling the economic, social and environmental impacts of the events. It monitors the entire event process from pre-event to post-event. Therefore, the content of ISO 20121 covers all related event parts. Furthermore, it adopts a "Plan-Do-Check-Act" approach to implement the principle of sustainability (ISO 2012). Thanks to this standard, there is now a uniformly documented and checkable management system. Due to its generic orientation, the norm only slightly touches on the characteristics of green meetings (Große-Ophoff 2012).

3.3 Green Globe Standard

Another one is the Green Globe Standard, the earliest international sustainable certification for the travel and tourism industry, which was created by Green Globe (GG), and is based on several international standards and agreements, such as the Global Sustainable Tourism Criteria, Global Partnership for Sustainable Tourism Criteria, ISO 19011 of audit programs, etc. The origin of this standard can be dated back to the UN Rio de Janeiro Earth Summit in 1992 where the Agenda 21 about sustainable development was proposed. It was then highlighted in 1999 at the UN Sustainable Development Commission and is reviewed twice a year in order to keep abreast with the updated international circumstances, which participates at various worlds' leading events, such as World Travel Market-London, ITB-Berlin, IMEX-Frankfurt, etc. (GG 2013a).

This standard is a structured evaluation to check the performance of event businesses and whether they are sustainable or not. It contains an entire set of indicators for sustainability criteria, certification policies and procedures, as well as auditor guidelines. It has four main areas. The first is Sustainable Management, which covers implementing a sustainability management system, legal compliances, employee training, customer satisfaction, accuracy of promotional materials, local zoning, interpretation, communication strategy and health and safety. The second area is Social and Economics, which includes community development, local employment, support for local entrepreneurs, employee protection and basic services. The third area is Cultural Heritage, such as code of behavior, historical artifacts and protection of sites and incorporation of culture. The last area is Environmental, which contains conserving resources, reducing pollution, conserving biodiversity, ecosystems, and landscapes (GG 2013b).

The Green Globe standard can apply to all types of events and provides certification standards for different kinds of industry sectors, such as attractions, congress centers, meeting venues, hotels and resorts, organizations, restaurants, transportation, cruise ships, etc. (GG 2013c). Businesses can use the standards to monitor the improvement of their processes and if their achievements are documented, certifications will be offered to their enterprises' sustainable management system. Through cooperation with the European Association of Event Centres, Green Globe has established itself as a pragmatic environmental management system in many countries including Germany. In addition, the certification supports the constant improvement process in the event centers. In this regard, it is not evident to external observers, how exactly the measures are put into place. It is however possible, that event centers voluntarily distribute this information. As it is very easy to achieve the Green Globe Standard, it does not offer a sufficient method for comparing a specific company to other event centers (Große-Ophoff 2012b).

3.4   APEX & ASTM Green Meeting Standards

The golden standard for the meeting industry is the APEX & ASTM Green Meeting Standards that were established by APEX, an organization of CIC that bolsters the improvement and performance of practices in order to promote the efficiency of the meetings, conventions and exhibitions industry, together with ASTM and in cooperation with the American EPA and GMIC (CIC 2013). The APEX & ASTM Green Meeting Standards were regarded as a milestone of achieving the sustainability in the meeting industry (Bair 2013) which seeks to provide available and applicable standards for developing more sustainable meetings.

APEX & ASTM has nine standards covering all the main aspects of the meeting industry: accommodation, audio-visual, communication & marketing material, destinations, exhibits, food and beverages, meeting venue, on-site office and transportation. Within each standard, eight areas are targeted: staff management and environment policy, communications, waste, energy, air quality, water, procurement and community partners. All these standards are measurable and specific, available throughout the whole meeting process, making both meeting organizers and suppliers responsible for the implementation and with the intention of gaining approval from other recognized standards in the meeting industry. The standards are international and have been discussed and modified by both meeting professionals all over the world and over 200 non-industry stakeholders. However, based on objective factors, such as the level of economic, social and technological factors, the standards are better implemented in and conformed to developed rather than developing countries. Nevertheless, these standards are the first, and only, comprehensive international standards for the sustainability of meetings (GMIC 2013).

The APEX & ASTM standards are special because only meetings that reach the established minimum green standards in all nine areas can call themselves "green meetings under APEX

& ASTM standards". If the meeting has just one positive green practice, it cannot claim to be "green" if the other practices are harmful to the environment (Scofidio 2010). In other words, the APEX & ASTM standards are like the "Bucket Theory": it has nine boards each with the same height, only buckets with the same height or higher than those of the standard bucket can fill themselves with the same amount or more of water. If one of the nine boards is shorter than the standard height, the whole bucket can just be filled with water depending on the shortest one and cannot belong to the standard bucket or superior bucket. Thus, the APEX & ASTM standards are comprehensive as they require green meetings to be comprehensive.

4 Discussion and conclusion

The standards make it clear that the majority of operating numbers that were used for managing green meetings were environmental numbers. In special consideration of the Triple Bottom Line (TBL) of Elkington (1999), it is apparent that there were not many social and economic operating numbers available. Additionally, some of the standards are very difficult to translate into the concept of green meetings due to their general orientation (Sherwood 2007). Countries such as Germany and organizers such as WIGF and DPEU have intiated some green meeting management practicing such as launching a green meeting program, increasing the awareness of environmental issues and enhancing the demand of green meetings, constructing many green accommodations and venues with environmentally friendly products and carrying out sustainable management systems for destinations, as well as making green meeting on-site management, marketing and communication for meeting organizers. However, the current focus is the environmental aspects of the implementation, although the international discussion regarding "greening events" suggests that health and social concerns should also be taken into consideration when planning a sustainable event (UNEP 2009).

Based on the environmental challenges society faces, the environmental focus of green meetings is important. First, green meetings can reduce costs by taking sustainable actions throughout the entire meeting process. For example, the Climate Change and Sustainability Global Summit 2013 held in February in New York saved $10,000 by reducing bottled water, $37,000 by using electronic materials and mobile apps instead of paper materials and $20,000 by locating the meeting venue with walk distance from the hotels. Second, green meetings are beneficial for participants because they provide a healthy and delightful meeting experience, while also acting as a catalyst for further green practices. Finally, but perhaps most importantly, green meetings can benefit the environment more than any other meeting by minimizing the consumption of resources and energy as well as reducing the amount of waste, and preventing air and water pollution (ANA 2004).

However, there are still challenges and difficulties when planning green meetings because there are many factors that influence their implementation, for instance, the development of technology in different countries, the degree of environmental awareness within various entities and the demand for holding green meetings (IMEX America 2014). These factors and the reflection about green meetings practical cases introduced above indicate that sustainability should be a new lifestyle pursued not only by the meeting industry but all of society. Approaches like "fairpflichtet" (see http://www.fairpflichtet.de) demonstrate how easy it is for companies to adopt and implement green meeting guidelines.

China is also experiencing a drastic transition. The government has established the target of ecological construction, "Ecological Civilization", and is focusing on the development of a low carbon economy that asks all industries to take action to limit carbon dioxide emissions and contribute to sustainable development. Sustainable action, such as requiring the green meeting concept for industry, is a necessary and important part of achieving the government's goals. Designing and implementing green meeting standards is the first step towards improving the sustainability of the meeting industry. In turn, this will have very practical significance. In order to establish green meeting standards and promote effective implementation, we prescribe the following:

(1) establish and coordinate working mechanisms to be led by the Chinese Municipal Development and Reform Commission, Chinese Science and Technology Commission and Chinese Municipal Environmental Protection Bureau, and support by the relevant departments who are responsible for the planning, organization, implementation, coordination, propaganda and technical,

(2) establish a working group constituted by government and relevant research institutes and universities technical team to be responsible for the coordination of the plan and provision of technical support,

(3) assess the implementation process, in order to optimize implementation and summarize the experience,

(4) spread the concept of green meeting in the whole society.

Acknowledgements

This work was supported by the [Humanity and Social Science Foundation by the Ministry of Education of China] under Grant [number 13YJC970003]; and [Interdisciplinary Studies Foundation by Shanghai University of International Business and Economics] under Grant [number JCXK-2014-008].

5   Literature

Ajzen, I. (1991), The theory of planned behavior. Organizational Behavior and Human Decision Processes, 50, 179–211.

Ajzen, I. (2001), Nature and operation of attitudes. Annual Review of Psychology, 52, 27–58.

Ajzen, I. (2011). The theory of planned behaviour: Reactions and reflections. Psychology and Health, 26 (9), 1113–1127.

Ajzen, I. and Fishbein, M. (1980), Understanding Attitudes and Predicting Social Behavior. Englewood Cliffs, NJ: Prentice-Hall.

ANA. (2004), ANA's Green Meeting Guide. Online: http://www.nursingworld.org/MainMenuCategories/WorkplaceSafety/Healthy-Work-Environment/Environmental-Health/EnvironmentalResources/GreenMeetingGuide.pdf (accessed on 7 December 2013)

Armitage, C. J. and Conner, M. (2001), Efficacy of the theory of planned behavior: A meta-analytic review. British Journal of Social Psychology, 40, 471–499.

Bagozzi, R., Dholakia, U. and Basuroy, S. (2003), How effortful decisions get enacted: The motivating role of decision processes, desires, and anticipated emotions. Journal of Behavioral Decision Making, 16 (4), 273–295.

Baker, B. (2007), Destination branding for small cities: The essentials for successful place branding. Portland, OH: Creative Leap Books.

Bair, B. (2013), APEX & ASTM sustainable standard on accommodations published. Online: http://meetingsnet.com/green-meetingscsr/apexastm-sustainable-standard-accommodations-published (accessed on 7 December 2013)

BSI. (2012), ISO 20121 Product Guide. Online: http://www.bsigroup.com/Documents/iso-20121/resources/BSI-ISO20121-Product-Guide-UK-EN.pdf (accessed on 20 October 2013)

Cai, L.A. (2002), Cooperative branding for rural destinations. Annals of Tourism Research, 29(3), 720–742.

Cai, L.A. (2009), Tourism branding in a social exchange system. In: L.A. Cai, W.C. Gartner, & A.M. Munar (Eds.), Tourism branding: Communities in action (pp. 89–104). United Kingdom: Emerald Group Publishing Limited.

CIC. (2004), CIC's Green Meetings Report. Online: http://www.conventionindustry.org/Files/CIC_Green_Meetings_Report.pdf (accessed on 21 October 2013)

CIC. (2013), APEX/ASTM environmentally sustainable meeting standards. Online: http://www.conventionindustry.org/StandardsPractices- /APEXASTM.aspx (accessed on 7 December 2013)

DPEU. (2013), Driving change through collaboration. Online: http://www.imex-frankfurt.com/media/195745/EU2012_Presidency_IMEX_-Sus tain_report.pdf (accessed on 20 December 2013)

Elkington, J. (1999), Cannibals with Forks: Triple Bottom Line of 21st Century Business, Auflage, Capstone: Oxford.

EPA. (2010), Greening your meetings and conferences: A guide for federal purchasers. Online: http://www.epa.gov/oppt/epp/pubs-/meet/greenmeetings.htm. (accessed on 23 October 2013)

GCB. (2013), Sustainability for success. Online: http://viewer.zmags.com/publication/cdb3ceef#/cdb3ceef/1 (accessed on 23 October 2013)

GG. (2013a), About Green Globe. Online: http://greenglobe.com/about/ (accessed on 7 December 2013)

GG. (2013b), GG Standard. Online: http://greenglobe-.com/green-globe-certification-standard/ (accessed on 7 December 2013)

GG. (2013c), Standard Criteria and Indicators. Online: http://greenglobe.com/standard/ (accessed on 7 December 2013)

GMIC. (2011), GMIC sustainable events standards summary. Online: http://c.ymcdn.com/sites/www.gmicglobal.org/resource/collection/2A2E-3AF1-0514-4AC9-B54077016F1DB197/GMIC_Sustainable_Event_Standards_Summary.pdf (accessed on 20 October 2013)

GMIC. (2013), APEX/ASTM sustainable event standard overview. Online: http://www.gmicglobal.org/?page=APEX (accessed on 7 December 2013)

Griese, K.M. (2014), Nachhaltigkeitsmarketing. Eine fallstudienbasierte Einführung, Wiesbaden, Gabler.

Große-Ophoff, M. (2012a), Was bringt die neue ISO 20121? In Tagungswirtschaft, Sonderpublikation Green Meetings, Frankfurt.

Große-Ophoff, M. (2012b), Green meetings & events: Nachhaltiges Tagen in Deutschland, in: Schreiber, M.-T. (Hrsg.): Kongresse, Tagungen und Events. Potenziale, Strategien und Trends der Veranstaltungswirtschaft, Oldenbourg, München, S. 173–186.

Hanna, S. and Rowley, J. (2011), Towards a strategic place brand-management model. Journal of Marketing Management, 27 (5–6), 458–476.

Hankinson, G. (2007), The management of destination brands: Five guiding principles based on recent developments in corporate brand theory. Journal of Brand Management, 14 (3), 240–254.

Hankinson, G. (2009), Managing destination brands: Establishing a theoretical foundation. Journal of Marketing Management, 25 (1–2), 97–115.

Hansen, J., Walker, B., Liverman, D., Richardson, K., Crutzen, P., and Foley, J. (2009), Planetary boundaries:exploring the safe operating space for humanity. Ecology and Society 14(2): 32. Online: URL: http://www.ecologyandsociety.org/vol14/iss2/art32/

IMEX America. (2014), IMEX America sustainability report 2014. Online: http://www.imexamerica.com/media/619737/14IMEX_SustainabilityReport_012215.pdf (accessed on 28.10.2015)

IMEX. (2013), IMEX-GMIC green awards., Online: http://www.imex-frankfurt.com/about-us/imex-awards-programme/green-awards/ (accessed on 15 December 2013)

ISO. (2012), Sustainable events with ISO 20121. Online: http://www.iso.org/iso/sustainable_events_iso_2012.pdf (accessed on 20 January 2014)

Meadows, D. L., Meadows, D. H., Randers, J., & Behrens, W. W. (1972). The limits of growth. Universe Books: New York.

Manning, M. (2009), The effects of subjective norms on behaviours in the theory of planned behavior: A meta-analysis. British Journal of Social Psychology, 48, 649–705.

Meinshausen, M., N. Meinshausen, W. Hare, S. C. B. Raper, K. Frieler, R. Knutti, D. J. Frame and M. R. Allen. (2009), "Greenhouse-gas emission targets for limiting global warming to 2 °C." Nature, 458 (7242): 1158–1163.

Merrilees, B., Miller, D. and Herington, C, (2012). Multiple stakeholders and multiple city brand meanings. European Journal of Marketing, 46(7–8), 1032–1047.

Rockström, J., W. Steffen, K. Noone, Å. Persson, F. S. Chapin, III, E. Lambin, T. M. Lenton, M. Scheffer, C. Folke, H. Schellnhuber, B. Nykvist, C. A. De Wit, T. Hughes, S. van der Leeuw, H. Rodhe, S. Sörlin, P. K. Snyder, R. Costanza, U. Svedin, M. Falkenmark, L. Karlberg, R. W. Corell, V. J. Fabry,

Scofidio, B. (2010), Looking ahead, Corporate Meetings & Incentives, 28(12), 20.

Sherwood, P. (2007), A triple bottom line evaluation of the impact of special events: The development of indicators, Melbourne.

Three Squares. (2013), 2012 Women in Green Forum Report. Online: http://www.imex-frankfurt.com/media/195751/IMEX.WomenInGre-enForumApplication.FINAL.PDF (accessed on 20 December 2013)

UN. (2013), Millennium development indicators. The official United Nations site for the MDG indicators. Online: http://unstats.un.org/unsd/mdg/-Default.aspx (accessed on 24 June 2014)

UNEP. (2009), Green meetings guide 2009. Online: http://c.ymcdn.com/sites/www.gmicglobal.org/resource/collection/47C838A0-D177-4D6A-84FA-0EC254420949/UNEP_2009_GreenMeetingGuide.pdf (accessed on 20 October 2013)

Xie, C., Bagozzi, R. and Oslie, J. (2013), Cognitive, emotional, and sociocultural processes in consumption. Psychology and Marketing, 30 (1), 12–25.

Probe into the Chinese event venue market – From an outside perspective

Gaida, Hans-Jürgen

探究中国会展场馆市场—从外部角度的分析

For the past decade, China has been the fastest emerging event market, in particular with regard to appropriate venues, i. e. exhibition centres, convention centres, (indoor/outdoor) arenas and performing arts centres. However, there is lack of published comprehensive overviews about the recent development and of reliable and comparable statistics. In the following essay, the author attempts to provide greater clarity on the numerous uncertainties prevailing in the various depictions of reality. After meticulous research, and despite only being able to analyse Chinese sources published in English, some significant findings were generated. Based on a number of selected examples, these findings reveal that a more differentiated approach should be applied.

在过去的十年中，中国是发展最快的新兴会展市场，尤其体现在合适场馆的供应上，比如展览中心、会议中心、室内外体育场及艺术表演中心。然而，目前缺少公开发布的有关当前行业发展的全面性概论，和可靠的、可比较的统计数据。在文章中，作者试图澄清目前在现状描述上的不确定性。尽管只能参考用英语发表的中国学术文章，在潜心研究之后，文章获得了一些重要发现。基于大量的案例的分析结果，本文建议应使用更多样化的分析方法。

1 Introduction

It goes without saying that any event of any kind can take place at any, or rather virtually any, kind of venue. Not only is there a great variety of events – there is also a reasonable number of venues that event organisers can choose from. They must decide which venue ideally matches the particular event. Hence nowadays, most event venues, despite many having been designed and built for a specific purpose, can be used as multipurpose venues. In practice, this means that, by making the relevant technical adjustments and providing the necessary services, venues can host a wide range of events.

Although the overwhelming majority of event venues are built, owned and run by the state, with the exception of hotels, the management has to operate in different related markets. It must cope with strong local, national and even global competition, and must be committed to strict customer-oriented entrepreneurship.

Furthermore, strong relations exist between event venues and where they are located, encompassing other players in the event business such as airlines, hotels (accommodation), shuttle and taxi services, related service suppliers, tour operators and local or national authorities.

The outside perspective is derived from the perspective of the German/European, American (USA) and Australian state of the art, contrasted with the current situation in China.

In the following sections, we will introduce and describe four of the most common and popular types of event venue in China from the perspective of the venue management. We will also outline a number of consequences of the outside perspective that may be considered in order to keep pace with the rapidly changing demands of the market (latest facts and figures as of February 2015).

- Exhibition centres
- Convention centres (also convention and exhibition centres)
- Arenas (or indoor stadiums)
- Performing arts centres
- To complete the picture, other additional types of venues are outlined.

2 The event venue market in China

In general, the pivotal questions in the event business are (to name but a few):

- What is the destination like (country/region/city)?
    - Size/population/catchment area
    - Accessibility (national/international) (airports/railway network (high speed)/highway network)
    - Importance and economic structure (industry/trade)
    - Science/education (universities, R&D institutes)
    - Socio-economic level
    - Political and administrative importance
    - Number of headquarters of national/international companies and organisations (government/associations/NPO/NGO/societies)
    - Scope of local, national and international mass media (coverage)
    - Number, capacity, quality and price level of hotels
    - Tradition and reputation as a trade fair/convention/event destination

- What is the venue like?
  - Site/location in the city
  - Type, size and capacity
  - Accessibility (public transport, parking lots, loading areas for trucks)
  - Infrastructure, functionality, maintenance
  - Public amenities on site

- How is the venue managed?
  - Price policy
  - Official/legal (local) rules and regulations
  - Levels of standard of facility management/TQM
  - Safety & security requirements
  - Scope of services (technical supplies, IT, catering)
  - Flexibility to provide services at short notice
  - Smooth operational processes (before, during and after an event)
  - Flexibility to cope with changes and unforeseen circumstances
  - Additional costs for modifications and amendments
  - Emphasis on sustainability and CSR (growing in importance)

These criteria, which may be used as a check-list, are standard practice worldwide. They focus on the prerequisites for success in the event business, and are therefore fundamental for all those involved: destination marketing organisations, the venue management, event organisers and the masses of people who visit a venue to experience an event.

3 Exhibition centres

All those active in the event industry know that exhibitions and trade fairs have been expanding rapidly in China, and continue to do so. Here is some information about the current situation.

3.1 Interaction between exhibitions and venues

Three particular circumstances that determine interaction between exhibitions and venues:

a. Appropriate dates for the exhibition in question, i. e. the right slot in the calendar
b. Amount of space available with regard to the rapid expansion of the individual exhibition due to rapid growth in the number of exhibitors and the space required
c. The need to explore scattered markets, i. e. rotating between different cities and regions

If the chosen venue is unable to provide the appropriate slot or additional space (very often, venues undertake to build new halls in time so as not to lose an exhibition), the organiser will be forced to look for another venue.

This example underlines the remarkable, but time- and effort-consuming, development.

The **China Sport Show (China International Sporting Goods Show)** has been organised since 1993 by the China Sporting Goods Federation (CSGF), a non-profit association founded in the same year. CSGF, directed and supervised by China General Administration of Sport and the Ministry of Civil Affairs, now has about 700 members. The domestic market, with more than 430 million frequent sports participants, is undoubtedly a solid basis offering good prospects.

Nonetheless, the exhibition started in Xi'an on a very small scale, taking up only 4,150 sqm in space. Since then, it has rotated annually between different cities, and has been growing rapidly by area and number of stands. In 2001, the show became international and moved to Beijing, now covering 65,000 sqm. One year later, the show was split into a summer show (Shanghai; 75,000 sqm with 4,000 stands) and a winter show (Beijing; 12,000 sqm with 400 stands).

While the summer show continued to developing rapidly, the winter show remained behind. For this reason, it was abandoned in 2011. In contrast, the summer show, this time taking place in Chengdu, covered 100,000 sqm, an area it reached as early as 2004. Due to the steady growth in development, the organiser had to choose new, bigger venues to suit the event.

The 32 shows that have been held to date – the 12th China International Sporting Goods Show Summer 2004 had to be cancelled due to SARS – rotated between exhibition venues in Xi'an, Fuzhou (3x), Tianjin, Nanchang, Wuhan (2x), Changsha, Changchun, Chengdu (5x), Beijing (11x), Shanghai (3x) and Harbin.

The China Sport Show now boasts 100,000 to 120,000 sqm exhibition space (5,000 standard stands), 1,000 exhibitors, 50,000 buyers from over 70 countries, 100,000 sports-minded visitors, and media coverage by 100 sources.

The 33rd edition in 2015 will be held at Fuzhou International Strait Conference & Expo Centre. SICEC is one of the biggest exhibition centres in China. The facility, built in iconic architectural design, offers 100,000 sqm covered exhibition space. The built-in conference centre covers an area of 86,000 sqm with 42 different sized meeting rooms.

3.2 General aspects of exhibition venue management

The majority of exhibition centres, convention centres, arenas, stadiums and performing arts centres were built and financed by governmental or municipal entities, sometimes also totally or partially in public-private partnership (PPP). In most cases, financial support includes contributions to cover the venue's (fixed) costs, such as investments, depreciation, interest and salaries.

The legal form of the company, which also affects the management, is manifold, and varies in all countries. In most cases, however, public authorities are behind the company, at least as members of the supervisory board.

Venue management generally comprises:

- Strategic management (corporate strategy, planning, budgeting, organisational development, booking policy/event portfolio, rental policy/pricing, local, national and international networking, shareholder and stakeholder issues, performance monitoring, CSR)
- Operational management (operational principles, scheduling, logistics preparation, room set-up, operations, dismantling staged events)
- Facility management (cost planning, controlling, contracting, maintenance, technical supplies, contracted services, security/safety, energy efficiency, waste, cleaning, TQM, "Going Green")
- Information and communication technologies and digital business
- Customer-focused services
- Risk and crisis management (financial issues, legal affairs, lease contracts and conditions)
- Human resource management (HRM)
- Marketing and public relations (market research; marketing mix)
- Catering, organisation of food & beverage (F&B)

This catalogue of duties can be compared with any other business management, albeit focusing on the particular prerequisites of events and the requirements of those involved. The most specific tasks include related services such as technical support, stand construction, catering, venue advertising and mass media relations.

Besides running and operating its venue, the business activities of an exhibition (trade fair) company may also include:

- Managing other venues
- Hosting exhibitions for external companies
- Planning and organising own exhibitions at the home venue
- Organising own exhibitions at other venues at home or abroad
- Organising joint participations of domestic exhibitors at overseas exhibitions.

The scope of the main business of Shanghai Expo Co., Ltd. (SEC), the management entity of the National Exhibition and Convention Centre (NECC) (see Discursion Case No. 1), describes best the corporate policy of a future-oriented venue management.

a. Ownership of venues and supporting facilities: to invest in and construct the complex, which integrates such functions as exhibition venues, comprehensive auxiliary services and supporting facilities into one building.
b. Venue operation: to undertake the daily management of the complex, including leasing the venue.
c. MICE development and management: to organise various exhibitions, meetings, conferences and major events at domestic or international levels as an organiser, co-organiser or contractor.
d. MICE-supporting services: to manage the office buildings and other commercial facilities, and to offer services such as stand construction, advertising design, exhibition con-

sultation, publication and information services, e-commerce, warehousing and logistics, food and beverage.

(Source: http://en.cecsh.com)

If the venue stages no exhibitions of its own, or at least not without the strong support of the related industry association, the management has to strive to acquire outside exhibition organising companies as their key clients. Several exhibition centres in China, or their subsidiaries, already organise a couple of their own exhibitions, a few of which even abroad. Yet the overwhelming majority of exhibitions are organised by other companies.

AUMA reports that there were 1,300 exhibition organisers in China in 2012. Of these, 820 (63 per cent) were domestic companies, 300 (23 per cent) were associations, 118 (9 per cent) were governmental or municipal entities, and 65 (5 per cent) were foreign companies or joint ventures (source CCPIT). The most active organisers in the latter group are REED Exhibitions (UK), UBM (UK), E.J. Krause (USA) and Messe Frankfurt (HK) Ltd., which now has branches in Beijing, Shanghai, Shenzhen and Guangzhou.

Some exhibition centre companies, notably in Europe and first and foremost in Germany, are not only owners and operators of exhibition halls, but also organisers of a couple of their own exhibitions – B2B and B2C.

Furthermore, starting in 1987 with the Messe Frankfurt and "interstoff Asia" in Hong Kong, a growing number of these companies have also been "cloning" their own exhibitions in foreign countries.

Many of these have subsidiaries, specialising in stand planning and construction, and running joint participations of their national exhibitors in foreign exhibitions. The China Council for the Promotion of International Trade (CCPIT), an independent organisation, has many years of success in these activities. Its subsidiary – China International Exhibition Center Group Corporation (CIEC) – has been following in its footsteps as a supporter of Chinese group participations at foreign exhibitions. However, it also organises nearly 20 of its own international exhibitions in China each year, and operates the China International Exhibition Centre (CIEC) and the large New China National Exhibition Centre (NCIEC) in Beijing.

3.3 Three main business models in the exhibition market

Briefly, there are three main business models in the exhibition market

A. Investor/owner:

Municipality/government – public-private partnership – private company

B. Venue management:

Municipality department – public/private joint venture – private company

C. Exhibition organiser:

Private – association(s) – government – venue management/subsidiary

It is not surprising that the aforementioned organisations experience an overlapping of cooperation and joint ventures as far as legal construction, financial ties, strategic and operational aspects, corporate policy and entrepreneurship are concerned. This overlap depends on many specific prerequisites in the world's different countries that cannot always be compared.

Most exhibition centres around the globe were financed, built and owned by the (municipal and/or regional) government [Model A]. The operating entities of most venues are also publicly owned (legally or financially supported); in some cases, they are operated by a private company (on behalf of the government) [Model B]. Some venue operators are also exhibition organisers on their premises [Model C]. In Germany, all big "Messe" companies (such as Messe Frankfurt and Messe München International) are a combination of all three models.

Excursion: The network of exhibition organisers and venue management companies in China

Here we give three examples of organisational structures in China. These examples show that there is already a remarkable variety of combinations of different models.

3.3.1 Case No. 1

- **China Foreign Trade Centre (CFTC)**

This centre is affiliated with the Ministry of Commerce of the People's Republic of China. It has been responsible for organising the China Import and Export Fair, also known as the Canton Fair, since its establishment in 1957. CFTC is the owner and operator of the **China Import and Export Fair Complex** (Canton Fair) on Pazhou Island, Guangzhou.

- **China Foreign Trade Centre (Group)**

A business entity affiliated with the **China Foreign Trade Centre (CFTC)**. It mainly conducts all forms of exhibitions, including foreign exhibitions in China and Chinese exhibitions both at home and abroad (http://www.ciefc.com).

- **China Foreign Trade Guangzhou Exhibition General Corp. (CFTE)**

This company is wholly owned by the **China Foreign Trade Centre (Group)**. It has four branches: CFTE Furniture Exhibition Company, CFTE Outbound Exhibition Company, CFTE Building & Decoration Exhibition Company and CFTE Business Development Exhibition Company.

CFTE is the organiser of large domestic exhibitions. In 2013, it completed ten exhibitions in China and three overseas, with a gross space of 1.5 million sqm. CFTE is also an important agent for many international trade events. In 2013, it helped Chinese companies to showcase their products in 35 exhibitions outside of China.

One of its major exhibitions is the China International Furniture Fair (CIFF), which takes place at the China Import and Export Fair Complex in March and September. The autumn version will be moved to the National Exhibition and Convention Centre (NECC) in Shanghai/Hongqiao.

- **National Exhibition and Convention Centre (NECC), Shanghai/ Hongqiao**

This centre, managed by **Shanghai Expo Co., Ltd (SEC)**, was jointly established by **China Foreign Trade Centre (Group)** and **Shanghai East Best International (Group) Co., Ltd.** in July 2011 in accordance with a cooperation framework agreement signed by the Ministry of Commerce and Shanghai Municipal Government.

- **Shanghai East Best & Lansheng International (Group) Co., Ltd.**

Although its core business is human resources and related services, the company also provides conventions and exhibitions, communications and trade services. Furthermore, the company has also successfully managed its own exhibitions, the most important being the China International Industry Fair (CIIF). The 17th CIIF in November 2015 will move from the Shanghai New International Expo Centre (SNIEC) to the National Exhibition and Convention Centre (NECC), which will remain its venue for the time being. The exhibition space, spanning up to 200,000 sqm, is expected to attract over 2,000 exhibitors and more than 120,000 trade visitors from China and abroad.

3.3.2 Case No. 2

- Intex Shanghai Co., Ltd.

The shareholders are **Shanghai Hongqiao E&T Development Zone United Development Co., Ltd., Council for the Promotion of International Trade Shanghai** and **Istithmar P&O Estates FZE**. The company, which owns and operates a smaller exhibition venue in Shanghai, organises exhibitions on its own, and accommodates other exhibitions (http://www.intex-sh.com/en/).

Together with **Shanghai International Exhibition Co., Ltd. (SIEC)** and **Ningbo New Shanghai International Property Management Co., Ltd.**, INTEX formed a management company in 2003, which was commissioned by the Ningbo Government to run and operate **Ningbo International Conference & Exhibition Centre**.

- **Shanghai International Exhibition Co. Ltd. (SIEC)**

Founded by CCPIT, Shanghai branch: In its 30 years in existence, **SIEC** has organised 580 exhibitions and 22 international conferences covering 105 industries and categories with a total exhibition area of 8,600,000 sqm, 134,000 exhibitors and 21,700,000 visitors (http://www.siec-ccpit.com/en).

- **Zhengzhou International Convention and Exhibition Centre (ZZICEC)**

Hong Kong – Shanghai Venue Management (Zhengzhou) Limited (VMZL), a private professional management company for **Zhengzhou International Convention and Exhibition Centre (ZZICEC)**, is a joint venture between companies in Hong Kong and Shanghai associated with the **Hong Kong Exhibition and Convention Venue Management China Limited** and the **INTEX Shanghai Company Limited**, respectively. VMZL's Management Agreement is controlled by the **Zhengzhou International Convention and Exhibition**

Company Limited (ZCL), an entity of the **Zhengzhou Municipal Bureau of Commerce** (http://www.zzicec.com/en).

3.3.3 Case No. 3

Finally, we come to one of the most outstanding examples, which is hard to replicate.

– **Shanghai New International Exhibition Center (SNIEC)**

SNIEC is jointly owned by German Exposition Corporation International GmbH, a joint subsidiary of Deutsche Messe AG, Messe Düsseldorf GmbH and Messe München GmbH, and Shanghai Lujiazui Exhibition Development Co., Ltd. This joint venture has become China's most successful exhibition centre.

SNIEC offers 17 column-free, ground-level exhibition halls, covering 200,000 sqm of indoor space and 100,000 sqm of outdoor space. Since its official opening on 2 November 2001, SNIEC developed rapidly, welcoming more than four million guests annually and hosting around 100 world-class exhibitions. As a multifunctional venue, SNIEC also caters to a diverse range of social and corporate events (http://www.sniec.net).

3.4 Excursion: Exhibition statistics

3.4.1 Metrics and occupancies

The basic key figures when contemplating exhibition centres are:

a. **Space sqm: property/construction area** – total premises/total floor space of the buildings (above plus, if applicable, under ground level)
b. **Space sqm: available** – indoor/outdoor. The indoor exhibition space usually corresponds to the overall size of the exhibition halls, and gives an indication of the size and maximum capacity of the venue.
c. **Space sqm: utilised by an organiser (gross)** – the proportion of **space available (b)** to accommodate a particular exhibition, i. e. exhibitor stand area, additional special presentations and access, escape routes and service areas.
d. **Space sqm: rented (net)** – the proportion of **utilised space (c)** rented by the organiser to exhibitors plus space used for additional presentations. As a rule of thumb, net space equals 50–55 per cent of gross space.
e. Sources in China use the term **exhibition space** to denote gross utilised space (c).
f. A so-called **space turnover factor** is sometimes calculated:

$$= \frac{\sum \text{utilised space (c) in halls by sqm (gross) per period/year}}{\text{total space available (b) in halls by sqm (gross)}}$$

Unfortunately, many statistic sources do not define which metrics apply.

Foreign exhibition organisers *) and exhibitors must become accustomed to the conventional Chinese way of indicating the capacity of exhibition halls. The maximum possible rented (net) space (bullet point d) is very often expressed by the total number of standard booths (3 x 3 m = 9 sqm) in the floorplans shown as a grid structure (50–55 per cent of gross space). This does not necessarily mean that stands have a uniform construction, since an exhibitor can rent as much booth space as he wishes to accommodate its individual stand design. However, it makes planning easier.

) In China, government entities, i. e. ministries or ministry departments, municipal entities, federations, associations, etc. often are called the "organiser" or "co-organiser". They usually act as initiators, hosts, sponsors or promoters, whereas planning and operational business is undertaken by professional companies, exhibition management, professional congress organisers (PCO), tour operators or similar enterprises. Since they are closest to the venues, the latter group is defined as the organiser in this essay.

3.4.2   An attempt to match disparate statistics

Today, a number of sources of information and statistics are available about the Chinese exhibition, convention and event market. Unfortunately, however, none of these is comprehensive, meaning that they are not very up-to-date or reliable. Nonetheless, they provide a certain picture, albeit with limited comparability. We therefore leave it up to the reader to decide which source to refer to.

Let us first focus on non-Chinese sources:

The Global Association of the Exhibition Industry – UFI Global Exhibition Industry Statistics March 2014 (figures from 2011/2012)

The report features 1,197 venues (with a minimum of 5,000 sqm indoor exhibition space), operated by 220 UFI members, with a total of 32.6 million sqm available space globally allotted to six regions. However, most venues are small or medium-sized. 689 (58 per cent) of these venues have less than 20,000 sqm exhibition space, 327 (27 per cent) have less than 50,000 sqm, and only 61 (5 per cent) provide more than 100,000 sqm indoor exhibition space (bullet point b).

According to an overview published by the German Association of the German Trade Fair Industry (AUMA) in 2014, these 52 worldwide "giants" featuring more than 100,000 sqm exhibition space include the following in China:

(4) 340,000 sqm China Import & Export Fair (Pazhou) Complex Guangzhou
(13) 204,000 sqm Chongqing International Expo Centre
(17) 200,000 sqm SNIEC Shanghai
(24) 150,000 sqm Wuhan International Expo Centre
(32) 120,000 sqm Yiwu International Expo Centre
(45) 106,800 sqm New China International Exhibition Centre Beijing
(47) 105,200 sqm Shenyang International Exhibition Centre
(48) 105,000 sqm Shenzhen Convention and Exhibition Centre

This list must be updated by adding the National Exhibition and Convention Center Shanghai (NECC), which has 400,000 sqm indoor and 100,000 sqm outdoor exhibition space (partly in operation since 2014, due to be completed in 2015).

Returning to the UFI metrics, the Asia-Pacific region encompasses 15 countries including China, Japan, Singapore, India and Australia. It has 184 exhibition venues spanning 6.6 million sqm exhibition space. China alone has 4.75 million sqm (bullet point b) spread over 101 venues, not all of which are UFI members. In the five years from 2006 to 2011, China's exhibition space increased by more than 1.5 million sqm, over 1 million on account of newly established venues, and 0.5 million sqm following the extension of existing venues. This was by far the largest expansion in the world. The second largest expansion occurred in the USA, which experienced a moderate increase of approximately 0.35 million sqm.

The net rented space (bullet point d) in the Asia-Pacific region amounts to 21.6 million sqm, 13.7 million sqm of which is located in China. This equals a space turnover factor (bullet point f) of approximately 3. This ratio appears to be small, but only with respect to the incomplete data compilation.

If we take a closer look at the exhibition industry in China, a lot of uncertainties surround the findings. So many facts and figures have been published, but none can really be compared with others. In order to find an informative and reliable solution, we apply a rather simple method. A comparison of five different data sources may provide an up-to-date overview of the scope of the Chinese exhibition venue market, despite not knowing the criteria and decisions behind each source. Even the simplest approach in which each city investigated must have one exhibition venue and must host at least one exhibition (annually) yields considerable differences.

a. UFI mentions Chinese 15 cities with exhibition venues that are UFI members.
b. The German AUMA database is comparatively comprehensive, listing 28 cities in mainland China with 315 exhibitions scheduled for 2015. Of these, 87 are organised by German companies, mainly trade fair companies. One such company, Messe Frankfurt, is the strongest and most widely established German trade fair company in the Chinese exhibition market.
c. The most comprehensive and constantly updated overview can be found on the websites of China Exhibitions.com, a privately operating company based in Hong Kong that covers the exhibition industry in Greater China. This overview presents 41 cities in mainland China that host various types of exhibitions.
d. A similar source, which is not always up-to-date, however, is China-Fairs.com, which features 44 cities.
e. The leading official compilation is published by the CCPIT in their Annual Report on the Chinese Exhibition Economy. This compilation lists exhibitions by host cities and refers strictly to trade exhibitions (B2B) only. The Report 2013 identifies 59 cities where 1,382 exhibitions were held at 104 venues. For promotion reasons, at least one city/venue is mentioned for each province, often listing only one or two exhibitions.

(By comparison, the m+a expodatabase, recognised in Germany, lists 550 trade shows in 46 cities at 131 venues for China.)

If we take the frequency of occurrence of the total of 74 cities registered by the five sources, not necessarily as proof of quality but rather as a position in the market, the well-known exhibition cities are the leaders (in alphabetical order):

- 11 cities are listed in all five sources
  Beijing, Shanghai and Guangzhou, as well as Chongqing, Dongguan, Nanjing, Ningbo, Tianjin, Yiwu, Shenzhen and Xiamen are among the front-runners.
- Ten cities are listed in four of the five sources
  Changchun, Chengdu, Dalian, Foshan/Shunde, Fuzhou, Hangzhou, Qingdao, Suzhou, Xi'an, Yantai
- 12 cities are listed in three of the five sources
  Changsha, Dongying/Guangrao, Harbin, Hefei, Jinan, Kunshan, Nanning, Shenyang, Taiyuan, Urumqi, Wenzhou, Zhengzhou
- Ten cities are listed in two of the five sources
  Guilin, Haiku, Langfang, Nantong, Shaoxing, Tangshan, Taizhou, Wuxi, Zhongshan, Zhuhai
- 31 can be found in only one of the five sources (mainly CCPIT)
  Baotou, Cangzhou, Changzhi, Changzhou, Daqing, Guiyang, Heye, Hohot, Huaian, Jilin, Jingdezhen, Jinjiang, Karamay, Kashi, Kunming, Lanzhou, Lijiang, Linyi, Luoyang, Nanchang, Quanzhou, Sanya, Shantou, Shijiazhuang, Weifang, Weihei, Xining, Xinjiang, Xuzhou, Yangjiang, Yongkang

Not one source can claim to be the "one-and-only" comprehensive overview of the Chinese exhibition industry.

In addition, the statistics published recently by China's Ministry of Commerce paint a very different picture *). For 2013, they listed 7,319 exhibitions, covering 93.91 million sqm exhibition space (an average of 12,830 sqm per exhibition). The top three exhibition heavyweights – Beijing, Shanghai and Guangzhou – hosted a total of 1,696 exhibitions (23 per cent), covering more than 25 million sqm exhibition space (26 per cent).

The surprisingly large number of exhibitions could be due to the fact that many smaller exhibitions are held on the same dates as part of a "main" exhibition, but are counted separately.

The regional allocation is as follows:

EAST (including Province Liaoning, Hebei, Shandong, Jiangsu, Zhejiang, Fujian, Guangdong, Guangxi, Hainan; Municipality Beijing, Tianjin and Shanghai)
       5,034 exhibitions (69 per cent)   65,940,200 sqm exhibition space (70 per cent)
minus the above top three
       3,338 exhibitions (46 per cent)   40,940,200 sqm exhibition space (44 per cent)

MIDDLE (including Province Shanxi, Inner Mongolia, Jilin, Heilongjiang, Anhui, Jiangxi, Henan, Hunan and Hubei)
       1,083 exhibitions (15 per cent)   14,565,100 sqm exhibition space (16 per cent)

WEST (including Province Shanxi, Gansu, Qinghai, Ningxia, Xinjiang, Sichuan, Yunnan, Guizhou, Tibet and Municipality Chongqing)

1,201 exhibitions (16 per cent)   13,413,800 sqm exhibition space (14 per cent)

) The author owes this information to Dr. Ding Ye of SUIBE

If we trace simple indications of the probable occupancy of related exhibition venues, we discover that the average exhibition space per exhibition is:

13,205 sqm in Beijing

15,050 sqm in Shanghai

17,310 sqm in Guangzhou

12,265 sqm in EAST (the figure is slightly higher for the whole region: 13,100 sqm)

13,450 sqm in MIDDLE

11,170 sqm in WEST

Bearing in mind that such average figures have to be considered with caution, they reflect a remarkable scale. The majority of all registered exhibitions must surely be much smaller.

Just to give an idea: the 2,181 exhibitions published in the UFI Euro Fair Statistics for 2013 used 22.1 million sqm rented space, averaging 9,630 sqm, hence the above-mentioned average dimensions of Chinese exhibitions are realistic.

It is assumed that some 90 exhibitions with more than 100,000 sqm exhibition space have been held so far.

The following conclusions can be drawn from the facts and figures outlined above:

- The statistical sources about the Chinese exhibition industry differ or overlap only partially
- The more exhibitions and space involved, the more confusing the findings are. This could be due to the fact that UFI statistics include areas as small as 5,000 sqm, which do not really reflect the impact of the industry
- Exhibition space alone has limited relevance. The more essential driver of further development is how strongly the exhibition theme is embedded in the related industry of exhibitors and buyers, and the exhibition's level of prestige.
- Although most Chinese venues call themselves "international", they do not really seem to be so yet because their international significance has so far not been proven
- exhibitionsSince there are so many exhibition venues (of all kinds) in China, it is advisable to differentiate between destinations and venues and to group them, for example, by taking the above-mentioned occurrence as first-tier (5 out of 5), second-tier (4 out of 5) and third-tier (3 out of 5) exhibition cities with their leading venues. This does not prevent the remaining destinations and venues from having potential, and provides better orientation on the market as a whole.

4 Convention centres

The most common type of convention centre is built to accommodate bigger assemblies of organisations, associations and societies. Events hosted there last between one and several days; they often take place annually at the same centre or rotate between national or international sites.

Characteristic features are:

- The majority are multipurpose and multilayer buildings
- One grand auditorium/theatre (flat floor or tiered; fixed or movable seats; build-in stage; a movable podium)
- A large number of meeting rooms (preferably with a flexible set-up) of varying sizes or capacities ("break-out rooms")
- Exhibition space (mainly for industry exhibitions and poster displays accompanying conventions)
- Public amenities (ticket sales, information desk, cloakrooms, restrooms, meeting point, cash dispenser, telephone box, first aid, service facilities, facilities for the disabled, etc.)

In Germany/Europe, most leading convention centres are incorporated in well-known exhibition companies, and buildings are adjacent to the exhibition halls (Congress Centrum Hamburg, CCH; International Congress Centre Munich).

A few convention centres are independent stand-alone buildings in the city centre, which have their own management and organisational structure. These include:

m:con Congress Centre Rosengarten Mannheim, Germany; Hannover Congress Centrum, HCC, Germany; Edinburgh International Conference Centre EICC, Edinburgh, United Kingdom; Walter E. Washington Convention Centre, Washington, D.C.; Moscone Center, San Francisco.

So far, the only Chinese venue that matches this type of convention centre is the China National Convention Centre in Beijing (CNCC). It is the only Chinese member of the highly ranked and recognised International Association of Convention Centres (AIPC). The significant shortcoming of the other venues is their lack of sufficient break-out rooms that are large enough to host major conventions and meetings.

In the USA, Canada, Australia and many other countries around the globe, these venues are called Convention & Exhibition Centres (widespread in China). They feature an architectural and functional combination of large convention facilities (meeting rooms) and ample exhibition space (halls), closely linked together but often operated separately according to the different events taking place simultaneously. Examples include:

McCORMICK Place, Chicago; the new International Convention Centre Sydney (set to open in December 2016); Shanghai World Expo Exhibition and Convention Centre SWEECC; and Hong Kong Convention and Exhibition Centre HKCEC.

Although many venues in China call themselves Exhibition and Convention Centres (or something similar), the relevant parts of the construction area can usually only accommodate smaller or medium-sized conventions and meetings, rendering it impossible for them to compete in the international convention business.

Hotels providing accommodation **and** facilities for a wide range of different events are tailored to particular needs. Smaller hotels focus on conferences, meetings and seminars (so-called **Conference Hotels**). Larger hotels – whether city or resort hotels – feature large multifunctional ballrooms, a large number of meeting rooms and even ample exhibition space, making them strong competitors for classic Convention & Exhibition Centres. Examples include:

ESTREL Berlin, Germany; Mandalay Bay, Las Vegas, Nev.; Oriental Riverside Hotel/ Shanghai International Convention Centre SHICC, Shanghai Everbright Convention and Exhibition Centre SECEC.

The convention and meetings industry in China is developing rapidly, and seems to be sound. Scientific associations, primarily in the medical and healthcare field, are the most important prospects for conventions as initiator or organiser, with their members representing the bulk of attendees. The more Chinese associations emerge, the greater their chances are of staging big conventions at the national and international level.

Although China's position on the global market is relatively good, it still has a long way to go to catch up with other countries. This is reflected in the ICCA Statistics Report. Published annually by the International Congress and Convention Association (ICCA), it is an informative indicator of the global enhancement of the association meetings market. According to strict ICCA definitions, the 2013 issue identified 11,685 regularly occurring association meetings that rotate between at least three countries and are attended by more than 50 delegates. The criterion of rotation fosters competition between countries and cities, but in return offers the opportunity to attract foreign associations to stage their convention there.

The USA ranks No. 1 (829 conventions and meetings), followed by Germany in second place (722) and China in eighth place (340). Beijing leads China's cities, ranking third in the Asia-Pacific region (after Singapore and Seoul), but is only in 18th place worldwide (105). The other Chinese cities rank as follows: Shanghai 9/29 (72), Hangzhou, Nanjing 30/148 (17), Chengdu, Guangzhou, Wuhan 48/206 (11), Xi'an 52/219 (10), Shenzhen, Suzhou 71/294 (7), Tianjin 79/328 (6) and Hefei 82/371 (5).

We can draw the following conclusions:

- A reasonable number of Chinese cities are already able to provide the venues, hotels and services necessary to host challenging international conventions and meetings
- The cities with an international reputation mentioned as convention and meeting destinations in the ICCA list are also the top exhibition cities in China; both segments of the market obviously have a mutual impact
- The widespread gap between the rank achieved in the Asia-Pacific region and the worldwide list is evidence of the tough competition between countries, cities and venues

- In order to strengthen China's position as a promising convention and meetings destination, all relevant key players, namely the Convention and Visitors Bureaus (CVB), should pool their strategic and operational marketing and branding activities

5 (Indoor) arenas and (outdoor) stadiums

Arenas were primarily built for sports events, and many still house sports clubs such as ice hockey or basketball clubs as "anchor users" hosting many events. Nowadays, arenas are venues that are able to host almost all types of events for large seated audiences of up to 20,000 people.

In most cases, they are colossal stand-alone buildings with the inside space built in an oval shape with fixed seats surrounding a large flat floor in the centre. Investors and owners are often municipal authorities or private shareholders. The management operates on an individual legal and economic basis. Examples include:

Mercedes-Benz-Arena Berlin; Olympiapark München with indoor and outdoor facilities; Lanxess Arena, Cologne; O2 World London; Palais Omnisports de Paris Bercy, Paris; Madison Square Garden, New York; Staples Centre, Los Angeles.

Many, acting as multifunctional halls, may be part of a large exhibition centre and may be operated by it as a department or subsidiary. Examples include:

Chongqing Yuelai International Convention centre (YLICC) with 1,010 exhibition stands or 25,000 seats, which is part of Chongqing International Expo Centre (CQExpo); National Exhibition and Convention Centre (NECC), Shanghai/Hongqiao.

Like arenas, **stadiums** were principally designed for sports events such as baseball, rugby, football or athletics. Some feature a retractable roof that can be closed completely in a short space of time, enabling them to be used like an arena, i. e. they are weatherproof.

Due to their large seating capacity (up to 100,000 people), they are increasingly being used for other events such as concerts (classic, rock and pop music), shows, religious or political assemblies, corporate events and even exhibitions. They are then comparable to **arenas**, as so-called indoor stadiums. A good example of such a stadium with a comprehensive range of events is the Millennium Stadium in Cardiff (UK), with a seating capacity of 72,500 (www.milleniumstadium.com).

Management's challenge is to additionally acquire non-sports public events that attract a large number of (paying) guests, enabling the venue to run economically if it is not making a profit. Examples include:

Olympiastadion Berlin; Wembley Stadium, London; National Stadium/ Bird's Nest, Beijing; Shanghai Stadium; Guangzhou Olympic Stadium; www.worldstadiums.com.

Two big privately owned and operating companies in the USA – Live Nation and AEG Anschutz Entertainment Group – have assumed the management of different types of venue, even worldwide, in addition to their activities as event organisers. AEG has a management portfolio of arenas, convention centres, theatres, stadiums and entertainment districts. As AEG OGDEN, the company manages many different types of venues in the Middle East, the Asia-Pacific Area and Australia.

In China, the MasterCard Centre, Beijing, and the Mercedes-Benz Arena, Shanghai, are managed by AEG. When it started this business in 2010, the management disclosed that the company also "provides design & construction advice to numerous cities in China who are in the process of building arenas, which shall become part of the AEG network in the country." The first, which went into operation in 2012, was the Zhongshan Centre in Dalian, an 18,000-seat arena with breath-taking architectural design.

The above-mentioned statement continues: "One challenge in China is that the majority of sports fans or entertainment consumers have never experienced a venue like the Mercedes-Benz Arena or the MasterCard Centre. And that's where AEG is creating real traction, helping its partners connect with the Chinese consumer who is, for the first time, getting the chance to experience major sports and entertainment events on a grand scale."

However, as is often the case in China, things are evolving rapidly. For example: the almost 18,000 tickets for the only concert in China given by American singer Taylor Swift in May 2014 at the Mercedes-Benz Arena sold out online in just one minute, making it China's fastest sale ever. Despite depending on active tour operators and the popularity of artists, the rock/pop concert market seems to be the fastest emerging sector in the event industry, offering suitable venues great opportunities, but also creating fierce competition.

In the world of sports, things have been put on a promising strategic track recently by the Dalian Wanda Group Co., Ltd. In February 2015, this company, which claims to be China's largest investor in the cultural and entertainment sectors, acquired Swiss-based Infront Sports & Media AG, the world's most respected sports marketing agency. With this 1.2 billion USD acquisition, it is expected to obtain great support in its bidding attempts to gain major international sports events, from which sports venues in China will undoubtedly benefit.

Due to their ability to host audiences of up to 25,000 and more than 50,000 people, respectively, **(indoor) arenas** and **(outdoor) stadiums** will undoubtedly play a major role in the future. Sports, music and entertainment LIFE (!) is an experience that cannot be replaced by other media, radio, TV, DVD or social networks. Be it Chinese stars such as Fay Wong and Chris Lee or the Japanese group ARASHI, the Rolling Stones or Justin Bieber (with VIP FAN package tickets costing 8,888 yuan for his concert at the Mercedes-Benz Arena in Shanghai, 2013), to name but a few, people love them and want to be as close to them as possible. Maybe even Germany's shooting star, singer Helene Fischer, who on her stadium tour in 2015 is going to perform 21 concerts in 16 stadiums (with an estimated total audience of about 1 million), will also attract an audience in China soon, requiring appropriate venues.

6 Performing arts centres: theatres, opera houses and concert halls

While these venues used to be strictly used in line with their purpose – performances and music – they are now increasingly becoming places for staging a variety of assemblies, entertainment and even marketing events. Examples include:

Wiener Staatsoper (Vienna State Opera); Metropolitan Opera, New York; and Sydney Opera House.

Surprisingly, new performing arts centres are emerging throughout China. In Shanghai, featuring numerous theatres and concert halls, the Shanghai Grand Theatre has already become a landmark, complemented by the Shanghai Oriental Art Centre in Pudong New Area. In October 2014, the brand-new Shanghai Symphonic Hall was opened, giving a home to the renowned Shanghai Symphonic Orchestra.

The spectacular China National Center for the Performing Arts (NCPA) opened in the capital Beijing in 2008. It is a multifunctional building with a 2,398-seat Opera House, a Concert Hall (2,019 seats), a Theatre (1,035 seats), a smaller hall (556 seats) a Fine Arts Gallery, and a large number of amenities for visitors, including restaurants, cafés and souvenir and arts shops.

In the first three years of its existence, NCPA staged 5,274 performances and shows involving almost 120,000 artists from all over the world, and attracting a total of 2,678 million visitors.

Advocating the core value of "arts change life", in its years of operation, the Centre has created a management model that strikingly demonstrates the current upheaval in performing arts venues: "Implementing brand management strategy, coordinating the relationship between art and business, providing professional and refined management and technical support, and providing personalized services, focusing on the different needs of the theatre troupes, artists and the audience."

Other cities in China also boast eye-catching venues with professional management. Examples include the Chongqing Grand Theatre, Dalian Development Zone Grand Theatre, Tianjin Grand Theatre (designed by German architects gmp), Wuhan Qintai Grand Theatre, and the recently inaugurated Guangzhou Opera House, designed by the acclaimed architect Zaha Hadid, to name but a few.

China's educated population takes great interest in classical music and performances, such as operas, ballet, concerts and recitals. One of the essentials of a vibrant music scene is the initiative of international performing arts agencies, like Wu Promotion in Beijing. Founded as a private company in 1991, it has become one of China's top performing arts promoters and event organisers, striving to enhance cultural exchange between China and foreign countries. In addition to organising 500 concerts in 20 foreign countries, the company has organised more than 3,000 concerts, recitals, performances and shows touring in excess of 30 cities in China. A large number of different venues was involved, giving citizens manifold opportunities to meet world renowned artists and to familiarise themselves with the world's classical and contemporary music.

7 Special event locations (unique venues)

In order to complete the list of event venues, other types should also be mentioned briefly.

Built for a particular purpose but also available for events (of any kind), this type of venue covers facilities/locations where a number of people (up to 100,000) can assemble to attend an event. A great variety of indoor and outdoor (open air) venues can be identified, such as universities/colleges, town halls, iconic buildings, movie theatres, museums/art galleries, shopping malls, (abandoned) industrial plants, train stations and airport terminals, to name but a few.

These unique venues are very often handpicked by event organisers with regard to the architecture and spectacular ambience matching the profile and orchestration of the particular event, especially in the field of marketing events.

Ancient ruins, urban spaces, streets, parks, bridges, beaches and lakes (with the stage built in the water like at Bregenz Festival, Lake Constance, Austria) serve as open air venues. These often require temporary precautions, particularly technical installations, life safety requirements, security provisions and catering services.

Whereas this part of the event business has developed very strongly in many countries, initiatives in China still seem to be in their infancy, with the exception of a number of music festivals, the City Marathons in Shanghai, Hangzhou and other destinations, and the spectacular Harbin Ice & Snow Sculpture Festival, which attracts ten thousands of spectators. One can easily imagine the meticulous planning and organising efforts of those responsible for smooth operations on a site prepared for temporary use only.

8 General aspects as a résumé

As we opened our essay with the assertion that any event of any kind can take place at a venue of any kind, we can resume at the end of our probe into the Chinese event venue market that this is obviously the case. There is a great variety of different venues as well as numerous events of different types, which match each other.

The global event venue market and the event business on the whole will continue to expand rapidly. Establishing and operating event venues is regarded as making a substantial contribution to the economic, cultural and social development of the community. Exhibition centres are scaled up everywhere, convention centres, arenas, stadiums and performing arts centres are being planned, newly built, expanded or refurbished.

In China, the situation is quite ambivalent. The fastest growth can be seen for trade fair facilities, with the most ambitious Hongqiao National Conference & Exhibition Centre (due to open in April 2015), which will rival in size the world's previously largest fair grounds of Deutsche Messe AG in Hannover, Germany. Due to the overcapacity of a number of exhibition venues, some market observers are already warning against long-term non-profitability. They probably disregard the fact that exhibition space may not be keeping pace with demand, but the latter could gain momentum in the future. Compared to the USA, China's exhibition industry is by no means mature – some challenges and opportunities remain before a solid profitable development can be achieved.

In order to boost the development of the exhibition industry, the State Council released guidelines for guaranteeing more market liberalisation in April 2015. A ministerial joint conference to be established is to coordinate the prospective market rules to be implemented by 2020. The central government plans to step back, giving greater influence to provincial-level authorities and private companies. The big national exhibition companies should be guided to acquire, merge with or buy stakes in foreign counterparts to establish multinationals. Smaller exhibition companies are to benefit from tax breaks and streamlined customs procedures to facilitate cross-border exhibitions. Furthermore, government plans include supporting exhibition-related industries such as transport, logistics, telecommunications, finance, tourism, catering and hotels. In order to lure global brand giants into taking part in exhibitions in China, the government promises to strengthen intellectual property rights protection to prevent massive counterfeiting. By taking these measurements, China seeks to become an exhibition centre "with a sound development environment and a high level of internationalization", which will be bound to affect exhibition venues, too (Shanghai Daily, 20 April 2015).

Although the convention and meetings industry in China is emerging rapidly, only the China National Convention Centre in Beijing can truly be regarded as being globally competitive as far as the size of the facility, the infrastructure and the professional services are concerned. Shanghai, which also operates successfully in the convention market, and other cities are still lacking in a similar venue. As far as the number of delegates is concerned, therefore, the size of potential national and international conventions will be limited.

The target groups and key clients of event venues to generate business are essentially the same. Event venues are differentiated according to their owners' individual objectives and policies, i. e. the local or national authorities, and the respective management.

- Exhibition organisers
- Convention and meeting organisers (PCOs, national or international associations, NGOs, NPOs, as well as the Government and, on a global level, organisations such as the UN, UNESCO and WHO)
- Corporate and incentive planners
- Concert agencies and tour organisers
- Decision-makers of national/international sports competitions, tournaments and championships
- The public as potential visitors, attendees and participants
- All important stakeholders, the media and other opinion-leaders

An intricate key to positioning a venue in the event market is a compelling favourable image, which is very much influenced by the destination. In this respect, cities, regions and nations are enhancing and strengthening their marketing initiatives. They all are active in a market of tough global competition. The intriguing question is: How can a positive appealing image and a strong market position of a destination in the event market be developed? In many cases, it turns out to be a long-lasting mutually affecting process with numerous creative and strongly backed initiatives by all parties involved. From a marketing perspective, it is similar to the branding of products or services.

The key to success has always been to monitor the ever-changing requirements of the market, i. e. clients and environmental factors, and to find the appropriate measures for meeting them, preferably in advance. The range of event-related marketing activities, tools and services are vast, but manageable. Since the internet is one of the most preferred instruments for a potential prospect to gather information, destination marketing entities and event venues should also offer their websites in non-Chinese languages, at least in English, including floorplans, seating plans, downloads of technical services, online ticketing, and so on. A number of Chinese event venues already have an excellent website, but a surprisingly large number of venues are struggling to keep abreast of the times.

The Chinese event industry undoubtedly has great prospects ahead, in spite of uncertainties about the development of the economy, e-commerce, government policies, society, the standard of living and lifestyle in China, open or latent global crises, threats and weaknesses inherent to the system, internal management proficiency, finance, HR, compliance rules, environmental challenges, and so on.

9 Literature

All facts and figures referred to in this essay were taken from sources retrieved from the internet in February/March 2015 (English version of the websites).

www.auma.de

Trade Fair Data Worldwide/Messemarkt China

www.ccpit.org.cn

2013 Annual Report on China's Exhibition and Convention Industry (released at the annual meeting of CEFCO China Expo Forum for International Cooperation)

www.chinaexhibition.com

Trade Shows and Events in China

http://www.china-fairs.com/

Trade Fairs and International Exhibitions in China

www. researchandmarkets.com

Research Report on China Convention & Exhibition Industry, 2013–2017

www.ufi.org

UFI 2014 Exhibition Industry Statistics;

UFI World Map of Exhibition Venues

Useful information about general aspects of event venue management:

Kirchgeorg, Manfred; Giese, Wilhelm; Dornscheidt, Werner; Stoeck, Norbert (2006): Trade Show Management: Planning, Implementing and Controlling of Trade Shows, Conventions and Events. Wiesbaden (Germany)

Lawson, Fred (2000): Congress, Convention and Exhibition Facilities: Planning, Design and Management, Oxford, United Kingdom, (Architectural Press)

Mahoney, Kimberley; Esckilsen, Lee A.; Jeralds, Adonis; Camp, Steve (2015): Public Assembly Venue Management – Sports, Entertainment, Meeting, and Convention Venues. Textbook published by the International Association of Venue Managers, Coppell, TX, USA (www.iavm.org)

Petersen, David C. (1997): Sports, Convention, and Entertainment Facilities, 2nd edition, Washington, D.C.

The Role of a Destination Management Organisation (DMO) in China, taking the example of Shanghai

Chen, Patrick

上海目的地管理组织的角色：以上海市旅游局为例

Shanghai International Conference Management Organisation (SICMO), under the Shanghai Municipal Tourism Administration (SMTA), was established in 2003 functioning as a Convention & Visitors Bureau (CVB). SICMO aims to assist the SMTA to promote and market Shanghai as one of the premier and attractive MICE destinations in the whole world. To reach the goal, SICMO has launched ten initiatives and programs in the past decade, including the Shanghai MICE Task Force, Shanghai Conference Ambassador Program and others. As a result, Shanghai has become an increasingly popular MICE destination in the Asia Pacific region as well as in the whole world.

Shanghai's Economy continues to grow at a relative fast pace. The scheduled opening of the National Exhibition and Convention Center (Shanghai), Shanghai Disneyland and Shanghai Tower in 2015 will have great impacts on the city's MICE industry. SMTA will spare no efforts to further market and promote Shanghai and help to build Shanghai into a world famous destination for both leisure and business travellers.

上海国际会议管理组织（SICMO）隶属于上海市旅游局，成立于2003年。它承担着会议旅游局的职责，以协助上海市旅游局开展目的地促销和营销活动，并使上海成为世界范围内一流的、有吸引力的会展业目的地。为此，SICMO在过去十多年间实施了包括会奖旅游工作组、上海会议大使项目等十条倡议和项目，上海也逐渐成为在亚太和世界范围内热门的会展业目的地。

上海的经济仍在不断高速发展，上海国家会展中心、上海迪斯尼乐园以及上海中心的开业将会深远地影响上海会展业的发展。SMTA将不遗余力地加深对上海的目的地营销，把它打造成休闲和商务旅游者眼中世界级的知名目的地。

1 Introduction

Shanghai Municipal Tourism Administration (SMTA), under the Shanghai Municipal Government, is a regulating arm in charge of drafting the master plans and strategies for developing the city's travel and tourism industry, implementing the trade policies and regulations, and coordinating the operations of related organizations and businesses in the industry. It is also responsible for promoting the travel industry and travel products in both domestic and overseas markets.

Under the SMTA, there is a specific department, the International Tourism Promotion Department, which is responsible for promoting Shanghai as an ideal MICE destination as well as the city's MICE industry. Its major responsibility is to market Shanghai in international meetings and events industry, coordinate the operation of meetings in Shanghai and provide training to the MICE industry people.

Under the SMTA, Shanghai International Conference Management Organization (SICMO) was established in December, 2003 to function like that of a Convention & Visitors Bureau (CVB) to assist the SMTA to promote and market Shanghai as a premier and attractive MICE destination in the world.

Shanghai Municipal Tourism Administration has been a member of ICCA (International Conference and Congress Association) since 2001. To upgrade the professionalism of the city's MICE industry and promote Shanghai as a popular MICE destination, SMTA has initiated various programs and projects in the past 14 years.

2 SMTA & ICCA

ICCA, the International Congress and Convention Association, is the most important global meetings industry association and the leader in the international association meetings sector. ICCA represents the main specialists in organizing, transporting, and accommodating international meetings and events, and comprises almost 1,000 member companies and organisations in over 90 countries worldwide. ICCA specializes in the international association meetings sector, offering unrivalled data, communication channels and business development opportunities. ICCA's mission is that ICCA is the global community for the meetings industry, enabling its members to generate and maintain significant competitive advantage (ICCA).

Shanghai is a destination for both leisure travellers and business travellers. In 2001, international arrivals to Shanghai were recorded with two million, among which 58 per cent were business travellers. To develop Shanghai into a popular destination of business events, it was significant to join ICCA. Before becoming an ICCA member, SMTA first became an observer.

Approved by the Ministry of Foreign Affairs, SMTA became the first organization in mainland China to join ICCA in July, 2001. By the end of 2002, there were 14 members from mainland China, among which five were from Shanghai. By September of 2013, the total number of ICCA members from mainland China was increased to 44, among which 11 were from Shanghai.

Every year, ICCA organized various events including training workshops, seminars and congresses, among which its most important event is its annual ICCA Congress. Since its founding in 1963, ICCA Congress never came to mainland China. If the meetings and events industry need to be further developed and the industry people in Shanghai as well as in whole China become more international and professional, an ICCA Congress seems to be the right platform.

In 2009, SMTA proposed to bid for the 52nd ICCA Congress to be held in 2013 in Shanghai. Shanghai from mainland China, Gold Coast from Australia and Houston from the United States were shortlisted after the first round.

In May 2010, SMTA led a team of the industry people in China to Frankfurt to present its proposal to bid for the 52nd ICCA Congress. The ICCA Board's decision to hold the 52nd ICCA Congress in Shanghai from 2–6 November 2013 was made at the IMEX 2010 exhibition in Frankfurt and was revealed on the last day of the show.

ICCA CEO Martin Sirk said: "The standard of bids received from our member destinations continues to improve each year, and Shanghai needed to produce an exceptional proposal in order to win this tough competition. Their bid involved members from all over China, it positioned the ICCA Congress as a key milestone in the strategic development of China's international meetings industry, was packed with creative concepts, and clearly communicated the enthusiasm and commitment of the host team. We anticipate that this will be a superb event, and look forward to working with our Chinese colleagues on a program that will expose ICCA members to China and its business potential, and which will transfer cutting-edge knowledge and expertise to the Chinese meetings industry."

The 52nd ICCA Congress was successfully held at the Shanghai International Convention Center from November 2–6, 2013. The Congress attracted 936 delegates from 61 countries and regions in the world. It was the largest ICCA Congress outside Europe. ICCA also celebrated its 50th Anniversary in Shanghai.

Shanghai scored the highest delegate evaluation in ICCA Congress history. Shanghai's organisational efficiency of almost 82 per cent is on par with best result ever. Martin Sirk, CEO of ICCA commented the Congress: "It's clear that the ICCA Congress has created an army of highly influential brand ambassadors for Shanghai!"

After the Congress, inquiries about Shanghai and interest in bringing meetings, incentives and events to Shanghai increase. Meetings and conferences have been secured in Shanghai like the 11th World Design & Health Assembly in 2015, the 7th Asian Tumor Summit & Viral Hepatitis Conference, the 9th International Air Transport Association Freight Conference, the 2016 Urban Future Convention, the 2016 Jeunesse Convention and 2020 Global Endometriosis Conference.

In September 2010, ICCA China Committee (Mainland) was officially established in Shanghai. The establishment of the ICCA China Committee (Mainland) will be conducive to better exchanges of experience in managing meetings and conferences, coordination and development of a cooperation mechanism among all ICCA members in China.

In 2001, when SMTA joined ICCA, the number of international association meetings held in Shanghai was 17 with Shanghai's ranking of No. 58. In 2013, the number of international association meetings was increased to 72 with Shanghai's ranking of No. 29. Below is the table showing the number of meetings and Shanghai's ICCA city ranking in the world from 2000 through 2013.

Table 1: Shanghai ICCA city ranking

	2000	2001	2002	2003	2004	2005	2006	2007	2008	2009	2010	2011	2012	2013
No. of meetings	9	17	32	14	45	46	43	45	57	58	81	72	64	72
Ranking	99	58	34	81	36	37	31	29	28	28	21	24	35	29

Source: ICCA Statistic Report 2014

3 Service-standards, research and promotion

3.1 Management & service standards for the conference industry in Shanghai

In September 2012, Shanghai Municipal Tourism Administration and Shanghai Municipal Bureau of Quality and Technical Supervision jointly released "The Management & Service Standards of the Conference Industry, Part 1: Conference Organizers". The standards were proposed by SMTA and drafted by SMTA and Shanghai International Conference Management Organization (SICMO). It is the first of the kind in China's conference service industry and fills the gap in the sector. This document contains provisions on the basic requirements for conference organizers as well as for conference services, conference management, continuous service improvement and compliance assessment. Comprehensive and feasible, the document is intended to help improve the service quality and professionalism of Shanghai's meetings industry.

The meetings industry is an important part and also an important starting point of the modern service industry. The past decade has seen rapid development of Shanghai's meetings market. This standard is developed to meet the requirements for the development of the service industry in the new period. It is developed based on the extensive research of the actual development of Shanghai's conference service industry and the market demand. It will become an important new yardstick used by the conference service industry to manage and evaluate itself and by the government to manage the conference service industry.

Under Shanghai Municipal Tourism Standardization Technical Committee, SMTA established Shanghai MICE Professional Committee in April, 2013.

In September 2014, the assessment of the first group of 17 conference organizers was completed. The announcement of those which pass the assessment is scheduled to be released in December, 2014. And the official website of Shanghai Meetings and Conferences Service Standards is soon to be released as well.

The Management and Service Standards of Conference Industry Part 2: Conference Venues are also scheduled to be released soon.

3.2 Research & report

One of the major jobs of the SICMO is to carry out market research of the meetings and events industry to provide valuable insight to SMTA. SMTA and SICMO have been successively producing Reports on Shanghai's International Meetings for the Year of 1997 through the Year of 2013.

The Report on Shanghai's International Meetings for the Year of 2013 provides a comprehensive analysis on various international meetings held in Shanghai in 2013. In 2013, a total number of 613 international meetings were held in Shanghai, among which 207 were corporate meetings, 175 association meetings, 203 seminars and forums, 28 government meetings and others. Out of the total 613 international meetings held in Shanghai in 2013, 24 meetings were attended by over 1000 delegates, 55 meetings by 500 to 999 delegates, 115 meetings by 300–499 delegates, the rest 419 meetings by under 300 delegates. The 613 international meetings attracted a total number of 198,983 delegates, among which 69,546 were overseas delegates. In terms of meeting duration, ten meetings lasted over six days, 241 meetings lasted three to five days, 362 meetings lasted one to two days.

In addition to the complete list of all the 613 meetings, the Report on Shanghai's International Meetings for the Year of 2013 also listed all the international association meetings held in Shanghai, which were included in ICCA database as well as the background of the important international meetings which take place in Shanghai every year.

3.3 Shanghai MICE Task Force

Shanghai MICE Task Force was officially formed in April, 2010 to bring together the players and partners of the meetings and events industry in Shanghai to enhance the development of the MICE industry. Meetings, seminars, workshops and inspection tours are organized on a regular basis to let the members of the Task Force to be updated with what's the latest development of the MICE industry in Shanghai and the industry trends in China as well as in the world.

The latest event organized for the Shanghai MICE Task Force members was a venue inspection tour of the National Exhibition and Convention Center (Shanghai) organized on July 17, 2014. Measuring 147,000 square meters in total construction area, the National Convention & Exhibition Center (Shanghai) is currently the world's largest single building and a complex for exhibitions, conferences and events. The construction of the National Convention & Exhibition

Center (Shanghai) North Zone was completed at the end of June in 2014, and the first exhibition will be held in the middle of October. The National Convention & Exhibition Center (Shanghai) has been discussed a lot in the MICE industry, and it will inject new vitality into the development of Shanghai's MICE industry and have great impact on the local economy. In order to help the members of Shanghai MICE Task Force gain a better understanding of the Center as soon as possible, the event was therefore organized and proved to be very popular.

To update, Shanghai MICE Task Force is joined by a total number of 38 organizations or companies from local PCOs, DMCs, convention centers, hotels and airlines.

3.4 Shanghai Conference Ambassador Program

The market of meetings and events industry has always been regarded as a high-end tourist market, and the international conference industry is a rewarding industry bringing both economic and social benefits. Successful conferences can not only promote local academic to the world's level, but also reap great economic benefits for the hosting city. Moreover, they can make their hosting city better well-known in the world. Attracting more international conferences to Shanghai cannot be solely achieved by one aspect of endeavour. It is a comprehensive and systemic task, which calls for the integration of the resources of the entire city and concerted efforts rendered by all walks of life.

Therefore, the SMTA developed the Conference Ambassador Program in 2006, a new initiative to formalize and cultivate the relationship between the SMTA and individuals who organize conferences in Shanghai on a voluntary, non-professional basis.

The programme recognizes the significant contributions of these "Conference Ambassadors", who will help develop Shanghai into a vibrant destination for international conferences. By creating a closer and more effective network of Conference Ambassadors, the programme facilitates the organizing of conferences in Shanghai – to the benefit of all parties. The programme seeks to make it as easy as possible to bring a conference to the city, from the creation of a tailored bid document through to venue selection and detailed conference organization.

Shanghai Conference Ambassadors are typically persons, who are influential in their respective professional and industry associations, as well as being industry specialists. They may already have practical experience securing and organizing conferences in their chosen fields, or have demonstrated the potential to do so.

In their ability to influence peers and promote locally held events, Conference Ambassadors often serve as spokespersons for Shanghai, especially while attending conferences and events overseas. They also serve a valuable role during the bidding process, where the local chapter of the international association is often required to lead the bid.

From the successful experience of countries and regions rich in hosting international conferences, the conference ambassadors are usually appointed by the city conference bureau. In some countries and regions, the appointment of conference ambassadors has a long history. For instance, major cities in Britain and Ireland have adopted such kind of program during the past ten years. There are over 100 celebrities of various circles appointed as the conference ambassadors in Manchester.

Since its establishment in 2006, a total number of 89 Shanghai conference ambassadors from various fields of industries have been appointed.

SMTA will support Conference Ambassadors to secure a conference for Shanghai under the following criteria:

1. Support for a site inspection to Shanghai by decision makers. Free reception service for decision makers for inspecting Shanghai's qualification for hosting corresponding conferences.
2. Supporting letter from the director of SMTA
3. Funding to design and produce bidding documents
4. Support with bid documents, supply of images, videos, DVDs, posters, etc.

Once the conference is secured, SMTA will support the organizers to a limited extent as follows:

1. Marketing the conference to delegates, support to local hosts attending conferences in intervening years to promote Shanghai, with such as print.
2. Contribute or support welcoming receptions for delegates in certain circumstances.
3. Shanghai tourist maps and guidebooks will be provided for conference delegates and Shanghai albums will be offered to VIPs.

3.5 Media (website, social media)

SMTA has been cooperating with major domestic and international leisure, MICE industry and other medias to promote and market Shanghai through various channels like publishing advertorials, exposing Shanghai's destination advertisements, reporting on the latest development of the MICE industry in the city. These medias include TripAdvisor, Travel & Leisure, Conde Nast Traveller, CEI, MeetingsNet, TTG, MIX, TravelWeekly, MICE China, Forbes, EuroSport, Business Traveller Asia Pacific.

The official website of Shanghai Municipal Tourism Administration (www.meet-in-shanghai.net) is a practical and authoritative guide for visitors to Shanghai and those engaged in planning and organizing meetings, incentives, conventions, exhibitions (MICE) and events in Shanghai. The website has five languages English, Chinese, French, Japanese and Korean with English as its homepage language. The English version website attracts over 100,000 total visitors with two million hits every month. It is updated by SICMO on daily basis with what is going on in Shanghai with a focus on the meetings and events industry in the city.

Additionally, ever since 2010, SMTA and SICMO also produce E-newsletter twice a week and a bi-monthly E-Magazine on the latest development of the meetings industry in Shanghai and are distributed among over 7000 industry people from home and abroad. Both E-newsletter and E-Magazine are available in English, Chinese and Japanese languages. Shanghai's MICE WeChat was also launched in January, 2013. It is pushed to about 3000 subscribers twice a week.

Industry medias from around the world are invited to do Shanghai Familiarisation (Fam-) tours on a regular basis. After the Fam-tours, all the invited travel writers and journalists are requested to report on the hardware and software of Shanghai's MICE industry.

4 Creating and using events for Shanghai's MICE-marketing

4.1 China (Shanghai) International Meetings & Conferences Forum

The idea of organizing China (Shanghai) International Meetings & Conferences Forum (CIMCF) was first put forward in SMTA's bidding document for the 52nd ICCA Congress. In our bid, SMTA promised to inaugurate an annual forum as of 2011. This new forum would offer local industry players the chance to exchange knowledge and experience with similar peers. The forum, leading up to the 52nd ICCA Congress in 2013 targeted estimated delegates at 150 for the first year and then with a gradual increment in target to estimated 250 in 2013.

The CIMCF took place in April, 2011 as scheduled and attracted over 200 delegates. Since it is becoming increasingly popular with the industry people, SMTA is encouraged to organize the Forum even after the 52nd ICCA Congress.

2015 will mark its fifth anniversary. With the success of the first edition jointly hosted by the SMTA and Hangzhou Tourism Commission, and the other three editions jointly hosted by the SMTA and Beijing Municipal Commission of Tourism Development, the CIMCF 2015 will be organized again by Shanghai International Conference Management Organization (SICMO). It will take place during April 15–17, 2015 at Shanghai International Convention Center. The CIMCF has been held in partnership with ICCA and supported by ICCA China Committee (Mainland) and aims to strengthen the international exchanges, share the international and domestic development trends and improve the professional standards of all the players in the meetings and tourism industry. Economists, industry professionals and experts from both international and domestic associations have been invited to share the knowledge and experience with all the delegates (http://en.cimcf.org/congress/en/index.shtml).

4.2 Shanghai Business Events Week

Shanghai Business Events Week was initiated by the SMTA in 2011 as part of its endeavour to carry out the decisions made at the Shanghai Tourism Industry Development Conference and promote the development of Shanghai's meetings and tourism industry. It is designed to provide access to the professionals of the meetings and tourism industry of China. The exhibitions, forums, training workshops and networking activities offer a great opportunity for the professionals and experts from hotels, travel agencies, PCOs & DMCs, meetings services suppliers, universities and PR firms to benefit from each other's ideas and experiences and strike deals. It is an exciting week of industry business, education and networking events when the MICE industry of the world comes together in Shanghai. Events taking place in middle April in 2014 include the China (Shanghai) International Meetings & Conferences Forum (CIMCF), IT & CM China (Incentive Travel & Conventions, Meetings China), IT&CM China Association Day, IMEX-MPI-MCI Future Leaders Forum, ICCA Association

Database Workshop, TTG China Travel Awards, Association Professionals Competencies Briefing, etc.

China (Shanghai) International Meetings & Conferences Forum (CIMCF) Learn how to organize and manage meetings and events successfully and professionally in China. Get expert advice through keynote speeches, panel discussions, educational presentations and case studies at this one-and-a-half day forum.

IT & CM China (Incentive Travel & Conventions, Meetings China) Since 2007, IT&CM China has established itself as China's leading international Meetings, Incentives, Conventions and Exhibitions (MICE) business, education and networking event, dedicated to "Promoting China to the World and the World to China". Bringing together Chinese and International MICE exhibitors and buyers in one dynamic marketplace, IT&CM China is the platform for international and leading Chinese players in the MICE industry to explore business opportunities on all fronts – inbound, outbound and domestic. Delegates to the 3-day event receive the best return on their investment in business, education and networking through structured business appointments, exhibition showcase, seminar sessions, official networking functions and tours. IT&CM China is part of the IT&CM Events series organized by TTG Events, a business group of TTG Asia Media. This event is co-organized by CITS International M.I.C.E. – a wholly-owned subsidiary of CITS (China International Travel Service), and MP International.

IT&CM China Association Day It was a one-day specially structured Association programme consisting of tailored education, networking and business engagement sessions catered for association decision makers.

IMEX-MPI-MCI Future Leaders Forum It was aimed at nurturing the future leaders of the MICE industry, this full-day program is catered to students pursuing degrees in meetings and events management, tourism or related business or administration studies. It offers the best and brightest students a chance to experience real-life industry challenges and an insightful glimpse into a dynamic MICE career. This event is held in conjunction with IT&CM China 2014.

TTG China Travel Awards The TTG China Travel Awards has been recognizing the best of Greater China's travel industry since 2008. This prestigious annual event honors stellar Travel Suppliers across Airlines, Hotels & Resorts, Serviced Residences and Travel Services segments in the region. Respected as one of the travel industry's most prestigious travel awards, The 7th Annual TTG China Travel Awards 2014 will applaud 60 exemplary industry partners for their success in maintaining quality standards to ensure a stellar experience for all. This TTG Travel Trade Publishing event is proudly organized by TTG China, with the support of TTG-BTmice China, TTG Asia, TTG India, TTGmice, and TTG Asia Luxury.

Association Professionals Competencies Briefing It was specially tailored for personnel working in societies and associations. Association Professionals Competencies Briefing is a higher education program based on the internationally acclaimed Certified Association Executive (CAE®) designation. It is co-offered by the Australasian Society of Association Executives and the Canadian Society of Association Executives. Hundreds of professionals have benefited from the CAE® programme. (http://www.itcmchina.com/article.php?article_id=2948).

4.3 Calendar of events

SMTA and SICMO have been producing Calendar of Events in Shanghai every year since 2008. It lists most of the exhibitions, major meetings and conferences, sport events, cultural and tourism festivals and events available at the beginning of every year. The Calendar of Events in Shanghai has proved to be very popular among all the industry people. They make full use of the information listed in the calendar to find business opportunities. It is distributed in early January every year among the industry people in Shanghai and at domestic and international industry trade shows.

4.4 Attending major domestic and international MICE industry trade shows

Every year, in order to further promote and market Shanghai as a popular MICE destination, local industry players and partners join SMTA to co-exhibit and participate in major domestic and international MICE industry trade shows including **IT & CM China** in April in Shanghai, **China Incentives, Business Travel and Meetings Expo (CIBTM)** in September in Beijing, **Asia Pacific Incentives & Meetings Expo (AIME)** in February in Melbourne of Australia, **IMEX** in May in Frankfurt of Germany, **EIBTM** in late November or early December in Barcelona of Spain. Through attending the industry trade shows, both SMTA's staff and industry people from Shanghai will get to know the industry's development trends in the world and meet buyers to get potential leads for the city as well as for the participating organizations and companies.

5 Conclusion

Through the above ten initiatives and programs launched by SMTA for the past 14 years, Shanghai has become an increasingly popular MICE destination in Asia Pacific region as well as in the world. Shanghai has received various awards including the "Best MICE Destination" Award at TTG China Travel Awards in 2010, the "IFEA World Festival & Event City" Award by the International Festivals & Events Association (IFEA) in 2011, the "Meeting & Incentive Destination (China) of the Year" Award at China Travel & Meetings Industry Award in 2013, the "2014 Edition of the Travellers' Choice Destinations Awards" in both 2013 and 2014. The scheduled opening of the National Exhibition and Convention Center (Shanghai), Shanghai Disneyland and Shanghai Tower in 2015 will have great impact on the city's MICE industry. SMTA will spare no efforts to further market and promote Shanghai and help to build Shanghai into a world famous destination for both leisure and business travellers.

6 Literature

Cimcf, http://en.cimcf.org/congress/en/index.shtml)

ICCA, http://www.iccaworld.com

ICCA Statistic Report 2014

Itcma, www.itcmchina.com/article.php?article_id=2948)

Report on Shanghai's International Meetings

The Management & Service Standards of the Conference Industry, Part 1: Conference Organizers

Opportunities and challenges for Shanghai Disneyland – A stakeholder analysis

Du, Jiayi

上海迪士尼乐园的机遇与挑战 – 个利益相关者的分析

This article takes a critical view on the potential effects of the Disneyland Park, on its stakeholders. Disneyland in Shanghai has been under discussion for more than ten years and will a milestone in Shanghai's tourism development. According to the official forecast, it will bring millions of billions economic benefits to the whole Shanghai economy and create more than 50,000 job opportunities. However, Shanghai Disneyland also faces challenges and risks. Themed parks are not new in China anymore. Shanghai Disneyland will face the direct competition from Hong Kong Disneyland, which was open in 2005 and did not make profits until 2012. Universal Picture will open a new Universal Studio in Beijing whose main target market is also the mainland China tourists. This paper will analyse these opportunities and challenges based on different stakeholders including Shanghai government, Disneyland's developers, local businesses, tour operators, local residents and potential employees.

本文从批判的角度评论了迪士尼乐园对其利益相关者存在的潜在影响。上海迪士尼项目曾经过长达十多年的谈判，其也将成为上海旅游业的一个重要里程碑。根据官方预测，它将为整个上海经济带来高达数万亿元的经济效益，增加五万多个就业岗位。但上海迪士尼乐园也同时面对挑战和风险。主题公园在中国已不是新兴概念。其将与香港迪士尼，一个2005年开张直到2012才盈利的公园形成直接竞争关系。环球影业也即将在北京开设新的环球影城主题公园，其主要目标市场也是中国大陆的游客。本文将基于包括上海政府、迪士尼开发商、当地企业、旅游运营商、本地居民和潜在员工在内的利益相关者的角度来分析这些机遇与挑战。

1 Introduction

The Disneyland theme park currently under construction represents a milestone in Shanghai's tourism development. It will help Shanghai become a premium family destination in Asia and is anticipated to bring great economic benefits to the whole Yangtze River Delta. However, in an area with limited space and resources, Shanghai Disneyland will also have a negative impact on Shanghai. This entertainment park will bring a lot of changes to local Shanghai residents.

In 2013, more than 113.69 million people visited Shanghai, most of whom came to buy tourism products and food and to experience culture (Dongfang Daily 2013). Shanghai has worked hard to develop sustainable tourism, successfully creating a positive image for its destination. With the opening of Shanghai Disneyland, it is necessary to consider the new opportunities and challenges facing Shanghai's sustainable tourism planning and development. This paper will analyse these issues based on different stakeholders, including Shanghai Municipal Government, Disneyland's developer, local businesses, tour operators, local residents and employees.

2 Shanghai Disneyland

2.1 Background

2.1.1 Shanghai

Shanghai, known as the 'Paris of the Orient', is famous for its dynamic and prosperous environment. Located at the tip of the Yangtze River Delta, Shanghai is considered to be one of China's international ports. It is a flourishing international metropolis, a golden trading market as well as a financial centre.

Every year, millions of tourists visit Shanghai; thousands of huge ships enter and leave Shanghai's ports; and hundreds of planes take off and land at Pudong International Airport every day. Shanghai is a globally respected city for tourism, known as a fine place for visitors, shopping and recreation.

2.1.2 Sustainable tourism development in Shanghai

In 2013, more than 113.69 million people visited Shanghai, most of whom came to buy tourism products and food and to experience culture (Dong Fang Daily 2013). Shanghai has worked hard to develop sustainable tourism, successfully creating a positive image for its destination.

2.1.3 Disneyland in Shanghai

Never satisfied with its tourism activities, Shanghai is continually seeking new opportunities to secure its image as a premium tourism destination in Asia. The launch of Shanghai Disneyland will represent a milestone in Shanghai's tourism development.

In fact, the idea to build a Disneyland theme park in Shanghai had been under discussion for more than ten years. At the beginning of the 1990s, Disney cartoon characters were already very popular with Shanghai residents. Shanghai Municipal Government was eager to develop an entertainment park in Shanghai and considered cooperating with the Walt Disney Company (WDC). In 1999, however, WDC chose Hong Kong over Shanghai as its park destination. In 2002, Shanghai Disneyland was raised once again by WDC, but negotiations between Shanghai Municipal Government and WDC failed, and the project was put on hold. In 2007, several news agencies reported that the Shanghai Disneyland project was soon to be realised. However, both Shanghai Municipal Government and WDC denied the news source. Finally, in 2009, WDC officially announced its decision to build its sixth Disneyland in Shanghai. Later in 2009, the project was approved by the Chinese Central Government. It was announced that the Park was scheduled to open at the end of 2015 (Shanghai Shengdi Group).

As a joint venture between Shanghai Municipal Government and the Walt Disney Company, the investment is estimated to be worth RMB 2,448 billion. Resembling the set-up in Hong Kong Disneyland, Shanghai Municipal Government has a 57 per cent stake, with WDC retaining a 43 per cent stake. Officials forecast that it would bring millions of billions of economic benefits to the whole Shanghai economy, creating more than 50,000 job opportunities. It is thought that 90 per cent of Chinese mainland tourists will visit Shanghai, along with tourists from other Asian countries. The area of the theme park will be approximately 286 acres (Shanghai Shengdi Group).

However, Shanghai Disneyland also faces challenges and risks. Themed parks are no longer a novelty in China. Shanghai Disneyland will face direct competition from Hong Kong Disneyland, which opened in 2005 and only started making a profit in 2012. Universal Pictures is set to open a new Universal Studio in Beijing whose main target market is also mainland China tourists.

The new opportunities and challenges for Shanghai's sustainable tourism planning and development created by the opening and operation of Disneyland require consideration. This paper will analyse these opportunities and challenges based on different stakeholders, including Shanghai Municipal Government, Disneyland's developer(s?), local businesses, tour operators, local residents and potential employees.

2.2 Analysis of challenges and opportunities based on different stakeholders

2.2.1 Analysis of Shanghai Disneyland's stakeholders

A sustainable destination should have a stable demand and supply; its level of sustainability depends on effective cooperation between all stakeholders in the whole tourism industry

(Carey & Gountas 1997). As a joint venture between Shanghai Municipal Government and WDC, there is no doubt that both partners are big stakeholders. An increase in the number of visitors to Shanghai will have both a positive and a negative impact on the city, so local residents and employees must also be considered when analysing the challenges and opportunities involved. The opening of Shanghai Disney will create competition with other tourism attractions in Shanghai and generate opportunities for local businesses. In addition, tour operators play an important role in the Shanghai travel industry. The analysis of the challenges and opportunities involved will therefore be based on this wide range of stakeholders.

2.2.2 Shanghai Municipal Government

In the report 'The Approval of Shanghai Disneyland Project' initiated by the National Development and Reform Commission in 2009, the area of Shanghai Disneyland was to be only be 286 acres, 25 acres smaller than Hong Kong Disneyland. According to the new statistics released by the Shanghai Shengdi Group, however, the actual area will be 963 acres.

However, Shanghai Municipal Government defended its investment and insisted that Shanghai Disney would promote the development of other industries. The top five industries that are expected to benefit from Shanghai Disneyland are the real estate industry, the tourism industry, the infrastructure industry, the logistics industry and the culture industry. For the government, its stake in the park represents a long-term investment.

Shanghai Municipal Government must also consider competition between Shanghai Disneyland and Hong Kong Disneyland. The target market of both Disneyland theme parks are tourists from mainland China. However, the two sides refused to admit there was any competition, emphasising that the Chinese market is so huge that two Disney Parks will have sufficient visitors. Compared with Shanghai, Hong Kong is better known as a family and shopping tourism destination in Asia. For some tourists, nothing compares to the shopping experience in Hong Kong. Shanghai Municipal Government should therefore start considering the park's long-term development.

2.2.3 Disneyland's developer

Before Hong Kong Disneyland opened, the theme park was expected to draw 5.6 million visitors in its first year. One year later, Bill Earnest, the park's Managing Director, admitted that the park had failed to meet its target (Los Angeles Times 2005).

While struggling to meet this target in its first year, HK Disney experienced massive complaints and a major error at the start of 2006. During the Chinese Lunar New Year holiday that year, Disney underestimated the number of people who would want to visit the park. Hundreds of visitors with valid tickets were turned away from the gates of HK Disney because the park had reached maximum capacity (Bradsher 2006).

Furthermore, another challenge from the public's perspective concerns how employees are treated at Disney. An early report last summer stated that employees of a southern Chinese factory that makes Disney products were underpaid and forced to work long hours without a break, and that only a few of them had health or accident insurance.

WDC is no newcomer to launching international parks and to imposing the American way of life on foreign tourists. When it opened its Disney Park in Paris in 1992, it hit the headlines for imposing its American style and image on the park by banning wine from its restaurants. In Hong Kong, Disney tried its best to localise the park, since its key target market was mainland China tourists. It introduced the first Chinese eatery in Main Street (Shuman 2006). Bill Earnest from the Park insisted that the company is still learning about Chinese culture (Fowler & Marr 2006). The localisation of Disneyland in Shanghai will be more important than it was in Hong Kong. For most mainland China tourists, Disneyland is still an unfamiliar foreign brand.

WDC expected to open more parks in Asia following the launch of Shanghai Disneyland. As a launching pad for further development in Asia, it is important that the Walt Disney Co. considers all of the challenges and doubts that the public and the media are expected to voice.

For WDC, it is also a difficult task to consider how to attract Chinese tourists. Chinese tourists know the Disney name, but lack the incentive to visit a theme park because they did not really grow up with Disney characters. Disneyland should learn how to educate tourists who 'don't understand Disney', which is also a great learning opportunity for Disney to understand Chinese tourists. For example, Hong Kong Disneyland has created a new programme, 'one-day trip guides' in Chinese, which clearly describes how to enjoy a visit to Disneyland (Shuman 2006). Furthermore, this learning process for Disney and tourists may raise the brand awareness and equity of Disney, since China has a huge potential market for Disney DVDs, toys and other products. Official forecasts that Chinese consumers will spend about USD 12.5 billion on toys. The main consumers will be 300 million children under the age of 14 (Los Angeles Times Mar 27 2006). "The best testimony we can have to the popularity of our characters is that manufacturers desire to put those characters onto merchandise," said Jeffrey Whalen, Senior Vice President with Warner Bros' consumer products unit (Los Angeles Times Mar 27 2006). All these experiences will be beneficial to Disney's future development in Asia since WDC is seeking to further develop consumer products, movie and television businesses in China (Fowler & Marr 2006).

2.2.4 Local residents in Shanghai

While the opening of Disneyland was expected to create a large number of new employment opportunities, the complaints of increasing real estate prices present a challenge to the Park's public image.

After the release of 'The Approval of Shanghai Disneyland Project', two Disneyland concept lands were auctioned at a high price. The whole Shanghai real estate industry was influenced by the Disney idea. While real estate developers and investors gain great benefits from the idea, the local residents will be hit by higher house prices.

Of the whole investment of RMB 2,448 billion in Disneyland, it is still not clear how much will be provided by Shanghai Municipal Government. However, it has been decided that part of the investment will come from the public treasury. This means that every Shanghai resident must pay in advance for the park. The question is whether these residents feel that the return on investment (ROI) is sufficiently high for them. The negative impact of an increasing number of tourists, such as traffic and environmental pollution, also influence local residents' attitudes toward Disneyland.

It is clear from the study by Oriental Morning Newspaper (2009) that local residents' perception of Shanghai Disneyland is very complex. A number of previous studies suggest that the key elements of sustainable tourism development are gaining local residents' cooperation and ensuring they have a positive perception of the project (Dyer, Gursoy, Sharma & Carter 2006). Factors that can influence residents' perception include interaction between local residents and visitors, the importance of the tourism industry to the local economy, and the development level of the tourism industry (Teye, Sonmez & Sirakaya 2002). Due to the close link between tourism and local residents, "development should be through local initiatives and consistent with local values" (Duffield Long 1981). Numerous studies have attempted to determine why people are favourably disposed to tourism or not, as the case may be (Kayat 2000). Ap (1992) introduced a model of a social exchange process to help us understand residents' perception of tourism. According to Ap, the driving force for the community to develop tourism is to improve its residents' economic, social and psychological conditions. Not all driving forces come from choices made by residents, and some may be imposed by decisions taken by others. In this case, residents will evaluate the benefits and costs they perceive will arise from tourism, and determine whether or not they will welcome it.

From the perspective of perceived tourism impacts, most residents regard tourism as a positive tool for the economic development strategy since the tourism industry creates new jobs, brings opportunities to locals and generates revenue (Gursoy 2004). However, the previous findings generated by analysing residents' perceptions of the social and cultural impacts of tourism development are contradictory and complicated (Dyer Gursoy Sharma Carter 2006). In Jurowski's study (1997) on residents from five counties surrounding the Mount Rogers National Recreation Area located in southwest Virginia, the results showed that residents' attitudes were determined by their evaluation of the impact of tourism, which was ultimately influenced by their values.

Understanding residents' perceptions and attitudes towards Shanghai Disneyland is essential to the long-term development of both Disneyland and Shanghai as a tourism destination.

2.2.5   Tour operators

In the case of Shanghai World Expo, more than 30 per cent of all visitors from other parts of China booked package tours. Visitors who booked through travel agencies and operators had the right to package the products. Tour operators also play an important role in establishing the image of destinations. Even independent tourists listen to advice and suggestions given by tour operators on a particular destination or product (Cavlek 2002). According to Sandra and Gountas (1997), each tour operator was instrumental in determining tourism demand, and the activities of tour operators influenced the sustainability of destinations.

For Shanghai Disneyland, it is essential to attract visitors from other parts of China, meaning that tour operators also play an important role. Disney should listen to the advice and suggestions of tour operators. Since tour operators have the right to select hotels, restaurants, shops and other products, Disney is trying its best to establish a stable and long-term relationship with them. In the case of Hong Kong Disneyland, Disney offers financial incentives for operators to include Disney in their tour packages, promising a commission of HK $2.50 per adult ticket (Fowler & Marr 2006).

2.2.6 Other local businesses

Happy Valley is the most well-known theme park in Shanghai at present. It opened in September 2009, and attracted more than three million visitors in its first year. Facing competition from Disneyland, Happy Valley stated that it is prepared to share the market with Disney. "Disneyland is definitely a big challenge to Happy Valley," stated Liu Chun Ping, President of the investment company of Happy Valley. However, he also mentioned that Happy Valley has a lot of different entertainment elements to Disneyland, and is capable of reaching its own target market.

Generally speaking, Disneyland can bring a lot of opportunities to other local businesses. For example, a huge number of construction jobs may be created in the building of the park and other infrastructure.

3 Conclusion and further studies

The planning, development and operation of Shanghai Disneyland is a new experience for both Shanghai Municipal Government and the tourism industry. For the Walt Disney Company, "Disney knows the theme-park business, but when it comes to understanding the Chinese guests, it's an entirely new ball game." (Hui 2006). For this reason, it is absolutely necessary for all of the stakeholders to work together to make Shanghai Disneyland a real success and bring benefits to Shanghai and its residents.

Literature

Ap, John (1992), 'Residents' perception on Tourism Impact', in: Annals of Tourism Research, 19(4), pp. 665–690

'California and the West; Hong Kong Disney Turnout on Track', in: Los Angeles Times 24 Nov 2005, C.2

Carey Sandra, Y Gountas (1997), 'Tour operators and destination sustainability', in: Tourism Management, 18 (7), pp. 425–431

Cavlek, Nevenka (2002), 'Tour Operators and Destination Safety', in: Annals of Tourism research 29(2), pp. 478–496

Christensen, Kim (10 Jan 2006), 'Disney Veteran Gets Top Spot at Hong Kong Park', in: Los Angeles Times, C.7

'Shanghai Tourism Statistics 2013', in: Dong Fang Daily, 16 May 2013

Dyer Pam, Gursoy Dursoy, Bishnu Sharma, Jennifer Carter (2007), 'Structural modeling of resident perceptions of tourism and associated development on the Sunshine Coast, Australia', in: Tourism Management, 28(2), pp. 409–422

Geoffrey A. F. and Merissa M (2006), 'Disney and the Great Wall: Hong Kong's Magic Kindom Struggles to Attract Chinese Who "Don't Understand Park"', in: Wall Street Journal, B.1

Geoffrey, A. F. and Merissa, M (2006), 'Chinese Lessons for Disney; At Hong Kong Disneyland, Park Officials Learn a lot From Their Past Mistakes', in: Wall Street Journal, B.1

'Hong Kong Disneyland Falls Short on Visitors', in: Los Angeles Times, 5 Sep 2006, C.3

Hui, Sylvia (12 Sep 2006), 'Hong Kong Disneyland's anniversary', in: Yahoo News

Jerry, W.J (7 Dec 2005), 'Disney park helps boost tourism in Hong Kong', in: Knight Ridder Tribune Business News

Jurowski C, Uysal M, and Williams, D.R. (1997), 'A theoretical analysis of host community resident reactions to tourism', in: Journal of Travel Research, 36(2), pp. 3–11

Lau, Justine (5 Sep 2006), 'HK Disneyland to provide lessons for visitors' in: Financial Times, p. 27

Mckercher, C. F. (2006), 'Living On the Edge', in: Annals of Tourism Research, 33(2), pp. 508–524

Powers, Scott (10 Aug 2006), 'Disney posts $1.1 billion profit', in: Knight Ridder Tribune Business News, p. 1

'Promise of world-class experience', in: Businessline, 15 May 2006, p. 1

Richard, V (12 Jan 2006), 'Iger, Eisner Get Bigger Payouts in '05; Disney shareholder reaction to the increases in compensation is largely subdued', in: Los Angeles Times, C.1

'Shanghai Happy Valley: how to differentiate itself from Disneyland', 24 July 2009. Online: http://www.bohaibbs.org/thread-127459-1-1.html

Shanghai Shengdi Group, 'Shanghai Disney Fact Sheet', Online: en.shanghaidisneyresort.com.cn

'Warner Plans China Rollout', in: Los Angeles Times, 6 Mar. 2006: C.2

The challenges posed by international trade fair projects

Kamphus, Manfred

绿色经济及旅游业

Virtually no company can take the liberty of not exhibiting their products at trade fairs. If a company operates internationally, it will inevitably showcase its products at major international trade fairs.

This article highlights, which processes are key to international trade fair projects.

It analyses, where to exhibit, how to manage cost control for international trade fair programmes and how to develop holistic fair concepts, which can be implemented globally. Advantages and disadvantages of centralised, decentralised and hybrid marketing are discussed, before it introduces different partners for implementing international trade fair programmes. Finally the article describes the situation of global acting German companies in the Chinese trade fair market: Together, Chinese and German employees nowadays create the balancing act to implement 3D activities in China.

事实上没有公司可以随心所欲地决定放弃在贸易展会上展示自己产品的机会。如果一个公司要想开展国际贸易，就将不可避免地参加国际主要展会。

本文着重介绍的了参与国际贸易展会中的几个重要步骤。

其分析了，在哪里展出、如何控制参展的成本以及如何发展出一个具有整体性的国际化展览概念。同时讨论了集中式、分散式和混合式市场营销的利弊。然后，文章将介绍在参加国际贸易展会过程中的各方合作伙伴。最后文章将叙述德国的国际化企业在中国贸易展会的现状。中德两国企业员工共同努力下在中国实现了 3D 立体活动。

1 Introduction

Virtually no company can take the liberty of not exhibiting their products at trade fairs. If a company operates internationally, it will inevitably showcase its products at major international trade fairs.

The individual presentation of the company within a temporary setting, establishing contacts to customers, engaging in discussions, viewing employees as brand ambassadors, showcasing the product and the exhibit at the stand, interactive media, perfectly staging the brand. Shape, colour, brand message, brand recognition. All of these factors are part of the 3D marketing strategy.

This logically derived statement necessitates a great deal of effort beforehand. By which I do not mean simply constructing an individual stand. The basic conditions required to ensure later success are created at a much earlier stage. And by the time fantastic stands are presented at the trade fair in Shanghai, many decisions will have been taken and strategies pursued by companies and their employees. I would now like to highlight which processes are key to success in this decision-making process.

2 Where to exhibit

Companies first have to ask themselves: At which trade fairs do we want to showcase our products? It is important to initially categorise the options into 'A', 'B' and 'C' fairs so as to be able to arrange and plan marketing budgets accordingly. The following basic questions must be answered:

- Where are our potential international markets?
- Which trade fairs are of major importance to our company (national, international)?
- Which fairs are vitally important from the perspective of (professional) visitors and also a fixed date in their trade fair calendar?
- At which trade fairs will our competitors be represented?

I suggest the following general classification: It is up to each company to decide on the exact classification.

'A' fairs:

- The most important trade fair in the industry
- All of the company divisions are represented at this fair
- The company's whole range of products and services is showcased
- There is a high proportion of professional visitors
- There is a large number of international exhibitors and visitors
- All competitors will most probably also be represented at the fair

'B' fairs:

- A well-known trade fair in the industry
- Some of the company divisions are represented at the fair
- Some of the company's products and services are showcased
- Mainly national exhibitors and professional visitors are attracted
- An industry gathering that fosters exchange with colleagues from the industry and associations
- Some competitors will also be represented at the fair

'C' fairs:

- A new fair in the industry (trial run)
- A small event often along the lines of "We just have to be there"
- The company has a small stand, often without any exhibits
- Only a few of the products and services are exhibited
- There are fewer professional visitors than at 'A' and 'B' fairs
- There are virtually no international professional visitors
- Some competitors will be represented

Initially, therefore, each company has to categorise the potential trade fair options. To achieve this, it is important and useful to discuss matters with colleagues from Sales and Product Management. The Controlling Department can provide statistics about the sales markets. The Marketing Department acts as the intermediary between the departments, sums up the results and creates proposals for further action. It is also often useful to attend eligible fairs before deciding whether or not to exhibit there. Useful information about international trade fairs can be found on the AUMA website (www.auma.de) or in the specialist literature provided by chambers of foreign trade in the respective country.

After having created a shortlist of the fairs where you wish to exhibit, a simple question is soon raised: How much does it cost to take part in these fairs? For planning purposes, all companies need to budget precisely and to make an accurate forecast of expenses in all areas. Despite undoubtedly being one of the most important marketing activities, trade fairs are also very expensive. It is therefore all the more important to analyse the costs precisely.

3 Cost control for international trade fair programmes

In order to determine the cost of participating in a fair, the following question arises: What does the fair budget include? How can costs be compared? Who can provide me with information about these costs?

At this point, I shall limit myself to the main costs concerning stand planning and stand construction, including implementation. (Hotel costs for staff, their travel expenses, internal logistics for machinery and exhibits, visas and customs are not considered further here.)

The main cost components for all fairs, whether at home or abroad, are:
1. Stand design for the fair concept
2. Floor structure and floor covering
3. Stand architecture (walls, doors, two storeys including stairs)
4. Ceiling systems with lighting technology
5. Power supply
6. Furniture
7. Media technology
8. Special structures for products and exhibits
9. Graphics and digital prints
10. Project management including on-site support during construction
11. Graphic design / media design
12. Logistics for getting to the venue and back
13. Assembly and dismantling of the entire installations
14. Services provided by the trade fair organiser, e. g. logistics at the exhibition centre, loading and unloading, storage of full and empty containers, equipment rigging points, electricity, water, internet connection, and so on.

To avoid having to plan each and every fair from scratch, the marketing manager should compile the costs for global programmes. Agencies, exhibition architects or full-service fair stand builders can provide assistance. These potential partners take different approaches. These partners' different work styles will be addressed later.

4 Holistic fair concepts

Considering fair concepts holistically has proven to be of great benefit to companies with an international orientation. To achieve this, it is necessary to classify fairs into 'A', 'B' and 'C' fairs, as described above. This classification leads to the emergence of approaches for the fair concept and exhibition design, and to decisions as to how much exhibition space to reserve. This means that the biggest stand is required at 'A' fairs, necessitating a highly detailed, top-quality fair display. Stands at 'B' and 'C' fairs are accordingly smaller.

Regardless of the stand area and the respective fair budget, it is always important to ensure that the brand is clearly recognisable. Brands can only be created and established by their repeatable presence at trade fairs and self-similar fair concepts. Branding is important, from easy recognition from a distance and zoning product segments to the clear, consistent presentation of products. In 3D solutions, shapes, colours and materials play a special role.

In contrast to 2D marketing, 3D stands enable visitors to walk into them and touch them. Customers can see, touch and feel the brand. They gain a spatial impression of the company and its products, also by engaging in communication with staff. The trade fair functions temporarily as the company headquarters, and is perceived by visitors as such. Shortcomings in quality or a poorly defined concept have a negative spill-over effect on the perceived quality of the company. For this reason, a fair concept – as a holistic approach – is crucial to the success of companies at trade fairs.

How can holistic concepts be implemented globally?

International companies have different forms of organisation in marketing when it comes to internal fair organisation. A differentiation can be made into three main forms of organisation:

1. Centralised marketing
2. Decentralised marketing
3. Hybrid marketing

1. Centralised marketing

The company headquarters gives all locally based marketing teams a strict definition of the complete set of guidelines for the global trade fair presentation. Fair concepts are developed, prepared and budgeted centrally, and awarded to partners. National and international branches are merely responsible for engaging with visitors at their local trade fair.

Advantages:

- Uniform implementation of the fair concept is ensured
- Rapid decision-making at the preparatory stage
- Clearly defined responsibilities for all marketing activities connected to the trade fair

Drawbacks:

- Headquarters needs a lot of time to prepare and control all of the activities
- Incorrect decisions may be taken due to a lack of experience and knowledge about the situation on the ground

2. Decentralised marketing

The company headquarters does not provide the local marketing teams with any guidelines for local trade fair presentations. Every branch is free to develop its own fair concept. The design is based merely on the brand guidelines arising from the company's corporate design. It is up to the local branch to decide whether or not to participate in certain trade fairs; they are also responsible for budgeting and for identifying partners to implement the actual stand.

Advantages:

- Speedy implementation of fair concepts
- Responsibility is delegated to branches
- Activities are budgeted within the framework of the branch's success

Drawbacks:

- There is a lack of awareness of the parent company's central marketing objectives amongst local staff
- Inconsistent brand images create a different perception of the brand on different markets
- Misguided savings by the local management lead to undesirable developments in marketing on potential growth markets

3. Hybrid marketing

The company headquarters and the central marketing team merely specify guidelines for global trade fair presentations. Fair concepts are further developed by the branches, and adapted to suit local characteristics. The headquarters are also partly responsible for budgeting. Either the headquarters or the respective competent branch can search for partners to implement the actual trade fair stand.

Advantages:

- The requirements specified by the central marketing team still form the basis of all trade fair presentations
- Local teams have a certain defined freedom of choice, motivating staff and transferring responsibility to local capacities
- Adaptation to local conditions thanks to experts on the ground who take decisions locally

Drawbacks:

- Differing understandings of what constitutes quality and of the importance of the brand image
- Wrong decisions may be taken owing to poor communication
- Less stringent controls by the central marketing team may lead to a dilution of the brand image, meaning that the actual objective will not be achieved

Each company should clearly determine which of the three forms described is ideal in its case, and then review this decision at regular intervals. There is a vast array of corporate and organisational forms, and hence approaches. With almost all companies, however, participating in a trade fair is the first step into a new market. Products are presented and market potential assessed, contacts are established and networks formed. Consequently, a company that adopts the approach of "Simply being there is everything" will never experience success. The structured planning and control of all activities are crucial factors in successful branding and effective sales. Event management and trade fair management are very communicative occupations. Regular consultation and clear hierarchies are key to the success of trade show participation and its preparation.

5 Partners for implementing international trade fair programmes

Once the target fairs have been defined and classified ('A', 'B' and 'C' fairs) and once the internal form of organisation (centralised, decentralised or hybrid) has been determined and communicated to all those involved, the organisers can start selecting partners.

Basic information about fair stand builders

Fair stand builders – a very broad term that everybody interprets differently and that, in reality, has a great many facets and characteristics. I would like to explain a number of key differences because they are also essential for budding event managers. It is important to understand the differences because approaches and cooperation with respective partners differ considerably.

There are four main orientations:

1. Agencies that focus on exhibition design
2. Architects who focus on trade fair planning
3. Fair stand builders dedicated to implementing fair stands
4. Full-service trade fair service providers

Regarding 1.:

Agencies that focus on exhibition design often originate historically from 2D marketing. In other words, they have already widely supported to the customer's brand. For example: development of brand messages, creation of print media and websites, and corporate and product catalogues. The agency knows the company and its marketing decision-makers. Based on this tradition, a number of agencies have devoted themselves to 3D marketing, and are involved in planning fair stands. Consequently, only a few agencies focus completely on the exhibition business. It is not usually the agency's core business.

Regarding 2.:

Architects who focus on trade fair planning. Architects are often hired to prepare tendering procedures for awarding exhibition projects. In other words, the aim is to purchase a precisely defined service on the market. To achieve this, precise and, most importantly, comparable statistics are required. Architects create this basis with the greatest of precision. From the definition of the first screw applied to the stand to the specifications of all components down to the last millimetre, exact product descriptions and brand names for the products used. Nothing is left to chance. The resulting calculation table is sent to potential fair stand builders at a later stage, who do their sums and complete the tender documents accordingly. The least expensive provider will be awarded the exhibition project, after carefully weighing aspects concerning reliability and capacity. The architect, who supports the project until its implementation, is paid an architect's fee for his services.

Regarding 3.:
Fair stand builders dedicated to implementing fair stands based on the agency's or architect's specifications (in this case, the term exhibition stand construction applies literally). Fair stand builders are specialised in implementing and constructing trade fair stands. Stands are produced in the builders' workshops. They construct furniture and exhibits. They arrange transportation to the trade fair, and provide installation teams for assembling and dismantling the stand. Professional fair stand builders know the exhibition venues, and are familiar with the conditions on the ground. They are perfectly familiar with effective time management and with coordinating complicated projects during the planning and implementation stage, which usually involves tight deadlines. They can draw upon skilled teams that are adept at recognising and, where applicable, effectively solving any planning problems that may arise.

Regarding 4.:
Full-service trade fair service providers concentrate their activities entirely on implementing 3D projects. In particular, these include trade fair events, as well as organising events and constructing showrooms and other permanent installations.

Trade fair service providers start dealing with the customer and its products at the development stage. They design the stand using their own professional 3D design teams. In-house architects then prepare the entire technical documentation for production. They communicate with the trade fair company, coordinate the logistics and all other aspects concerning exhibition stand construction (media, graphics, etc.). They plan and construct the stand using their own teams or by awarding contracts to close partners (subcontractors)

The trade fair market in China
My reflections about the structure of the trade fair landscape and the possibilities arising from it are focused to a great extent on the current situation in Germany.

In fact, the Chinese exhibition industry has undergone rapid development in recent years, and will continue to develop in this direction. A large number of exhibition centres have sprung up in all major cities. Modern centres of communication are gaining in importance in China.

Some were initially only built so as to give the city a contemporary new look. These centres were planned as a source of income, without adequate expertise about how to fill them effectively. This development process is understandable, however. Nowadays, a great many of the trade fairs are prepared very attractively, with an international-level conceptual orientation. Growing numbers of exhibitors and visitors, particularly an increased inflow of international guests, clearly demonstrate this positive development. China is starting to establish key leading trade fairs. Shanghai, Beijing and Guangzhou in particular are the top centres of the international trade fair industry in China at present.

The Chinese market promises to remain a good sales market for German companies, hence trade fairs will continue to be a very important factor and develop further in this region. This development is also clearly visible in the quality of stands implemented in China. Details are increasingly important, alongside professionalism in the presentation, the quality of the design and the clear message conveyed to customers.

International trade fair exhibitors in China

Major international groups of companies and enterprises have been operating in China for years. In the past, however, many of these companies attached little importance to participating in trade fairs. They were reliant on other marketing activities in order to get to know customers and strengthen ties with them. The market was profitable, and many competitors were not yet active on this market.

This situation has changed considerably over the past ten years. Virtually all companies recognise the importance of the Chinese market, and envisage potential sales markets for their enterprises, too. Numerous branches were established in China, and increased pressure from competitors prompts companies to deal more intensively with implementing 3D marketing activities. In an increasingly tight market, only companies that understand marketing in detail and are able to make effective use of it will be able to market their products successfully.

Here, companies that have already positioned themselves effectively in other international markets by conducting trade fair activities, for instance, are especially able to gain an advantage; companies that have already built up an internally functioning 3D organisation and that can pursue a carefully thought-out strategy.

Local trade fair exhibitors in China

At present, local Chinese trade fair exhibitors have more of a problem presenting themselves at trade fairs in China. One reason for this is that many companies have a marketing strategy that is not so strictly defined. There is usually no trade fair management department, nor an organisational structure. Subsidiaries are usually lacking in a marketing department or staff responsible for trade fairs. Instead, the sales team helps organise the trade fair. Decisions are taken on a case-by-case basis, concepts are developed and abandoned at the next trade fair event. The almost proverbial transition of Chinese society is also making itself noticeable in the exhibition world. However, this presents a danger to consistent brand development.

The company and the brand are presented at the trade fair. This also has consequences for the quality of the implementation of the stand. In the past, an extreme neglect of quality was discernible with many Chinese companies. The stand had to be implemented quickly and cheaply. "Build and burn" was the order of the day. It was not important or necessary to consider sustainability or the re-use of resources.

This attitude is increasingly changing. Chinese companies now also recognise the importance of marketing and the impact a trade fair event has on the company. Quality in the implementation of a stand is starting to become more important. They are learning from established companies and adopting a great many details, also interpreting them for their own presentation.

6 Internationalisation in exhibition stand construction focusing on China

The globalisation of companies has also led to internationalisation in the exhibition industry. The logical consequence of the German trade fair market being highly developed is that German fair stand builders, exhibition architects and agencies were quick to set up their own offices and representations in China. The direction was one-sided to begin with. German companies exhibited in China. They needed support, and resorted to their established, familiar German networks of partners.

At the next stage, the initial development trend changed slightly. Chinese branches established their own marketing departments in China. Some exhibition stand projects in China were developed by Chinese subsidiaries on their own account. In addition, the number of Chinese fair stand builders has grown tremendously, and there is an almost overwhelming supplier market in the area of exhibition stand construction that is constantly changing. New exhibition stand construction companies are being established every day. All means are used and lots of promises made to attempt to gain market potential from competitors. Aggressive pricing is one of the methods applied by new companies to gain customers.

However, top quality can never be gained at the cheapest price, neither in Germany nor in China. It is a well-known contradiction. Companies therefore have a change of thinking, having experienced the consequences of wrongly purchased exhibition services. Clear quality specifications and reliable partners are required. After all, the actual time spent at the trade fair is usually short, and there is too much effort involved in terms of time and money to create a bad impression due to planning errors and quality deficiencies. Ultimately, all providers should take this maxim on board. It is immaterial whether a Chinese or a German provider is hired. The result alone counts.

The trend towards having more Chinese decision-makers in the marketing departments of exhibiting companies has at the same time led to Chinese employees in the original German stand construction companies gaining more responsibility. Together, Chinese and German employees nowadays create the balancing act required by international enterprises to implement 3D activities in China.

7 Trade fair management as a process

Taking a critical look at the exhibition presentation is an important element of trade fair follow-up work. Companies often want to monitor the success of every trade fair, but it is difficult to furnish proof of success. What should be monitored and used to measure performance? The number of people who visited the stand? The number of discussions held? The number of transactions concluded at the stand? What can be measured reliably, and guarantees success?

Ultimately, it is the sustainable impact of exhibition activities. Activities related to fair concepts do not bring immediate success – they are part of a process. A process that must be an integral part of the management's actions and the exhibiting company's organisational structure.

Trade fair management should be grasped and embraced holistically as an important element of corporate strategy.

Chinese companies at European trade fairs

Müller-Martin, Rolf

在欧洲展览会上的中国公司

For decades, the majority of European global companies have enjoyed a well-established global branding awareness within their trade and consumer target groups. Virtually no Chinese brands have this advantage, although China is the world champion in the export business. One possibility to demonstrate the power of a successful brand is to participate in leading trade fairs in Europe, especially in Germany. Whereas European blue-chip companies spend enormous amounts on their company presentations at fairs, Chinese brands with a worldwide market share of up to 50 % in their respective branch often resemble medium-sized enterprises. Chinese companies are not good at telling customers their own international success story. Only a few act as established global players, but most Chinese exhibitors remain in total anonymity, although almost 11,000 exhihitors from China participated in German trade fairs in 2013 – one third of all foreign exhibitors. There is enormous potential for future improvement.

几十年来欧洲的主要国际企业已在它们的贸易和目标消费者群体中享有了悠久的全球品牌知名度。虽然中国是世界的出口贸易冠军，但几乎没有中国品牌具有这个优势。参与在欧洲特别是在德国的知名展览会不失为展示一个成功品牌实力的好方法。与欧洲的蓝筹企业在展会上投入巨资展示自己的品牌相比，一些在全球市场上拥有高达50%份额的中国品牌却表现得像个中型企业。中国公司不擅长向消费者宣传他们在国际上的成功历程。虽然有少数企业以成功的世界级企业展示自己，可绝大多数参展商仍表现得默默无闻。尽管在 2013 年有 12350 家中国参展商到德国参展，占德国国外展商总数的三分之一，但在未来仍然存在着巨大的改善空间。

1 How the European market differs from the Chinese market

The People's Republic of China is the world's biggest exporter, having overtaken Germany a few years ago. The WTO predicts that Germany will resume the leading position in 2014. In any case, the two countries are the most powerful industrial export nations on this planet. China's second largest buyer of export goods is the EU, mainly Germany, France, the UK and Benelux. However, the majority of European consumers are still very prejudiced against Chinese products, stating partly unsubstantiated arguments such as: Chinese companies copy everything, they produce low-quality products and fail to meet Europeans' design expectations. The old saying is true: myths are more powerful than facts.

The image and awareness of Chinese products in general has changed immensely in Europe over the past five years: from the cheap mass production of plastic toys, artificial flowers and T-shirts to world-level products in fields such as solar energy, computers, TV and LED technology, mobile communication and cooling systems.

Most European global companies have enjoyed well-established worldwide awareness of their brands among their trade and consumer target groups for decades. For instance, Adidas, AUDI, Mercedes, Volkswagen and BMW are so strong in their worldwide branding positioning that they no longer need to show their company name. In their international promotion campaigns, they simply use their logo without having to include the company name. The majority of these dominant firms with strong brands are based in Germany. A number of fashion companies such as Gucci, Hermes and Calvin Klein also use only their logo. A number of US brands, e. g. Apple, Nike and McDonalds, have a similar standing worldwide and use only their company logo in their promotional activities. None of the companies mentioned need to show the company's name. Their established brand logos are self-explanatory. No more than ten leading enterprises throughout the world can claim this degree of uniqueness.

In addition to these strong leading brands, there are numerous European companies that have an outstanding worldwide reputation among the public and industry: Bayer and BASF in pharmaceuticals, Nivea in cosmetics, MAN in the truck industry, Porsche and Jaguar in sports cars, Rosenthal and WMF in consumer goods, Fissler, Braun, Nestle, Siemens, Olivetti, IKEA, and so on. All of these brands have been established and well known in their respective markets for decades, sometimes centuries. When most people in Europe – and sometimes even in Asia – hear or read one of these company names, they have an idea of the kind of products these brand names represent. However, it takes decades rather than years to establish a brand like those mentioned above and to position a company name where it is to remain in the future. Reliability, quality, design, service, distribution, a global image and awareness of the product are the key factors for success. Brand awareness is quite common and important to European consumers. They prefer and are used to living with, using and consuming products that have a certain "product image". A product's attractiveness increases in line with its image. Price is often of secondary importance.

In China, the term 'national product image' is virtually unknown. Almost all Chinese brands lack this advantage compared to European products. The only consumer product that has become an established brand in China and Southeast Asia is Tsingtao Beer, which has been around for more than 30 years. Today, just a handful of Chinese enterprises are truly global players, despite only having been on the global market for a few years. These include Lenovo, Haier, Huawei, Hisense, Suntech and Konka. By comparison: it took South Korea's three leading brands – Samsung, KIA and LG – only ten years to conquer the entire world. Their secret was to act nationally, but think global.

Chinese companies are not good at telling their customers and the public about their success stories. The new strength of Chinese financial and economic power can be demonstrated by a few examples: Lenovo purchased the entire IT section of IBM, one of the largest US companies; Geely took over the Swedish car plant Volvo; Huawei bought 49 per cent of Electrolux/AEG shares. Other recent Chinese acquisitions include Pfaff sewing machines, Liebherr construction cranes, Dual sound technology, Schimmel pianos (Perl River Piano has now become the world's largest piano manufacturer). Hisense, unknown in Europe, is the top manufacturer of air-conditioning systems in Asia and the second largest in the US. Galanz is the second largest computer chip producer. Haier has a 20 per cent share of the global market in household appliances. All of these brand names are relatively young and anything but well established and well known in European consumer and trade target groups. However, Chinese export-oriented firms are constantly gaining in self-confidence, intensively pursuing their goal to establish their brands in European markets. "Zou chu qu" is the motto for many Chinese companies – spread out to new horizons. A number of Chinese enterprises are already producing high-tech products in a level of quality that the world requires and has come to expect. They no longer want to be recognised as Chinese brands, but as global suppliers.

2 The European trade fair market

One way to demonstrate the power of a successful brand is to participate in leading trade fairs in Europe. "Companies that participate in trade fairs will be recognised by visitors and customers and they will talk about it. Companies that are absent from a fair will face serious problems: they will be neglected by their target group and will no longer be in the limelight." This statement was made in 1960 by the then German chancellor Ludwig Erhard during his inauguration speech at Messe Hannover, which even then was the largest fair in the world. Today, 55 years on, his comment still holds true.

It is not unusual for European companies to spend more than 35 per cent of their total marketing budget on presenting their products at fairs. Some leading brands reserve entire fair halls or stands with an area of up to 2,000 square metres – almost the size of a football field. The larger a company's stand, the more respected and impressive the exhibiting company's image is. On the other hand the average stand size of European exhibitors on trade fairs is only 55 square metres.

According to a recent survey of over 15,000 enterprises in Europe conducted by AUMA (Association of the German Trade Fair Industry), 80 per cent of the respondents exhibit their products or services at national or international trade fairs regularly or frequently. The global players are participating even up to 95 %. The majority of the respondents expect the importance of participating in trade fairs to increase in the future, meaning that their budget for fairs could increase to more than 40 per cent of their entire marketing budget.

In contrast, around 15 per cent of small and medium-sized European firms have never exhibited at a fair or included a fair in their marketing mix plan. In many cases, this negligence is not due to inadequate financial resources, but simply uncertainty and a lack of know-how about professional and successful fair participations. If these figures reflect the situation in Western Europe with highly industrialised countries such as Germany, the Netherlands, Italy, Spain, France and Austria, the figures for China are bound to exceed European statistics by far.

3 Chinese exhibitors in Europe

More than 900 Chinese companies have their own branches and subsidiaries in Germany; an estimated 1,200 are represented in Western Europe. With the exception of a few internationally operating enterprises, the vast majority of Chinese representations are medium-sized companies in China.

Managers of Chinese companies are used to exhibiting their products at European trade fairs. In 2013, almost 11,000 (!) Chinese exhibitors presented their products at German trade fairs, representing 34 per cent of all exhibitors from abroad. Other nations that used to top the list, such as Italy, France, the US and the UK, have fallen below the 20 per cent mark. China has been the most well-represented foreign country at German trade fairs since 2011. The following figures demonstrate the huge scale of Chinese participation in trade fairs: 490 Chinese companies participated in Berlin's IFA (the world's largest consumer electronics trade fair), 605 in Medica (the world leading trade fair for the medical industry) in Dusseldorf, 510 in Frankfurt's Ambiente (the world's largest consumer fair), 665 in Automechanika (the world's leading trade fair for the automotive industry), 425 in Hannover's CeBIT (the leading fair of the digital industry), 550 in the International Household Goods Fair in Cologne, 390 in Munich's Intersolar (the world's largest trade fair for the solar industry) and 345 in Nuremberg's International Toy Fair, just to mention China's largest involvements in German fairs. In 2013, 65 Chinese companies even participated in the relatively unknown exhibition Interlift (international trade fair for lifts and elevators) in Augsburg. Augsburg is not known in Germany as an international fair city with a number of successful exhibition events. The more surprising it is, therefore, that so many Chinese companies went to the Bavarian city to show their products.

A total of 11,000 Chinese exhibitors does not necessarily equate to 11,000 individual stands at various fairs in Germany. Some small companies share stand space with other exhibitors to reduce costs, but are registered in the fair catalogue as individual exhibitors.

The general problem with Chinese exhibitors, mainly small and medium-sized companies, is that too many of them are unaware of the fact that they are no longer selling their products to Chinese customers in Europe, but to international target groups: Indian customers come to

Germany to buy products made in South Africa; American customers order merchandise made in Thailand; Swedish visitors purchase products made in Brazil. Chinese exhibitors need to accept that international trade fairs in Europe are meeting places for entire industries, and that trade fairs are sensors of future developments, they set trends in industries, and are the best way to compare one's products with those of competitors. For European business people, attending and visiting a fair is a very serious business matter – and an expensive one, too. Organisers of leading trade fairs in Europe usually charge an entry fee of between € 40 and 60 per person per day. This is only a small share of the expenses incurred when a visitor attends a fair: travelling expenses (plane, train, taxi or car), hotel accommodation, restaurants, and so on, can easily total € 500 or more per day.

Many Chinese exhibitors in Europe are experienced in dealing primarily with Chinese or Asian customers, and are used to an exhibition atmosphere that differs completely from any exhibition in Europe. The majority of fairs in China resemble a place for a family outing, including children. Charging a high entrance fee to keep families out is unknown in China – except for very few international fairs in Shanghai, Beijing and Guangzhou/Canton. It often seems as though families are visiting a fair as an alternative to going to the zoo or an amusement park. The seriousness of attending a fair in China and Europe is often worlds apart, and sometimes creates an enormous culture clash for Chinese exhibitors. They suddenly have to deal with the whole world in their respective branch. Chinese exhibitors very often simply ignore the high, professional "fair culture" in Germany or Europe. The top priority of an exhibiting German company is to impress their existing and new customers with a stand that immediately reflects the company's philosophy – either presenting themselves as modern, future-oriented companies that lead their field with state-of-the-art products and the latest technologies, or as traditional companies with sound experience based on one hundred years of production knowledge.

These are the most common mistakes that many Chinese exhibitors make in Europe:

- The stand is cluttered with products, making it look like a warehouse. Potential visitors are put off by the quantity of goods on display
- Printed information material is not available in English or the language of the country in which the exhibition is being held. It is useless having information in Chinese only
- People manning the stand are unable to discuss and inform visitors in English or any other European language. No interpreters are present
- People manning the stand fail to approach visitors who stop in front of the stand and show an interest in the goods on display. The chance to make initial contacts to a prospective new customer is lost
- Visitors are asked to present their business cards before the conversation has even started
- People manning the stand sit together at a table having breakfast or lunch, even when an interested visitor stops in front of the stand. It is extremely impolite and discourteous to visitors to consume food at the stand
- Empty boxes, luggage and coats are visibly stored in a corner of the stand. A built-in lockable store room (1 x 1 m) for hiding all unnecessary items is a must for every stand, even small ones
- Carpets, glass cases and shelves are not cleaned each morning. The stand looks untidy

- Chinese symbols such as dragons, lanterns or characters are used for decoration, even though they usually bear no relation to the products shown
- Reams of written information about the company and its products on the walls and huge photos of production plants will not encourage anyone to stop at the stand. Customers are only interested in the product, the price and the delivery conditions, not the size of the production plant
- Huge photos of products are displayed on the walls and the original products are shown on shelves or tables

In recent years, an increasing number of Chinese exhibitors have become aware of the importance of presenting a corporate image in the international arena on a long-term scale, rather than merely generating on-the-spot sales orders. Big brand exhibitors had a comparatively difficult starting position in terms of professional presence at international trade fairs. Even brands with a worldwide market share of 25 per cent or more often resembled medium-sized enterprises. Since 2010, an increasing number of Chinese companies have started exhibiting in Europe using much larger stands, with "Western style" stand designs and much better trained stand personnel. They have come to expect a stand design and feel resembling those of European exhibitors – in the same construction quality, with light effects, graphics, audiovisuals and on-time delivery by the construction firm. In fact, they want to look like an established modern company from a European country without any hint of a Chinese background.

Unfortunately, these exhibitors represent only a small minority because 92 per cent of all Chinese exhibitors either participate in so-called National Pavilions (joint presentations of many companies from one particular industry at the same fair) or have mini stands seldom featuring more than 15 square metres stand space. In contrast, only 10 to 15 per cent of German companies that participate in international fairs outside Germany exhibit in a German pavilion.

The easiest, most cost-effective way to participate in a fair abroad is to join a pavilion. Everything is organised for exhibitors by the association of the respective branch or by an agency: stand space reservations, transporting the exhibited goods from China to the fair venue and back, customs clearing, constructing a simple stand including furniture, carpet, shelving and the company name signage, visas, hotel reservations, flights and, in some cases, financial support – all at a fixed price. The exhibitor simply has to place his products on the shelves the day before the fair opens and wait for the arrival of customers.

However, group participations have a major disadvantage: all stands are standardised and look exactly the same as dozens of others in the pavilion. No individual creativity or design ideas are permitted on the stand, no special colours, large graphics or text panels are allowed, and it is not possible to place the company logo at the entrance to the stand. Joint presentations in any national pavilion are generally not very exciting; they look rather monotonous, with rows and rows of identical stands to the left and right. It is virtually impossible to attract visitors to the stand.

At the beginning, Chinese companies were understandably unfamiliar with European fair markets. After a few years of gaining experience in pavilions, seeing the European way of doing business and comparing their own company presentation to that of competitors "outside" the pavilion, more and more Chinese exhibitors are becoming aware of the importance of displaying their products in an independent, sales-oriented manner. They are looking for alternatives to raise awareness of their company and to improve their success by having their own individual stand, designed and built according to their own budget and requirements. They want to show their products in a fresh, modern style without the restrictions imposed on pavilions.

The year 2012 signalled a breakthrough: a large number of previous small exhibitors from China increased their stand sizes substantially at German and other European trade fairs. For the first time, Chinese companies were seen by fair visitors as serious and modern exhibitors with the same level of professional appearance as other established exhibitors from Europe. Many of the stands were designed and constructed like the majority of Western stands.

It may take a few more years for the 92 per cent of users of standardised national pavilions to fall drastically. After all, most small and medium-sized Chinese companies are still afraid and insecure about leaving the safety of a pre-organised pavilion. If the pace of change can be maintained, hundreds or even thousands of brave Chinese exhibitors will have their own independent stands in the future. Once managers of Chinese enterprises have decided to present their company independently, they will never return to the confinement of a pavilion.

All of the work required to organise a stand abroad, previously dealt with by an association or agency, then has to be performed by the exhibitor.

Here is a list of the most important steps demonstrating the future workload for new exhibitors in chronological order:

- Appoint a project manager to act as a link between the company management and the organiser of the exhibition. This person will be responsible for all activities involving participation in the fair
- Use the data available to select the "right" exhibition to reach potential target groups
- Request and order a stand of the chosen type and size
- Calculate and release the budget
- Register to the selected fair; await admission from the fair organiser
- Select a stand construction company
- Brief the design and stand construction company
- Order organisational services such as interpreters, temporary staff, catering, security, and so on
- Supporting advertising options during the fair
- Opt for events on the stand to attract more visitors
- Ship merchandise to the fair venue, considering import and export regulations
- Select and train people to man the stand
- Apply for visas and reserve and book hotels and flights
- Ship merchandise back to the country of origin

Almost all exhibiting companies in Europe, especially in Germany, have at least one person on the payroll who is in charge of all activities regarding participation in trade fairs. This job is rarely outsourced to an external company because they lack internal knowledge of the company structure, and are not linked to various departments such as the management, marketing, PR, product developments, distribution and the sales force.

The person appointed to assume this important position in the exhibiting company may be employed permanently as Project Manager Fairs and Exhibitions, with full responsibility, or only temporarily. This depends entirely on the number of fairs the company participates in each year. Large enterprises often have an independent well-staffed exhibition department. They do not work as sub-departments of the advertising or sales department, but are very often placed directly under top management with direct access to decision-makers.

What is very common in Europe remains an exception in China. Only big brands work with trained, professional internal project managers or have established a dedicated fair and exhibition department. Most small or medium-sized companies temporarily appoint a secretary or another clerk from the company to organise and execute fairs. They train themselves by way of "learning by doing". Once they have organised a few fairs and learnt the various steps required for successful participation in fairs, they are able to perform this job without any problems.

4 Literature

All data and information in this article have been retrieved from China features in weekly magazines or newspapers like Der Spiegel, Focus, Die Welt, FAZ and trade fair publications like m+a report, TradeFairs, EXPO, events – and of course boundless information from AUMA in Berlin.

Why China needs more Professional Congress Organisers (PCOs)

Seifert, Frank,
Ding, Yi

中国为什么需要更多的 PCO？

After the generalisation and analysis of the current situation in the Chinese meeting industry, the article claims that the industry has developed dramatically but is still in its youth. This is mainly shown in the low usage of PCOs in the Chinese meeting organisation and management. Since the establishment of ICCA and IAPCO, founded in the 1960s, a PCO's role and function has been recognised by the international meeting industry. Hence, the Chinese meeting industry should develop more PCOs to increase its efficiency, which relies on the co-efforts of the educators and the practitioners.

文章对中国会议业的发展现状进行了总结和分析，认为中国的会议经济在过去的几十年间有了长足的发展，但仍然处于发展的幼稚期，这主要体现在会议的组织与管理中使用 PCO 的比例相对较低。随着上世纪 60 年代 ICCA 和 IAPCO 的成立，PCO 对会议业发展的作用和功能已被国际会议界广泛认可，因此中国的会议业的发展需要更多 PCO 的加入来提高效率，而这有赖于教育界和行业的共同努力。

1 The development of Professional Congress Organisers (PCOs)

The meetings and event industry in China is developing very fast. Many national Chinese meetings/events are taking place and there is a great need for intensifying the communication between people within companies, government, private entities and other by means of meetings/events. In addition there is the wish to participate in the international meetings and event business. That is also why many new meetings facilities have been built.

Therefore there is a growing need of companies or single persons who are able to manage and organise these meetings/events, the so called Professional Congress Organisers (PCOs). How did the profession of Professional Congress Organisers develop? Its concept is going back to the year 1962 when two travel agents from Mexico City and Paris came together to take advantage of the then-new phenomenon of international association meetings travelling round the world being stimulated by the introduction of commercial aircrafts and airlines. They wanted to discuss how to share information about the rising meetings business and to obtain competitive advantage and win a bigger slice of the travel revenue from this fast emerging market. Five more travel agents from other regions of the world became involved and in 1963 they founded the International Congress and Convention Association ICCA.

So the beginning of the PCOs profession was the travel business. But very soon the travel agents recognised that their clients, the international associations were not only looking for travel assistance but they also wanted to receive service in organising their meetings and that is why these travel agents added to their travel services those of organising meetings, the Professional Congress Organiser was on the map.

This leads to the fact that not only travel agents organised meetings but more and more specialists came into the business who concentrated on the organisation of meetings without the travel option. Therefore some PCOs decided in January 1968 to create a new group to develop systematically the PCO business and founded the International Association of Professional Congress Organisers, IAPCO, whereas ICCA took care for the meetings business in all its aspects.

In the sixties and seventies the meetings market was fast growing and not only international associations organised meetings but more and more companies came into the business. More services in the organisation of these meetings were asked and especially the development of technical innovations demanded more specialisation by the PCOs.

Let us have a look into the spectrum of services of Professional Congress Organisers.

1.1 The role of the PCOs in the MICE industry

Many service providers are responsible for the success of a meeting or an event: Venues, hotels, airlines, travel agents, technicians, caterers etc. The Professional Congress Organiser, PCO, plays an outstanding part in organising a meeting or an event.

The PCO is a company, which specialises in the management of meetings and events. He will act as a consultant to the organising body, enacting its decisions whilst utilising the experience and knowledge it has gained over many years in organising meeting and events. He is the partner of the initiator of a meeting or event.

To better understand the diversity of the PCO business let us have a look into the duties of a PCO. His work divides into the following parts:

1. **Meeting place**

The first step is to analyse the needs of the meeting/event and of the initiator, what are the targets of the initiator, what is the expected size of the meeting/event, in which year and at what time of the year will it take place, are there any pre-settings where it should be organised. Next step is the search for the suitable meeting place. After the decision is taken, the PCO has to find the meeting venue, negotiate the requirements and prices and book the meeting rooms and other necessary facilities, like exhibition space or rooms for the meeting secretariat. He has also to book the technical equipment and technicians.

2. Programme conception work

Following the specifications of the initiator the PCO assists in developing the programme and the programme structure of the meeting/event. He is putting together an organisation chart with responsibilities to ensure a smooth management of the meeting/event. A detailed time table helps being always at the right stage of the planning.

3. Budget/Finances

At the earliest possible stage the PCO has to develop the budget for the meeting/event, which the initiator has to agree and approve. This will be the guideline for all preparation activities. The PCO is also responsible for the frequent budget control and as to give a regular status report to the initiator.

Another duty is to find sponsors for the financing along with a discretionary finance management. It goes without saying that after the end of the meeting/event the PCO has to draw up the final account.

4. Marketing/Advertisement

Important responsibility of the PCO is the promotion of the meeting/event in order to get as many participants as possible. Part of this promotion is the production and print of the programme and to develop the internet presentation of the programme.

5. Hotels

Months, sometimes even years before the beginning of the meeting/event, the PCO has to book the hotel room allotments to assure that there is enough hotel accommodation for the participants in different hotel categories. He has to do the administration of the hotel room allotments following the registrations of the participants, including the booking of the finally needed hotel rooms and to send out the booking confirmations to the participants.

6. Administration of participants

One of the main tasks is the registration of participants and the collection of the participation fees. This activity includes the sending of invoices and of the participation confirmations. Needless to say is that the whole communication with the participants is the duty of the PCO. The preparation of the meeting/event kids and the on site registration are part of the administration of participants.

7. Lecturer administration

All lecturers have to be registered. The lecturers' technical requirements have to be coordinated. Travel organisation and organisation of VIP transfers for the lecturers are other duties. The PCO has to manage the travel expense accounting and the on site registration and assistance to the lecturers during the whole meeting/event.

8. Exhibition/Poster exhibition

Following the decision of the initiator the PCO has to organise the linked exhibition or poster exhibition to the meeting/event. The administration of the exhibitors and poster presenters include the preparation of the exhibitor's manual and the guidelines for the posters.

9. Abstract handling

PCO's duty is the collection and administration of abstracts and the production of the meeting/event documentation, the proceedings. This can be done in a printed or electronic way with abstracts or full manuscripts.

10. Translation

Early enough should be done the booking of simultaneous interpreters and necessary translation equipment, followed by the administration of the interpreters.

11. Social programme

The PCO is responsible for social activities like the conception and handling of technical visits, sightseeing tours, organisation of receptions and the organisation of galas, evening events and dinners.

12. Employment of staff

The PCO has to book the on site personnel (hostesses and other temporary assistant staff). The briefing and supervising of the on site personnel is very important.

13. On site management

After all the preparation activities the work of the PCO starts with the on site management: Installation of registration counters, installation of a fully equipped meetings/events secretariat, coordination of technical equipment and technicians, organisation of coffee breaks and luncheons, decoration, signposting and transfers

1.2 The development and characteristics of the China MICE Industry

1.2.1 Exponential growth resulting in the rank of eight in the global meeting market

There was hardly any international meeting held in China until the reform in 1980s when China swiftly merged into the international society. The China Meeting Market has developed in an exponential growth (ICCA 2014a), According to ICCA's statistics, China has taken the 8th position in the global meeting market with 340 international meetings held in 2013 (ICCA 2013).

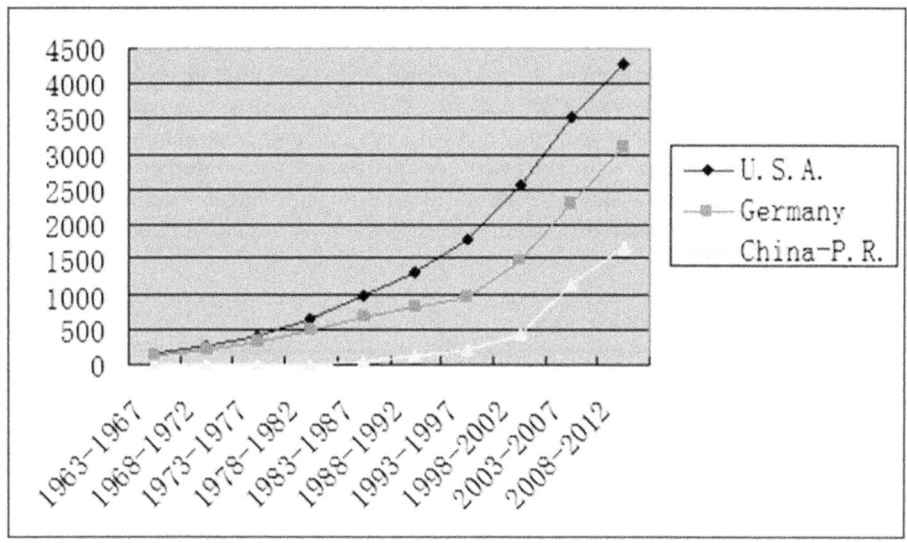

Image 1: The developing trend of meeting industry in USA, Germany and China from 1963 to 2012 (ICCA 2014a).

1.2.2 Meetings distributed with a 'More in East China, Fewer in Central and West China' geographical pattern

45 per cent of meetings are held in East China, followed by North China with 16 per cent. North China ranks No. three with 14 per cent of meetings. Central China, South West China and North West China have relatively fewer meetings, taking ten per cent, eight per cent, and five per cent respectively. South East China sees the fewest meetings with only two per cent share of the whole market (CTHA 2013).

According to ICCA, the top ten meeting cities in China are Beijing, Shanghai, Hangzhou, Nanjing, Chengdu, Guangzhou, Wuhan, Xian, Shenzhen and Suzhou. Four cites come from East China, namely Shanghai, Hangzhou, Nanjing and Suzhou. Two cities are from South China, which are Guangzhou and Shenzhen. North China, South West China and North West China each have one (ICCA 2013). This demonstrates again the geographical pattern of 'more in East China, fewer in central and West China'.

1.2.3 The ratio of international meetings over domestic meetings is 1:41

According to the survey made by CTHA in 2011, there were 377 international meetings in the total of 15980 meetings, showing the ratio of international meetings over domestic meetings is 1:41. It is worth mentioning that the criteria of being an international meeting are not the same between China and ICCA. ICCA asserts that international meetings should be rotated in more than three countries, whereas China entitles any meeting with delegates coming from three or more countries or districts (Hong Kong, Macau and Chinese Taipei are not included) an international meeting. Therefore, usually the number of ICCA's international meeting is fewer than what China counts.

1.2.4　More than 98 per cent of meetings held in hotels

ICCA claims that the most popular venues for international association meetings are hotels, which takes the share of 45.4 per cent (ICCA 2011). This aligns with the China's case except for the percentage is 97 per cent and only 3.1 per cent meetings use conference centres (CTHA 2013). This again agrees with Davidson's results, except that conference centres take a share of 13.9 per cent, which indicates PCOs usually manage larger meetings naturally requiring bigger venues. Davidson further concludes that a higher usage of hotels shows that most meetings in China are corporate meetings (Davidson 2013).

Tab. 1:　Venues used in China Meeting Market.

	CTHA etc. (per cent)		Davidson (per cent)	
Hotels	Business Hotels	80.7	81	
	Resorts	16.1		
Convention centres	3.1		13.9	
Others	0.1		University	1.3
			Other	3.8
	100		100	

1.3　The main suppliers of the China MICE market

1.3.1　Venues

1. Venues show the same geographical pattern as the number of meetings: 'More in East China, Fewer in Central and West China'

The table below shows that the distribution of Chinese meeting venues also complies with the same geographical pattern of the number of meetings: 'more in East China, fewer in Central and West China'. Although both data of CTHA and ICCA support the view, ICCA's data shows a higher percentage in North China in both meetings and venues. The reason is that Beijing is located in North China, which has attracted more international meetings. Also, more venues in Beijing have become the members of ICCA.

Tab. 2:　Geographical pattern of venue distribution in China Meeting Market.

	CTHA (per cent)		ICCA (per cent)	
	meetings	venues	meetings	venues
East China	45	47	42	27
South China	16	12	6	27
North China	14	12	38	37
Central China	10	10	4	0
South West	8	9	6	9
North West	5	4	3	0
North East	2	6	1	0
Total	100	100	100	100

2. The number of China hotels remains stable in recent five years

In the recent five years, the number of hotels remains stable with a small fluctuation from 13500 to 14000 (National Bureau of Statistics 2014). As mentioned previously, almost 97 per cent of meetings are held in hotels. This indicates that the hotels have satisfied the needs of the meetings because the largest initiators are corporate and government and the size of the meetings are relatively small.

1.3.2 PCOs

1. Most of China meetings managed by initiators rather than PCOs

The majority of the meetings in China are organized by the initiators themselves with a small percentage organised by PCOs. According to CTHA, the former occupies 88.1 per cent and the latter 11.9 per cent (CTHA 2013). The reasons are two-folded: firstly, Chinese enterprises or institutions have long followed the 'small and fully equipped' rule, which means all processes from the production, distribution and marketing are integrated fully in each organization with very little corporation with others, this results a lower specialized industry in China. Traditionally, the administrative department takes care of meeting organization. Secondly, in their interpretation, using their own staff rather than the outside PCOs is more cost efficient. One thing worth mentioned is that there are many in-house PCOs in government and big-scaled enterprises which perform at a high standard. However, how many they are is not available currently.

2. PCOs under rapid growth with various developing history

PCOs were developed initially after 2000. Presently, there are 16 members under the Meeting Management sector of ICCA (ICCA 2014b). These PCOs can be categorized into four types: firstly, domestic PCOs, which takes 33 per cent of the PCO market. Secondly, a branch of an international PCO, such as Triumph Group in Italy and MCI in Switzerland. This type occupies 13 per cent of the market. Thirdly, domestic PCOs originated from other MICE suppliers, such as airlines or venues. For example, Shanghai Airlines Event Management Company, this category owns 13 per cent of the market. The last one also the largest one is evolved from name branded Chinese travel agencies, such as China CYTS MICE Service Co. Ltd, and CTS MICE service Co. Ltd, they have taken 44 per cent of the market.

The evolution from travel agencies to PCOs has taken the advantages of being travel agencies, which are the experiences in venue selection, accommodation arrangement, events planning and group registration. Furthermore, Chinese government believes that MICE belongs to 'high-end tourism' and has promoted this transformation strongly by the means of policy and monetary support. Meanwhile the Tourism Industry Association has strengthened the training in conference management for their members, and a new sector 'MICE Committee' was set up accordingly in 2011 (CTHA 2013).

One more thing should be noted is that some well-established overseas PCOs have operated in the China MICE Market. These companies possess excellent professional skills, communication capacity with international clients and customer database. Therefore, this force becomes an inevitable competition in the industry.

1.4 The role of the PCOs for the development of the MICE industry in China

The PCO is not only a service provider, but he has also a responsibility in developing the business in his country and city where he is active, not least in a vested interest.

That means that the PCO has to develop marketing activities towards a potential clientele which is keeping contact with national and international associations, national and international big companies and government organisations. In addition the PCOs should communicate with national and local Convention and Visitors Bureaus and venues and convention hotels to join forces in convincing the target groups to held meetings continuously in the country and their home cities and in bidding processes. Another important activity of a PCO is to convince government authorities that the meetings and events business is a big economic factor for cities and the country in the whole. Let us have a look into the benefits of a meeting:

- Additional local/regional income (hotels, shops, restaurants, pre- and post-tours)
- Additional tax revenues from commerce (hotels, shops, restaurants etc.)
- Increase in the number of tourists after the meeting (delegates who are coming back for holidays)
- Generation and protection of employment (hotel staff, restaurant staff, temporary staff etc.)
- Image

As an example, here the economic significance of meetings to the US economy[2] in 2011:

- Total economic output to the US economy: 907 billion USD = 5.606 billion CNY
- Total economic output, contribution to GDP: 458 billion USD = 2.830 billion CNY
- Total economic output, in labour income: 271 billion USD = 1.675 billion CNY
- Total economic output: 6.3 million full-time and part-time jobs
- The US meetings industry directly supports 1.7 million jobs

In 2011 the income of the meetings industry for Beijing was 1.017,2 million CNY, for Shanghai 659,8 million CNY (CIC, US Convention Industry Council 2011)

This is additional income, additional purchasing power for the cities generated by the meetings business. And the figures are only showing the primary effect. They are even higher if you add the secondary effects like employment, taxes etc.

The PCO can very much contribute to the development of the MICE industry in China through his own activities especially his marketing work. As he has an interest to develop his own business, he will keep contact with his national potential clients, that means national associations, companies and government authorities. Moreover he will be interested in international business and focus on international associations and international Non Governmental Organisations (NGOs) as they generate most of the international meetings business on a continuous level. Therefore it is essential for a PCO to have close contact with for instance the International Union of Associations UIA for the development of his client database or be part of his professional organisations like the International Congress and Convention Association ICCA or the International Association of Professional Congress Organisers IAPCO to exchange business with colleagues on an international level and use the ICCA database of international associations.

2 What to do to develop the PCO business

The meetings business in China is still very young and actually in the process of fast development. That is one of the reasons why PCO business is still at the beginning of its development. We have shown under 3.2.1 that only 11.9 per cent of the meetings in China is organised by PCOs. One of the reasons is that there are not as many PCOs on the market, only 16 following the ICCA Meeting Management sector. And these are concentrating only in four cities: Beijing (6), Shanghai (8), Xiamen (1), Hangzhou (1). And the Chinese initiators of meetings have to realise that it is not very cost-effective to hold own staff for the organisation of maybe one or two meetings a year but to pay salary for the rest of the year. It is more economic to let a PCO organise the meeting and to pay a reasonable price for this service and to save overheads.

Why more PCOs in China are needed? If we are only looking into the international business: In 2013 340 international meetings have been held in China with about 225,000 participants which on average is about 660 participants per meeting.

A skilled and well organised PCO can handle about six meetings of that kind per year. Keeping in mind that 660 is only an average figure, there are many meetings with more than these 660 participants but with 1,000 up to 3,000 and more. If we relate these six meetings per PCO with the 340 meetings held in China in 2013 we should have about 55 PCOs in China. Actually, to look into the ICCA list of PCOs in China there are just 16 PCOs which means a lack of 39 PCOs at present. And the meetings business in China is growing fast. And if the domestic business is more and more looking for the professional services of a PCO, even 55 PCOs will not be sufficient in the future.

So what to do to get more PCOs into the market as there is enough business – more education and training is needed. More education programmes are needed like the programme of the Shanghai University of Business and Economics. And it needs entrepreneurship of those who finished these education programmes.

The tourism authorities and here especially the Convention and Visitors Bureaus also have a responsibility to encourage whether their own staff or people in their business environment to start into the PCO business and to give them any necessary support. The volume of the PCO business, as shown above, is actually already very high and it is still increasing.

The same applies for venues (more the Congress Centres than the hotels). They could even think of establishing an inhouse PCO under their own control.

The past experience has shown that even in times of economic recession, the meetings and events business was growing from year to year, especially on the international level. And this development will continue and the business in China being just at the beginning of its development will continuously grow in the coming years. Good reasons for PCOs to establish an own business. 16 PCOs at present, there is surely enough place for far more PCOs. The market will need them.

3 Literature

CTHA (ed.) (2013), *China Tourist Hotel Association: Statistic Report on China Meeting Market*, Beijing: Tourism Education Press

Davidson, Rob (2013), *China MICE Buyers Report* (Chinese Meeting Planners' Site Selection Survey). Beijing: CIBTM

ICCA (2011), *Statistic Report 2002–2011: International Association Meetings Market*. Online: http://www.iccaworld.com/newsarchives/archivedetails.cfm?id=3195 (accessed 06 Oct. 2014)

ICCA (2013), *2013 ICCA Statistics Report*. Online: http://www.iccaworld.com/npps/story.cfm?nppage=3537 (accessed 06 Oct. 2014)

ICCA (2014a), *ICCA 50-year statistics: International association meetings market shows exponential growth*. Online: http://www.iccaworld.com/npps/story.cfm?nppage=3823 (accessed 06 Oct. 2014)

ICCA (2014b), *Membership Directory*. Online: http://members.iccaworld.com (accessed 06 Oct. 2014)

McCabe, Vivienne; Poole, Barry; Weeks, Paul & Leiper, Neil (2000), *The Business and Management of Conventions*, Queensland: John Wiley & Sons Australia, Ltd.

National Bureau Of Statistics (2014), *The general statistic of Tourism market*

CIC (2011), *Economic Significance of the Meetings and Events Industry to the US Economy*, conducted by Pricewaterhouse Coopers US. Online: http://www.conventionindustry.org/Files/2012%20ESS/CIC%20Meetings%20ESS%20Update%20EXECUTIVE%20SUMMARY-FINAL.pdf

How to organise successful meetings in China

Gao, Frankie

如何在中国主办成功的会议

Following the rapid growth of the Chinese economy, the Chinese MICE industry has played an increasingly important role to be part of the economy. Focusing on the international association meetings, the article suggests a successful meeting should be able to generate profits, impact the local industry positively and provide business opportunities for the attendees. Also, the article discusses the bidding process, congress organisation, sustainability and digitalised meetings in China.

随着中国经济的发展，会议业已经成为经济发展的重要组成部分。文章聚焦于协会会议，提出衡量一个会议是否成功的三个因素，即是否能够盈利，会议的主题对当地行业是否带来积极影响，以及是否会为参会人员带来生意机会。文章还就会议的竞标、会议的组织、可持续发展和数字化会议等议题进行了讨论。

1 Introduction

Since China joined in WTO in 2001, the government has developed a blueprint plan for the China's meetings and exhibition industry's future development. The Olympics Beijing 2008 and Shanghai World Expo 2010 have also pushed China in the spotlight of the global stage after receiving much positive feedback from international delegates and audience around the world sitting in front of the TV. The people, who had never been to China were impressed by China's capability of organizing such large-scaled events. This convinced the government to further support action to promote the local meetings industry. China's meetings and exhibition industry grew by 15–20 % in the following years and it is predicted in the China's 12th Five Year plan that the industry value will surpass China Renminbi Yuan (CNY) 300 Billion in 2015 (Meadin 2012).

Also from the point of view that China is the world's second-largest economy in 2013 by total Gross Domestic Product (GDP), which is the accumulated contribution of diversified industries, the shortage of talents has become a challenge for the country. The desire for local talents has encouraged new knowledge, business exchange opportunities and places to share their ideas and thoughts. Meetings, especially international meetings, provide exactly the platform to fill any gaps. Industry experts, new talents and company representatives want to attend international and local meetings to acquire new knowledge and extend business opportunities. National associations are also working with international associations to explore education and business opportunities for local communities.

The focus of this article is on international association meetings, which are drastically different from government or corporate events. Bringing international congresses to China is one important objective of local governments. The reason is obvious – the international congresses are normally large, longer and involve more programmes, which have a bigger impact on the related industries and the economy. In addition, the government also encourages the global PCOs (Professional Congress Organiser) and PEOs (Professional Exhibition Organiser) who possess advanced expertise in meetings and exhibition management to establish branches in China. This article will offer some guidelines and new trends in congress bidding, congress management and how to measure a successful meeting.

Sustainability adapted to meetings is not common in China. This article will introduce some concept of the sustainability solution, too.

Thinking of a Press Conference in the year 2005 in China, every journalist held a camera and a heavy laptop. At present, they carry just an iPhone or Pad. Technology is changing the way of organising a meeting as well as shifting our life style. The article will also cover the topic of the latest meetings' technology at the last page.

2 Types of meetings

Meetings can be categorised into three main types with respect to their organisers:

- Corporate meetings
- Association meetings
- Government meetings

Each type of meeting has different goals, budget sources, target audience and decision-making processes.

Tab. 1: Comparison between different types of meetings.

	Meeting samples	Goals	Audience
Corporation-Internal	Training Board Meeting Incentive program AKM (Annual Kick-off Meeting)	Education/Information Performance Improvement	Internal staff
Corporation-External	Investors Meeting Road show Client meeting Sponsoring / exhibiting event	Information Client Experience Enhancement Sales Goals	Shareholders, Clients Distributors
Association-Internal	AGM Board Meeting Committee Meeting	Information Decision-making	Board members Staff
Association-External	Association-External Congress Annual Meeting Trade shows	Education Business exchange Standards Reputation	Members Non-members Partners
Government and Institutions	C-level meeting	Information Governance Lobby Appeal	Officers Press

Source: Carey, T. Professional Meeting Management – A European Handbook, MPI-Foundation, 1999, Brussels

Definition of International Association Meetings:

The leading global meetings industry network – ICCA (International Congress and Convention Association) defines the international meetings as having three characteristics: (a) they must be held on a regular basis; (b) they must have at least 50 delegates; (c) and they should rotate between at least three countries. Congress is a common terminology to describe a large association meeting and will frequently be used in this article.

3 International congress – bidding process

According to the ICCA 2013 Statistics Report, China has moved to 8 in 2013 from 10 in 2012 by the total international meetings number, as an attractive congress destination in Asia, which means China will have increasing opportunities in bidding international congresses in the future. From the destination bidding to a successful congress management, it normally takes more than one year, or sometimes even more than two years for large and less frequent meetings. There are some standard procedures and guidelines for participating in a congress bidding.

3.1 Bidding process

Figure 1 gives a simple introduction of a complete congress bidding process, which a large number of associations are following.

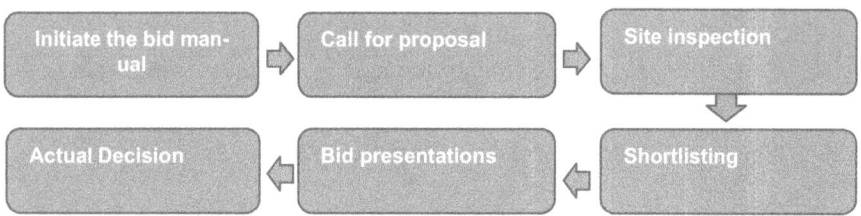

Figure 1: International congress – bidding process.
Source: ICCA Intelligence: International association meetings: bidding and decision-making

Here is an example of a step-by-step pathway. Some associations may have additional stages in their process, whilst others will have shorter and less complex processes (ICCA Intelligence 2014)

- Call for proposals/next "Open Year" communicated.
- Interest expressed (by either members or suppliers, depending on whether local members are required to be the formal bidders).
- Evaluate if bidders qualify to make a bid.
- Bid manual/guidelines/rules made available to interested parties.
- Bids created by local members/suppliers.
- Bids submitted.
- Site inspections (many associations conduct the shortlisting stage without visiting all candidates)
- First round evaluations by association staff, volunteer leaders or consultants/contractors.
- Shortlist decided and announced.
- Detailed site inspections and negotiations.

Revised bids submitted.

Formal bid presentation.

- Final shortlist or final selection.
- Negotiations.
- Decision made.
- Decision announced.
- Feedback to losing bidders.
- Draw up and sign contract or letter of agreement.

3.2 Decision makers

Decision makers differ from association to association. In general, the decision makers are single volunteer leaders (e. g. President or Chairman), association executive (e. g. CEO) or a group of people, e. g. Board of Directors, Congress Committee, National representatives or all members (e. g. via online referendum).

Tips on the congress bidding

- Get government's support
- Study the local market, if there is a strong academic community, who helps to generate local influence on the targeted audience and the society
- Know the competitors and demonstrate the unique selling points in the proposals
- It is necessary to organise a supportive and competent Local Bidding Committee (see Figure 2), generally consisting of government representatives or CVB (Convention Visitors Bureau) key opinion leaders of the industry, and a PCO.

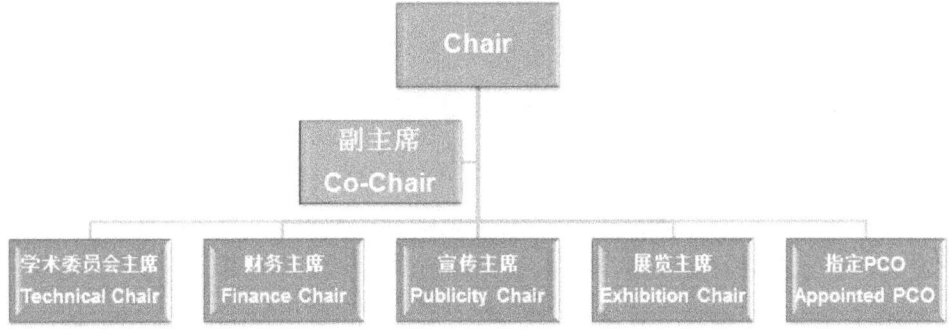

Figure 2: Structure of the Local Bidding Committee, Source: MCI

A PCO can play an important role in the congress bidding process with its rich knowledge about the congress management (see Figure 3). In the past 30 years in China, state-owned associations like the CICCST (China International Conference Center for Science and Technology) and CMA (Chinese Medical Association) dominated the international and domestic congresses' organization. Nowadays, it is common to involve professional PCOs to organize international congresses in China (Wu 2008).

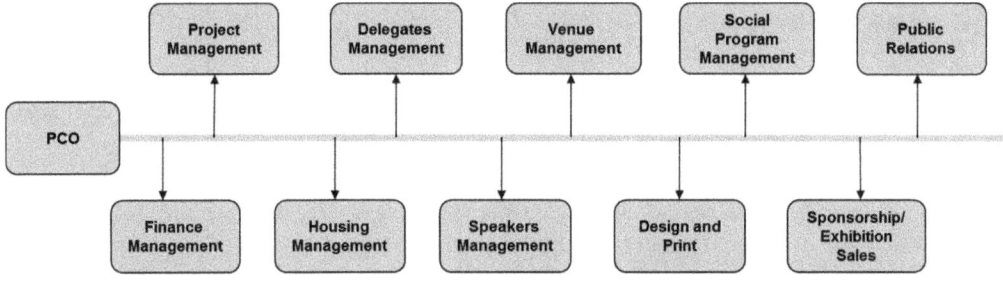

Figure 3: PCO's main responsibilities in the congress management. Source: MCI

4 International congress organisation

This section will focus on changes and trends in the following key steps in the congress organization.

4.1 Local congress committee:

Generally speaking, the international congresses are organized by a Local Congress Committee, which consists of the three committees (see Image 4):

- Academic Committee: normally the committee members are experts of the respective industry of the congress or board members of the association who are responsible for generating the congress theme and topics.
- Executive Committee: the PCO usually assumes this role and is in charge of all the perspectives of the congress management.
- Finance Committee: include representatives from both international associations and the PCO. The PCO is good at cost control and profit generation which supports the healthy financial status of the international congress.

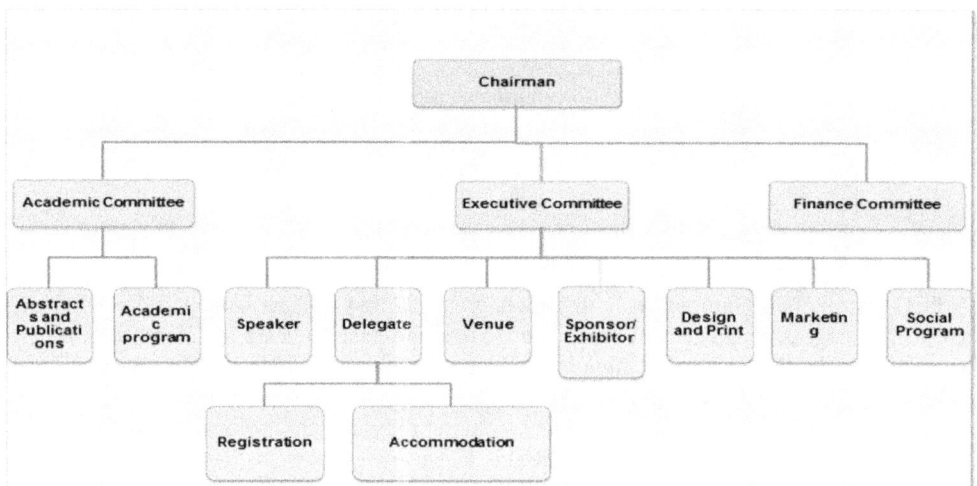

Figure 4: A General Structure of a Local Congress Committee.

4.2 Venue

Increasing investments have been made in China's meeting infrastructure in recent years, which offer PCO more options for organising congresses. The new meeting infrastructure and incentives policies from the local governments are apparently alluring for PCO when selecting a venue, but key elements to keep in mind also include the experience of organising congresses with the same scale as well as the professional level of the venue staff, which also means a lot for a successful meeting. When selecting a city, it is necessary to consider the city's characteristics – Macau is a perfect place for incentive event, but the gambling heaven is absolutely not the right place for academic meetings. Also accessibility is crucial for international congresses – how many direct international flights connect this city.

4.3 Registration

Signing into a congress is getting easier than before! Registration is not limited to your name, job title and email. QR-code and social media accounts are also needed for the registration, enabling the delegates to immediately connect to their social media community members and exchange personal contact information. With an acquisition strategy for additional key markets, more delegates outside of the country will be attracted to the congress as well.

4.4 Sponsorship and exhibition

The sponsors and exhibitors will not be limited to the same industry. Companies from information and communication technology (ICT) can also sponsor a medical meeting. For example, GoogleFit, a newly released healthcare platform and Samsung's Simband, a wrist band which can track health status, are also targeting the healthcare industry. Let's think big with a continuous learning mind!

4.5 Marketing

Digital marketing is making an increasing impact on the overall event marketing strategy. In China, promoting an international congress is not constrained to an email or a call. Posts and videos on social media is a must-do tactic. It is equally important to recognise local key opinion leaders and leading associations to spread the words, normally quite useful.

5 Measuring a successful congress

Below are the three key judging criteria to decide if this congress is successful or not, but it is not limited to these three.

– A profitable business model

Generally speaking, a financial goal was set up before a congress begins. Not like company events, which normally have a fixed budget, associations usually can acquire additional income by organising an international congress. A profitable congress in terms of a satisfactory

ROI (Return On Investment) is very important for an association, supporting the organisation to grow sustainably and create sustainable value to its members.

– The congress topics have positive impact on the local industry

Top of the congress objectives for most congresses is education and knowledge sharing. A high quality meeting contains cutting-edge knowledge for local audience. With the new technology, the meeting content is also reachable by extended online audience.

– Provide business opportunities

Nowadays, more new forms of interaction are designed before, during and after the congresses to maximize the business opportunities. Business Exchange Sessions like eight minutes fast-meetings are set apart from the trade show to create more exchange opportunities. Social media, congress mobile app and devices like Spotme (a smart device enables immediate e-business card exchange) also accelerate the efficiency of business exchange.

6   Sustainability

Many multinational companies and international associations take sustainability seriously: they are dedicated to the engagement in the sustainability activities and even release annual CSR (Corporate Social Responsibility) Report. The benefits of adapting sustainability strategies include, but are not limited to:

– Build brand reputation
– Reduce the operation cost
– Accelerate innovation
– Sustainability consists of three pillars: people, planet and profits.
– "People" pertains to fair and beneficial business practices toward labour and the community and region in which a corporation conducts its business.
– "Planet" refers to sustainable environmental practices – require a corporation not to harm and minimize environmental impact.
– "Profit" is the economic value created by the organization after deducting the cost of all input (Wikipedia).

Many global corporations add sustainability in their vendor evaluation form as one criterion. Hence, as a Meeting Solution Provider, PCOs shall also be equipped with sustainability knowledge and capability of executing sustainability events. There are actually lots of new ideas for a congress from reducing waste and pollution to improving staff health and wellbeing, from planting a tree to spending time with minorities.

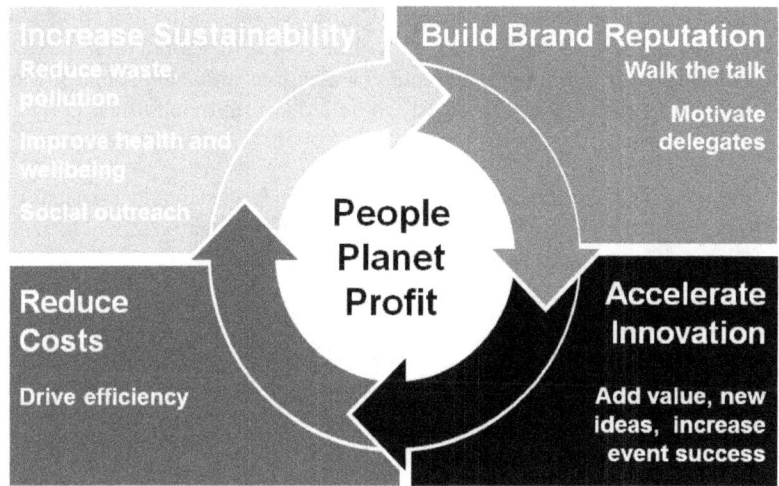

Figure 5: Sustainability Values. Source: MCI

7 Digitise the meeting business

Though the physical meetings are still dominating the meetings industry in China, tremendous development in the digital world has been changing the way we communicate and capture knowledge. Besides, the sluggish economy forces lots of companies to cut back the travel budget and invest in electronic equipment for online meetings and reduce the face-to-face interaction opportunities. People are also ready to welcome the online meetings too with equipped devices (smart phones, pads, laptops) and online tools (Mobile apps, social media network, chat tools). The obvious values of digital meetings include but are not limited to the following:

- Diverse audience experience
- Enhanced, sharable content
- Personalized schedules
- Take networking to a new level
- Make changes on the fly
- Put sponsors front and centre
- Get real-time analytics
- Customization options
- Gamify your event
- Keep the conversation going

These changes are impacting the meetings industry in China. Mobile communication has been integrated into events; virtual or hybrid meetings will be more and more common. We expect technology to help drive outstanding results into our meetings and events, and if it is not a digital meeting, it shall be run digitally. Be ready to be a platform transformer, content copyrighter and technology owner!

With the increasing number of ICCA members and MPI (Meeting Professionals International)-members from China, we expect to see a more mature meetings industry in China with talents with increasing expertise, and with passion!

8 Literature

ICCA-Statistics Report 2013, http://www.iccaworld.com/npps/story.cfm?nppage=3537

ICCA Intelligence 2014: International association meetings: bidding and decision-making Online: http://www.iccaworld.com/cdps/cditem.cfm?nid=4089 (assessed on 31.Dec.2014)

MCI-group, http://mci-group.com/en

Meadin 2012: Online: http://res.meadin.com/areaAnalysis/73534_1.shtml

Wu, Shaoyuan 2008: 2008 Meeting of the International Association for Earth-quake engineering – successful bidding case study. Online: http://www.meetingschina.com/news145.html

The evolution of the Chinese events market – An agency perspective

Dams, Colja M.

德国会展公司分享在中国发展的经验

This article explores the specifics of the Chinese event industry and how it has evolved over the past decade. Based on the exemplary development of VOK DAMS China, it examines the particularities of the Chinese events market ten years ago compared to their importance and relevance today. Analysing and juxtaposing the past and present, the article closes with a brief outlook on the future and the trends that will shape the events industry not just in China, but all over the world.

本文探讨了中国会展行业的特点，以及其在过去十年的演变。基于 VOKDAMS 在中国的发展样本，文章总结了中国会展市场在十年前的特征，并重新评估其在当今的重要性和关联性。在把过去和现在进行对照分析后，文章在结尾对会展行业的将来和发展趋势做一个简短的展望，这个展望不仅是针对中国，更是对全世界而言。

1 Introduction

It was as early as in 2003 that the event agency VOK DAMS first started thinking seriously about expanding into China. Intense research was initiated and funded to identify the potential, the opportunities and challenges of such an endeavour. At that time, very little was known about the events market in China. Although large corporations had been expanding to China and the Chinese economy was booming, there was only a limited number of rather small-scale agencies that focused on PR and marketing activities, and also offered events.

However, with the biggest event in the world – the Olympic Games – looming on the horizon in 2008, it became obvious that China had a huge, untapped potential for events and event planning.

Since the market research funded by VOK DAMS also stressed China's potential – it estimated that the Chinese events market grew by 41 per cent in 2003 – VOK DAMS aimed to find out how best to open an office in Beijing. After having originally started out with a joint venture partner, it soon became obvious that it would be quicker to establish a self-contained marketing company that would be more successful and much more flexible. However, VOK DAMS was adamant that local expertise and know-how had to be substantially integrated into the office to ensure the agency's continued success. We believed that a solution of merely "implanting" a German or European team into the Chinese market would be doomed to failure. Hence this was the start of the (simple but efficient) recipe for the successful story of VOK DAMS in China: combining a high standard of quality with local know-how; combining international expertise with local creativity.

This was particularly the case because we had identified large German corporations with branches in China as our main target group for the Chinese market. The idea was that German companies with experience in operating successfully with VOK DAMS in various locations in Germany and Europe would view VOK DAMS as a familiar partner in China. However, it was also clear that these corporations would have to be given the same high standard of quality to which they had become accustomed in other markets. We knew that we would only achieve this if we focused on, integrated and embraced Chinese know-how and expertise, merging it with the industry standards and principles that had evolved in Western markets over the past two decades.

It may sound simple, but this approach in which "the best of both worlds" was exploited was the foundation of our success. The tenth anniversary of our office opening in Beijing and the fifth anniversary of our Shanghai office, both of which we celebrate in 2014, are the best proof of the success of this strategy.

It goes without saying that the decision to open a branch in China was also prompted by our clients – primarily our automobile clients – who were increasingly asking us to help them establish, design and implement events in China. The automotive industry, which soon discovered China as an important market, was experiencing growing competition. Volkswagen in particular felt that, what had once almost been a monopoly position in China's automotive market, was increasingly being threatened by competitors. Let us recall: Volkswagen had a head start in China, where it established connections as early as in 1978 and had enjoyed a leading position for more than 25 years.

The automotive industry had long embraced events and live marketing measures as essential features for brand communication and for retaining existing customers and gaining new ones. It would almost be fair to say that the growth and expansion of the automotive industry, and competition within it, directly influenced the growth and expansion of the Chinese events industry (and, of course, competition within it). Even now, many of our clients are from the automotive industry, which can be viewed as a 'pace-maker' for events and live marketing.

However, two additional decisive factors were instrumental in professionalising and expanding the Chinese events industry: the Beijing Olympics in 2008 and the Expo 2010 in Shanghai. The former in particular played a highly influential role for events and the development of the events industry in China. Successful cooperation between Chinese artists – such as internationally acclaimed filmmaker Zhang Yimou as General Director, choreographer Zhang Jigang and composer Qigang Cheng – and creative and production experts from the American branding agency Jack Morton Worldwide is a perfect example of the huge potential, the appeal and success of events hosted in China. This was even more the case because they were created following the perfect merger of "the best of both (or rather: several) worlds".

In contrast to some agencies, which merely flew in teams to help support events surrounding the Olympic Games and opened "event camps" to be left and evacuated, or resumed and re-assembled depending on market demand, VOK DAMS had always been adamant about the necessity to establish fixed teams and offices if it was to succeed in China. We had a nucleus of experts, a well-developed supplier network and a wide range of freelance experts who could be hired, depending on the expertise required. In addition, we could always rely on a large body of steady, established colleagues, some of whom had been with us from the very start. They "grew up" with us, and now embody this mixture of local know-how and expertise paired with international quality standards and proficiency.

After all, we have learned one thing: in order to succeed in China long term (not merely picking up the crumbs left over whilst others host a major, internationally-appealing event such as the Olympic Games), you have to know the country, and know it thoroughly. European concepts cannot be adopted one-to-one; they have to be adapted to fit Chinese culture, whilst adhering to international standards. Key messages and emotionalisation have to be shaped and adapted, never losing sight of the identity of the international brand. This is the greatest challenge.

Hence a strong team is required that is likewise familiar with international events (and their standards) and Chinese culture. For this reason, we invested in "developing" and attracting these types of colleagues and event experts: international specialists who feel "at home" in China and who speak Chinese, as well as Chinese experts who have spent time abroad (e. g. studying) and who are familiar with the western way of life. This team, which is simultaneously international and local in outlook, goes through all the different process steps of an event: from the event design to its implementation. Particularly when it comes to implementation, it ensures the existence of qualified event specialists who can supervise and control the quality of services offered by suppliers, making sure that the high quality expectations of our clients are met.

In this article I will give a snapshot of the Chinese events industry a decade or so ago, touching on what we identified as crucial factors for success in China in 2004, giving an impression of what the Chinese market was like when we encountered it. In the next section we will juxtapose these original success factors with how we experience target group expectations today, and examine whether or not what was crucial for success in China is still relevant today, providing a good idea of current target group expectations and requirements in China. In the last section we will provide an outlook of what we believe will be inevitable developments in the events industry in China and elsewhere in the world. The aim of the article is therefore to provide insight into the past, the present and the future of the events industry in China as we perceived it then and perceive it now, always from the perspective of an agency that was an international pioneer in China. Let us first, then, go back ten or so years, to when we first started out in China.

2 Past differences

Although we had read all of the literature and learned all there was to learn about Chinese culture, we still managed to "put our foot in it" in a number of typical, almost clichéd situations. The biggest difference – or, shall we say, the one that most contradicted our "German" way of working – was the differentially nuanced ways of saying "no". This was sometimes so polite that we mistook it for meaning "yes", and were surprised when things we assumed had been agreed on were not delivered or were not available in the quality we thought we had ordered them. Similarly, our Chinese counterparts were probably surprised about the length of time it took us to grasp the situation; we must have seemed rather impolite when we kept coming back again and again to ask when the work would be finished – we had obviously not taken "no" for an answer. It would be unrealistic to say that we never fell into many such cultural "traps", despite having done our homework and read the literature, but it would be fair to say that we did so less and less. This was obviously helped by integrating several young Chinese colleagues into our teams, some of whom had lived abroad and in China, and who served as "cultural interpreters" between the two cultures.

Besides the cultural differences we experienced in our everyday work, there were several differences regarding the expectations we encountered (and continue to encounter today), which required similar tact and sensitivity. One example is that Chinese journalists who are invited to a PR event expect to be given a monetary expense allowance to pay for travel expenses incurred, whereas western journalists would view such payment as a bribe more than as an incentive.

Let us turn the clock back to 2003 and 2004, when we started out in China, to examine what was crucial for success in event management at that time. In the next section we will then examine whether these success factors continue to be relevant. In 2004, we also compiled our "eight golden rules for success in China" – of course playing with the importance of the lucky number eight. Indeed, when we started out in China, there were many differences. Clients were looking for familiar faces, which was probably one of the reasons why we made such a good head start. At that time, the main focus was on differences. In order to write this article, I referred to this whitepaper again to get (and give) an impression of what we started out with.

Ten years ago, China was thought to be very different. There were certain cultural aspects that were particularly important when planning and executing successful marketing events. For one: the importance of hierarchies. Events that "gave face" to individuals, that focused on being exclusive and formal, played a particularly important role. This hierarchy had to be an important feature in every event – making sure that VIPs were not just treated as VIPs, but also demonstratively and ostensibly so, in order to make all those present also perceive their importance. This had all kind of effects, from seating and serving arrangements to the kind of events that were focused on, such as galas and award shows.

Another important issue, which we termed the "one-for-all" factor at the time, was the group-oriented culture that still permeated Chinese society in the early 2000s. Stemming from Confucianism, this submission of the individual to the group, obedience and almost self-sacrificing loyalty towards one's family and superiors, were perceived as characteristic and major elements of Chinese culture – and also had a profound impact on successful marketing events and measures. As a Chinese manager of a large German automotive company aptly put it: "In China, the most important thing is people, not product." More so than in Europe or the US, family members had to be taken into account when organising events. In addition, the so-called 'Shouren', the 'inner circle' was always in the foreground when it came to passing on privileges, always trying to go beyond the individual.

Ten years ago, another feature of the relatively small but emerging middle class was the importance attributed to status symbols. Certain brands were not just seen as incredibly desirable; they gave their owner an air of status, elegance and exclusivity. This was another feature that had to be considered when planning events, from offering expensive cigarettes, exclusive liquor and luxury give-aways to presenting a product in a surrounding that would highlight its appeal and turn it into a status symbol, and attempting to give it a permanent place on the hierarchy measuring rod. For a product to succeed, it was deemed important that it benefited from the phenomenon of emulation purchases. A product was to be positioned and presented such that it could be associated with the values of material success and the improvement or development of one's position. It had to become desirable, as it clearly correlated to certain (not least economic) conditions.

This was particularly true of all things Western. When the Chinese market and society opened up to the rest of the world, Western products became highly desirable. Extensive surveys showed that Western products were associated with creativity, competence, quality and reliability. This, of course, had a direct impact on advertising and marketing, which also benefited from this nimbus. Let us not forget that, ten years ago, advertising and marketing were perceived more by Chinese people as a source of information about new products and desirable lifestyles. In fact, a survey we conducted in 2003 as part of an extensive market entrance study revealed that Western or Western-oriented advertising was usually regarded in a more positive light than domestic advertising:

- "more creative" (93 per cent)
- "more memorable" (92 per cent)
- "more innovative" (91 per cent)
- "more dynamic" (87 per cent)
- "more original" (83 per cent)
- "more humorous" (79 per cent)
  (Dams 2004)

"Bargain buy" is what we called another of our success factors. Indeed, it was commonplace in China to provide consumers with detailed explanations and information about a product. The product had to be tangible and comprehensible. In contrast, cold calling and promotions were doomed to failure from the outset – they were perceived to convey a feeling of urgency, haste and impersonality, which were – surprisingly – seen to deeply contradict Chinese business practice (at the time).

Prices were haggled over in protracted, detailed discussions to ensure that, ultimately, both parties would part thinking they had just made a good deal. These two elements – long negotiations and extensive information – therefore had to be taken into account and combined when transferred to the world of events and live marketing measures. Bonus and incentive schemes, promotions providing free samples for extensive testing, and special price promotions were therefore seen as promising marketing tools. Time was another important factor:

Chinese consumers and dealers had to be allowed ample time to gather detailed information about a product. It was thought that sufficient contact with the product would trigger purchase decisions. For events, this meant that the need for information had to be combined with special discount promotions, the offer of customer clubs or dealer incentives which, in addition to the product, also offered unique experiences, events or offers. This was the perfect way to combine the need for information with the feeling of having got a good deal.

"Go for gold" was another of our success formulae. The 2008 Olympic Games in Beijing were expected to hugely stimulate the then emerging events industry. The pervasive feeling was indeed "going for gold" – with an expected increase in live marketing measures and, particularly, a growth in consumer events. We advised our customers to get a head start so as to exploit these benefits. In fact, we prepared ourselves to enable us to provide our clients with whatever services they required surrounding the Games.

By "China blend" we meant the importance of striking a good balance between Western and Chinese elements in an event. This meant that both international and Chinese companies endeavoured to combine Western and Chinese elements in their presentation, giving themselves an identity that offered a projection surface for both cultures. This meant that certain colours and spatial structures or names had to be scrutinised with regard to potentially negative meanings. It also meant that marketing had to be adapted to the Chinese value system. At the same time, positive perceptions vis-à-vis Western products had to be clearly considered and exploited when positioning a product. West and East, Taoism and Neo-Confucianism, Western and Eastern values, tradition and the modern age had to be brought into line. In addition, both Chinese and Western elements had to be clearly identifiable by all participants, providing identification.

In short, ten years ago it was important to integrate both Chinese and Western elements into an event. The features of a successful event were:

- Combining Western and Asian elements
- Paying special attention to traditional Chinese meanings (numbers, colours, feng-shui, and so on)
- Introducing identifiable traditional and modern elements to provide projection surfaces (Dams 2004)

The importance (and relative impenetrability) of *guanxi* has been written about extensively. Indeed, networks were and remain an integral component of Chinese culture. This naturally fits (and fitted) our industry perfectly. What better way is there to substantiate and fortify these stable and secure networks than to host events, especially regarding relationships to employees, dealers and journalists? Live marketing creates and intensifies relationships, which are deepened and emotionally anchored. This may also account for the huge growth of the events industry in China. This is particularly the case because companies discovered the potential of live marketing measures at an early stage, and still apply experience-oriented marketing today to strengthen and further substantiate such networks.

Whilst the entire events industry benefited from this, it was also *guanxi* that formed an important element of supplier relationships, acting as door openers with some clients and making the seemingly impossible become possible – literally opening doors (e. g. to event locations) which had previously been securely locked. To strengthen our agency position, we had to build on our Chinese colleagues' existing bonds and to start establishing new ones. Admittedly, at the beginning we sometimes lost pitches due to the apparently "better" *guanxi* that others had with some clients. This proved to be a steep learning curve for us – further stressing that our approach to employ and combine "the best of both worlds" was working. Local know-how was indispensable to our success, as was the importance that our international staff embrace the Chinese culture and language.

What do we perceive when considering our outlook on China ten years ago? A society on the move. A small, but fervently emerging and growing middle class. A country where everything was possible. A certain "gold rush mood" amongst international companies that flocked to China and were then relieved to find familiar faces and agencies that they could collaborate with. An economy in which having a head start truly mattered. And an events industry that was only just emerging – with a view to the Olympic Games in 2008 – and hoping to benefit from its hype. Boom, hype and growth, excitement and opportunities, pristine, undiscovered locations, target groups that were grateful and excited rather than fastidious and pampered, mixed in with a touch of being "lost in translation", a feeling that characterised a lot of the many expatriates who were required to organise their international corporations' marketing endeavours – the perfect ingredients for successful growth. And it did indeed grow. In 2009, we opened our second Chinese office in Shanghai – to ensure we had competence available on site, and permanently so, rather than having to fly in experts from Beijing. Looking back, I am very proud of the success of our China offices – featuring substantial growth, exciting projects, substantial market expertise and – as far as our good retention rates show – good client relationships. Our growth is substantial, yet still manageable, and we have a team that has "grown up" together with VOK DAMS China. However, the Chinese events industry has also developed, namely at a remarkable pace.

3 Present similarities

When comparing notes of what was happening ten years ago to what is happening and 'in' nowadays, one cannot fail to be astounded at the pace of change in China. After all, it is economic development and the emergence of a strong middle class that have considerably shaped, influenced and changed the "rules of the game" in China – not only concerning the events industry.

Let us now look at what was important and vital for success then, and check whether and to what extent it is still applicable today.

Hierarchy and exclusivity are still important, albeit to a lesser extent, more or less resembling the situation in other countries. We now find that it is much more important to give everyone the feeling that they are VIPs. It is also more difficult than before to identify who tops the hierarchy. One example is the recent VIP launch of a very prestigious luxury car brand in Beijing where most of the guests were in their mid-twenties and dressed in jeans and baseball caps.

We have also witnessed a remarkable decline in the feeling of belonging to a collective, of group orientation. It is now the individual and the product that matter – and ten years of evolvement have disproven the Chinese automobile manager's statement cited above, although, of course, direct family ties are still very important – as they are in most countries of the world. Individual communication, individual approaches and individual product features are now important, and have replaced the earlier almost self-sacrificing feeling of loyalty towards one's superiors or the importance of passing on privileges to one's inner circle.

A drastic change can be perceived in what we termed "cool cult" – the importance attributed to status symbols. The middle class now no longer regards certain status symbols as attributes of their success. In fact, displaying expensive items is considered rather vulgar, a "lower class excess" of proof of affluence, paired with a lack of style. Indeed, style, class and quality are now considered distinctive features to a much greater extent. Brands now have to prove themselves much more than before. They have to be stylish, classy and of a high quality; origin no longer matters.

This is directly connected to the loss of nimbus experienced by Western products. Simply being Western is no longer a mark of distinction, and will not suffice to make a cool brand. Instead, as Chinese brands and products are becoming increasingly better, so is their perceived image. 'Made in China' is no longer a mark of "cheapness", but is increasingly becoming a trademark for quality, gaining in the "coolness factor" with incredible speed. Let us take the example of China's favourite, indispensable 'toy' – the mobile phone. In this industry, Chinese brands are not just catching up, but overtaking Western ones due to an increase in quality and quality awareness. A similar increase in quality and raised quality awareness are also visible when it comes to events.

The hype surrounding the Olympic Games and the Expo in Shanghai influenced this – especially regarding the quality of suppliers and event personnel and the perception and understanding of event standards. Yet it is fair to say that, interestingly enough, most events surrounding the Olympics, for example, were organised for companies that were not (and are still not) based in China. For established event agencies, therefore, these two major events proved to be more of an impetus for increased quality in terms of suppliers and personnel – a more differentiated understanding of quality, even – albeit to a lesser extent for prolonged business relationships with clients on the ground.

When we started out in Beijing, bargain buys and haggling were distinctive features and important elements to be taken into account when planning marketing measures. This is now well and truly a thing of the past. In fact, China is now the biggest market for online purchases, where no haggling is involved or possible. Of course the Chinese still like to strike a bargain and buy reduced items, but this is the case across the globe. Nowadays, however, haggling in shopping malls is taboo, seen as vulgar or lacking class by many Chinese people. Regarding the importance of receiving sufficient information about a product, this may still be the case, as long as the information is presented in an entertaining way, involving the user. Protracted sales speeches, however, are 'out'. The more the product information involves online and virtual elements, the better and more effective it will be. The Chinese are "married" to their smartphones, even more so than in European countries. They tend to look up information on the web, scan through it and then make up their mind about a product or brand. Social media and online communication have replaced the protracted, detailed haggling and purchasing process, accelerating it considerably.

Let us look at what we called the "China blend", by which we meant the importance of combining Chinese with Western elements. When we started out, this was often key to the success of our events. Now, however, it is no longer a matter of ensuring that sufficient, blatantly obvious Chinese elements, such as a kung fu performance, and Western elements are integrated. If at all, is it about striking the right balance. However, we generally find that this need to integrate both worlds is in decline. Clients pick and choose whatever suits their objective. It is much more about having an overall, holistic understanding of the respective target group's lifestyle and overall brand positioning – as is the case in Europe and the US. International marketing concepts beat traditional values. The coherence of a brand is what makes it successful. We only need think of the coherently branded experiences found all over the world upon entering an Apple Store, a Starbucks or a Nike Store.

The last item on our list was the overwhelming importance of *guanxi*. This seemed to be the key factor of economic success in China. Without it, you were doomed to failure. With it, everything was possible. While I would not go so far as to say that *guanxi* has been abolished altogether, it has lost a lot of its business-relevant halo. Networks and networking are certainly important, as in any other country in this world. Likewise, having good networks can smoothen, accelerate or ease business endeavours substantially. Yet *guanxi* alone will not get business done or sell an event concept. A great concept will most likely benefit from having good client and supplier relationships; a mediocre concept will not be bought simply on the basis of *guanxi*. Ultimately, it all comes down to quality, creativity and know-how, not good connections.

If we look at ourselves now and ten years ago, when we were international pioneers in a largely unknown Chinese market, it is apparent that we have grown and matured with the market. One aspect is particularly striking – the features we identified as crucial for marketing success were very much the features of society undergoing change, with an evolving (but relatively small) middle class. It was a society that was increasingly coming into contact with products and brands that were previously inaccessible to them, a society that was also coming to terms with aligning its culture with influences from all over the world and, most of all, a society that witnessed tremendous economic growth. Ten years ago, China was considerably less exposed to the West than it is now. And all things Western had a certain charismatic appeal, simply because they came from the West. This has changed considerably. It is now a matter of quality, style and brands – and not origin.

The pace at which this change occurred was incredible. It almost feels as though the standards, rules and norms that took 30 to 40 years to develop in Western countries – the changes we have witnessed in attitudes, behaviour, expectations and communication – changed society in China's main cities in a matter of ten years. The pace was truly remarkable.

It goes without saying that most of the features mentioned here are predominately features of China's urban middle class, and a lot of what we witnessed as change may be rather different in rural China. And yet the urban middle and upper classes are the core target groups for marketing events, which may explain why we have focused on the changes we perceived in behavioural patterns here. Generally, however, I would leave it to anthropologists or sociologists to establish the extent to which we are all turning into "citizens of the world" and being homogenised regarding attitudes to brands and products, the expectations fostered and the changes we have witnessed – and the extent to which shopping areas are gradually coming to resemble one another throughout the world.

This development is visible in the photos taken at the 2014 Auto China Beijing, where our team at VOK DAMS China supported Volkswagen in designing, staging and implementing their trade show booth.

Figure. 1:VOK DAMS Auto China Beijing 2014.

Figure 2: VOK DAMS Auto China Beijing 2014.

Figure 3: VOK DAMS Auto China Beijing 2014.

If asked where these photos were taken, it would be difficult to pinpoint the location. This is, indeed, the main development – brands are cohesively staged around the world, and cultural differences and specifications no longer matter. They need to be taken into account regarding dietary requirements, religious rules and possibly a superstition of certain numbers, but these are features of events all over the world, because target groups have also become culturally mixed. Since the number four is considered unlucky in China, it is rarely found in Chinese buildings, but neither is the 13th floor – indeed, we find that both Chinese and Western habits are taken into account and merged. Target groups are increasingly becoming "citizens of the world" with individual and specific preferences and animosities. Knowing these and catering for them individually is what matters most – and thus events have to be individually geared towards target groups, offering the most individual service whilst preserving and transferring the holistic brand experience, the nucleus of which is identical across the globe.

Nevertheless, for us as live marketing specialists it is vital to explore the characteristics and features of a society, examining its psychology and culture, its desires, attitudes and values. In Germany, we often apply so-called Sinus Milieus to target groups, where people are grouped according to their views of life and lifestyles. After all, knowledge of our target groups is the key to our success. In our business, you need to know how people tick in order to emotionalise, motivate and inspire them. This must never be perceived as being artificial or false, but must be as authentic as possible, involving the target group and turning them into protagonists rather than mere passive onlookers, bystanders or guests.

In the events industry more so than in others, it is crucial for success to remain ahead of the game, to find out what is happening all over the world, the latest trends and developments, and how they can be utilised best to enthuse, fascinate, motivate and have a lasting effect on event target groups. One of our main tasks is therefore to look at and examine trends and shape certain developments. In the last section I will now outline what we believe will shape the events industry all over the world – in Beijing and Shanghai as much as in Berlin, London, Paris, New York or Prague.

4 Future outlook

When looking at current trends in events, a lot has obviously changed in the past few years – not just in China but all over the world. New formats are ever more in demand since the internet has changed attitudes, expectations and the live experience of events, which are increasingly being complimented and interlinked with so-called MoSoLo (mobile applications, social media and location-based services) elements. We call such events "hybrid events".

Every marketing professional knows that attention is the currency of the 21st century. Although basic communication processes are unaltered – a sender still wants to embed a message as deeply as possible within a recipient – communication channels have fundamentally changed. In times of the mobile internet, there is an abundance of information at one's disposal at all times. More importantly, anyone can simultaneously join in this communication as a dialogue partner.

What does this mean for traditional brand communication?

One needs to be heard, and the respective message needs to appeal to the recipient, offering added value. This, in turn, requires a mind shift in communication. Consumers no longer want one-way communication; they seek dialogue. Recommendations from peer group are what trigger people's purchase decisions.

Which communication tool offers the best opportunity for engaging in dialogue?

The answer is obvious: live encounters and the internet: live marketing measures represent an enormous depth of contact; the internet stands for a very large number of real-time contacts.

The most obvious solution would therefore be to sensibly combine the two. This is what "hybrid events" are all about. It is striking to note that China is definitely leading the way here: in our European events, 74 per cent of all client requests for bids and briefings in events contain hybrid elements; in China, this figure is closer to 100 per cent. Indeed, in all events in China we have to address and integrate social media elements to ensure that we truly unleash the event's full success potential.

I find it particularly striking that "hybrid events" are a good example of where China is well ahead of Western events. Whilst Western marketing executives are increasingly grasping the potential of integrating social media and mobile applications, these elements have become an integral part in almost all events in China. This is a good example of how China has changed from a trend follower to a trend setter.

Whilst "hybrid events" are increasingly becoming a standard feature, in our industry it is vital to keep looking beyond what is happening and to analyse what will happen next. Let us now take this further and look beyond the current trends in events. If we examine the developments that shape our era, we find that a new (and inevitable) development is taking place in events. A number of important socio-cultural trends that will have an inevitable impact on designing successful events in future are given below.

No. 1: Egolution
"Me, myself I" – self-realisation will become increasingly important.

No. 2: From society to 'weciety'
The impact of peer groups will continue to grow, and people will increasingly define themselves via their peer groups. This is directly linked to the first trend about self-realisation: one may belong to several peer groups, but it is within these groups that people aim to find self-fulfilment, as joint experiences with others becomes a means of self-realisation.

No. 3: Word of mouth 2000
This is the most effective marketing tool. Recommendations by peers (see No. 2) will become the most important guide in an increasingly confusing world with ever more choices and options.

No. 4: Co-creation

People come together to create something big, to brain-storm and find solutions together. Why? Simply because it is possible nowadays, and because they want to achieve something. Makerspaces, hackerthons and co-working places are all examples of this. The focus is always on the search for a pragmatic solution to a problem.

No. 5: Appetite for stories

People have always loved a good story – this is not a trend; but content marketing is. However, it can only succeed if the content is relevant and offers the target group added value. The more "beautifully wrapped" a story is, the more it becomes a story to retell and share with one's peers. Hence if you want to market content effectively, all you need to do is turn it into a good story and (let others) spread the word!

What do these interlinking trends have in common? What do they signify for effective event marketing? It is actually rather simple (but difficult to achieve): communication has to be authentic, emotional, relevant and offer added value.

What does this mean for events? Other media channels, such as TV, print or PR, are increasingly being integrated into events. In turn, the event becomes the epicentre of the overall marketing campaign – it becomes a live campaign. What makes a live campaign different is that the event is not just a "one-off" occasion, but generates content, which in turn can be communicated over a long period of time.

A live campaign is also a platform for joint, interactive working and thinking – which can be started (virtually or in person) before and/or continued after the event. Live campaigns can therefore first emerge in the virtual world and then develop into an event at a later stage.

Hybrid event elements are what drive the live campaign – it is communication before and after it, joint collaboration and content generating and sharing between participants and beyond (PR, media) that make a live campaign, ensuring cohesive, permanent and most effective communication.

Live campaigns are therefore not just a trend, but an inevitable development. They are here to stay, not just in China or Europe, but all over the world. And not just regarding the events industry, but also communication and marketing in general. When I look at the speed at which China's society has not only caught up with, but in some ways even assumed trend-setting qualities in events, I believe that we will witness a lot of live campaigns in and coming from China.

When I wrote this article, I found myself musing about how we started out in China, in the days when we were pioneers in a market that was only just starting to evolve. This has changed substantially. Nowadays, almost all major events and branding agencies have at least one subsidiary in China, and Chinese agencies have grown and become big players in the market. We also find all kinds of agency designs, from small agencies to big players, from international agencies that fly in experts from abroad to those that prefer to work only with employees on the ground, from mixed teams of Chinese and Western employees to all-Chinese teams. Everything is possible; and everyone seems to have found and shaped a (suitably large) niche to suit them, depending on their customer expectations and demands.

It goes without saying that competition has also grown, as have the standards and expectations of clients and event guests alike. Again, although the development was expected (and it was this anticipation that induced us to get a head start back in 2003), the pace at which it occurred still astounds me. However, it is a very healthy development, as the criteria for what makes a good event and an effective event concept have also developed. It is quality in implementation that matters most, paired with an event concept that combines creativity, authenticity and emotions to leave a truly lasting impression. Ultimately, it does not matter where you are based, but these criteria will continue to matter in the future – in China as much as elsewhere in the world.

5 Literature

Dams, Colja M. (2004), *Das Phänomen China - Lösungen für Live-Marketing* (Research Report on Live-Marketing in China), Wuppertal: VOK DAM: ILM Institut für Live-Marketing GmbH

A City Brand Personality Model for international event marketing: An empirical research across multiple cultures

Milewicz, Chad,
Griese, Kai-Michael,
Ding, Yi

城市品牌人格化模型在国际会展营销中的运用：跨文化的实证研究

Cities, regions and countries compete globally for skilled workers, business investment and tourists. Place branding is the application of brand strategies and concepts to differentiate a city, region or country in order to create experiences that people desire based on the places where they live, work and visit. Due to the importance of the city brand in China, we examine how city brands are experienced in order to provide an insight into to how event managers can integrate city brand considerations into their marketing planning and strategies. Our research indicates that there are similarities in how people in North America, Europe and Asia personify cities. Additionally, we find evidence that these similarities can be measured by a shortened, easy-to-use version of Aaker's brand personality scale. Based on this brand personality scale cities are able to measure the personality of a city. The results are interesting for stakeholders of a city, for example, because it helps them to understand the personality of their respective city.

各个城市、地区甚至国家都在全球范围内为技术性人才、商业投资和游客竞争。地方品牌是品牌化战略和概念的一种实际运用，从而来区分一个城市、地区或国家来营造出人们基于生活、工作和访问而产生的期望和体验。由于城市品牌化在中国的重要性，本文将调查城市品牌化的经验，来深入探讨如何让会展管理者在策划市场营销战略时，将城市品牌的因素融入其中。我们的研究显示，北美、欧洲和亚洲在评价城市人格化上有很多相似点。除此以外，我们也有证据表明，这些相似点可以用简易版的 Aaker 品牌人格量表来衡量。基于这样一个品牌人格标准，城市可以用来测量自己的城市性格。比如，城市的利益相关者可能认为研究结果相当有趣，因为这帮助他们了解了城市的性格。

1 Introduction

Cities, regions and countries compete globally for skilled workers, business investment and tourism. Places increasingly apply marketing theories and tactics as they compete and branding is a critical component of place marketing (Hankinson, 2007; Hanna and Rowley, 2011). Place branding is the application of brand strategies and concepts to differentiate a city, region or country in order to create experiences that people desire based on the places they live, work, and visit (Hanna and Rowley 2011; Hankinson 2007). This definition highlights the strategic management of the brand and the consumption experience of the brand.

The importance of the city brandings has been recognized in recent years, especially in China and has thus been examined from different perspectives (Go and Zhang 1997; Mercille 2005; Owen 2005; Xu 2006; Li and Kaplanidou 2008; Zhang and Zhao 2009; Meng and Li 2011). Reasons for this are high growth opportunities in tourism and the increasing attractiveness of a relevant representation of a city brand for investors and workers (Zhang 2009; Ding 2011).

Due to the importance of the city brand in China, we are going to examine how city brands are experienced in order to provide an insight as to how event managers can integrate city brand considerations into their marketing planning and strategies. Specifically, we will focus on the city brand personality component of city brands. First Principles were developed for this purpose in the 1970's by Mayo (1973), Hunt (1975) and Crompton (1979). These days the city brand of a destination is one of the most frequently measured constructs in empirical research (Dolnicar and Grün 2012). Our goal is to identify the components of city brand personality that are generally recognizable across multiple cultures. In doing so, we hope to provide a city brand personality model that can be effectively applied to international marketing practices.

In general, brand personality is "the set of human characteristics associated with a brand," (Aaker 1997, 347). Thus, the city brand personality construct represents the ways in which individuals personify their overall beliefs about a city. A city's brand personality has been shown to be distinct from the city's overall brand image (Ekinci and Hosany, 2006) and brand personality, in general, can have a positive distinct impact on customers' trust and loyalty towards a brand (Siguaw et al. 1999). Research indicates that people associate human personality characteristics with cities, although the types of personality characteristics tend to vary across cultures (Ekinci and Hosany, 2006; Kaplan et al. 2010). We will now take a closer look at these existing unique city brand personality constructs, compare them with research on Aaker's (1997) brand personality construct for products and propose a city brand personality model that can be more generalizable across cultures.

After we have proposed our model, we will provide the results of a study consisting of three samples, one from China, one from Germany, and one form the US, which suggest that our model can be applied across cultures for international marketing purposes.

2 A four-factor City Brand Personality Model

Aaker (1997) developed a five-factor brand personality model for products based on research administered in the US. These factors are sincerity, excitement, competence, sophistication and ruggedness. Sincerity consists of a product being perceived as down-to-earth, honest, wholesome and cheerful and is measured using 11 descriptive items. Excitement is also measured with 11 descriptors. The Excitement factor captures perceptions of a product being daring, spirited, imaginative and up-to-date. Competence consists of three facets, being reliable, intelligent, and successful. This factor is measured using 9 descriptive items. Sophistication is characterized by being perceived as upper class and charming and is measured by six items. Finally, ruggedness is measured by five items and is characterized by the facets of being outdoorsy and tough. Thus, this model has five factors, 14 facets, and 42 items that are used to measure the facets in each factor.

We have four goals with our proposed model. First, we want to identify a model that is generalizable and theory-based, so we will build on existing work rather than trying to define new factors, facets and measures. Thus, we will try to only utilize factors, facets, and measurement items that are part of Aaker's (1997) five-factor model brand personality model. Secondly, we want to make sure that our model is consistent with the city brand personality construct. To do this, we will look for for consistencies between existing city brand personality models and Aaker's (1997) model. In this way we are building on a body of city brand personality research. Thirdly, we want our model to be applicable in international marketing contexts, so we will research literature that extends Aaker's (1997) model of brand personality to multiple cultures, even if it is not in a city branding context. The purpose of this is to identify if any brand personality factors, facets, and measures are consistent across cultures but may have not yet been considered in city branding contexts. Fourthly, we want to identify the most parsimonious measurement model possible so that it can be easily utilized by place and event marketers.

Table 1 summarizes the measures that were used by Ekinci and Hosany (2006) in a city brand personality context as part of a study of adults from Great Britain. Their research utilized a sample of 20 British participants to evaluate Aaker's 42-items measuring brand personality to evaluate which ones were reasonable for use in city branding context. Their work led to 27 items being identified and the items were representative of each of the original five factors. As shown in table 1, an exploratory factor analysis identified only three city brand personality factors, not five. Moreover the only factors that were characteristic of any of the original five were the sincerity and excitement factors. It is interesting to note that some of the items their study uses to measure sincerity and excitement are items that were originally used to measure other factors in Aaker's (1997) original model. Thus, for the purpose of building our model we keep the sincerity and excitement factors, but we only utilize the measurement items that were consistently grouped in each factor by Aaker (1997) and Ekinci and Hosany (2006). These are the first two factors in our proposed four-factor city brand personality model.

Next, we looked at the work of Aaker et al. (2001) who studied the brand personality construct in a product context but outside of the US and Great Britain. As shown in table 1, the factors of sincerity and excitement are again identified in both Spanish and Japanese samples. Also, at least one of the measurement items in each factor are the same as used for the respective construct in the city branding work done by Ekinci and Hosany (2006). Aaker et al. (2001) also identify the sophistication factor in both the Japanese and Spanish samples, although different measures were used for each factor. Additionally, some of the measurement items in these factors were items that were related to other factors in Aaker's (1997) original work. Recalling that our goal is cross-cultural applicability, we include the sophistication factor in our model, but only utilize measures that were consistent with the original US-sample tested model (Aaker 1997).

Our research identified one other extension of Aaker's (1997) brand personality construct to the context of city branding, the work by Kaplan et al. (2010) for several cities in Turkey. Kaplan et al. (2010) utilize a list of measures that go beyond the 42 items used by Aaker (1997), so we have not presented their work in the table. However, for the purposes of our research it is sufficient to note that excitement was identified, again, in a city branding context and competence also captures in this city branding context, along with ruggedness.

To summarize, sincerity, excitement and competence are all found in at least two brand personality studies completed in different countries, and each of these factors have been previously identified in at least one city brand personality context. Additionally, sophistication was recognized in brand personality studies in Japan, Spain, and the US, although these were all in product contexts. Moreover, for each of these four factors, at least two measurement items are consistent with those used in Aaker's (1997) original conceptualization of brand personality.

Thus, we propose a four-factor city brand personality model for international marketing. The model consists of an excitement factor that is measured with five descriptors and captures perceptions of a city being spirited (three measurement items), exciting (one measurement item), and up-to-date (one measurement item). It also contains a sincerity factor that has three measurement items that represents the honest facet of this factor, a sophistication factor with three measurement times that represent the upper-class facet of this factor, and a competence factor that has three measurement items representing the successful facet of this factor. Each of these factors, facets, and measurement items are part of Aaker's (1997) original brand personality construct, they have been at least partially identified in at least one other city brand personality context, and they have been at least partially identified in at least two other international contexts. Thus, the conceptual nature of the model is based on existing theory and empirical research.

3 Testing a four-factor City Brand Personality Model

In this study we will examine the extent to which our proposed 4-factor city brand personality model can be applied in international settings. Specifically, we will test the hypothesis of how our proposed 4-factor city brand personality model is applicable across cultures, thus being suitable for application in international marketing.

We will test this hypothesis using a confirmatory factor analysis of data collected from three samples. One sample consists of 217 Chinese college students attending a University in China, a second sample consists of 110 German college students attending a German University, and a third sample consists of 112 American college students attending a US University. In German and Chinese sample participants were instructed to read the provided list of descriptive words and use a 5-point scale to indicate the extent each word described the city where they attended school. The scale points ranged from "not at all descriptive" and "extremely descriptive". In these samples, participants also had the option of indicating that they did not understand the meaning of a descriptor in relation to a city. In the US sample, students read the same set of descriptors and responded using the same scale to indicate how the extent to which each word described the city in which thy attended school. Students in the US sample were not given the option of indicating that they did not know the meaning of a word in relation to a city because we had reason to believe they were easily understood in the US, based on the reliability results presented in study 1.

Results. Table 2 shows the confirmatory factor analysis (CFA) results for our study. Almost all factor scales exceed the minimal desired threshold for reliability, with composite reliability and coefficient alpha scores all over .600 (Bagozzi and Yi 1988). The only scale which does not have at least one of these measures of reliability meeting the threshold is the competence scale in the Chinese sample (composite reliability = .594; coefficient alpha = .518). Thus, overall, the scales appear to have sufficient measures of internal consistency across our three samples. Additionally, the AVE estimates are all above the strictest threshold of .500 in the US sample, and we find mixed results in the AVE estimates in the Chinese and German samples (Fornell and Larcker 1981). The AVE estimates therefore indicate that there tends to be more measurement error present in the Chinese and German samples than in the US sample. Overall, we believe that there is sufficient evidence in to suggest that these scales can be viewed as reliable for use in each of the three cultural settings we tested.

To asses our hypothesis that the four-factor city brand personality model can be used to understand city brand personalities in international marketing, we examine the fit indexes resulting from our CFA for each sample. Researchers suggest consulting multiple fit indexes to assess how well a hypothesized model performs in a CFA (Hatch 1994; Sivo et al. 2006). We considered four recommended indexes to test hour hypothesized model. The respective optimal cutoff points for concluding if a model is acceptable are .95 or higher for the CFI index, .88 or higher for the NFI index, .06 or lower for the RMSEA index, and a chi-square statistic that is less than two times the value of the model's degrees of freedom (Hatcher 1994; Sivo et al. 2006). As shown in Table 3, three out of four fit indexes for the US sample and Chinese samples meet or exceed these optimal criteria. In the German sample, the respective indexes do not meet these optimal criteria. Thus, we conclude that our proposed four-factor model of city brand personality is acceptable in the US and China samples, but not in the German sample. However, a post-hoc analysis of the German sample reveals that a two-factor model consisting of the excitement factor and the sincerity factor is an acceptable model of city brand personality (CFI = .964; NFI = .889; RMSEA = .059; χ^2 = 26 with 19 degrees of freedom).

4 Conclusions

Our research indicates that there are similarities in how people in North America, Europe and Asia personify cities. Additionally, we have found evidence that these similarities can be measured with a shortened, easy-to-use version of Aaker's (1997) brand personality scale.

Our four-factor model of city brand personality clearly indicates that individuals in our China and US samples recognize excitement, sincerity, sophistication, and competence as identifiable personality traits of cities. Results from our German sample suggest that sophistication and competence may either be city brand personality traits that are less identifiable by people from European cultures or that they need to be understood differently than how our scales measure them. However, it appears that individuals in Germany, China, and the US are clearly able to associate excitement and sincerity as elements of a city's brand personality.

Based on these results, marketers should be confident use the proposed 14-item city brand personality scale for research purposes in China, Germany and the US. When using these scales to research Chinese customers' city brand perceptions it may be worthwhile to pre-test the excitement and competence scales because of the size of the average variance extracted measures we found for those scales in our Chinese sample. For the same reason, similar precautions may be useful when using the sophistication and competence scales with German customers.

5 Recommendations for event marketing

It is critical for marketers to understand how brand experience affects customers. A customer's affective and cognitive responses throughout the searching, purchasing, and consumption processes of an event represents the event's brand experience (Brakus, Schmitt, and Zarantonello 2009). As such, an event's brand experience is not detached from the city in which it takes place. In this way, the city's brand, which includes the city's brand personality, is connected to the event's brand experience. We provide a theoretically-grounded four-factor model of city brand personalities. This model provides marketers a way to view the commonality of how individuals experience cities. Our model can complement what is already known about the unique characteristics of a given city when marketing to international customers.

For example, in our Chinese sample, the target city was rated most highly on Excitement and Competence. What our research suggests is that a US customer attending an event in that Chinese city will likely identify with those same factors as prominent elements of the city's personality. This is because our US sample also recognizes excitement and competence as valid factors of a city personality. Of course, there are other elements of the US customer's brand experience in the Chinese city that will be unique or new to the customer, but these will be in addition to brand elements the person already associates with cities, in general.

Knowing what city brand personality factors customers tend to perceive as generalizable across cities and what factors are seen as unique to a given city, can help marketers better differentiate and position their events in the cities in which they are located. Knowing that some city brand personality factors are consistent across cultures is particularly helpful in international marketing contexts.

Our research suggests that our four-factor city brand personality model can be measured using only the 14 measurement items shown in Table 2. Thus, marketers can easily and effectively assess how a target city rates on these common city brand personality factors. We provide multiple measures of reliability and a conservative estimate of potential measurement error based on our samples from China, Germany, and the US. Thus, depending on the target audience where these scales are applied, a researcher should be able to anticipate which measurement items, if any, may require additional translating or need to be analysed with more caution when being used in a particular market.

Finally, our four-factor city brand personality model can be applied to understand generational differences in how people experience a city. For example, a given city may have high ratings on excitement by an older generation, but relatively lower ratings by a younger generation. Testing for such differences can help event marketers connect the desired brand experience of their event in a city with its target audience. For example, in the US we tested our scales on an older adult sample and compared the ratings to the student sample. The reliability and validity measures were equally strong, as expected. However, on average the older adults rated the same target city as significantly lower in regards to competence and excitement relative to the younger adults. It is possible that the difference in how each generation experiences the city may influence differences in how each generation experiences or anticipates experiencing an event in that same city.

6 The fundamental relevance of the City Brand Personality Model

Based on the results of the investigation, a variety of benefits of the City Brand Personality Model can be derived.

1. The benefits of the City Brand Personality Model by measuring the personality of a city: Especially for international events it's important to understand that the city's personality effects the event experience and vice versa (e. g. Echtner and Ritchie 1991; Kearns and Philo 1993; Ankomah, Crompton and Baker 1995; Um 1998; Richards and Wilson 2004). The City Brand Personality Model is helpful for the event industry and other stakeholders because they can now measure the personality of a city and compare it with other cities. Moreover, it is possible to understand and compare different perceptions of different people from different countries (e. g. perception of Frankfurt/Germany by the Chinese or perception of Shanghai/China by the Germans).

Tab. 1: Overview of Previous Adaptation of Aaker's (1997) Brand Personality Construct and Scales.

Author (Date): Context	Sample sizes and Methodology	Measures Reported	Factors Reported
Ekinci and Hosany (2006): City brand personality	Sample 1: 148 British adults	Sample 1 (12 items): Reliable, *Sincere*, Intelligent, Successful **Wholesome**	*Sincerity*
		Exciting, **Daring**, Original, *Spirited*	*Excitement*
		Friendly, Family-Oriented, Charming	Conviviality
	Sample 2: 102 British individuals	Sample 2 (11 items): removed "Reliable," kept the rest	
Aaker et al. (2001): Product Brand Personality	Japanese Sample 1: 1,495 Japanese adults	Japanese Sample (36 items): Warm, Thoughtful, Kind	*Sincerity*
	Japanese Sample 2: 114 Japanese students	Talkative, Funny, Optimistic, Positive, **Contemporary**, Free, Friendly, Happy, Likable, Youthful, Energetic, *Spirited*	*Excitement*
		Consistent, Responsible, **Reliable**, Dignified, Determined, ***Confident***, Patient, Tenacious, Masculine	*Competence*
		Shy, Mild-Mannered, Peaceful, Naïve, Dependent, Childlike	Peaceful
		Elegant, **Smooth**, Romantic, Stylish, Sophisticated, Extravagant	*Sophistication*
	Spanish Sample 1: 692 Spanish adults		
	Spanish Sample 2 101 Spanish adults	Spanish Sample: *Real*, ***Sincere***, **Down-to-Earth**, Considerate, Thoughtful, Well-Mannered	*Sincerity*
		Happy, Outgoing, Fun, **Daring**, *Young*, *Spirited*, **Unique**, **Imaginative**, **Independent**,	*Excitement*
		Good Looking, ***Glamourous***, Stylish, Confident, Persistent, Leader	*Sophistication*
		Affectionate, Sweet, Gentle, Naïve, Mild-Mannered, Peaceful	Peacefulness
		Fervent, Passionate, Intense, Spiritual, Mystical, Bohemian	Passion

NOTE: **Bold** = measurement item loaded onto same conceptual factor as Aaker (1997) and factor is part of Aaker (1997) BPS. *Italics* = measurement item and factor is in used in our IPBPS.

Tab. 2: Proposed City Brand Personality Scale for International Marketing and Evidence of Scale Performance in China, Germany, and United States.

Personality Traits	Factor	Factor Loadings (Composite Reliability / Coefficient Alpha)			Average Variance Extracted	
		US Young Adult Sample	China Young Adult Sample	Germany Young Adult Sample		
	Excitement	(.897 / .891)	(.721 / .700)	(.793 / .773)	China:	.348
Exciting		.889	.769	.723	Germany:	.439
Cool		.730	.597	.815	US:	.636
Young		.727	.540	.528		
Up to Date		.872	.558	.632		
Spirited		.754	.437	.576		
	Sincerity	(.882 / .875)	(.689 / .648)	(.736 / .787)	China:	.431
Honest		.903	.734	.879	Germany:	.493
Sincere		.883	.708	.661	US:	.716
Real		.745	.504	.518		
	Sophistication	(.849 / .845)	(.814 / .763)	(.612 / .558)	China:	.596
Good-looking		.798	.751	.754	Germany:	.354
Glamorous		.857	.675	.477	US:	.653
Charming		.766	.876	.516		
	Competence	(.899 / .898)	(.594 / .518)	(.654 / .561)	China:	.344
Confident		.915	.685	.520	Germany:	.400
Leader		.815	.350	.511	US:	.748
Successful		.862	.663	.816		
		Fit Indices				
CFI		.962	.950	.821		
NFI		.904	.873	.719		
RMSEA		.071	.049	.091		
χ^2 (do)		111.27 (71)	108.13 (71)	143.75 (71)		

2. The benefits for stakeholders in a city: The results are also interesting for stakeholders of a city, because it helps them to understand their city's personality. Based on the results, the stakeholder in a city may decide how they can improve the personality of the city for existing events or how they can check out the city and new planned and future oriented events fit together. Furthermore they can understand how a city (e. g. Shanghai) can attract clients from other countries (e. g. Americans).

3. The benefits for the international event industry: The results are interesting for the event industry, because it helps them when deciding where to develop new international events. The city's personality can have a positive effect on the event. In addition, it

helps with deciding which kind of elements of a city's personality could be implemented into the advertising for the relevant events.

4. The benefits for a brand: The results are interesting for brands (e. g. Mercedes Benz) because it helps them in deciding which city's personality is more or less relevant for exhibitions due to the high coherence with their own brand.

7 Literature

Aaker, J. L. (1997), 'Dimensions of Brand Personality', in: *Journal of Marketing Research*, 34(3), pp. 347–356

Ankomah, P., Crompton, J. L. and Baker, D. A. (1995), 'A study of pleasure travellers' cognitive distance assessments', in: *Journal of Travel Research*, Fall, pp. 12–18

Bagozzi, R.P. and Yi, Youjae (1988), 'On Evaluation of Structural Equation Models', in: Journal of the Academy of Marketing Science, 16(1), pp. 74–94

Brakus, J.J., Schmitt, B.H., and Zarantonello, L.Z. (2009), 'Brand Experience: What is It? How is It Measured? Does It Affect Loyalty?' in: *Journal of Marketing*, 73(1), pp. 52–68

Crompton .L. (1979), 'An Assessment of the Image of Mexico as a Vacation Destination and the Influence of Geographical Location upon that Image', in: *Journal of Travel Research*, 17(4), pp. 18–23

Ding, S. (2011), 'Branding a Rising China: An Analysis of Beijing's National Image Management in the Age of China's Rise', in: *Journal of Asian and African Studies*, 46(3), pp. 293–306

Dolnicar, S. and Grün, B. (2012): 'Validly Measuring Destination Image in Survey Studies', in: *Journal of Travel Research*, 52(1), pp. 3–14

Echtner, C. M. and Ritchie, J. R. B. (1991), 'The meaning and measurement of destination image', in: *Journal of Tourism Studies*, 2(2), pp. 2–12

Ekinci, Y. and Hosany, S. (2006), 'Destination Personality: an Application of Brand Personality to Tourism Destinations', in: *Journal of Travel Research*, 45(2), pp. 127–139

Fornell, C. and Larcker, D. (1981), 'Evaluating Structural Equation Models with Unobservable Variables and Measurement Error', in: *Journal of Marketing Research*, 18(1), pp. 39–50

Go, F., and Zhang, W. (1997), 'Applying importance-performance analysis to Beijing as an international meeting destination', in: *Journal of Travel Research*, 35(4), pp. 42–49

Hankinson, G. (2007), 'The Management of Destination Brands: Five Guiding Principles Based on Recent Developments in Corporate Brand Theory', in: *Journal of Brand Management*, 14(3), pp. 240–254

Hanna, S. and Rowley, J. (2011), 'Towards a Strategic Place Brand-Management Model', in: *Journal of Marketing Management*, 27(5–6), pp. 458–476

Hatch, L. (1994), *A Step-by-Step Approach to Using SAS for Factor Analysis and Structural Equation Modelling*, Cary: NC, SAS Institute, Inc.

Hunt, J.D. (1975), 'Image as a factor in tourism development', in: *Journal of Travel Research*, 13(3), pp. 1–7

Kaplan, M.D., Yurt, O., Guneri, B., and Kurtulus, K. (2010), 'Branding Places: Applying Brand Personality Concept to Cities', in: *European Journal of Marketing*, 44(9/10), pp. 1286–1304

Kearns, G. and Philo, C. (Eds) (1993), *Selling Places: The City as Cultural Capital, Past and Present*. Oxford: Pergamon Press

Mayo, E.J. (1973), 'Regional Images and Regional Travel Behaviour', In Research for Changing Travel Patterns: Interpretation and Utilization. *Proceedings of the Travel Research Association, Fourth Annual Conference*, pp. 211–18

Meng, F. and Li, X. (2011), 'The 2008 Beijing Olympic Games and China's national identity building', in: E. Frew & L. White (Eds.), *Tourism and national identity: An international perspective* (pp. 93–104). New York, NY: Routledge

Mercille, J. (2005), 'Media effects on image: The case of Tibet', in: *Annals of Tourism Research*, 32, pp. 1039–1055

Owen, J. G. (2005), 'Estimating the cost and benefit of hosting Olympic Games: What can Beijing expect from its 2008 Games?', in: *Industrial Geographer*, 3(1), pp. 1–18

Richards, G. and Wilson, J. (2004), 'The Impact of Cultural Events on City Image: Rotterdam, Cultural Capital of Europe 200', in: *Urban Studies*, 41 (10), pp. 1931–1951

Siguaw, J.A., Mattila, A., and Austin, J.R. (1999), 'The Brand Personality Scale', in: *Cornell Hotel and Restaurant Administration Quarterly*, 40(3), pp. 48–56

Sivo, S.A., Fan, X., Witta, E.L., and John, T. (2006), 'The Search for "Optimal" Cutoff Properties: Fit Index Criteria in Structural Equation Modelling', in: The Journal of Experimental Education, 74(3), pp. 267–288

Um, S. (1998), 'Measuring destination image in relation to pleasure travel destination decisions', in: *Journal of Tourism Sciences*, 21(2), pp. 53–65

Li, X. and Kaplanidou, K. (2008), 'The Impact of the 2008 Beijing Olympic Games on China's Destination Brand: A U.S.-Based Examination', in: *Journal of Hospitality & Tourism Research*, 37(2), pp. 237–261

Xu, X. (2006), 'Modernizing China in the Olympic spotlight: China's national identity and the 2008 Beijing Olympiad', in: *Sociological Review*, 54(2), pp. 90–107

Zhang, L., and Zhao, S. X. (2009), *City branding and the Olympic effect: A case study of Beijing*. Cities, 26, pp. 245–254

Zhang, J. (2009), 'Spatial Distribution of Inbound Tourism in China: Determinants and Implications', in: *Tourism and Hospitality Research*, 9(1), pp. 32–49

Education for China's event industry

Fit for the future? Some thoughts on event education in a changing world

Schwägermann, Helmut

适应未来？在变化的世界中对会展专业教育之思考

The mission statement of both our event management programmes is: We educate Future Leaders for the Event Industry!

The employment rate of IEMS graduates regularly exceeds 95 per cent. However, we must realise that our graduates will lead an active working life in the event industry until 2050 and beyond! The half-life of knowledge is becoming dramatically shorter. At the same time, mega-trends will strongly influence the working environment as well as customers' needs and demands. Some of the knowledge that students acquire on their study programmes will soon be obsolete.

For this reason, this article addresses the following two questions: Do we equip our graduates with the skills and competencies required to be fit for the future? Is the event education system able to provide appropriate education, and what has to be changed?

In this article, we discuss job profiles of event managers, the concepts of employability, key qualifications and lifelong learning, and offer suggestions concerning future education in the event industry.

对我们中德双方两个会展管理专业来说，其使命宣言都是：我们为会展行业培养未来的领导者。

对于上海国际会展经济与管理专业的毕业生，应届生就业率超过百分之九十五是习以为常的事。但我们也必须意识到，毕业生将在会展行业中工作到2050年甚至更久，而用于这半辈子工作的知识却日见其短。与此同时，宏观趋势将显著地影响着工作环境以及顾客的需求与需要。因此，学生们在大学学习中获得的专业知识不久就会过时了。

本文就此展开讨论两个主要问题：我们是否赋予了毕业生合适的技巧和才能以适应未来？此专业的教育系统是否有能力提供适当的教育，或者哪些应有所改变？

本文论述了会展管理者的工作概况、就业能力的概念、核心素质和终生教育理念，并在最后为将来的会展行业教育提出一些建议。

1 Introduction

The mission statement of both our event management programmes in Osnabrück (Business Events) and Shanghai (International Event Management Shanghai IEMS) is: *We educate Future Leaders for the Event Industry*! Being a *university of applied sciences*, our focus lies on theories and developments that our students can apply in their future working environment. As the name of our programme suggests, we focus on business events as well as the services associated with them.

Our Chinese programme has won several awards for successfully integrating theoretical knowledge with practical experience. The employability of our graduates is one of our main priorities when drawing up the curriculum. The employment rate of IEMS graduates regularly exceeds 95 per cent, including those who go on to pursue a Master's degree anywhere in the world.

However, we must realise that our graduates will lead an active working life in the event industry until 2050 and beyond! The half-life of knowledge is becoming dramatically shorter, and the number of jobs that our graduates will have over the course of their working lives will increase. At the same time, mega-trends will strongly influence the working environment as well as customers' needs and demands. Some of the knowledge that students acquire on their study programmes will soon be obsolete.

For this reason, this article addresses the following two questions: Do we equip our graduates with the skills and competences required to be *fit for the future*?

The second aspect of this article involves exploring the quality and future of the event education system: Is it able to provide appropriate education, and what has to be changed?

In this article, we discuss these challenges, introducing the concepts of employability, key qualifications and lifelong learning. We also offer suggestions concerning future education in the event industry.

2 The profile of today's event managers

2.1 Event managers are live communication specialists

Events can be defined as all kinds of gatherings of people who share a common goal. They can last for days or just for some hours, and must therefore be prepared very efficiently and effectively. In contrast to the length of the event, it can take months or even years to prepare an event. Events meet the needs of different target groups for one main purpose: they want to communicate face to face with other people, whether customers or peers. As we understand it, events are therefore *special instruments for live communication!* The target groups, topics and types of event (exhibitions, conferences, corporate meetings, etc.) may vary, but they all involve the same challenge: all participants have to be there on time; and service providers have to deliver their services on time and in the expected quality and quantity; speakers and exhibitors have to perform as best they can – after all, the event offers them only one chance to convince their peers or customers. Special people with distinct profiles are required for this special quality of live communication and the constant time pressure demands involved. The task of event managers is therefore to organise these special communication tools between small and large groups of people.

Events are increasingly regarded as *projects*, which is why they are managed using project management methods and tools. Today's event managers must therefore fully embrace the strategic and operational dimensions of the "art of project management".

Event managers must also have a thorough understanding of *quality management,* which not only involves avoiding errors (which has a special dimension in live communication), but also constantly satisfying their customers in order to establish a loyal relationship with them.

As a project manager responsible for directing event teams, the main tasks performed by an event manager can be described as: planning, deciding, leading, communicating, consulting and controlling. The event manager is in charge of the entire process of events from the initial idea to the completion of the project.

The tasks undertaken by event managers vary according to their specific jobs and companies. However, they may include developing new event concepts; advertising for exhibitors, visitors and sponsors; defining programmes and processes; choosing locations; coordinating and controlling all internal and external service providers; calculating and controlling event budgets; and, last but not least, controlling the results.

Irrespective of the type of event involved, events are always a *peoples business* which means that, for the majority of event managers, their overall tasks include communicating with people and coordinating them.

2.2 Requirements placed on today's event managers

The significance of events has grown substantially in the last thirty years or so, which is a worldwide trend. Due to the increasing lack of efficiency of traditional communication tools as well as an "information overflow", companies and non-profit organisations are investing ever-greater sums in events focused on target groups. Consequently, the demand for professionally educated event managers has increased. Nowadays, the market needs event managers who have an extensive knowledge of the event industry and who can offer their internal and external customers high-quality communication solutions.

So-called *soft skills* are becoming increasingly important for event managers, particularly those working in an international environment. These soft skills include foreign language skills, personal communication skills in all situations, social skills and intercultural skills. At the same time, special *technical skills* (social media, special event technology, etc.) are becoming increasingly relevant as core competences.

Most of these skills can be acquired at university. However, those wishing to pursue a successful career as an event manager must have a number of *personal characteristics*. These include flexibility in terms of time and mobility and, more importantly, always having to expect the unexpected and develop solutions at very short notice. In addition, event managers must be able to take decisions independently. After all, the relevant line manager cannot always be consulted in time when a problem surfaces thousands of miles away and in a different time zone.

Hence event managers must be able to cope with frustration and stress.

The event industry is characterised by a high degree of labour division. Small and medium-sized service providers offer a wide range of highly specialised services. Event managers have to set up individual project teams for each event; special services from external companies are routinely required. For this reason, leadership skills and the ability to develop people are additional key requirements. In a way, the job profile of an event manager resembles that of an entrepreneur, who must excel in the core competencies of goal orientation, flexibility, communication skills, efficiency and leadership. Event managers often work on projects for a variety of industries (such as automotive, pharmaceuticals, IT, etc.) either simultaneously or in quick succession. Another core ability event managers must have is therefore the ability to grasp the structure, processes and business models of different industries quickly, enabling them to communicate efficiently with their customers.

3 Developments and trends in event education

3.1 Development of event education

Event education programmes have only been offered at universities worldwide for two decades. Before then, event or exhibition companies had to recruit staff from graduates of other programmes, such as marketing or languages. Ten years later, in 2004, the first Chinese event management majors were admitted in Shanghai (Shen 2007).

As the event industry raised its profile over the years and was simultaneously recognised by governments all over the world, many universities and colleges started integrating this special programme for event management in their portfolio.

In the process, each university has to decide whether it wants to offer an event management programme featuring exclusively event-related courses, or a programme that is based on and integrated in a broader field of education, such as business management, tourism or communication. It goes without saying that the latter option is less event-specific, but offers students a broader perspective. The content and curriculum would invariably differ substantially.

Furthermore, universities have to decide whether they want to specialise in certain kinds of events, such as business events, or whether they prefer to offer general education for all kinds of events (see also the introduction). We decided to focus on *business events*, including trade fairs and exhibitions, conferences and meetings as well as corporate events. In addition, we provide education on the management of service associated with those events, namely the management of venues, destinations and event agencies.

Some education programmes focus on a special tourism-related event module such as destination management. We decided to educate our students as event organisers. They are trained to plan, realise and monitor the entire production chain of events and to be responsible for the success of the event in all aspects. These aspects include the content and topic of the trade fair/congress, the location and venue, the quality and quantity of participants, participants' satisfaction, and the Return On the Event (ROE). Our students therefore learn how to conceive, plan and organise events according to participants' needs and expectations. We educate them not only as project managers, but also as marketing managers and quality managers!

How, then, can we balance the relation between theory and practice in event education? The lack of practical experience, social skills and capacity to act has been criticised for years, especially in China, resulting in universities taking new approaches.

As the name "University of Applied Sciences" suggests, in Osnabrück we maintain close relations and open dialogue with the event industry. We involve members of the event industry in the education of our students as lecturers, internship providers and partners. All professors at a university of applied sciences have had management experience in the relevant area of teaching. Event industry associations play a special role since they represent their individual members' needs and arguments. Every semester we offer practical projects and internships, and lectures delivered by event industry leaders are part of the curriculum in both Osnabrück and Shanghai.

In the last decade, a number of international initiatives have evolved that give event education a common structure and greater relevance for the event market. We will now briefly discuss two of these initiatives, namely *EMBOK* and *Meeting Architecture*.

3.2 The EMBOK model

EMBOK (The Event Management Body of Knowledge) was developed by a group of international event lecturers in 2004/2006. They developed a three-dimensional description of the knowledge and skills required to create and organise an event. They were obviously inspired by the framework of PMBOK (Project Management Body of Knowledge). The aim of EMBOK was to create a framework to meet the needs of various cultures, governments, education programmes and organisations in organising events of all kinds.

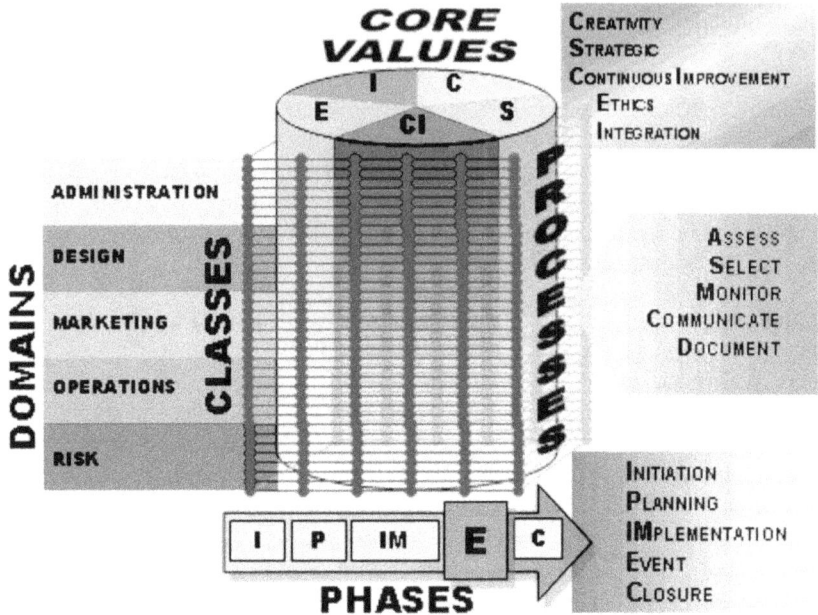

Figure 1: The EMBOK model (EMBOK 2006)

The EMBOK model comprises three dimensions: Domains, Phases and Processes. It provides a comprehensive overview of the principal tasks to be performed by an event manager. The EMBOK model is therefore also a valuable reference tool for any kind of event education. Even if we do not explicitly refer to this model in Osnabrück and Shanghai, we found EMBOK useful and inspiring.

3.3 The meeting architecture

In 2009, Marten Vanneste suggested in his "Meeting Architecture Manifesto" that meeting planners should think, plan and act like architects, who analyse the special needs of their customers before starting to develop a custom-made concept for houses or office buildings. He stated that many special service suppliers in the event industry were too narrow-minded, and only interested in the logistical perfection of their own service, without caring about the overall goals that customers/organisers seek to achieve with their events.

Following this basic idea, which was much applauded in the event industry, he teamed up with a number of colleagues from the event industry to develop a *Meeting Architecture Curriculum* for an MBA programme, shown in Figure 2 (Vanneste 2009).

As we can see, this curriculum is shaped like an onion with several skins, namely (from the outside inwards): cycle, sciences, industries, tools, time and terrains. In a much broader sense than traditional event curricula, it describes which areas should be addressed within the study programme.

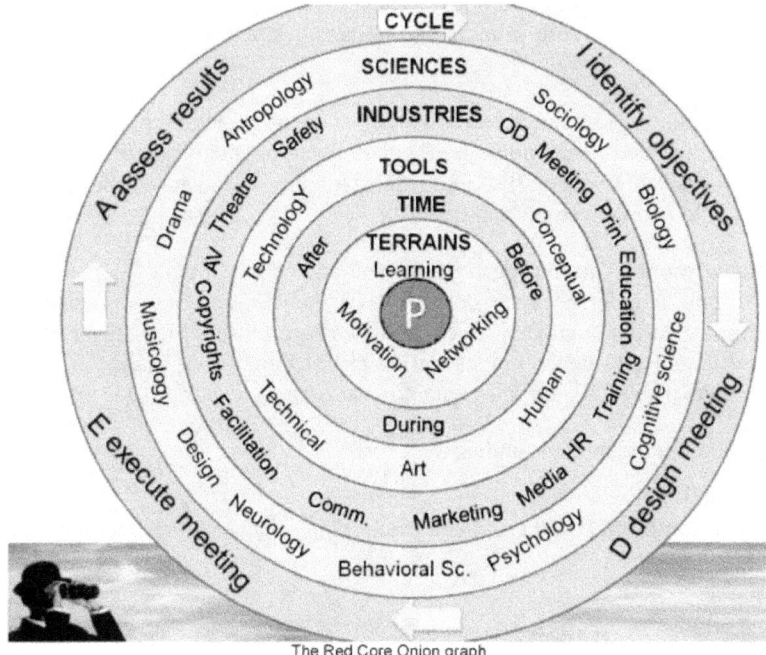

Figure 2: Meeting Architecture Curriculum, 2009

This approach is certainly a valuable discussion point for a number of traditional event service-oriented study programmes. In study programmes where students learn to think and act as organisers and are trained to control the whole value chain of the event, however, Vanneste's criticism does not apply. Nonetheless, these programmes should also discuss whether and how some of the new ideas can be integrated in existing curricula without losing sight of their focus (Schwägermann 2010).

4 Key competences and employability

4.1 Key competences

For years, politicians, employers and scholars have been discussing the increasing significance of so-called "key competences" or "soft skills" in achieving a successful working life as opposed to "hard skills". Although no standard definition exists, experts tend to conclude that hard skills comprise specific, teachable abilities that can be defined and measured. Examples of hard skills include the ability to use software programs; they often refer to accounting, statistics and financial modelling, which may be some of the occupational requirements for a job. These skills are often connected to students' intelligence or GPA

(Grade Point Average). The adoption and reproduction of knowledge and such skills were key elements of education at both schools and universities, especially in China's education system.

By contrast, soft skills are less tangible and harder to quantify. Soft skills include personality-driven skills such as verbal and non-verbal communication and other *people skills*, including negotiation, persuasion, active listening, delegation and leadership. Soft skills have a closer connotation to people's emotional quality.

In the Recommendation of the European Parliament and of the Council on key competences for lifelong learning, competences are defined "as a combination of knowledge, skills and attitudes appropriate to the context. Key competences are those which all individuals need for personal fulfilment and development, active citizenship, social inclusion and employment". Furthermore, it suggests the following *eight key competences*:

1) Communication in the mother tongue;
2) Communication in foreign languages;
3) Mathematical competence and basic competences in science and technology;
4) Digital competence;
5) Learning to learn;
6) Social and civic competences;
7) Sense of initiative and entrepreneurship; and
8) Cultural awareness and expression (EU, 2006:13).

In a recent study, the University of Kent identified "the top ten skills that employers want". These were ranked as follows: 1. Verbal communication 2. Teamwork 3. Commercial awareness 4. Analysing & investigating 5. Initiative & self motivation 6. Drive 7. Written communication 8. Planning & organisation 9. Flexibility and 10. Time management. According to this study, graduates who are equipped with these competences are increasingly sought after by employers (University of Kent, 2014).

In a more event-related study, UFI, The Global Association of the Exhibition Industry, asked their members' HR managers to state which core competences they expect from their future employees. Marketing exhibitions (83 %), sales techniques (72 %) and the development of new exhibitions (72 %) were the key issues (UFI 2013).

Staff who excel in these competences are required by companies and organisations in the service industry, particularly in the event industry, where face-to-face communication is a core characteristic. This observation is also in line with various customer satisfaction models. These have identified the following success factors for service providers: *reliability* (the ability to perform the promised service dependably and accurately); *responsiveness* (the willingness to help customers and provide prompt service); *assurance* (employees' knowledge and courtesy and their ability to inspire trust and confidence); and *empathy* (caring, individualised attention given to customers) (cf. Zeithaml, Bitner 2003: 9).

These findings are fully in line with the requirements placed on event managers (cf. 1.2). Event education programmes are therefore strongly recommended to integrate these key competences in their curricula.

4.2 Employability

As mentioned before, however, it is not only the initial employment rate that counts – our graduates' active working lives will span forty years or more. They are also likely to want to change jobs, employers or even industries for a variety of reasons. We have to widen our perspective from focusing on initial employment after graduation to the comprehensive perspective of their entire working life. For this reason, authors such as Greinert underline three aspects of employability:

1. The ability to *gain* initial employment;

2. the ability to *maintain* employment and make 'transitions' between jobs and roles within the same organisation to meet new job requirements;

3. the ability to *obtain new employment* if required, i.e. to be independent in the labour market. They are willing and able to manage their own employment transitions between and within organisations (Greinert 2008:10).

Similarly, employability can also be defined as a person's capability of gaining and maintaining employment (cf. Hillage 1998:2).

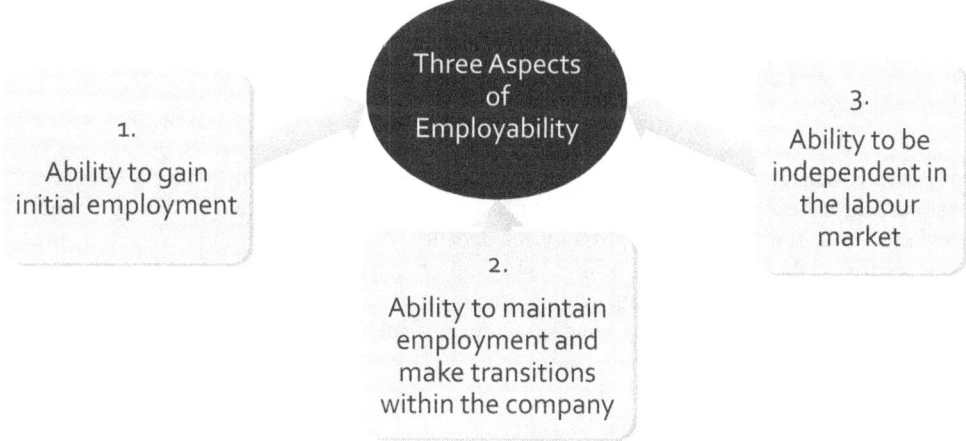

Figure 3: Three aspects of employability

These abilities are sometimes termed *transferable skills* or *employment skills* in the sense that graduates will use these skills when changing jobs within the company or elsewhere on the labour market. These transferable skills are more or less similar to *soft skills* and *people skills*. Employers obviously consider employment skills to be equally important as job-specific or technical skills. Most graduates will change jobs several times in the course of their working lives. Whether or not they have these skills will make a difference on the labour market. This comprehensive concept of employability poses challenges not only to universities that offer event management as a major subject. They need to qualify their students so that they can find a job and contribute to the company's success after graduation. However, they also need to train them so that they will be able to manage their entire professional life in the event industry, if desired, or leave the event industry after a few years if preferred! Universities obviously have to shift their focus to transferable or personal skills without neglecting to teach the special technical skills required by event managers.

How, then, can universities manage to do this? First they have to ensure a balanced provision of special knowledge of the event market and soft skills. In our event programmes, we place special emphasis on training these key competences. We make sure that our students have a good command of English, good communication, presentation and intercultural skills, as well as the ability to work in a team. Our programmes involve more practical experience than those at other universities, meaning that our graduates are highly sought after, and not only in the event industry. In fact, our graduates in Shanghai are also sought after by multinational companies outside the event industry in China, which are looking for young talents with our students' profile.

In addition, however, universities must carefully analyse the past and present driving forces behind their business, as well as those that may dominate it in the future. The job environment and corresponding tasks will change in the years to come. Business models will change. Nobody can be sure about future developments, but we have witnessed several changes in the past that have had a major impact on our professional and private lives. We call such trends 'megatrends'. Their impact on education is discussed in the next section.

5 Megatrends in the event industry

Megatrends can be defined as social, economic, political, environmental or technological changes that have a major impact. Once in place, megatrends influence a wide range of activities, processes and perceptions, possibly for decades. A number of trend research institutes have identified 20 megatrends (z-point 2015), others have defined just 11 (Zukunftsinstitut 2015). In their study on the impact of megatrends on the meeting industry, the German Convention Bureau identified the following seven megatrends:

- Globalisation and internationalisation
- "Peak everything" – shortage of resources
- Urbanisation – city of the future
- Demographic change, feminisation and diversity
- Technology in work and life
- Sustainable development
- Mobility of the future and
- Security and safety

These trends will most certainly have an impact on how we do business in the event industry, and are already doing so today. How, then, can we train our students to meet these changing requirements as future event managers? We will now discuss three such megatrends: *globalisation, sustainable events and technology*.

5.1 Globalisation and intercultural skills

The first massive impacts of globalisation were also felt by the event industry at the end of the last millennium, when the influence of the internet became apparent. By the financial crisis at the latest, it also became more than evident that neither capital flow nor successful ideas, services or products can be stopped by national borders or language barriers.

Enterprises and associations increasingly act globally. Consequently, in addition to using upcoming web-based communication, they also apply live communication instruments such as trade fairs, conventions or marketing events and meetings to achieve a more global market position and/or worldwide influence. In China, the first phase of internationalisation started in the 1980s in the form of Deng Xiaoping's opening policy. Multinational companies, including foreign exhibition companies, flocked to China from the 1990s, establishing joint ventures and later wholly foreign-owned enterprises (WFOE). It is easy to predict that the event business will be increasingly international, and that a good command of (ideally) several languages and intercultural skills will be essential (cf. Steinkuhl et al.).

How can event programmes respond to this trend? Even in the course of their degree programmes, our students should be able to interact professionally with organisers and clients from different cultural backgrounds. After all, our future leaders are very likely to work at least temporarily in foreign countries or at home with foreign customers or partners.

Intercultural skills should not only be trained in lectures, projects and workshops. The best way to gain these skills is to experience people from other cultural areas at university whilst living and working abroad – either on an exchange semester abroad or during an internship in a foreign country.

Students from Osnabrück University of Applied Sciences today can benefit from our comprehensive internationalisation strategy, which includes an international network of more than 100 partner universities in all continents, enabling personal experience abroad. Study abroad is a *compulsory element* of all international study programmes, and highly recommended and encouraged in all other types of study programme. Even in Germany, for instance, 18 per cent of students at Osnabrück's Faculty of Business Management and Social Sciences are international students, providing ample opportunity to gain intercultural skills. The partnership with SUIBE is of great significance to event management students from Osnabrück, many of whom spend a semester studying in Shanghai.

In the other direction, 12 IEMS students from China are invited to attend a language and cultural summer school in Osnabrück each year. In addition, up to ten IEMS students spend an exchange semester abroad in Osnabrück, many of whom are awarded scholarships to do so.

It would make sense to set up a *multi-country Master's programme* for event management where students can study for one or two semesters at different universities, in different countries. Universities are bound to create many more answers to address the megatrend of *globalisation*.

5.2 Sustainable events

A growing number of event organisers and participants around the world believe that it is necessary and a matter of course to ensure their decisions and actions contribute to sustainable event management, and hence to a sustainable world.

The German event industry, led by the German Convention Bureau (GCB) and the European Association of Event Venues (EVVC), introduced a series of special events called *Green Meeting & Events* in 2009. In this connection, they focus on aspects such as reducing the carbon footprint of events and raising awareness of sustainable management among managers and staff from the event service supply industry.

Event lecturers from Osnabrück University of Applied Sciences have been members of the advisory board of this initiative from the outset, providing valuable input to the debate. They were also able to reflect upon the debate within the event industry in their lectures at the university. Sustainable event management is therefore by all means one of the core competences of Osnabrück University of Applied Sciences. The first Bachelor thesis on Green Events was written by a Chinese student from SUIBE as early as 2009. This topic was chosen by several other students in the ensuing years, reflecting Chinese students' great interest in this issue. In 2013, we launched a Sino-German research project on Green Meetings, resulting in an article on Green Meetings in this handbook. Our colleagues at SUIBE are becoming increasingly competent in this field, and are able to teach students accordingly. We believe that event managers throughout the world should gain competence in this field and that universities should take this new topic on board.

5.3 Technology

Following the rapid development of the internet and the diffusion of the digital world to all spheres of life, events have also changed substantially in the past 20 years. Whereas the content of events often developed gradually, communication before, during and after the event has changed dramatically. Web-based and mobile event apps for individual registration and "match-and-meet" functions as well as special offers in the social media raise the prospects of establishing valuable contacts during events.

Even if virtual events have not and will not replace real events, so-called hybrid events combine the strengths of both communication channels. Especially in China, the new buzz-word "O2O" is already used widely not only in e-commerce, but also for events. This term is translated as "online-to-offline". Even now, event managers use various online instruments to attract customers to the offline *point of sales,* which is the real event.

All in all, events are more and more technology-driven, and all forecasts predict that it will be a stable trend. How, then, can universities respond to this trend?

At IEMS, we conduct experiments with all kinds of blended learning, since German lecturers only travel to Shanghai during the teaching period (blocks). We therefore communicate regularly via e-learning platforms and Skype, or use videoconferencing to exchange with our students. Videoconferencing is even used for students to orally defend their Bachelor theses. Thus, although a start has been made, we still need to embed this area in our curriculum. However, there is stiff competition between the different platforms in the world – facebook, twitter and Whatsapp are banned in China; similar Chinese applications such as Weibo and Wechat not only replace these western applications, they also have a number of advantages over them. Due to these circumstances, Sino-foreign educational programmes are unable to make consistent use of these new technologies for internal training or communication purposes. In addition, the half-life of knowledge is becoming dramatically shorter; the estimation for the IT sector (including new event-related apps) is only three years, meaning that this specialist IT knowledge becomes obsolete after this space of time!

The debate on these megatrends provides additional evidence that we must not focus our education on transferring specialist knowledge alone – we must develop long-term, sustainable concepts, such as the one introduced in the next section: lifelong learning.

6 Development of a lifelong learning concept for the event market

In a changing world, universities must make sure that students recognise, accept and manage ever-changing society, markets, enterprises and their own job profile, in other words, that they are prepared for lifelong learning. Fischer suggests that lifelong learning is a necessity rather than a luxury. Lifelong learning is more than adult education, it is a mindset and a habit for people to acquire (Fischer 2000: 268). Arnold and Rohs regard the attitude of lifelong learning as a new way of life (Arnold, Rohs: 22ff). Tao points out the difference between the concepts of lifelong education and lifelong learning: whereas lifelong *education* emphasises the aspect of the education system providing individuals with access to education and opportunities for organised learning, lifelong *learning* emphasises that potential learners are not limited (by time, place, occupation or group) in their acquisition of knowledge and self-promotion. They can decide on the pace of their learning according to their own wishes and needs (Tao 2009:255).

Lifelong learning is obviously a necessity for individuals, as well as for societies and their organisations. As organisations, universities cannot therefore be made responsible alone – all stakeholders involved must cooperate in order to manage constant change.

For the event market, we have identified *four stakeholders* that must be involved in developing a lifelong learning concept: universities, professors, the event industry and students (see Fig. 4).

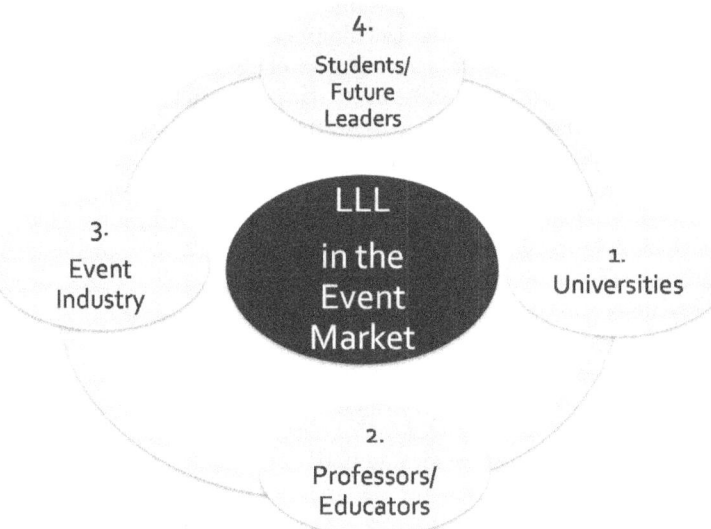

Figure 4: Lifelong learning concept for the event market

6.1 Challenges for *universities*

It goes without saying that universities and academies have to be addressed first, since they are the core institutions for research, higher education and learning. Universities should *per se* see themselves as learning and developing organisations that are change agents and promoters of new knowledge and ideas. They therefore have to continuously adapt and update their curricula/teaching plans according to the changing requirements of the market. They must make sure that professors are aware of the latest developments and are able to teach the "state of the art". This has to be a precondition within the certification and recertification process, which all universities have to undergo. However, universities should also acknowledge the ever-declining half-life of knowledge, and offer updated knowledge to their alumni and interested practitioners, if they are qualified to attend these courses.

The practical experience gained by our graduates is a hot topic not only but especially in China, where the traditional teaching and learning model emphasised the acquisition of knowledge to the detriment of application skills. Case studies and information about how to integrate practical experience at university are presented later in this article as well as in the article on education systems in this handbook.

Concerning the major in event management, at least some universities in each country should offer Continuing Professional Development (CDP) programmes. Osnabrück University of Applied Sciences is currently contemplating establishing a *Centre for Continuing Event Education* with the philosophy of an *Open University*, using methods of blended learning. A similar *institution* for Shanghai could be discussed soon.

Such an education centre would have three potential tasks:

- Offer seminars and courses to event management graduates and practitioners to enable them to continuously update their knowledge and skills
- Offer certificate programmes to practitioners to enable them to obtain a Bachelor degree in event management whilst working
- Offer additional programmes such as summer schools that could focus on special issues within event management.

Universities that offer event management also have to recognise the megatrends occurring in the event industry and integrate certain aspects of these trends in their curricula to ensure their students are fit for the future. And yet it is not only the institution 'university' that has a responsibility in this respect – the professors in charge of teaching and education also play a role.

6.2 Challenges for *event professors/educators*

Professors in the event industry must also constantly ensure that they teach according to the state of the art. Professors who conduct research are aware of the latest trends in their specific research field. In addition, all event professors at universities of applied sciences in Germany must have a track record of at least five years of management expertise in their respective fields. They must also retain close contacts to the event industries and their respective associations. In China, most event professors have no working experience, but embarked on an academic career immediately after graduating.

It is therefore of paramount importance, particularly in China, that professors and lecturers

- gain *practical experience* in the event industry before starting to teach
- have *regular contact* with the event industry
- are *members* of national and international *event associations*
- initiate *joint projects and research together* with the event industry
- attend special training courses

and also commit themselves to the concept of lifelong learning.

6.3 Challenges for the *event industry*

The concept of lifelong learning is obviously of paramount interest for the event industry and its companies, represented by associations and organisations. However, if event companies are interested in well-educated and motivated employees who can contribute to the success of the company, they should retain closer contacts to universities and academies; try to provide advice on new university topics; and go out of their way to meet top talents. The event industry has extensive experience in all kinds of events, but is also interested in the research and development of new applications. They should invite universities to go on *excursions* to their company; give students the chance to *volunteer* at their events; initiate interesting *event projects* in cooperation with universities; and give students the chance to undertake *real internships*. They should initiate and co-fund special research projects, which can be applied in their strategic or operative planning. They should set up a *personal development plan (career plan)* for their own staff, and determine *seminars and courses* that may be useful in the further development of their staff. Event companies can also try to influence concepts and curricula for the event business. Together with universities, event companies could develop the concept of *Continuing Professional Development for Event Managers*. The event industry, especially in China, must also ask why highly talented event graduates opt to take their first job in other areas, rather than remain in the event industry. We believe it is not just the attraction of being able to earn more in other industries. It is also the case that event managers demonstrate a lack of effort and patience towards students who are still in the learning phase.

In summary, event companies should learn to think and act like *learning organisations*, and integrate the concept of lifelong learning in their corporate culture!

6.4 Challenges for event *students/future leaders*

Last but not least, we come to the students – future leaders in the event industry: more than ever before, we have to teach our students how to learn by themselves. They must expect continuous changes or, even better: be change managers! They have to understand that future employers expect a mixture of professional and personal skills, and that professional knowledge has a shorter half-life than personal, transferable skills, which also have to be adapted outside the classroom. They have to find the right active approach towards the event industry now (proactively!) and gain practical experience at university. They must try to recognise new megatrends and respond to them earlier than others, enabling them to gain a strategic advantage in their career and on the labour market. Even if it is not a compulsory element of their study programme, students should venture abroad and experience different cultures on an exchange semester, during an internship or simply during *work and travel*. To sum up: students have to accept and grasp the concept of employability and lifelong learning at the earliest stage possible.

7 Conclusion: are we fit for the future?

Today's event managers have a special profile that is dominated by transferable skills such as communication, flexibility, team orientation, etc. The event business is a people business. People skills are transferable skills. This is definitely an advantage over other industries, which are dominated to a greater extent by specific technical skills.

Although different approaches to event education exist, universities have to try to find ways of shaping their profile and simultaneously improving the employability of their students.

Event management graduates must be experts in live communication in an international environment, influenced by many overlapping trends. As pointed out in this article, the future will bring about dramatic change in the living and working environment, not only in the event management industry. Some of these potential changes have been already identified (megatrends). The concepts of employability and lifelong learning will therefore be key factors for the continued success of these universities and their graduates. Forward-looking education must strike a healthy balance between specific professional/functional skills and soft skills. Moreover, this article demonstrates the need for closer cooperation between all stakeholders involved in the fields of learning and education.

Fit for the Future? This article takes a rather optimistic view of the education of event managers, but also states the preconditions that have to be met if the event industry wants to master the challenges of the future with the help of adequate manpower. Thus the significance of events as a unique communication instrument is also ensured for the future.

8 Literature

Arnold, R., Rohs, M. (2014) Von der Lernform zu Lebensform, in: Schönherr, K.W., Tiberius, V., Lebenslanges Lernen, Wiesbaden, p. 21–28

Commission of the European Communities (2006) Adult learning: It is never too late to learn COM (2006) 614 final

EMBOK (2006) Event Management Body of Knowledge, www.EMBOK.org

European Union (2006) Recommendation of the European Parliament and of the Council on key competences for lifelong learning (2006/962/EC)

Fischer, G., (2000) "Lifelong Learning – More Than Training," Journal of Interactive Learning Research, in: Training and Life-Long Learning (eds.: Richiro Mizoguchi and Piet A.M. Kommers), 11(3/4), p. 265–294.

German Convention Bureau (2013), Meetings and Conventions 2030: A study of megatrends shaping our industry

Green Meetings & Events, www.greenmeetings-und-events.de

Greinert, W.-D. (2008) Beschäftigungsfähigkeit und Beruflichkeit – zwei konkurrierende Modelle der Erwerbsqualifizierung, BiBB, BWP 4/2008, p. 9–12

Hillage, J. (1998) Employability: Developing a Framework for Policy Analysis, Research Report RR85, Department for Education and Employment

Schubarth, W., Speck K. (2013) Employability und Praxisbezüge im wissenschaftlichen Studium, HRK-Fachgutachten

Schwägermann, H. (2010) Bildungscontrolling, ROI und Meeting Architecture: Neue Wege zu effizienten Meetings? in: Zanger, Cornelia (ed.), Stand und Perspektiven der Eventforschung, Wiesbaden, p. 119–131

Schwägermann, H. (2011) Studium Business Events in Osnabrück: interkulturell, grün, hybrid und praxisverlinkt, TW Tagungswirtschaft 4/2011, p. 25–26

Shen, X. (2007) Shanghai Education, Shanghai

Steinkuhl, C., Gray, C., Metz, A. (2015) Lecturing key competencies in China and the challenge of transnational education, in: Schwägermann, H., Mayer, P., Ding, Y. Handbook Event Market China, Berlin 2015

Tao, W., Cheng, J, Dong, J., Wang, J. (2009) East Asia Lifelong Learning Community 2020: Objective, Organization and Operation, Springer-Online

UFI (2013) ufi education survey, http://www.ufi.org/Medias/pdf/thetradefairsector/surveys/2013_education_survey.pdf

University of Kent, http://www.kent.ac.uk/careers/sk/top-ten-skills.htm

Vanneste, Marten (2009) The Meeting Architecture Manifesto, www.meetingarchtecture.org

Zeithaml, V.A., Bitner, J.B., Gremler, D.D., (2006) Service Marketing, 4th edition

z-point (2015) www.zpunkt.de/fileadmin/be_user/englisch/D_Downloads/Megatrends_Update_EN.pdf

Zukunftsinstitut (2015) http://www.megatrend-dokumentation.de

The event industry and its human resources: A view based on the characteristics of the industry

Mao, Daben

会展与人才 – 基于行业特点的会展人才观

After a fast-paced boom for more than 20 years, China's Event Industry is suffering from a worsening scarcity in its human resources. The gap between the supply and demand is becoming wider in all areas of the industry, including organisers, official constructors, official freight forwarders or service agents. This article summarises the characteristics of Chinese event industry and its required human resources, and gives some suggestions on the event education and the development of the students.

The event industry is a people industry, is an industry that combines lots of practices, an industry that service is itself, and an industry that involves teamwork. The human resources of the event industry should develop planning, integrative, marketing, and executive skills. The event education should combine the theory and practice together, should cultivate internationalised talents, also it should develop the students' capacities to use new technologies such as big data, cloud computing, internet platforms and mobile internet. As for students, the success of their future career comes from the book knowledge, communication skills and a down-to-earth working attitude.

经过二十多年的高速发展，中国会展业人才匮乏的局面存在恶化的趋势，无论是会展主办方、会展设计搭建方、会展场馆物流方和会展代理方都面临着越来越大的供需差距。文章阐述了中国会展业的行业特点和人才需求特点，并对会展教育和学生的发展提出了一些建议。

会展是人，是实践，是服务、是团队。会展业的人才需要具备策划能力、整合能力、营销能力和执行能力。会展教育要加强理论与实践的结合，注重国际化人才的培养，还要开发学生使用大数据、云计算、平台、移动互联等新科技的能力。对学生来说，未来职业的成功来自于课本知识、沟通技巧和脚踏实地的工作态度。

1 Introduction

The event industry has been booming in China for more than 20 years, and now features a complete industry chain on a remarkable scale and with many benefits (Jiao 2013). According to statistics made available by China Convention/Exhibition/Event Society, 7,319 exhibitions were held, totalling an area of 9,391 square metres and a direct output of 387 billion yuan. Universities around the country have recently established Event Management as a major subject. Forty per cent of China's students majoring in Event Management are enrolled at Guangdong, Zhejiang and Shanghai, with 5,700 in Guangdong, 3,700 in Zhejiang and 3,100 in Shanghai (CCES 2014). However, fast-growing event education is unable to meet the need for sufficiently qualified employees for the industry (Wang and Li 2011). Table 1 shows that the gap between supply and demand is very large in all areas of the event industry, be it organisers, official constructors, official freight forwarders or service agents in the event industry. Industry insiders believe it is very difficult to find project managers who are able to plan, manage and carry out whole projects independently. It is even difficult to find people who can take on part of the work, such as sub-projects.

Tab. 1: The ratio between the supply and demand of qualified employees (own calculation)

	2005	2006	2007	2008	2009	2010
Organisers	13:1	12:1	15:1	16:1	15:1	18:1
Co-organisers	12:1	14:1	13:1	17:1	19:1	21:1
Official constructors	10:1	8:1	8:1	15:1	17:1	25:1
Official freight forwarders	11:1	13:1	9:1	10:1	13:1	20:1
Service agencies	5:1	7:1	9:1	6:1	10:1	12:1

What are the reasons for this lack of qualified employees? Is the salary too low? The answer is no. Salaries have risen in line with the development of the industry. The annual pay of a project manager is several hundred thousand yuan, which is not low. The next question is: where do qualified graduates end up? Does the content of degree programmes fail to meet companies' requirements? As a CEO of an exhibition company with 24 years of experience in the event industry, I hope that this paper will help stakeholders in the industry to find out more about the real needs of the industry, and to provide advice and thoughts on how to improve university-level event management. The following paper consists of four parts. Three issues will be discussed in the first three parts, namely the characteristics of the event industry, the demands placed on qualified employees in companies, and employees' needs concerning the future event industry. Advice on how to develop university-level event management will be provided in the final section.

2 Characteristics of the event industry

The event industry differs considerably from other industries, which means that qualified employees should adapt to the characteristics and development of this industry to the greatest extent possible.

2.1 Events focus on people

Events are like circles, starting from contacting people, reaching a peak during the event, then continuous contacting people after the event until the next event starts. An exhibition in China usually starts from communication with the industry association and the approval from the government on the topic and the range of exhibits. Then the exhibitors and potential visitors are contacted, which takes time. During the event, visitors, exhibitors and the media come to the venue, where they can communicate with each other, and so bringing people together in the whole event process. Communication does not stop once an exhibition finishes. Face-to-face communication will continue in the form of clearing up the deals with suppliers, summarising the event and expressing thanks to the partners. This business circle repeats constantly.

Compared to other communication platforms, exhibitions feature the most direct and close contact, which is best for multilateral communication between people. Table 2 shows that events involve clients more than other platforms, such as TV, radio, shopping centres and credit cards, and involve more face-to-face communication. Although virtual events on the internet feature a growing number of the aforementioned functions, they still lack face-to-face communication and business talk.

Since events focus on people, their willingness and ability to communicate with others are obviously important. The event industry requires employees to do research, contact, serve, organise, coordinate and lead people. Meanwhile, it also requires that employees have the composure to deal with all kinds of problems maturely and appropriately.

Tab. 2:   Comparison of platform participants. Source: VNU

Platform	Constructor/ Supplier	Client 1	Client 2	Client 3	Whether to meet	Whether to negotiate	Interaction
TV/media	TV/ radio station	Visitor/ audience	Advertising company		No	No	Unilateral
Shopping centre	Investors	Customer	Manufacturer		No	No	Unilateral
Credit card	Bank	Customer	Company		No	No	Unilateral
Meeting	Organiser	Audience	Lecturer	Advertising company	Yes	No	Unilateral
Exhibition	Organiser	Visitor	Exhibitor	Media	Yes	Yes	Multilateral
Internet	Internet company	Browser	Manufacturer	Advertising company	No	No	Multilateral

2.2 Events need practice

The event industry is an industry with a high practical orientation. Outsiders consider us to be white-collar workers in offices when they see us in suits at exhibitions. In fact, only insiders know that a lot of dirty, hard and dangerous work has to be completed beforehand. In the process of inviting exhibitors, you do not only have to sell the space successfully but also please your clients with a satisfactory service. If exhibition managers have no practical experience, it is virtually impossible to realise these two aims by learning from books alone. In the course of arranging exhibitions, project managers have to do a lot of dirty, hard and dangerous work to conduct on-site management, such as keeping a close eye on the exhibition halls all the time, preventing illegal practices and ensuring that stand decorations are not at risk of collapsing when supervising constructors. Project managers must also check the hall in order to inspect security equipment, liaise with venue workers, constructors and exhibitors, and solve all emergencies. In all, therefore, our colleagues have to walk between 10 and 15 km a day during the lead up to and opening of the exhibition. It must be ensured that everything has been organised perfectly so that everyone else is clear about matters. It therefore takes a while for a novice in the event industry to become a mature project manager.

Events cannot live without practice. Operations are related to many aspects. Wherever problems occur, the quality of an exhibition will potentially be directly affected. In order to operate a project efficiently and to prevent problems from occurring, you experience many sleepless nights, starting from two months before the opening ceremony. Figure 1 gives an accurate description of the processes that have to be considered in order to implement an event project successfully. It covers many practical aspects, from time and monetary budgeting, supplier management to previous events' data collecting.

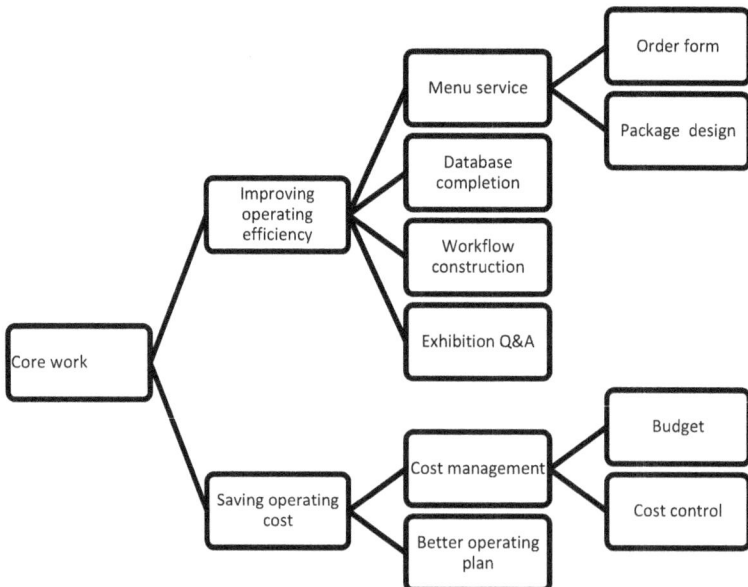

Figure 1: Core work performed by the operating department.

The dual education system at DHBW Ravensburg, Germany is really admirable. The school provides education for some students coming from an event company and they will go back to work in the same company after the graduation. Some students even come from companies. They usually spend three years at university – half of which is spent learning theories, and the remainder practicing. In other words, three months of every semester are spent studying theory and three months are spent undergoing practical training at event companies. Thanks to this kind of dual education system, students are able to improve their theoretical knowledge as well as their practical skills (Zhang 2004).

2.3 Event equals service

The event industry is a high-level service industry. This is because it has become an engine for economic development with a pulling effect for economic growth usually 10 to 30 times higher than in general service industries (Chen et al. 2011). Taking the result of the survey concerning Hamburg Exhibition Company (HMC) conducted by Munich-based ifo-Institute for Economic Research as an example, every euro gained from the HMC, Hamburg's retail sales, rental industry, catering industry, hotel industry, etc. benefit from an additional 7.6 euros. A total of 266 HMC employees created 6,450 employment opportunities in the logistics industry, handcraft industry, catering industry, etc., 4,093 of which are in Hamburg (Annual Report of HMC, 2014) this is why Shanghai is building four centres: the international economic centre, the international financial centre, the international shipping centre and the international trade centre. When planning the construction of the international trade centre, the government placed much greater emphasis on the development of the event industry than ever (Xin 2010).

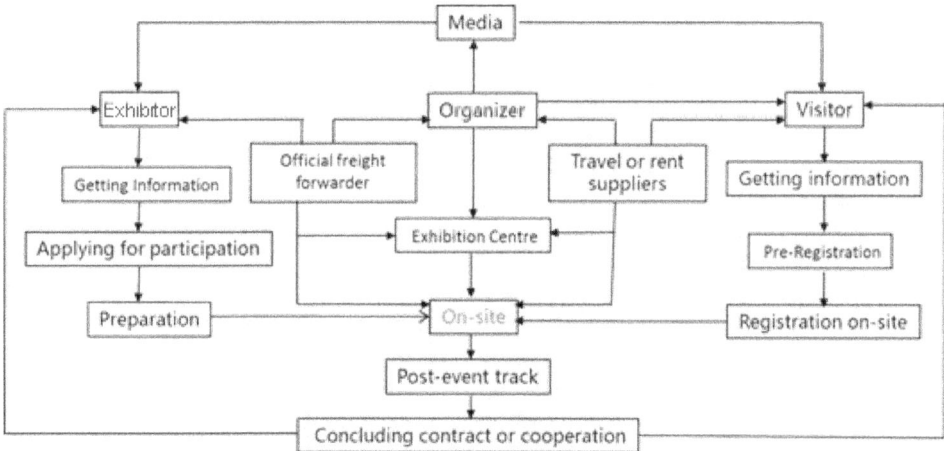

Figure 2: Service diagram of exhibitions.

Being a part of the service industry, services should be considered seriously. Willingness to help others is very important in providing good services to the organiser's three main customers: exhibitors, visitors and the media. Figure 2 shows the whole service process provided to the three main customers by the organiser. This process takes one year, while the actual exhibition will only last for three or more days. In this one-year process, services are provided from beginning to end. First, services are provided to the media, enabling them to obtain information about the industry quickly. Second, services are also provided to exhibitors to ensure that they know the exhibition well and can prepare for it fully. Services are provided to visitors in order to give them a more satisfactory experience. 'The customer is god and experience is best' are goals pursued by everyone in the exhibition company.

2.4 Events involve teamwork

An exhibition is related to many different aspects of services. Every node of the industrial chain can affect the operation and management of companies, so the work cannot be done by one person alone. 'Being a team player' is the most basic requirement for talents in the event industry. Cooperation is the most important core value in our company. The success of an exhibition requires the cooperation of every employee in the company, even part-time workers. Large exhibitions involve around 50 part-time workers, making cooperation within the team even more difficult.

3 Demands placed on qualified employees in event companies

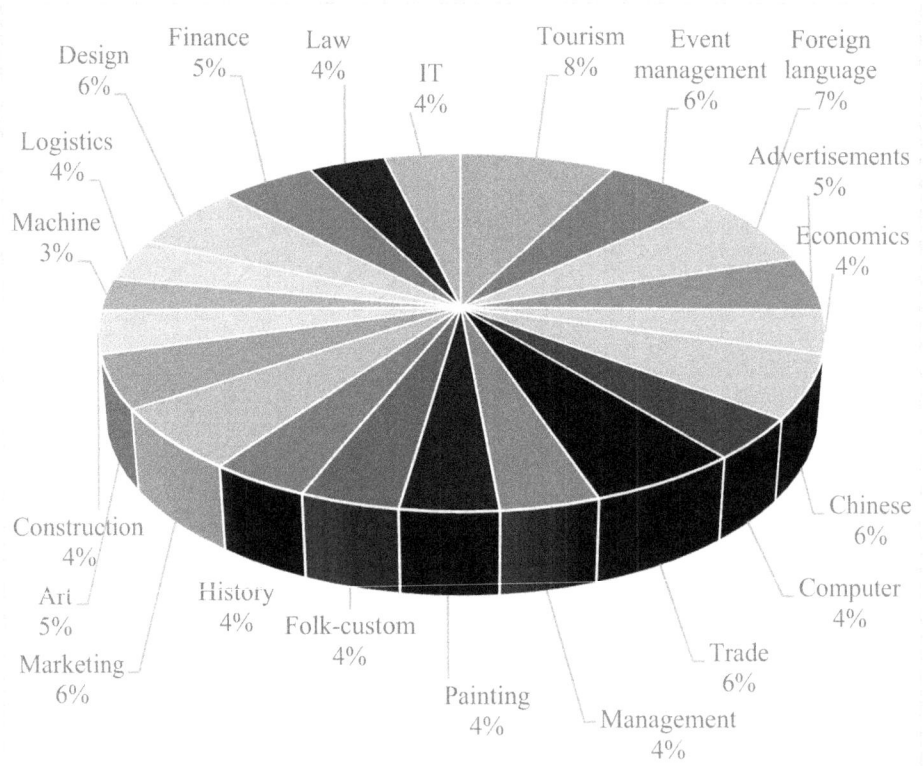

Figure 3: Educational background of employees in the event industry.

3.1 Event management requires planning skills

Figure 3 shows that education background of the people working in the event industry is rather balanced, which means the industry requires various knowledge to generate creativity. Creativity sounds fancy however is based on the understanding of customers' needs and discovering their unmet requirements. Although the 7,200 exhibitions held each year in China cover almost all industries, there are still a number of unsatisfied needs that remain to be discovered. It is up to talents in the event industry to find them.

3.2 Events need integrative capabilities

When it comes to exhibitions, the organiser acts as a 'bridge' and 'platform'. All of the stakeholders are brought together on this platform. Talents in the event industry should have the capability to make full use of their advantages and to integrate them. As Figure 4 shows, a feasibility report should first be prepared according to the industry's needs. After obtaining recognition from industry associations and government approval, the project can be launched. When information about industry association members is used properly, exhibitors can be recruited more smoothly; Government in China usually provides financial support to large size exhibitions (for example, an exhibition with 100,000 square metres), this is also a good financial resource to integrate if the number can be reached. After agreeing on the exhibition, organisers may need help from downstream service providers in the industry chain, such as the media, the contractor and the transporter. The core competencies of talents in the event industry comprise knowing how to exploit their advantages, finding key people and associations so as to achieve the goals, and drawing upon mutual benefits.

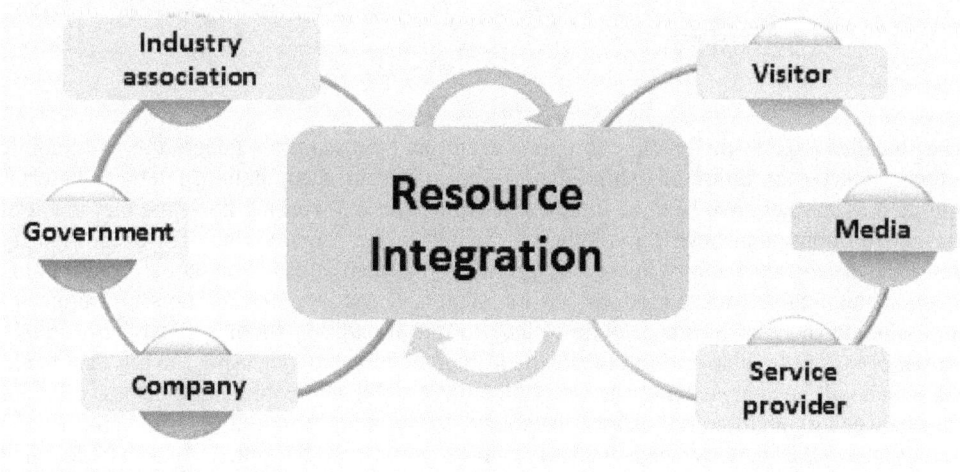

Figure 4: Resource integration.

3.3 Events need marketing capabilities

If we take creativity and planning as the starting points for marketing, finding creative tools is a must to boost the marketing efficiency. Nowadays, in the era of big data, information spreads rapidly and intensively; the traditional 4P theory seems not enough. On the basis of developing the traditional 4P marketing theory, we need to master many innovative methods and logic, such as integrating the transmission (integration) of online and offline marketing methods as well as integrating the internet and mobile internet, which has already changed not only relationships between people, but also our traditional way of thinking. Furthermore, as to the innovation of marketing, another two Ps should be taken into consideration, namely People and Presentation. Being people oriented and serving people with our hearts require us to present well to convey this kind of service to our clients. An outstanding presentation is the main key to success.

3.4 Events need executive capabilities

A successful event requires all kinds of tasks to be done. Organising and managing an event is like operating a delicate machine. As mentioned above, an error with any part can cause the whole project to fail. Details decide about success or failure, which means that the project manager should be able to control each section completely, efficiently and accurately. Event talents should therefore be clear-minded, highly efficient, and result- and action-oriented.

4 Requirements of talents for the future event industry

The so-called 'o2o event' (offline to online event) and the seamless integration with mobile internet will be the future of exhibitions. As big data, cloud computing, internet platforms and mobile internet have become inseparable from people's working lives, the placement of the new economy and new technology will be key to the pace at which the event industry develops. As Figure 5 shows, the event information system is based on modern information technologies that provide a platform for interaction. It encourages exhibitors to present information on this platform and invite visitors to join in, aiming simultaneously at hosting a virtual event on the platform. It collects their interactive behaviour using the big data method, which will be analysed and used to build a more stable and continuing business relationship between exhibitors and visitors. Therefore, today, with the rapid development of technology, the event industry needs managers who keep up with the times. As well as learning traditional knowledge, people should also ensure they understand and use modern information technologies, which will become the key skills required to lead the event industry in the future.

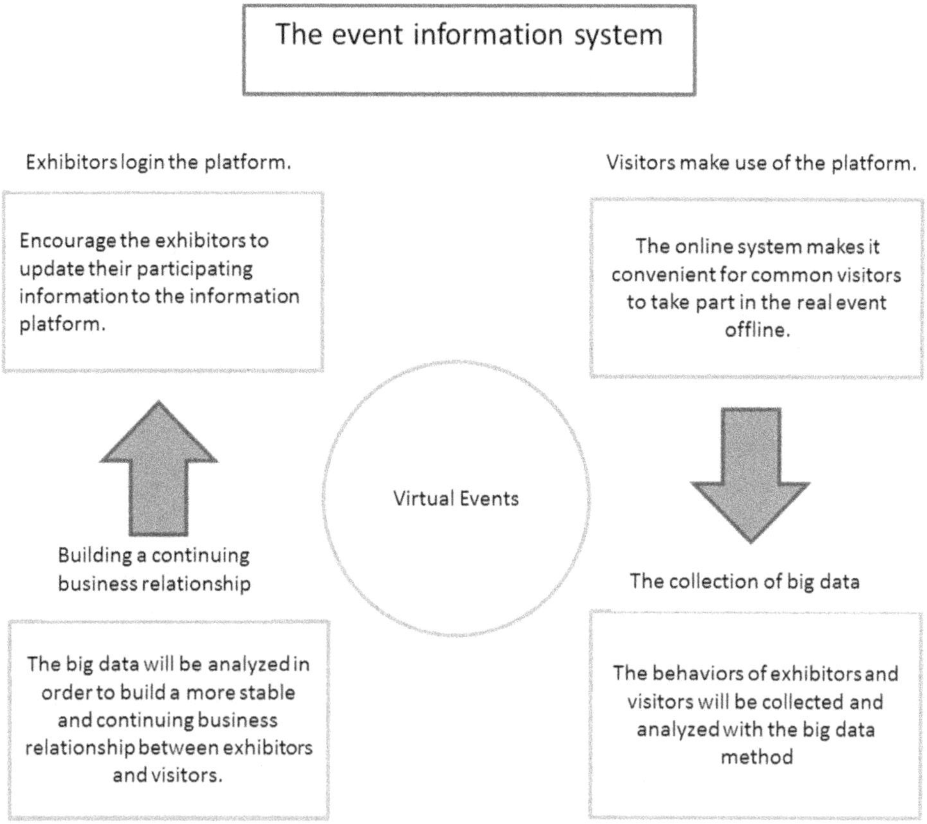

The event information system

Exhibitors login the platform.

Encourage the exhibitors to update their participating information to the information platform.

Visitors make use of the platform.

The online system makes it convenient for common visitors to take part in the real event offline.

Virtual Events

Building a continuing business relationship

The collection of big data

The big data will be analyzed in order to build a more stable and continuing business relationship between exhibitors and visitors.

The behaviors of exhibitors and visitors will be collected and analyzed with the big data method

Figure 5: The event information system.

5 Suggestions to event educators

From our experience as event initiators, we can make the following suggestions to event educators.

1. Systematically combine event education and event companies, and explore dual education.
2. Teaching and training are both important when cultivating event talents.
3. Economic globalisation will definitely lead to the globalisation of events. Train more international talents.
4. Greater attention should be paid to the new economy such as mobile internet, which is bound to change and lead the development of the event industry

Finally, here are five suggestions for students interested in entering the event industry.

1. Learn more theoretical knowledge at school. The two most important subjects are marketing and project management, which will equip you with a sound theoretical foundation.
2. Work hard to learn English well, which will make you more competitive, ensuring there are no barriers to your career.
3. Go to event companies. Work in a call centre. After half a year of hard work, you will have improved considerably. If you were the star employee in the course of those six months, project managers will be wanting to recruit you.
4. Participate in events. Work as a trainee and, at the same time, watch, join in and take notes as much as possible. There is no doubt that you will be chosen to join the best event companies.
5. In your event career, these three elements will make you outstanding.
   - Ten per cent is professional knowledge at university, which gives you a sound theoretical foundation.
   - Forty per cent is communication skills, helping you to gain support from your clients and cooperation partners.
   - The remaining 50 per cent depends on your reliability. Reliability will help you gain the continuing trust of your partners and clients, ensuring their permanent support.

6 Literature

China Convention and Exhibition Society/CCES (2014): *China Event industry Development Report in 2014*

Wang, J. and Li, J. (2011), *Investigation and Analysis of the Needs for Professional Exhibition Talents-Shanghai as an example*. Online: http://www.cces2006.org/yjcg/2011-5/6845.shtml (accessed on 30 Jun. 2014)

Xin, S. (2010), *Shanghai Released a White Book for the Four Centre Construction* [上海发布四个中心建设白皮书]. Online: http://finance.sina.com.cn/stock/y/20101112/01108941128.shtml (accessed on 05 Jul. 2014)

Zhang, J. (2004), *Investigation and Analysis of the German Exhibition Education System*, Issue 17 in 2004

Jiao, W. (2013), *Research on Present Situation and Countermeasures of China's Exhibition Industry*, Issue 18 in 2013

Chen, T., Yuan, Y. and Yuan, P. (2011), *The Definition, Characteristics and the Connotation of China High-level Service Industry*, Issue 13 in 2011

Hamburg Exhibition Company/HMC (2014), *2014 Annual Report*

Xu, J. (2014), *Event Education* [会展教育应做到"起点宽、内容广、接地气"]. Online: http://expo.ce.cn/sy/gd/201411/14/t20141114_3906105.shtml (accessed on 07 Oct. 2014)

Education of event management in Germany and China: A comparison

Ding, Ye,
Gaida, Hans-Jürgen,
Schwägermann, Helmut

会展管理教学在德国与中国的比较

Events of all kind have a long tradition in all countries and all cultures of the world. In the course of the globalisation, the need of a professional management of these events became obvious. However, until the end of the last century, there was no professional education available for those, who wanted to work in exhibition companies, event agencies or convention centres. It was only in the early 1990s, when event management appeared on the study programmes of the universities in Germany and some other countries around the world. Today, in Germany almost 50 universities, universities of applied sciences, academies and various other institutions are active in the event education system. In China, event education started in the universities in 2002. In 2011, already 187 universities and vocational schools offered event management as a major in China. This article gives an insight into the two event management education systems.

各式各样的展会在全世界各种各国文化中都有着悠久的历史。
在全球化的进程中对于展会的专业化管理的需求也变得日益明显。然而直到上世纪末，对于一些想在展览公司、展会服务中介、会议中心工作的人都无法获得相关的专业教育。直到上世纪九十年代早期，一些会展管理专业才在德国和其他国家的大学成立。当今，在德国有将近50所大学、应用技术大学、学院和各类其他机构积极活跃在会展教育系统中。在中国，大学会展专业始于2002年。在2011年，在中国已有187家大学和职业学校设置了会展管理专业。本文将深入分析两国会展专业教育体系。

1 The framework of event management education

All countries and cultures of the world have a long tradition of hosting all kinds of events. Gatherings have always been held for a wide variety of purposes: exchanging information, entertaining, doing trade, taking decisions, hosting competitions and games, and for all kinds of religious and cultural purposes. Initially, many of these functions were integrated in a few comprehensive events. Over time, however, many of these events were "professionalised": they have grown in importance; they are visited by an ever-growing number of individuals; and their budgets and the risks involved have grown accordingly, meaning that they must be planned and organised more professionally.

At the end of the last century, however, there was still no professional higher education available to those intending to embark on a career with an exhibition company, an event agency or a convention centre. Only professional associations and private companies offered seminars and other courses, but these were not recognised as being work towards a degree. This situation changed at the end of the last millennium, when universities started offering degree programmes in event management.

As mentioned in the introduction to this handbook, the *event market* consists of various types of events that differ considerably. It is therefore virtually impossible – and in most cases not pertinent – to cover them all. For this reason, most universities that offer event management as a degree programme specialise on certain aspects of the market, e. g. business events.

The second aspect covered by university programmes is the *management of events*. This involves aspects such as service management, quality management and project management. Universities also have to decide whether they wish to teach their students to plan, organise and control the whole event production process as the *initiator (producer) of events* or whether they would prefer to concentrate on training them to perform certain *event-related services*, such as destination or venue management.

In addition, universities have to decide whether they wish to offer event management as an entire study programme or whether they would prefer to include event management modules in other basic programmes, such as business management, media management or tourism management.

This decision obviously depends on the national and local situation of the university, its profile compared to its competitors, and how the future employability of its graduates is assessed (cf. Schwägermann, *Fit for the Future?* in this handbook).

2 The higher education system in Germany

The fields of higher education in Germany are manifold. Due to the federal structure of Germany, each of the 16 constituent states is responsible for the administration of its science, education and cultural affairs. In order to give a brief overview of the system, we refer to a number of statistics provided by the DAAD (German Academic Exchange Service, www.daad.de). There are over 380 officially recognised universities, which can be divided into three main types:

- 109 universities, which focus on methodological and theoretical knowledge transfer
- 216 *universities of applied sciences* (应用科技大学Ying Yong Ke Ji Da Xue), which are more practically oriented. (Some of these are *cooperative universities*, which have an even stronger vocational orientation)
- 55 *colleges* of art, film and music

In all, 240 universities are administered and funded by government. Nonetheless, universities and, increasingly, universities of applied sciences work autonomously. Almost 100 institutions are privately run. A relatively large number of these are state recognised, which means that they are entitled to confer Bachelor degrees and, in some cases, even Master's degrees. If this is not the case, these institutions may cooperate with officially recognised universities in Germany or abroad to ensure that their students can gain an academic degree. Privately run universities charge tuition fees, which may total over € 30,000 for a six-semester study programme. In contrast, government-supported universities do not charge tuition fees, or if they do so, it is usually only a nominal amount.

The higher education system in Germany envisages three main ways of obtaining a university degree (cf. Figures 1 and 2).

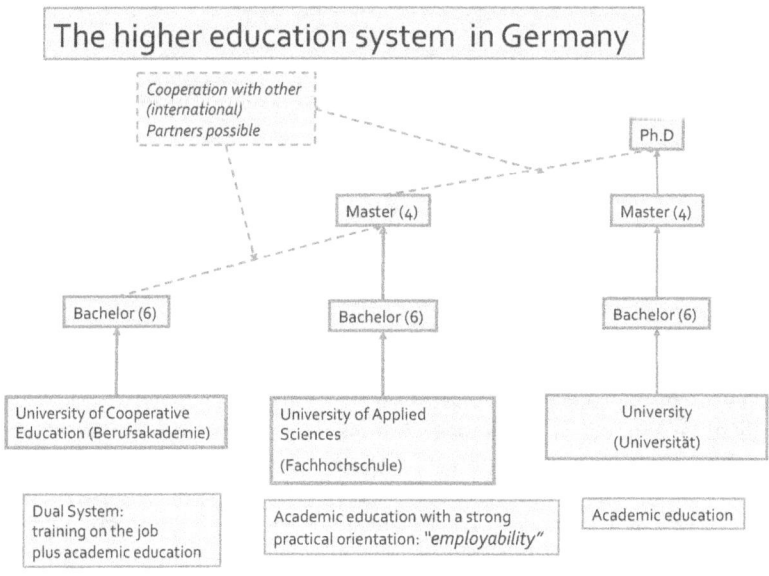

Figure 1: The higher education system in Germany (Schwägermann, 2008)

In order to be accepted by a university, applicants usually require a general higher education entrance qualification (or a special one, depending on the chosen type of university). This qualification is usually gained upon passing final secondary school examinations (*Abitur*). In addition, applicants sometimes have to pass an individual admission test held by the university. These may vary slightly, as the Federal Republic of Germany has 16 federal states, which are in charge of culture and education.

Within the context of the Europe-wide "Bologna Process", which commenced in 1999, Germany's higher education institutions conducted the largest reform of higher education in decades. This reform process succeeded in establishing internationally accepted degrees, improving the quality of study programmes and enhancing the international mobility of students. Courses had to be harmonised (not standardised) as modules with clear module descriptions, which also included the student learner's outcome and the credit points (ECTS) that students could obtain. The European Credit Transfer and Accumulation System (ECTS) is a student-centred system based on the student workload required to achieve the objectives of a programme (cf. www.bmbf.de).

Germany's higher education system is currently influenced by several factors. Demographic developments result in declining numbers of applicants. And yet the public funding allocated to a university is dependent on its number of students. Hence universities are increasingly having to compete for students. Student satisfaction is just one of the criteria on which the ranking of universities in Germany is based (CHE Ranking). Quality management was introduced years ago. Universities are increasingly endeavouring to sharpen their profile and to improve their uniqueness. Internationalisation strategies and international cooperation are one of the key developments in recent years. Universities of applied sciences, which traditionally focused on teaching, have been encouraged to engage more deeply in research.

3 Event management education in Germany

3.1 Development of event management education in Germany

No academic event management programmes existed anywhere in the world before the 1990s. Since then, the number of Bachelor and Master's programmes in event management has grown, most of which are part of tourism, hospitality, leisure, recreation or sports management courses. The George Washington University in Washington DC was an early pioneer in offering a concentration in event management within a graduate programme. In 1994, it launched an entire certification programme in event management (Getz and Wicks, 1994). Today, universities in the UK, Ireland, France, Australia, Canada and the USA offer several event management courses with different focus areas.

Event management appeared on study programmes at German universities as late as the early 1990s. This is quite astonishing, since Germany's exhibition association AUMA recently celebrated its 100th anniversary. The Berufsakademie Ravensburg, which then had the status of vocational college and is now called the Cooperative University Baden Württemberg (DHBW), launched its Trade Fair Management programme in 1986 (Congress and Event Management were added later). Osnabrück University of Applied Sciences was the first university in Germany to offer Event Management focusing on business events. Today, almost 50 universities, universities of applied sciences, academies and various other institutions are active in the event education system.

Germany's "dual system", referred to frequently in China, usually includes *vocational training*, which has a long tradition in Germany. Vocational training in the Federal Republic of Germany is provided on the job and at vocational training schools. Based on the *dual system*, practical vocational training is provided at work. This practical training is backed up by theoretical training and general education provided at vocational training schools, usually attended for one or two days a week. In Germany, there are currently around 350 officially recognised occupations that require training. The occupation of "Event Manager" (*Veranstaltungskaufmann/-kauffrau*) became a recognised occupation requiring training in 2001. This model of vocational training is clearly becoming increasingly interesting for China, too. According to *China Daily*, the Chinese government announced plans in May 2014 to increase the number of vocational students by one third by 2020 (China Daily).

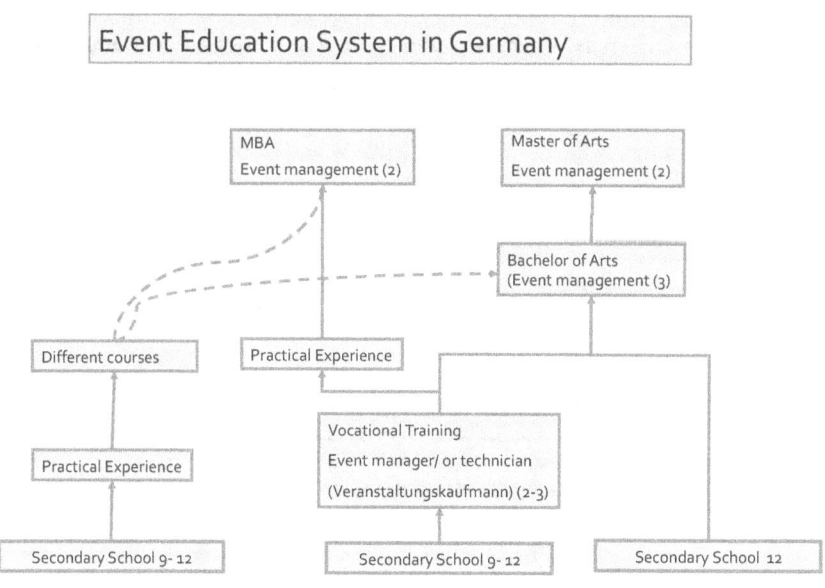

Figure 2: The event education system in Germany (Schwägermann 2008)

The dual study concept of cooperative state universities such as Ravensburg integrates academic studies with workplace training. DHBW cooperates with companies and social institutions all over Germany – so-called corporate partners. These corporate partners select their own students as employees, and are responsible for their workplace training. Students receive monthly remuneration from these partners. In the course of their three-year study programme, students regularly switch between university and the company/social institution providing workplace training. The advantage of this dual concept is, of course, that it features a strong practical orientation. The disadvantage however, is that the academic education is rather limited, and practical training takes place exclusively in the corporate partner's specific event domain. In any case, there are several ways to train to become an event manager and various ways to obtain access to universities that offer event management.

3.2 Event management programmes

A number of general insights can be gleaned from a recent survey of event management programmes in Germany (cf. Gaida 2013).

A total of 46 institutions offer 67 event-related courses, 51 of which lead to a Bachelor of Arts (B.A.) or Bachelor of Sciences (B. Sc.) degree, and 16 to a Master of Arts (M.A.) or Master of Sciences (M.Sc.) degree. The vast majority of these event management programmes are offered by universities of applied sciences; only a few are offered by cooperative universities.

Only two German universities offer event management courses: the University of Cologne focuses on trade fair management; Chemnitz University of Technology offers event marketing.

Following the respective university's general orientation, event courses are "embedded" in general studies of

- Business management
- Tourism management
- Sports management
- Media & communication management

Of these 46 institutions, 14 are funded by the Federal Government, 23 are privately run and have state recognition, and nine are privately funded institutions.

Table 1: Structure of event management programmes in Germany

	Business management	Tourism management	Sports management	Media management	Event management	Total
Funded by the Federal Government	7	11	–	2	2	22
Private, with state recognition	6	13	6	10	–	35
Private	2	2	1	5	–	10
Total	15	26	7	17	2	67

According to the principles of the Bologna process, the standard length of Bachelor courses is six semesters, plus four semesters for a post-graduate Master's course. An internship and/or study abroad is optional or even compulsory on Bachelor courses at some universities.

There is no general standard concerning the structure of courses and the event-related topics covered. Each university has its own scheme. It goes without saying, however, that some of the main topics are similar. These include macroeconomics, microeconomics, business management, finance management and accounting, marketing and human resource management.

Based on the general scope of the respective programmes, most courses start with the principles of the event market, followed by the principles of event management and supplemented by courses on special aspects of events or event services.

In 2008, the *Event Dozenten Forum* (Event Lecturers' Forum) was initiated by Osnabrück University of Applied Sciences at IMEX in Frankfurt. This was the first regular meeting between event management professors and lecturers in Germany. Initially, only 12 professors attended this forum; now, some 50 colleagues attend it. Examples of the topics discussed include the curricula offered by the participating universities, and trends in education and event management. Representatives from leading German event associations use this forum to report about their activities and to maintain contacts to event academia. In order to avoid misunderstandings, irritations and false expectations, and to give students a clear reliable orientation, a group of innovative universities of applied sciences founded the *Quality Circle of Event Studies* in 2011. The aim of this body is to outline the principle requirements for event studies backed by sound theory and firm practice.

3.3 Case study: *Business Events* at Osnabrück University of Applied Sciences

The mission statement for event management programmes at Osnabrück University of Applied Sciences is: *We educate the future leaders of the event industry – since 1993*. Osnabrück regards itself as one of the pioneers in German event education. It was the very first university (of applied sciences) to offer event education. Osnabrück University of Applied Sciences regards events as special target-oriented forms of live communication; it focuses its education on business events.

Business Events is a specialisation of the generic modularised Bachelor programme *Business Management*. After completing their first year of study, when they attend general management courses such as marketing and logistics, financial management, accounting, controlling, strategic management, business law, human resources management, etc., students choose a specialisation. The core courses of *Business Events* comprise six modules worth 30 credit points (ECTS). Together with the selection of other event-related activities, students can achieve up to 75 (out of 180) event-related credit points throughout their degree programme. However, our clear philosophy is that we base our event management specialisation on a sound management foundation. We regard this management know-how as a sound basis for our students' employability.

In Osnabrück, the focus is on business events, i. e. events that address participants from companies and organisations as their target group. Consequently, we specialise in the management of exhibitions, congresses and corporate events and the management of special event services required in the production chain of business events. These services include the management of event centres, destinations and service agencies. The main topics of the six event-related modules from the *Business Events* programme are:

- Introduction to the event market
- Principals of event management
- Management of special events, such as exhibitions, congresses, corporate events, cultural events
- Private and public event law
- Purchasing management
- Dramaturgy and staging of events
- Management of event services (event centres and destinations, service agencies).

As a university of applied sciences, we maintain close relations and open dialogue with the *event industry,* which we involve in the education of our students as lectures, suppliers of internships, and partners. Industry associations of the event industry play a special role, as they represent the needs and views of their individual members. Osnabrück University of Applied Sciences is the only German university that is a member of the *International Congress and Convention Association* (ICCA). It also has close relations to the leading German exhibition association AUMA, the German Convention Bureau (GCB), the European Associations of Event Centres (EVVC) and FAMAB, an association of event service suppliers.

We are also strongly involved with IMEX in Frankfurt, which is the leading European exhibition for the Business Travel and Event industry. Together with IMEX, Osnabrück University of Applied Sciences developed the Future Leaders Forum (FLF), which now takes place in several countries worldwide, including China. The ability to participate in IMEX also gives our students invaluable insights into event practice and networking options.

In addition, each semester we offer practical projects in cooperation with the event industry. During such a project, students are asked to devise solutions for special problems encountered by our partners. As stipulated by Germany's universities of applied sciences, all of our professors must prove they have at least five years' management experience in their respective field. The event management programme in Osnabrück therefore strikes a good balance between event theory and practical issues.

4   The higher education system in China

Education in China is differentiated into three stages, which reflect the typical pattern of other educational systems around the world. The stage of basic education is followed by higher education. After this, the stage of adult education is implemented (cf. Figure 3). China's education system is the largest in the world. In 2015, 9.42 million students sat the National Higher Education Entrance Examination (Gao Kao) in China. Admission to university depends on the results achieved in this examination. Programmes leading to a Bachelor degree usually take four years to complete. If they pass the entrance examination, graduates with a Bachelor degree may pursue a Master's degree, which is usually awarded after two to three years of study. Investment in education accounts for about 4 per cent of total GDP in China. The higher education sector is also growing. China is seeking to improve its quality of education by conducting a major reform of the curriculum. China has increased the proportion of its college-age population in higher education to over 20 per cent, compared to 1.4 per cent in 1978 (cf. CHE; China Education Center; UNESCO).

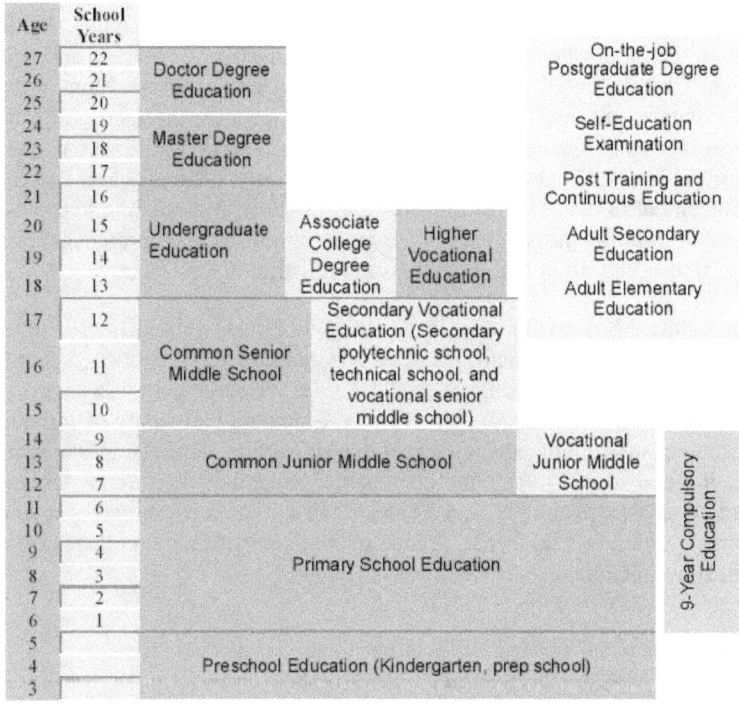

Figure 3: Higher education system in China, *Source*: National Centre for Education Development Research, 2008, quoted from UNESCO 2011

5 Event management education in China

5.1 Development of event management education in China

Since the beginning of the 21st century, the Chinese event industry has rapidly developed into an important part of the national economy and a booster to regional economic development in China. By the end of 2012, there were 286 exhibition venues in China, with 8,524,800 square metres of indoor exhibition space. Over 8,000 exhibitions were held in 2012 (Guo, 2013). According to the International Conference and Congress Association

(ICCA), China ranked 8th in the world with a total of 332 international association conferences (ICCA 2014). After the successful implementation of mega events such as the 2008 Beijing Olympics and the 2010 World Expo, China's event industry entered a new period.

In contrast to the rapid development of the industry, there has been a shortage of talents. University education is currently the main form of China's event management education. In 2004, China's Ministry of Education (MOE) defined event economy and management as its 'category management', *public administration sub-class, professional code 110311S (MOE, 2012)*. Another discipline that is closely related to the event business in China is *exhibition art and technology*. Eight Chinese universities and colleges offer this discipline. Most of the events such as cultural events, political and state events, sport events, and especially the mega events such as the Olympics Games and the World Expo and other hallmark events, were initiated and organised by the Chinese government. Accordingly, officials classified the discipline of event management in the *public* administration sub-class. Many Chinese professors and experts argue that both business events (such as exhibitions and conferences) and event management should be reclassified in the *business* administration sub-class.

In 2002, event education started being offered at universities in China. Beijing International Studies University, Guangzhou University and Shanghai Normal University launched event-related courses in their respective tourism schools. In 2003, event management was set up as a new discipline in Beijing International Studies University, Shanghai University of International Business and Economics (formerly Shanghai Institute of Foreign Trade) and Shanghai Normal University. At the end of 2011, 187 universities and secondary vocational schools offered event management as a major in China. 10,176 students studied event management, including 7,915 students in colleges (Liu, 2012). A total of 55 universities and colleges offer event management education in China.

Table 2: Education of event management at universities and colleges by geographical distribution

Province/ City	Quantity	University or college
Shanghai	1	Shanghai Normal University
	2	Shanghai University of International Business and Economics (Shanghai Institute of Foreign Trade)
	3	Shanghai Institute of Technology
	4	East China Normal University
	5	Shanghai Second Polytechnic University
	6	Fudan Pacific Institute of Finance
	7	University of Shanghai for Science and Technology
	8	Shanghai Business School
	9	Shanghai Industry and Commerce Foreign Language College
	10	Shanghai Jianqiao University
	11	Donghua University
Guangdong Province	1	Sun Yat-sen University
	2	Guangdong Business School
	3	Guangzhou University
	4	South China University of Technology
	5	Shenzhen Tourism College of Jinan University

Province/City	Quantity	University or college
Zhejiang Province	1	Zhejiang University City College
	2	Zhejiang Wanli University
	3	Zhejiang University of Media and Communication
	4	Hangzhou Normal University
	5	Zhejiang Shuren University
	6	Jinhua Polytechnic
	7	Tourism of Zhejiang China
	8	Zhejiang Economic and Trade Polytechnic
	9	Yiwu Industrial and Commercial College
	10	Zhejiang Yuying College of Vocational Technology
	11	Ningbo City College of Vocational Technology
Beijing	1	Beijing International Studies University
	2	Beijing Union University
	3	Beijing University of Agriculture
	4	Beijing City University
Chongqing	1	Chongqing University of Art and Science
	2	Chongqing Technology and Business University
	3	Chongqing University of Technology
Shandong Province	1	Shandong Jiaotong University
	2	Qindao Hotel Management College
	3	Shandong Tourism College
	4	Shandong Institute of Commerce and Technology
Fujian Province	1	Xiamen University of Technology
	2	Fujian Hwan Women's College
Heilongjiang Province	1	Harbin University of Commerce
Jiangsu Province	1	Wuxi City College and Vocational Technology
Tianjin	1	Nankai University
Sichuan Province	1	Sichuan University
Liaoning Province	1	Liaoning University of International Business and Economics
Guangxi Province	1	Guangxi University of Finance and Economics
Yunnan Province	1	Yunnan University of Finance and Economics
Hunan Province	1	Hunan University of Commerce
Hubei Province	1	Hubei University
Henan Province	1	Henan University of Finance and Economics
Hebei Province	1	Hebei University of International Business and Economics
Hainan Province	1	Hainan University
Liaoning Province	1	Shenyang Normal University
Shanxi Province	1	Xi'an International Studies University
Inner Mongolia Province	1	Inner Mongolia University of Finance and Economics

Source: Authors' compilation based on online data

Table 2 shows that almost all provinces and municipalities have universities or colleges that offer event management education. Shanghai, Guangdong Province, Zhejiang Province and Beijing take the lead in event management education, which is relevant to the development of the event economy. After all, Shanghai, Beijing and Guangzhou are the key cities in China's event industry.

5.2 Course design in event management education

The subject area of event management is progressing as a discipline, with an increasing number of qualifications being offered with 'event' in the title. In addition, anecdotal evidence suggests that there are hundreds of modules covering the principles of event management within tourism, management, leisure and communication courses.

China's event management education at university level generally offers courses at three levels. We shall now explore the course design of event management at Guangzhou University as an example (cf. Table 3).

Table 3. Event management education courses at Guangzhou University

Level	Professional competence	Description	Courses
Level 1	Basic knowledge	Master the basic theory of economics and management	Principle of Economy, Management, Statistics, Accounting, Marketing, Finance Management
Level 2	Key knowledge	Master the planning, organisation and operation of conferences, exhibitions, special events and business tourism	Event Introduction, Management of Exhibition Planning and Organising, Management of Convention and Conference Planning and Organising, Event Project Management, Event Marketing, Event English
Level 3	Advanced knowledge	Master the knowledge relevant to events and business tourism	Event Law, International Trade, Venue Management, Participation in Exhibitions and Trade Fairs, Business Writing, Advertising

(Source: Liu, 2012)

The course design at *Guangzhou University* is a typical example. The course design for the first two levels is similar to other Chinese universities such as Shanghai Normal University, Shanghai University of International Business and Economics and Beijing International Studies University, which started offering management education at a much earlier stage. Differentiation usually takes place at level 3.

Shanghai Normal University (SNU) offers more courses that are relevant for special events, such as the principles and methods of special event management and an introduction to the creative industry. *Shanghai University of International Business and Economics* (SUIBE) focuses more on business events. Consequently, it offers more modules that are relevant for this area, such as participation in exhibitions and trade fairs, venue and event destination management, communication and key competences.

After reviewing most of the course designs in event management in China, we draw the conclusion that the course design of event management in China is similar to that in foreign countries at the foundation level. However, the course design in China starts to differ at level 3, depending on the respective university's preference. The event industry offers a wide range of aspects and facets. Event management education at universities should be professional. It is impossible for one university to cover all aspects of all kinds of events at the level of quality required.

5.3 Lecturers in Chinese event management education

When we entered the key words *teachers event management education* to search for teachers on LinkedIn, the most popular international social network website for professionals, we got 1,031 hits. These event management teachers included trainers at event consultancies, and university lecturers and professors. Most of these teachers had an educational background in management or tourism management (LinkedIn 2014). The situation is similar in China: when China started offering event management education at universities and colleges, no professors or lecturers had graduated with a major in event management. Most event management courses were offered at tourism schools. Event management education in China therefore got off to a difficult start. Lecturers educated in tourism management or business management were proficient in the theory of management or tourism, but had no theoretical knowledge or own experience in events.

Universities took one of two measures to resolve this problem: some universities invited experts from event enterprises in China to work as full-time or part-time lecturers. At the same time, they sent their own lecturers abroad to study event management. For example, SUIBE sent teachers to Germany every year and SNU sent teachers to the United States.

Cooperation in event management with foreign universities is another way to train teachers. SUIBE cooperates with a German university; Shanghai Industrial and Commercial Foreign Language University cooperates with an Australian university. By taking these measures, Chinese lecturers' competency in event management education developed rapidly, including teaching team building.

5.4 Four ways to include practical education

Event management is not only a sub-domain of management, making use of most management theories. It also has close links to the fields of business, industry, tourism, sports and communication. All of these fields have a lot of practical aspects, which cannot be covered by theory and classroom teaching alone. Practical teaching and enabling students to gain their own practical experience are indispensable aspects in event education today.

Nearly all universities and colleges encourage their students to volunteer to work at exhibitions or conferences. But this is not taking it far enough. There are *four essential ways* to include practical education in China's event management programmes.

First, *the study programme is divided into theoretical semesters and practical semesters,* where students work as an employee at the enterprise for a whole semester. For example, the Inner Mongolia University of Finance and Economics offers an eight-semester Bachelor programme in event management. The first four semesters are spent studying on campus. This is followed by three further semesters of work in an event-related enterprise. The final semester is set aside for preparing a dissertation. This model is similar to the dual study concept in Germany.

The second method is *orientation training within school/enterprise cooperation*. In this case, renowned enterprises such as exhibition companies and meeting companies are involved throughout the teaching period of university event management education. General managers or other executives from these enterprises deliver lectures to students on campus, and offer them the opportunity to volunteer or do internships in their companies. After graduation, the companies give priority to these students when it comes to taking on new staff. For example, SUIBE has cooperated with two renowned event companies in this way for years. The first company is Shanghai Baiwen Exhibition Company, which owns and organises the largest beauty exhibition in China. The second is MCI, a globally operating communications and event management company.

The third method involves *self-organised campus exhibitions*. In this case, an exhibition is designed, planned, operated and managed totally by students. The lecturer accompanies them as a coach, and helps them to overcome any problems they encounter. In this way, students can apply the knowledge they have gained in the classroom to event practice. As an example, students from Guangzhou University planned China's first Divorce Exhibition in 2012 in Guangzhou. Since 2006, students from SUIBE have hosted a Campus Beauty Show. The CBS has now been held nine times.

The fourth method is *participating in events* organised by the event industry itself. For example, event students participate each year in competitions sponsored by the international event association, such as in the 'Future Leaders Forum' at the IT&CM in Shanghai. Selected students also attend the annual meetings of international event associations such as the International Convention and Conference Association (ICCA).

By applying these methods, event management students gain additional practical experience that cannot be taught in the classroom.

5.5 Case study: *IEMS* at SUIBE

In cooperation with Shanghai University of International Business and Economics (SUIBE), Osnabrück University of Applied Sciences started offering a Bachelor programme in *International Event Management Shanghai* (IEMS) especially for Chinese students in October 2004. IEMS offers its students a double degree: a Bachelor of Arts (B.A.) from Osnabrück and a Bachelor of Management (B. Mgmt.) from SUIBE. For this reason, the structure, quality requirements and examination regulations have to comply with both education systems. IEMS is a six-semester Bachelor programme embedded in the eight-semester Chinese Bachelor programme. From the German side, the first two semesters are regarded as propaedeutic semesters.

Teaching takes place solely at SUIBE in Shanghai. Half of the lectures are held by German professors and lecturers in block events. Modules include the fundamentals of business management such as accounting, services marketing, macroeconomics, mathematics and management tools and concepts. Nine special event modules (core modules) include event management, management of trade fairs, congresses and exhibitions, management of marketing events, management of venues and event destinations as well as trade fairs and exhibitions in China. All courses, including tests, are held in English. A few basic event management courses delivered in Chinese are offered to students in their first two semesters.

In 2003, SUIBE deliberately chose a German partner for this new major, as Germany's experience in organising trade fairs and congresses is renowned throughout the world. Osnabrück University of Applied Sciences was mainly chosen on the basis of its practical orientation and its interactive teaching style.

The degree course is supported by scholarships for summer language courses, student exchange and sur-place scholarships from the German Federal Ministry for Education and Research and the German Academic Exchange Service as part of the programme "German higher education abroad".

IEMS offers internationally oriented event education, where students are trained to be decision-makers and leaders in the international event industry. IEMS's slogan is: *"We educate China's Future Leaders in the Event Industry"*.

One element of the practical orientation of this programme is strategic cooperation with German and Chinese event companies, which offer work experience for volunteers during the programme and internships before writing a Bachelor thesis. All of the German and some of the Chinese lecturers have practical experience working in their respective fields. IEMS students founded their own exhibition company, called *Wonder Fairs; they* organise a Beauty Show each year on campus for their fellow students.

The interactive teaching style includes discussing problems in class, working in project teams, and often giving presentations in teams rather than writing tests or essays.

Students gain international and intercultural skills, as English is the official language of the programme. Since the lecturers come from Germany and other countries with different cultural backgrounds, students are confronted with the different appearances, habits and lifestyles of their lecturers and exchange students from Osnabrück. In addition, each year 12 IEMS students are awarded a scholarship for a six-week language and cultural summer school in Osnabrück. Last but not least, eight students are selected to spend an exchange semester in Osnabrück, five of whom are given a full scholarship by the DAAD. This means that 25 to 30 per cent of our students have the chance to study and live in Germany during their study programme. Thanks to Osnabrück's membership of the ICCA, one IEMS student each year is awarded a scholarship to attend the ICCA Congress (for more information, visit: http://www.wiso.hs-osnabrueck.de/international-event-management-shanghai.html?&L=1).

6 Conclusion

Event education is a relatively new phenomenon at universities worldwide. The event industry is a comparatively new industry that is developing rapidly in China. As key tools of communication in modern society, events are growing in importance, increasing the need for more and better educated talents for this industry. Our analysis of the German and Chinese systems of event education has revealed many similarities. Although China's universities got off to a late start, they have adapted and learnt very quickly. This article provides insight into modern event education in China. The future of China's event management education appears to be very promising.

7 Literature

BMBF, Federal Ministry of Education and Research, www.bmbf.de

Brandenburg, U., Zhu, J., (2007), Higher education in China, Arbeitspapier No. 97, 2007

China Daily (2014) Fit for the job, Cover story September 5–11, 2014

China Education Center, www.chinaeducenter.com, retrieved in June 2015

CHE university ranking, www.che-ranking.de

Gaida, H.-J., (2013) Eventstudium, Study on event education at German universities, presentation at Qualitätszirkel Eventstudium, Frankfurt, 2013

Getz, D. Wicks, B. (1994) Professionalism and certification for festival and event practitioners: Trends and issues, Festival Management and Event Tourism 2(2):103–109.

Getz, D. (2002) Event studies and event management: On becoming an academic discipline. Journal of Hospitality and Tourism Management, 9(1), 12–23.

Guo, J. (2014) Report of China's event economy development in 2013. Shanghai: Social Science and Academic Publishing.

HK 24 (2014), Vocational Training in Germany – The Dual System, document 15402, retrieved on 13 April 2014

ICCA (2015) Statistics Report 2014

LinkedIn (2014) Key word: *teachers event management education*

Liu, S. (2012) Research and practice of the module of event's talent cultivation and social service two-way drive. Chongqing: Chongqing University Publishing

Ministry of Education, http://www.moe.gov.cn/moe_2792/

Schwägermann, H. (2008) Event Education in Germany, Presentation at the Exhibition & Convention Education and Research International Conference, Shanghai 2008

UNESCO (2011) World Data on Education, VII Ed. 2010/11, People's Republic of China

Where do they want to go? Expectations of Chinese talents from their future employer

Schinnenburg, Heike,
Walk, Marlene,
Jin, Quan

职业选择之路 – 中国人才对他们未来雇主的期望

Highly qualified talents are scarce in China's tough labour market. In particular, the generally small companies of the service and event industry are struggling to compete with multinational companies in terms of payment and internal career paths. So how can companies become attractive employers for the young generation in China? How can the expectations of young talents be met to foster long-term commitment and satisfaction? This chapter uses data from an empirical study in Shanghai and discusses the implications for human resource management in event management companies.

在中国竞争激烈的人才市场中高素质人才稀缺。特别是小型服务和会展业公司由于薪酬和内部职业生涯规划的原因无法和跨国公司竞争。因此如何能成为对中国的新生代来说是有吸引力的雇主？怎样能满足年轻的人才对公司和工作的期望以培养他们对公司长期的责任感和满意度？这篇文章使用从上海获得的统计研究数据来讨论会展公司中的人力资源管理的实际运用。

1 Introduction

Well-qualified and experienced talents are scarce in China. This scarcity enables them to choose their employer and negotiate contracts. Young talents are also more likely to change their job if new opportunities arise. Their behavior can be interpreted as "boundaryless" especially in a psychological meaning (Lau et al. 2013). High turnover rates constitute a challenge for a stable customer-relationship management in the service sector and strategic HR Planning and Development in China. Companies continuously have to recruit new, often inexperienced employees, train and retain them. In the service sector, many small companies, like event management agencies, cannot compete with multinational companies (MNC) in terms of payment and internal career paths. It is therefore important for them to meet the expectations of young talents to foster long-term commitment and satisfaction. In this chapter we discuss the expectations of students from business programs at Shanghai University of Business and Economics (SUIBE), China, concerning their future employer and their life. We draw on data from a multinational survey conducted among business management students in India, China, and Germany (Walk et al. 2013). For this chapter we particularly focus on the Chinese portion of the data investigating the career orientation and work expectations of young talents. Additionally we use results from a poll of students from the sino-foreign programme International Event Management Shanghai (IEMS) looking at their changing priorities over time. In the discussion of the resulting HRM challenges in the field of service and event management we prioritize the practical implications of the findings.

2 HRM in the Chinese service sector

The economic liberalization led to the growth of the Chinese service sector and an increasing demand for employees with diverse skills and qualifications in a highly competitive market. Consequently the importance of HRM and HR Development rises to manage people in order to be successful in a *"cutthroat competition"* (Ananthram and Pearson 2008: 33).

For this chapter, we particularly focus on event companies, which comprise one part of a quite heterogeneous service sector (Zheng et al. 2008). Typically Event Management Companies work with only a small core of permanent workers. Additionally temporary workers have to be recruited, introduced to their tasks and monitored for the short period of an event. This may lead to a split approach of HRM: Whereas for the temporary workers a "high performance – high commitment"-HRM practice, including performance appraisals, reward systems and a strategic oriented HR development, does not seem to be realistic, different requirements arise for the core employees. They need managerial skills and have to foster stable customer relationships, organize the events and coordinate the temporary workers. Especially in the relationship-orientated businesses in China high turnover rates of core managers endangers long-term customer connections (Zhang and Bright 2012: 5).

In this "people business" one may assume that the 'soft' side of HRM practices is emphasized for qualified talents to develop a sustainable service culture on the one hand and commitment to the company and its goals on the other hand. However labor intensive service businesses like hospitality – with similar challenges in HRM as Event Management – are mostly dominated by poor working conditions and cost-minimizing HR strategies (Legge 1995). Whereas there is not much valid data about the event sector, the combination of a quite young business, mostly small companies and a high amount of temporary workers indicates a similar approach. Furthermore many graduates in China do not possess the suitable qualifications the companies require (Guthridge et al. 2008: 9). This *"shortage among plenty"* in China (Lau et al. 2013: 248) presents an additional challenge to train and develop young people with little practical experience who nevertheless expect fast promotions and status symbols (Schinnenburg and Dankert 2009).

For China, Akha et al. (2008) found that *"a valid set of strategic HRM practices (training, participation, results-oriented appraisals, and internal career opportunities) affect both product/service performance and financial performance. Employment security and job descriptions contribute uniquely to product/service performance, whereas profit sharing contributes uniquely to financial performance"* (15). Particularly for the Chinese service sector Zheng et al. (2008) discuss recruitment, training, support resources and skill development as main HR approaches to enhance employee commitment, which shall result in increasing service quality and organizational success. Interestingly, their research shows that

1. Formal, innovative recruitment methods increased the service quality of the company but led to a higher turnover rate whereas informal recruitment, such as word of mouth and employee referral, were connected to higher employee retention.
2. HR development was *"significantly related to building more harmonized relationships between employer and employee but does not relate to enhancing service capacity"* (8) and
3. Skills development was positively related to the performance indicators but negatively connected to employee retention (Zheng et al. 2008: 7 f).

These findings show a dilemma for the service sector: Strategic HRM approaches tend to improve service quality and business results on the one hand. However, HR Development leads to more visible career capital and higher employability which increases retention problems on the other hand.

Therefore the question arises how small event management companies can find ways to obtain commitment of highly-qualified young talents, who seem to be less loyal to one company and value different aspects of life than the older generation (Walk et al. 2013).

3 Boundaryless Careers – new opportunities and requirements for the young generation

The challenges summarized above are in line with career concepts such as protean or boundaryless careers, which have been widely discussed in the literature. Both concepts are concerned with attitudes, which focus on individual, independent and career plans. For the boundaryless career, Arthur and Rousseau (1996) find that they do not depend on *"traditional organizational career arrangements"* (6). Hall (1996), even states for the protean career that the *"traditional psychological contract in which an employee entered a firm, worked hard, performed well, was loyal and committed, and thus received ever-greater rewards and job security, has been replaced by a new contract based on continuous learning and identity change"* (8). Instead of walking the internal career paths of companies, well qualified talents tend to act more self-directed, independent and opportunity-seeking (Briscoe and Hall 2005).

Companies are drivers of this new psychological contract through HR policies of lean management, restructuring, and continuous strategic changes on the one hand (Baruch 2001). On the other hand they are affected by the results of these changes since HR development investments are easily lost through job transitions.

Tab. 1: Protean and Boundaryless Career Attitude

Traditional Career	Protean Career attitude	Boundaryless Career attitude
Long-time Commitment to one company	Self-directed orientation, independent and flexible to change plans and job	Unlimited options, not bound to a company
Progress in one company: upwards	Development according to own values and goals	Physical and psychological mobility

(Table: Based on Lamb and Sutherland 2010 and Sullivan and Arthur 2006)

These contemporary career concepts require a high degree of planning, flexible adaptions to new situations and autonomy of individuals. Inkson and Arthur (2001) describe people with such a career behavior as Career Capitalists. Such a successfully pursued career path results in high employability through visible and marketable individual career capital. It allows to choose between options and to bargain contracts. However it has to be recognized that career attitudes are also embedded in a framework of culture and the respective labor market on the one hand and personality structures, gender (expectations and duties) on the other hand (Schinnenburg et al. 2014).

Originally discussed for western countries, especially the US, these subjective career expectations and plans are also found in China (Lau, Hsu and Shaffer 2013). This is in line with changing values for the young generation, which integrate western thinking and Chinese traditional values (Ralston et al. 1999). In their Global workforce study 2005 TowersPerrin conclude: *"Employee loyalty is waning. In the wake of company reorganizations resulting from reengineering efforts as well as mergers and acquisitions, employees are rethinking the wisdom and feasibility of building a long-lasting career with a single organization"*(5). A boundaryless mindset with an individuals' focus on agentic behavior therefore may be a learned attitude *"to cope with uncertain career environments"* (Briscoe et al. 2013: 314).

Thus it is important for a young sector such as event management to know more about the work expectation and career orientation of young graduates in managements programs, preferable with a specialization in event management.

4 Empirical research:

4.1 Methods

Recruitment and Sample

This study is based on a sample of convenience of undergraduate management students enrolled in IEMS, International Business and International Trade and Economics program at SUIBE in Shanghai (N=404). The same data has been used in a previous publication that focused on a comparison of China, India and Germany (Walk et al. 2013). Looking at the whole sample, 36.23 % were female. The average age was 21.83 years (SD=.91).

Students were recruited in a classroom setting. They were assured that their participation is completely voluntary and that they could terminate participation at any time without their data being used. The survey instrument was administered in English language.

Survey Instrument/Variables

Socio-Demographics: Age is a continuous variable measuring clients' year of birth. *Gender* is dichotomized for female and male (male=1, female=0).

Work Expectations: Students were asked to rate 22 items related to work expectations on a 5-point Likert-Scale ranging from very important (5) to very unimportant (1). Work expectations fall onto two dimensions: extrinsic (10 items, e. g., "making a lot of money") and intrinsic work expectations (5 items, e. g., "opportunity to do something worthwhile") (Walk et al., 2013). Extrinsic work expectation achieved high (α=.79), intrinsic work expectations acceptable internal consistency (α=.69).

Career Orientation: Career orientation was assessed using 8 items such as "I am career-oriented". Rating was done on a 5-point Likert Scale from Strongly Agree (5) to strongly disagree (1). This scale achieved high internal consistency (α=.80).

Analysis

To serve the purpose of this chapter, we draw on correlations between career orientations and the two work expectation scales. Furthermore, we investigate the ranking of the individual work expectation and career orientation items to get a better sense of the relative importance of these items among the sample of Chinese students.

4.2 Results

Table 1 presents descriptive statistics and correlations between the work expectation dimensions and career orientation. Intrinsic work expectations are highly correlated with extrinsic work expectation and career orientation among this sample of students. We also find a medium correlation between extrinsic work expectations and career orientation.

Tab. 2: Descriptive Statistics and Correlations

Variables	Range	M	SD	Career Orientation	Extrinsic Work Expectations	Intrinsic Work Expectations
Career Orientation	1–5	3.69	0.58	0.80		
Extrinsic Work Expectations	1–5	4.1	0.46	.30****	0.79	
Intrinsic Work Expectations	1–5	3.98	0.55	.46****	.43****	0.69

Note: Coefficient alpha shown on diagonal. *p≤.05, **p≤.01, ***p≤.001, ****p≤.0001. Values are rounded to two decimals.

To contrast the relative rank ordering of the career orientation items, we first display our previous findings in Table 3 (see Walk et al. 2013, for the complete findings comparing China, India and Germany).

Tab. 3: Relative rank ordering of all Work Expectation items in China

Item Description		Rank	Mean
Promotion possibilities	n. s.	1	4.34
Work-life-balance	EWE	2a**	4.31
Good standard of living	EWE	3a**	4.29
Appropriate pay	EWE	4	4.27
Being successful	EWE	5	4.25
Learning new things	IWE	6	4.22
Good relationship with colleagues	n. s.	7	4.21
Social benefits	EWE	8a+	4.15
Work environment	EWE	9a*	4.13
Make my own decisions about how to do the job	n. s.	10	4.03
Recognition through supervisor	EWE	11a***	4.00
Making the world a better place	IWE	12b+	4.00
Helping people in need	IWE	13	3.99
Having a well-defined career path	n. s.	14	3.99
Compliance with the contractually agreed working hours	n. s.	15	3.98
Possibility of a leadership position	n. s.	16	3.97
Opportunity to do something worthwhile	IWE	17	3.96
Organizational reputation	EWE	18	3.90
Location of company	EWE	19	3.90
Making a lot of money	EWE	20	3.87
Making use of own knowledge	IWE	21	3.73
Work-related travel	n. s.	22	3.48

Note: Items are abbreviated for convenient presentation. +p≤.10, *p≤.05, **p≤.01, ***p≤.001, ****p≤.0001. a) women rate higher, b) men rate higher. EWE = extrinsic work expectations, IWE = intrinsic work expectations, n. s. non-salient, not part of work expectation dimensions, but asked on survey (Source: Walk et al. 2013)

Table 4 displays the relative rank ordering of the career orientation items. Overall students rated all items above the mid-point. Professional development was hereby rated as the most important considering the mean scores, followed by the willingness to contribute more than others and having concrete ideas of one's future life.

Tab. 4: Relative rank ordering of Career Orientation items

Item Description	Rank	Mean
Professional development	1	3.99
Willing to contribute more than others	2	3.96
Having concrete ideas of future life	3	3.94
Invest time to develop professionally	4	3.83
Knowing the kind of work after graduation	5*b	3.57
Doing overtime is natural part of the job	6*b	3.52
Career-oriented	7***b	3.48
Give up personal over professional interests	8**b	3.25

Note: Items are abbreviated for convenient presentation. $*p \leq .05$, $**p \leq .01$, $***p \leq .001$, $****p \leq .0001$.
a) women rate higher, b) men rate higher.

We find statistically significant differences between women and men on four of the items. Male students in our sample had a clearer idea of the kind of work they wanted to do after graduation (t(393)=−2.11, p=.0359), they felt that overtime was part of a job (t(394)=−3.20, p=.0015), were more career-oriented (t(392)=−3.30, p=.001) and more likely to give up personal interests over professional interests (t(393)=−2.66, p=.0082) compared to females.

4.3 Motivators for IEMS-students: Poll in class

Particularly for the group of IEMS students a short poll was run in class by hand signal since 2006. In particular students were asked to raise their hands to vote for the three motivators such as pay, incentives, additional benefits, career opportunities, HR development programs, work tasks, company culture (supportive climate, such as recognition through supervisors), reputation of the company, and work environment that were most important to them. Table 5 presents the results of the rankings. Class size ranged from 68–75.

Incentives were interesting for the students if they were visible through status symbols, especially a company car was highly valued in the discussion afterwards. Additional benefits (medical insurance and loans for houses) were always seen as relevant but never in the top 3. These benefits, however, might become more attractive later in life (e. g. when thinking about starting a family).

Tab. 5: Ranking of work expectation in IEMS groups from 2006–2013

	2006	2007	2008	2009	2010	2011	2012	2013	2014
No 1	Pay	Pay	Incentives (Company Car)	Career Opportunities	Career Opportunities	Career Opportunities	Pay	Career Opportunities	Work environment
No 2	Career Opportunities	Incentives (Company Car)	Pay	Work Environment & Company Culture*	Pay	Work tasks	Company Culture	Development Programs	Pay
No 3	Work tasks	Development Programs	Work Tasks		Work tasks & Company Culture*	Company Culture	Career Opportunities	Pay	Development programs

* Both items were ranked equally

The overview shows a growing relevance of soft facts, such as company culture and development programs, but students perceive pay as very important. Further discussion with the groups revealed that many students feel obliged to be successful in order to support their parents in their old age, since the social security system in China is not well developed yet. Therefore professional development and career opportunities in a company are seen as an investment into a successful future with a high employability on the labor market and a good salary.

5 Implications for HRM in the Chinese service sector

Not surprisingly the findings show that it might not be easy for small event management companies to be regarded as attractive employers. Very often they will not be able to compete with perks such as high salaries or career opportunities usually offered by MNC. Moreover young talents tend to see their careers as boundaryless without long-term loyalty to a company. But the results also show that diverse motives exist and the meaning of non-financial benefits increases. In their cross-sectional study TowersPerrin (2005) come to similar results, for instance *Learning and development* was seen as Top Attraction Driver number one. We find similarly that Work-Life-Balance plays an important role for the students (Table 3) as compared to the wish for *low-or no-stress work environment* which has been found as one of Top Retention Drivers in TowersPerrin (2005).

Based on our findings, we offer some suggestions for companies in this sector to successfully recruit and retain talents:

1. **Establish close cooperation with Chinese universities**

Rapidly growing companies, especially those with international customers may consider strategic co-operations with Chinese universities. Recommendable are universities with study programs for the service sector, to get access to talents who like to work in this field. Ideally these programs have international components and study periods abroad and/or ties with international guest lecturers and universities. These international connections ensure that graduates get a basic understanding of intercultural topics and are used to more creative, problem-solving learning styles [see also Gray et al. in this handbook]. Through close relationships, companies can send employees to hold guest-lectures or to co-teach specific subjects of practical relevance, e. g. case studies, to the students. This combination of theory and practice improves the competencies of graduates and establishes relationships with young talents. Additionally the companies can give suggestions for curriculum design in a fast changing sector and provide attractive internships or projects for Bachelor thesis.

2. **Encourage informal ways of recruitment, especially for internships**

As internships are popular in China, especially in joint programs like IEMS, companies can use this instrument for recruitment and selection of young talents who mostly have no practical experience. This requires a professional approach to get an indication of the potential and motivation of the intern on the one hand and to create a positive work environment on the other hand. The goal is to encourage the best-fitting talents to stay in contact for temporary jobs or as student trainee while completing their degree or during a practice-based Bachelor thesis and then to start with an entry-level job after graduation. Respectively, this allows students to gain more experience and facilitates their transition between university and their first position. For the company this approach establishes a long-term relationship with a talent through an internship as a kind of probationary period and introduction into the field of work.

3. **Professional leadership for internships and entry level jobs**

During internships companies may be able to showcase interesting work tasks, learning opportunities and a supportive environment to potential talents. But this is easier said than done: Such an approach needs an investment in time to explain procedures, trust to hand over parts of the responsibility for projects, supportive coaching during the task and encouraging feedback after a project has been completed. Professional leadership is needed to ensure that supervisors invest the time and know-how to motivate their team members. This requires a professional HR function to care for the development of mostly quite young supervisors and support them to fulfill their responsibilities in this important leadership role. At the end of an internship a feedback meeting with the intern should be regarded as an important ritual to show that the individual is highly valued by the company. In addition to feedback and praise for the intern, his/her ideas and experiences can help the company to improve the internships for the future and to enhance application rates through informal networks. Entry-level jobs and development opportunities can be discussed.

4. Supportive company culture – beyond boundaries

Even with limited funds for Human Resources, event management companies can focus on a core business that is perceived as interesting working field for young individuals. Furthermore a growing event market enables the transfer of responsibility for projects after a short time, if employees perform well and are willing to contribute their energy to the goals of the company. In such a way young employees continuously learn new things and experience themselves as successful in their jobs (No. 5 and 6 in Table 3). However, it needs more to make them stay in the company. A positive work climate with trust between colleagues and encouragement through supervisors is needed to increase employee retention (No. 7 and 11 in Table 3). Furthermore HRM in this field should accept that – similarly to some consulting companies – after a time of learning some employees will leave and find new challenges. A company culture that values these steps of a boundaryless career and considers it a normal aspect of HR development is important. It is recommendable to establish structures that enforce knowledge management across team members, which enables insights in procedures and customers independent of individual employees. Otherwise the company loses valuable information and perhaps customer relationships in case somebody leaves the company.

6 Literature

Akha, Syed R.; Ding, Daniel Z. and Ge, Gloria L. (2008), 'Strategic HRM Practices and their impact on company performance in Chinese enterprises', in: *Human Resource Management*, Spring 2008, 47 (1), pp. 15–32

Ananthram, Subramaniam and Pearson, Cecil Arthur Leonard (2008), 'The Impact of Macro Level Drivers of Globalization on Organizational Reform Measures in Indian and Chinese Service Organizations: An Exploratory Insight', in: *South Asian Journal of Management*, 15 (4), pp. 7–43

Arthur, Michael B. and Rousseau, Denise M. (eds) (1996), *The Boundaryless Career: A new employment principle for a new organizational Era*. Oxford

Baruch, Yehuda (2001), 'Employability: a substitute for loyalty?', in: *Human Resource Development International*, 4 (4), pp. 543–566

Briscoe, J. P. & Hall, D. T. (2005). The interplay of boundaryless and protean careers: Combinations and implications. *Journal of Vocational Behavior, 69,* 4–18.

Briscoe, J. P., Henagan, S. C., Burton, J. P. and Murphy, W. M. (2012), 'Coping with an insecure employment environment: The differing roles of protean and boundaryless career orientations', in: *Journal of Vocational Behavior*, 80, pp. 308–316

Guthridge, Matthew; Komm, Asmus and Lawson, Emily (2008), *Making talent a strategic priority*. Mc Kinsey Quarterly, Issue 1, pp. 48–59

Hall, Douglas T. (1996), 'Protean Careers of the 21st Century', in: *Academy of Management Executive*, 1996 10 (4), pp. 8–16

Inkson, Kerr and Arthur, Michael B. (2001), 'How to be a successful Career Capitalist', in: *Organizational Dynamics*, 30 (1), pp. 48–61

Lau, Victor P.; Hsu, Yu-Shan and Shaffer, Margaret A. (2013), 'Global Careers in China'. In: Reis, C. and Baruch, Y. (eds.), *Careers Without Borders*, 13, pp. 247–266

Legge, Karin (1995), 'HRM: rhetoric, reality and hidden agendas', in: Storey J. (ed), *Human Resource Management – a critical text*, London, New York, pp. 33–62

Ralston, David A.; Egri, Carolyn P.; Stewart, Sally; Terpstra, Robert H. and Kaicheng, Yu (1999), 'Doing business in the 21st century with the new generation of Chinese managers: A study of generational shifts in work values in China', in: *Journal of International Business Studies* 30(2), pp. 415–28

Schinnenburg, Heike and Dankert, Inga (2009), 'Mitarbeiterbindung als unternehmerische Herausforderung in China', Kull, St. and Schinnenburg, H. (eds), *Auf gelben Spuren. Menschen, Management und Märkte in China*, pp. 65–82

Schinnenburg, Heike; Böhmer, Nicole; Walk, Marlene and Handy, Femida (2014), *Young talents: Individualistic, boundaryless and disloyal? Challenges for International HRM and Development*. Submitted for the IHRM Conference 2014, Krakow: "Uncertainty in a Flattening World: Challenges for IHRM"

Sullivan, Sherry E. and Arthur, Michael. B. (2006), 'The evolution of the boundaryless career concept: Examining physical and psychological mobility', in: *Journal of Vocational Behavior*, 69, pp. 19–29

TowersPerrin (2005), *Global Workforce Study. Managing the Workforce for Competitive Advantage. China.* (www.towersperrin.com.cn)

Walk, Marlene; Schinnenburg, Heike and Handy, Femida (2013), 'What do talents want? Work expectations in India, China, and Germany', in: *German Journal of Research in Human Resource Management*, 27(3), pp. 251–278

Zhang, Shuai and Bright, David (2012), 'Talent definition and talent management recognition in Chinese private-owned enterprises', in: *Journal of Chinese Entrepreneurship*, 4 (2), pp. 143–163

Zheng, Connie; Lamond, David and Kam, Booi (2008), *The Impact of Selected HR Practices on Service Firm Performance in Asia*, Paper submitted to the 6th Asia Academy of Management Conference focusing on 'the New Faces of Asian Management', Taipei, Taiwan, December 14–16, 2008

Learning style of Chinese event management students

Louw, Mattheus J.,
Louw, Lynette,
Li, Yanxia

There is a demand for social development in China by establishing, inter alia, a framework focusing on the employability of university graduates and developing self-directed learners. The key to achieving this would be to gain a better understanding of how learning styles, as one of the cognitive factors, contribute towards academic performance in order to provide meaningful learning experiences. The purpose of this study is to gain an understanding of learning styles and how they influence the academic performance of selected students on the International Event Management (IEMS) programme at Shanghai University of International Business and Economics (SUIBE). As such, the aims of this exploratory quantitative study are to describe and analyse: learning styles; the relationship between learning orientations and learning styles; the relationship between learning styles and academic performance; and the relationship between gender and the learning styles of selected 2nd year 2010 and 2011 IEMS student cohorts (f = 140) at SUIBE. Since the two most dominant learning styles in this study were Divergers and Accommodators, the most dominant learning orientation for these two learning styles was concrete experience. Overall, most of the students in each learning style performed at the satisfactory academic performance level, and females obtained higher scores than their male counterparts in all learning styles.

中国的社会发展尤其需要建立一个制度集中发展大学毕业生就业能力和自主学习能力。实现这一目标的关键在于更好的了解学习风格，它作为一个认知要素是如何改善学习表现的，从而总结出更有意义的学习经验。本文的研究意义在于深入了解不同的学习风格，并分析其对被挑选的上海对外经济贸易大学的会展专业（IEMS）学生的学习表现的影响。此次探讨性的定量研究目标在于描述并分析：学习风格类型；学习导向和学习风格之间的关系；学习风格和学习表现的关系以及性别和学习风格的关系，研究数据来源于就读大学二年级的 IEMS2010 级和 2011 级 140 位学生。由于研究结果中最主要的学习风格是发散型学习（divergers）和调节型学习（ accommodators），说明这两种学习风格的最主要的学习导向都是具体经验（concrete experience）。总体来说，每个学习风格中的大多数学生的学习表现令人满意，并且在所有学习风格中女生的成绩要高于男生。

1 Introduction and context

The overall education status in China gained great progress when China's reform and "opening-up policies" were launched in 1978. Free compulsory education (including primary and junior middle education) has become the norm in urban and rural areas. In the meanwhile higher education has reached a new stage of popularisation. The development of education has improved the quality of human resources and made a significant contribution to economic growth (The Chinese State Council 2010).

The function of fostering young talents and professionals has been further emphasised as the central task in college and university work (Hao 2005). The higher education system in China has been criticised a great deal for the fact that the graduates cannot meet the demands of industry. The students are weak in their adaptability to society, and the shortage of innovative, practical and versatile professionals has been an acute problem that draws great attention (Li and Lan 2013). Scholars believe that an education system based on graduate employability can help solve the problem (Xie and Song 2005). The core of employability-based education is to develop the potential of the students, and transfer the focus of the education process from the teachers' teaching to the students' learning (Hao 2005). This is also referred to as "'self-directed learners" where the learners are "learning to be self-aware" (Robotham 1999: 7) and the approach is learner-centred rather than teacher-centred. Pan and Che (2009) maintain that in order to improve the employability of graduates, some provincial universities and colleges should differentiate their position from traditional research-orientated to application-orientated, and focus on the development of skilful talents and professionals. Similar points were proposed by premier Li Keqiang on Feb 26th 2014. Accordingly, the government needs to transform the graduate employment policy by focusing on employability rather than the employment rate, and integrate the employment policy into the higher education process to build a new policy system based on cooperation, colleges and employers (Zhang, Liu, Yu, Jiang and Xue, 2009). Consequently the government is building a new framework including Higher Educational Institutions (HEIs), research institutes, industries and enterprises to better cultivate talent and professionalism in order to meet the demand of social development (The Chinese State Council 2010).

Another serious challenge in the higher education system in China is burnout (Lian, Yang and Wu, 2006) which is mainly due to the following:

- Lack of study purpose (Wang, Zhang and Fu 2010). This lack can be attributed to the extreme desire to get a university certificate so as to be employable. In this process students experience external push from parents to pass the entrance examination to university, known as "Gaokao".
- Lack of professional commitment (Lian et al. 2006). The high income in certain industries and positions guides the students' choice of majors such as finance, management, law and informational technology. The future career and income rather than interests and talents become the standard when parents choose majors for their children. The external push from parents and teachers rather than internal interest becomes an important motivation to learning for students in China, and many students do not like their major subjects.

- Low professional adaptability (Wang et al. 2010). Many students get low academic results initially because they battle with establishing a learning strategy and building in-terpersonal relationships immediately after leaving the monitoring environment and assistance from their parents and teachers in high school.

There is a demand for social development in China by establishing a framework focusing on the employability of the graduates from universities, and developing self-directed learners. Hun, Loy and Milah (2013: 1957) stress that it is important for HEIs to be aware of the ways in which students learn, in order to provide meaningful learning experiences. Furthermore, the quality of students is considered as the key index of higher education effectiveness (Sun, Shen and Guan 2012), therefore learning has received significantly more attention in China since 1980s.

According to Robotham (1999: 1), students: "will develop a way or style of learning, and refine that style in response to three groups of factors: unconscious personal interventions by the individual, conscious interventions by the learners themselves, and interventions by some external agent." In this study, it is argued that both the unconscious and conscious interventions by the learner and the learner's response to external interventions are influenced by cognitive and non-cognitive factors. Cognitive factors relate to how information is processed, the role of intelligence, learning strategy, and learning style, while the non-cognitive factors include personal psychological and environmental elements.

Even though there are many factors that contribute to predicting academic performance, progress and persistence (such as selecting incorrect majors and degree choices, being under- and unprepared, and the lack of study purpose, adaptability, motivation and commitment as well as socio-economic factors), in this study the focus will be on the learning styles as one of the cognitive factors and its relationship with academic performance. Intelligence has been proved to have a direct influence on academic performance. Garavalia and Gredler (2002); Huo, Cai, Zou, Feng, Zhu, Xu, Geng, Zhang and Mao (1997); Rosander and Bäckström, (2012: 820) have found that the cognitive factor "learning style" directly influences students' academic performance The cognitive factor, learning style is among predictors of academic performance (Chang, Kang and Wang 2005; Drysdale, Ross and Schulz 2001; Gauss 2002; Kvan and Yunyan 2004; Lu 2005). Wu (2004) examined the relationship between learning strategy, learning style and learning achievement, and found that the research supported the direct influence of both learning strategy and learning style on students' learning achievement. Even though multiple ways have been used to describe students' learning and studying processes (Tait and Entwistle 1996: 100), the most commonly used are students' learning styles (Hun et al. 2013: 1958). Andreou, Andreou and Vlachos (2008: 665) describe a learning style as "a student's preferred mode of perceiving, organising and retaining information". A student responds to and uses stimuli in their learning environment through behaviours incorporating their individual learning style (Drysdale et al. 2001: 273).

Even though the cognitive factor (learning style) directly influences students' academic performance, it is important to note that the emotional factors (learning willingness and achievement motivation) indirectly influence academic performance via cognitive factors.

Students' learning attitude (Yin 2008; Zhang and Geng 2009), learning motivation (Huo, et al. 1997; Tu 2013), personality types (Gauss 2002), goals and sub-goals (Riordan 2002), coping strategies and study skills (Abatso 1982) are predictors of academic persistence, and significant influences on academic performance. Positive affective variables such as self-esteem (Tu 2013) and perceived self-efficacy (McSorley 2002) can help improve academic performance, while negative affective variables such as anxiety about difficulties (Nie, Zhao and Shan 2000; Tu 2013) are negatively related to academic success.

The financial and educational status of the family is also proved to influence students' academic performance. Huang and Xin (2007) argue that the family background significantly influence students' academic achievement; students from families with an ample collection of books showed higher performance than their classmates with fewer books. Sun, et al. (2012) found students' family financial status and Party membership significantly influence their academic performance.

However, for the purpose of this study the focus will be on gaining an understanding of the cognitive factor, learning styles, and their influence on academic performance of selected students in the International Event Management (IEMS) programme at the Shanghai University of International Business and Economics (SUIBE).

SUIBE has established extensive partnerships with its overseas counterparts from more than 80 countries, and now offers 12 joint programmes in cooperation with institutions of higher education in Australia, the United Kingdom, Canada and Germany. One of these is the International Event Management Shanghai (IEMS), a cooperative programme between SUIBE and Osnabruck University of Applied Science (HSOS) from Germany, which has the most developed MICE industry. IEMS is one of the first two programmes that got the approval on event management from the Ministry of Education in China in 2000. In addition, it is the first international cooperative programme of event management in China. The teaching activity is conducted by faculty members from HSOS and SUIBE. Fifteen core courses of IEMS modules are offered in English, which are cooperated by both German professors and Chinese faculty members. In the fourth year, the students must write a thesis in English and pass the oral defence given by both Chinese and German supervisors, to get the degree from both universities. After the successful implementation of the IEMS programme over the past ten years, more than four hundred students have graduated from both SUIBE and HSOS. IEMS has now built its human resource development system for event management talents, which covers the key processes in event management. The system also covers the cooperation with industry and enterprises in event industry.

The purpose and aims of this study will be provided in the next section. In this chapter an overview of theoretical perspectives on learning styles and learning orientations, learning styles and academic performance, and learning styles and gender will be given. The re-search methodology of this study, findings and concluding remarks are also given.

2 Purpose and aims of the study

The purpose of this study is to gain an understanding of learning styles and their influence on academic performance of the selected students in the International Event Management (IEMS) programme at the Shanghai University of International Business and Economics (SUIBE).

More specifically, the primary aims of this study are to describe and analyse the following:

- The learning styles of the selected IEMS students at SUIBE;
- The relationship between learning orientations and learning styles of selected IEMS students at SUIBE;
- The relationship between learning styles and academic performance of the selected IEMS students at SUIBE;
- The relationship between gender and learning styles of selected IEMS students at SUIBE.

A more comprehensive overview of the learning styles will be provided in the next section.

3 Theoretical overview on learning styles

3.1 Learning style frameworks and theories

Extensive research has contributed towards the development of conceptual frameworks for better understanding of learning preferences, approaches to knowledge acquisition, information processing, and learning styles. Particularly relevant to this study are the varioius conceptual learning styles frameworks and theories that have been used to describe students' preferred modes of learning (Komarraju, Karau, Schmeck and Avdic 2011: 472, Rodrigues 2005: 610). Some widely used learning style frameworks and theories are the Approaches to Studying Inventory (ASI), Inventory of Learning Processes (ILP) and Learning Styles Inventory (LSI) based on Kolb's Experiential Learning Theory (ELT).

The ASI was originally developed by Marton and Säljö (1976, cited in Diseth and Martinsen 2003: 196) and is used to explore interrelationships between various factors leading to differences in learning and studying. The ILP developed by Schmeck, Ribich and Ramanaiah (1977, cited in Komarraju et al. 2011: 474), is a widely used learning style framework that is able to show which learning strategies can help students improve their academic performance. The ELT was developed by Kolb (1984, cited in Kolb and Kolb 2005: 194) and, according to Kayes (2005: 250) and Rodrigues (2005: 610), describes different but interdependent learning styles according to the different learning abilities of students (Kayes 2005: 250; Rodrigues 2005: 610). Descriptions of different learning styles as identified by the ASI, ILP and ELT learning style frameworks and theories are summarised in Table 1.

Tab. 1: Summary of the ASI, ILP and ELT Learning Style Frameworks and Theories.

Approaches to Studying Inventory (ASI)	Inventory of Learning Processes (ILP)	Experiential Learning Theory (ELT)
Deep approach – Intention to understand – Motivated by interest – Meaning orientation – Relating ideas – Using evidence	*Synthesis-analysis* – Processing information – Forming categories – Organising into hierarchies	*Diverging style* – Preference for learning through creating – Generating new ideas – View concrete situations from multiple perspectives
Surface approach – Rote learning intention – Motivated by fear of failure – Reproducing orientation – Syllabus-bound	*Elaborative processing* – Connecting and applying new ideas – Uses existing knowledge base – Uses learner's personal experiences	*Assimilating style* – Preference for learning by drawing on different sources of information – Organising information concisely – Value logical soundness of theories
Strategic approach – Intention to achieve best grades with minimum effort – Motivated by competition – Achieving orientation – Adapting to assessment demands – Managing time and intellectual resources	*Methodical study* – Careful and methodical – Completing assignments on time – Traditionally emphasised in most academic environments	*Converging style* – Preference for learning through solving practical problems – Good at decision making – Dealing with technical tasks rather than interpersonal issues
Apathetic approach – Non-academic orientation – Lack of direction and interest – Negative attitudes – Improvidence	*Fact retention* – Processing information in order to memorise it – Goal of doing well and not understanding of meaning	*Accommodating style* – Preference for learning through taking action and risks – Comfortable in leadership roles – Rely heavily on people for information

(Source: Adapted from Cassidy and Eachus 2000: 311; Diseth and Martinsen 2003: 196; Entwistle and McCune 2004: 33016; Kayes 2005: 250; Komarraju et al. 2011: 474; Kvan and Yunyan 2005: 21).

Although there are various frameworks and theories of learning styles (Komarraju et al. 2011: 472) – three of which are described in Table 1 – Kolb's ELT has been the most influential (Andreou et al. 2008: 665) and is widely used in learning styles research at the tertiary level across multiple academic disciplines (Kolb and Kolb 2005: 196; Kvan and Yunyan 2005: 22; Drysdale et al. 2001). Kolb developed the learning styles inventory (LSI) to validate his ELT theory. Kolb developed the first LSI instrument in 1976, after which further refinement of LSI-2 appeared in 1985, LSI 2A in 1996, and the LSI-3 in 1999 (Kayes 2005: 250). For the purpose of this study, an amended version of the LSI-3 marketed by BK One (BK One Corporate Training 2011) was used to determine the students' preferences for the different orientations which determine their preferred learning styles. According to Lynch, Woelfl, Steele, and Hanssen (1998: 62) the LSI is a "well-validated method for assessing learning style preferences" in a variety of situations, and it has been applied in China by Kvan and Yunyan (2004: 19).

3.2 Kolb's Experiential Learning Theory (ELT)

The ELT portrays the learning process as a cycle during which a learner will recursively experience, reflect, think and act in response to the requirements of an encountered learning situation (Kolb and Kolb 2005: 194). The ELT therefore proposes four interdependent orientations to learning, namely, concrete experience (feeling/experiencing), reflective observation (reflecting/observing), abstract conceptualisation (thinking/facts) and active experimentation (acting/performing) (Kayes 2005: 250).

According to the ELT, learners will process information along two dimensions, namely the vertical and horizontal dimensions. As shown in Image 1, the vertical dimension (axis) provides insights into how students assimilate information either through concrete experience (CE) by means of emotions (feelings and people involved) or abstract conceptualisation (AC) by means of thoughts and facts (objective and factual). How students understand or input information is further processed or transformed through either reflective observation (RO) by reflecting on the experience (introvert) or active experimentation (AE) by acting out the experience (extrovert), as shown by the horizontal dimension (axis) in Image 1 (Rodrigues 2005: 610). An orientation towards concrete experience (feeling/experiencing) entails learning by engaging through direct experience, emphasising experiential learning, whereas an orientation towards abstract conceptualisation (thinking) entails learning through developing analytical theories and concepts to create meaning and direct action (Kayes 2005: 250; Lynch et al. 1998: 62). On the other hand, an orientation towards reflective observation (reflecting) entails learning through considering multiple perspectives which include existing experience and new knowledge, before executing an action, while an orientation towards (action) active experimentation describes a preference for learning through taking action and risk taking (Kayes 2005: 250; Lynch et al. 1998: 62).

Some positive researchers have found that learning styles and orientation are strongly influenced by culture. Research by Joy and Kolb (2009) shows that people from countries that are high in in-group collectivism, institutional collectivism, uncertainty avoidance, future orientation, and gender egalitarianism, tend to be dominant in the abstract learning orientation (AC). Joy and Kolb (2009) also found that people from countries that are high in in-group collectivism, uncertainty avoidance, and assertiveness, are more dominant in the reflective learning orientation style (RO). Researchers from Asia are of the opinion that the learning style preference is culture-sensitive, and that the scales developed in the USA need to be further validated (Hyland 1993; Isemonger and Sheppard 2007).

Although learners will use aspects of the four orientations to learning during a learning process, they tend to develop a preference for using one or two of these orientations, which then become their particular learning style (Kayes 2005: 250). The ELT thus identifies four particular learning styles which are determined by preferences for the different orientations to learning (Kvan and Yunyan 2005: 21). The four learning styles according to the ELT as measured by the LSI are therefore: diverging, assimilating, converging, and accommodating (Andreou et al. 2008: 665).

Learners with a diverging learning style have a preference for concrete experience and reflective observation learning orientations. Rather than take action, divergers prefer to consider situations from many different perspectives and come up with new ideas (Kayes, 2005: 250; Kvan and Yunyan 2005: 21). Consequently these learners, who are reflective in nature, are inclined to need more time to consider and process the different perspectives before taking action. Divergers have been referred to as "creative learners" (Lynch et al. 1998: 62) who are likely to specialise in the arts discipline (Kolb and Kolb 2005: 196).

The assimilating learning style uses the reflective observation and abstract conceptualisation learning orientations. Assimilators are able to understand and concisely organise information from many sources, are logical, and value sound theories (Kvan and Yunyan 2005: 21), and are referred to as the theorists. These learners prefer developing concepts or unifying theories inductively to explain their observations (Lynch et al. 1998: 62). Consequently, learners with the assimilating learning style show more interest in concepts and theories rather than people, leaning towards specialising in information and science disciplines (Kolb and Kolb 2005: 197).

The converging learning style emphasises the abstract conceptualisation and active experimentation learning orientations. Convergers are therefore learners who have a preference for practical problem solving through deductive reasoning, are good at decision making, are comfortable with taking action as part of their learning process (Kayes 2005: 250; Kvan and Yunyan 2005: 21; Lynch et al. 1998: 62), and pragmatic in nature. As convergers prefer to deal with technical tasks rather than people, they tend to lean towards the specialist and technology disciplines (Kolb and Kolb 2005: 197).

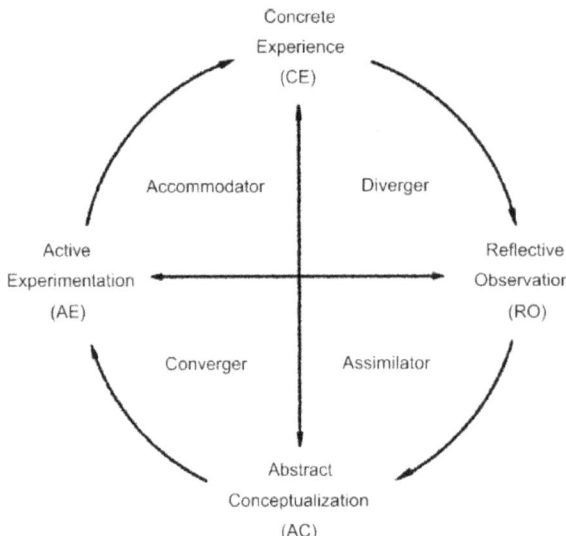

Figure 1: The Experiential Learning Cycle, Learning Orientations and Learning Styles. (Source: Adapted from Kolb, 1984 cited in Kvan and Yunyan 2005: 21).

Lastly, the accommodating learning style uses the active experimentation and concrete experience learning orientations. Learning for accommodators therefore typically involves taking action, relying on their intuition rather than logical analysis, (Kayes 2005: 250; Kvan and Yunyan 2005: 21) and are activists in nature. Accommodators are also comfortable with new experiences and commit quickly to action and leadership roles, and tend to be more effective in action-orientated disciplines like marketing and sales (Kayes 2005: 250; Kolb and Kolb 2005: 197). A summary of these four learning styles can seen in Table 1.

Based on their preference for concrete experience or abstract conceptualisation and reflective observation or active experimentation, a learner can thus be classified into one or two of these learning styles (Kvan and Yunyan 2005: 21). The four learning orientations and resultant learning styles can be represented by an experiential learning cycle, as shown in Image 1. Kolb and Kolb (2005: 194) describe experiential learning as a cyclical learning process that will use the four learning orientations, albeit to varying degrees. Emphasised preference for a certain learning stage (orientation), results in an individual learner's particular learning style (Kvan and Yunyan 2005: 21).

3.3 Managing the learning process using the ELT

As mentioned previously, the ELT can be used to assess learners' individual learning styles by using Kolb's self-report instrument, the Learning Style Inventory (LSI). When learners are conscious of their individual learning styles, they focus more on beneficial habits that will lead to a more effective learning experience (Lynch et al. 1998: 66), facilitate better under-standing of fellow students, enhance team work, and assist in task completion and procrastination (Connelly 2010). Being aware of one's learning style, according to Andreou et al. (2008: 672), can lead to improved attitudes, behaviour and motivation due to increased self-knowledge and awareness. The increased self-awareness, in turn, contributes to academic and social integration, and has implications for level of confidence and career development (Connelly 2010). As such, students should be empowered to identify and address developmental areas in their learning styles, and consequently have a sense of control over their academic performance and social integration.

From the academic faculty's perspective, knowledge of learning styles of their students could assist Faculty members in different ways such as facilitating the proposed shift in teaching orientation towards a student-centred approach, as highlighted in the introduction and context of this chapter, and considering different teaching and assessment methods. In this regard a shift would be required in approaches to learning from a low quality (surface) learning to a high quality (deep) learning approach. The shift would be towards a student-focused deeper learning experience away from the narrow focus on solving particular problems to where "the interest of the individual is not confined to an instrumental approach to learning where task completion is the only aim, there is also on interest in the learning process" (Robotham 1999: 2). In deep learning, the intention is to understand the material as motivated by an interest in (Diseth and Martinsen 2003: 196) and looking for meaning in (Rosander and Bäckström 2012: 820) the subject matter, and to substantiate with evidence. According to Diseth and Martinsen (2003: 196), operation and comprehensive learning strategies are included in deep learning.

On the other hand, surface learning refers to operation learning and the focus is on reproducing learning material by means of different forms of rote learning (Diseth and Martinsen 2003: 196) and memorising content in isolation without understanding the content (Rosander and Bäckström 2012: 820). Deep learning has been positively related to high achievement (Diseth and Martinsen 2003: 196) and academic success (Entwistle and Wilson, 1977, cited in Cassidy and Eachus 2000: 311). Faculty members could be more informed on how to adjust their methods of instruction, namely teaching methods and assessment, to accommodate the most dominant learning styles in a cohort of students so as to encourage deep learning. It has been asserted that matching the methods of instruction with learning styles, optimises the students' learning and academic performance (Vawda 2005: 11; Andreou, et al. 2008: 672; Charkins, O'Toole and Wetzel 1985; Dunn 1984). However, it is cautioned that there should be a balance between structuring methods of instruction according to the dominant learning styles versus a balanced approach across the learning styles. There are various reasons for this, that fall beyond the scope of this chapter. However, it is important to note that there are strong arguments for an instructional delivery approach that is more balanced across the learning styles, enabling greater learning versatility and contributing to the development of a student-centred approach (Pedrosa de Jesus, Ameida, Teixeira-Dias and Watts 2006: 109; Ruble and Stout 1993; Friedman and Alley 1984; Cronbach and Snow 1977).

Kolb and Kolb (2005: 196–197) propose that: divergers learn most effectively in groups, benefit from personal feedback, and enjoy activities such as brainstorming; assimilators benefit from readings, lectures, using analytical models, and need time for reflecting before responding; convergers learn best through exploring new ideas, simulations, practical assignments and solving technical issues; and accommodators benefit from group assignments, field work and exploring different ways of accomplishing tasks. Developing habits that are beneficial to one's particular learning style could therefore lead to enhanced academic performance (Lynch et al. 1998: 66).

4 Learning style and academic performance

Past research has established that learning styles and approaches to the learning process have a bearing on the academic performance of learners (e. g. Hun et al. 2013; Komarraju et al. 2011; Kvan and Yunyan 2005; Cassidy and Eachus 2000; Drysdale et al. 2001; Lynch et al. 1998). Learners' dominant learning styles can therefore affect academic performance (Rosander and Bäckström 2012: 825). Furthermore, learning style differences can be observed across disciplines (Kolb and Kolb 2005: 195) as briefly discussed earlier in the section on Kolb's ELT.

Lynch et al. (1998) for instance, used Kolb's LSI to measure the learning styles of learners and to determine the relationship between learning styles and academic performance. The research by Lynch et al. (1998) explored the learning styles of third-year medical students and found that convergers and assimilators (with their preference for abstract conceptualisation) performed better on single best answer multiple choice examinations. Based on this result, medical students were therefore found to employ analytical and abstract approaches to learning, which were beneficial for their discipline. Kolb and Kolb, (2005: 202–203) further propose that learning in the management discipline, is a scientific and largely text-driven learning process that emphasises theory. In this regard, the management discipline is seen to emphasise an abstract learning orientation. A study by Drysdale et al. (2001) on the cognitive learning styles and academic performance of 19 first-year university courses confirms that there is a significant correlation between academic performance and learning styles. Their study further confirms that maths-related disciplines are better suited to learners who think logically and sequentially, and that all the learning styles are suited to the liberal arts and social sciences.

5 Learning style and gender

As personal factors such as gender can have an influence on the learning process (Vermunt 2005: 205, 207), learning style research has also examined gender differences with regard to preferences for particular learning styles. For example, Philbin, Meier, Huffman and Boverie (1995) found that female learning styles were predominantly divergers or accommodators and they preferred non-traditional learning and concrete learning experiences, while males were more likely to be assimilators and preferred traditional and analytical learning environments. Andreou et al. (2008) in their study of English 2nd language learners confirmed that females leaned more towards a divergent learning style than the males. The study by Peng, Ma and Li (2006) confirmed these findings. Peng, et al. (2006) found significant gender difference in the cognitive styles of the university students: male students preponderated in the thinking and sensing (AC), female students preponderated in the feeling and intuition (CE). A study by Dee, Nauman, Livesay and Rice (2002) of Biomedical engineering students in the Netherlands confirms the findings of Peng et al. 2006).

Zhou (2007) found that female and male students showed different learning styles such as visual style, hands-on style, impulsive style and teacher-independent style, and explained the possible reason from the perspective of socialisation. Females were also found by Vermunt (2005: 229) to be more social and less individualistic in their learning. Finally, Rosander and Bäckström (2012: 825) found that females were more motivated by a "fear of failure" and "aim of qualification", in their academic performance, which resulted in adopting a surface approach to learning. It is also pointed out that studies that do not find differences in learning styles between genders could be attributed to a variety of factors such as sample size, mixture of students, and type of instruction (Jones, Reichard and Mokhtari 2003).

6 Research methodology

The positivistic research paradigm was followed, in which the data collected was quantitative in nature (Collis and Hussey 2014: 44). As such an exploratory and descriptive approach was used to describe and analyse the learning orientations, styles and academic performance of the 2nd year IEMS students at SUIBE.

A non-probability convenience sampling was used in identifying all the 2nd year 2010 and 2011 IEMS cohorts at SUIBE (f = 140). The reasons for selecting the past two 2nd year co-horts were that their academic results from their 1st semester in their 2nd year of study could be calculated and they had had time to settle into university learning after having completed their first year of study. The results from this study could provide useful insights for their own study and for faculty members to consider in the second semester of the 2nd year and the 3rd year of study. Participation was voluntary and with consent. Since the data gathered over the two years was similar, only the overall findings are reported in this chapter.

As previously mentioned, the adapted version of Kolb's LSI-3, marketed by BK One (BK One Corporate Training 2011), was used in this study. This research instrument was administered during the first semester of the 2nd year of study. Students were requested to respond to 36 statements by selecting one of two statements from columns A or B and C or D that most closely described them. The first 18 statements pertain to the horizontal axis, as shown in Image 1, and represent the continuum from being an AE to RO (active – observer continuum). The scoring for these statements is obtained by subtracting B from A (A-B). A positive AB score is indicative of a more active orientation (AE) while a negative (B-A) score is indicative of a more reflective (RO) learning style. The second 18 statements pertain to the vertical axis, as shown in Image 1, and represent the continuum from being an AC to CE (abstract – concrete). The scoring for these statements is obtained by subtracting D from C (C-D). A positive CD score is indicative of a more abstract orientation (AC) while a negative (D-C) score is indicative of a more concrete (CE) problem-solving and learning style. The AB (AC-CE) and CD (AE-RO) scores are plotted on perpendicular axes, as shown in Image 1, placing the respondent into one of the four quadrants. Each of these quadrants corresponds to one of Kolb's four learning styles, namely, convergence, divergence, assimilation, and accommodation. By joining the two learning orientation scores with a line, the quadrant of the most dominant learning style is shown. The scores from each column were captured into an Excel spreadsheet, and the mean values for each learning orientation and learning style were calculated for the two cohorts of students as a whole. According McFarland (1997 cited in Vawda 2005: 65) the reliability of this LSI instrument ranges from 0.52 to 0.86. Consistent with previous research, Kayes (2005: 254, 255-6) provides evidence for the internal reliability of Kolb's LSI-3 scales, with Cronbach's alpha scores for the four dimensions ranging between 0.77 to 0.82 and the "combined scores for AC-CE and AE-RO of 0.77 and 0.84 respectively". There is also support for the internal construct validity of Kolb's LSI-3 instrument (Kayes 2005: 256). One potential limitation of the measuring instrument is its ipsative nature, where respondents have to compare two options and then choose the most preferred, also referred to in psychology as "forced choice" scale. Consequently a "high score on one dimension results in a correspondingly low score on another dimension" (Kayes 2005: 252). Despite this potential limitation it is accepted that ipsative measures "pose few problems when an instrument is used for self-diagnosis" (Kayes 2005: 253), which was the case in this study.

Assessment of the academic performance was based on the first semester of the second year of each cohort's Grade Point Average (GPA) scores. The GPA score is calculated by determining the average score for each student, based on the class and exam mark for all the courses completed in the semester in which study was undertaken. The types of assessments range from single best answers, multiple-choice questions to assess knowledge, short case scenarios, to presentations and group assignments. The GPA mean scores for both cohorts are categorised according to the following groupings: below 60 per cent – fail; 60 to 69 per cent – pass; 70 to 79 per cent – satisfactory; 80 to 89 per cent – good; and 90 to 100 per cent – excellent.

Data was analysed by means of descriptive and inferential analyses. Given the exploratory and descriptive nature and the small sample of respondents, descriptive statistics such as mean scores and frequency counts which were converted to percentages were tabulated to describe the learning styles, the cross tabulation of learning styles with a academic performance, while mean scores were used in the cross tabulation of learning orientations with learning styles. The frequency counts were used to explain the cross tabulation of learning styles with gender. The relationship between the learning styles and academic performance was analysed by using regression analyses. All the data was captured into an Excel spreadsheet and the regression analysis was done by using SPSS 19.0.

7 Findings

A response rate of 94,28 per cent was received based on the participation of 132 out of 140 students from both the 2010 and 2011 cohorts. Overall there were 96 female and 36 male respondents.

As mentioned previously, only the overall findings for the two cohorts will be reported on in this chapter.

The distribution of the four learning styles is presented in Table 2. From Table 2 it can be seen that that all four learning styles were represented in the whole sample. Most of the students' dominant learning style was Diverger (f = 73, 55 per cent), followed by 40 students who were Accommodators (30 per cent), 13 Assimilators (10 per cent) and the six Convergers (5 per cent). A majority of studies (Kvan and Yunyan 2005; Lynch et al. 1998; Kolb 1981) find all four learning styles to be represented, although they may differ on the dominant learning style and be influenced by the discipline of study (Kolb and Kolb 2005).

Tab. 2: Learning styles for whole sample.

	f	per cent
Diverger	73	55
Assimilator	13	10
Converger	6	5
Accommodator	40	30
Total	132	100

The learning orientations are cross-tabulated with the learning styles in Table 3 based on mean scores. As shown in Table 3, the Divergers seem to be using Reflective Observation (RO) (mean score 5.28) the most, followed by Concrete Experience (CE) (mean score 4.86), Active Experimentation (AE) (mean score 4.01) and Abstract Conceptualisation (AC) (mean score 3.88). Assimilators seem to use more Reflective Observation (RO) (mean score 7.23) which means that they are tentative and reflective in their learning. The Assimilators combine Reflective Observation (RO) with Abstract Conceptualisation (AC) (mean score 6.92) and use significantly less Active Experimentation (AE) (mean score 3.23) and Concrete Experience (CE) (mean score 2.54). Convergers also seem to use more Active Experimentation (AE) (mean score 6.67) which suggests that they are performers, action orientated, who learn through experimentation. The Convergers seem to closely combine Active Experimentation (AE) (mean score 6.67) with Abstract Conceptualisation (AC) (mean score 6.00) which indicates that they are fact-orientated, relying on logical thinking and rational evaluation. To a lesser extent the Convergers use Reflective Observation (RO) (mean score 3.33) and Concrete Experience (CE) (mean score 3.0) on an equal basis. Accommodators use Active Experimentation (AE) (mean score 7.00) which means that they are hands-on and learn through experimentation and Concrete Experience (CE) (mean score 5.93) most, which means they combine an action orientation with an experienced based approach to learning. These learners use Abstract Conceptualisation (AC) (mean score 4.00) and Reflective Observation (3.25) significantly less in their learning.

Tab. 3: Cross tabulation of learning orientations with learning styles.

	Diverger	Assimilator	Converger	Accommodator
	Mean	Mean	Mean	Mean
AE	4.01	3.23	**6.67**	**7.00**
RO	**5.38**	**7.23**	3.33	3.25
AC	3.88	6.92	6.00	4.00
CE	4.86	2.54	3.00	5.93

7.1 The relationship between learning styles and academic performance

Table 4 shows the descriptive cross tabulation for the four learning styles and the academic performance according to the GPA categories. It should be noted that none of the students failed or received excellent GPA scores. From Table 4 it is evident that in all four learning styles, most of the students in each category performed at the satisfactory level as follows: 50.68 per cent of divergers; 46.17 per cent of the assimilators; all the convergers; and 66.67 per cent of accommodators. Relative to the other learning styles, a higher percentage of the assimilators (23.08 per cent) performed in the good category. Overall, there was no real trend.

Tab. 4: Cross tabulation of learning styles and academic performance.

Learning style	Pass	GPA Satisfactory	Good	Total
Accommodator	6	26	7	40
	(15.38 per cent)	(66.67 per cent)	(17.95 per cent)	(100.00 per cent)
Assimilator	4	6	3	13
	(30.77 per cent)	(46.15 per cent)	(23.08 per cent)	(100.00 per cent)
Converger	0	5	0	6
	(0.00 per cent)	(100.00 per cent)	(0.00 per cent)	(100.00 per cent)
Diverger	23	37	13	73
	(31.51 per cent)	(50.68 per cent)	(17.81 per cent)	(100.00 per cent)
Total	33	74	23	132
	(25.38 per cent)	(56.92 per cent)	(17.69 per cent)	(100.00 per cent)

Table 5 shows the results of the regression analysis between the four learning styles and the academic performance according to the GPA categories. Based on the regression, no significant relationships between learning styles and academic performance were found, as shown in Table 5.

Tab. 5: Correlation matrix between learning styles and academic performance.

	GPA	Accommodator	Diverger	Assimilator	Converger
GPA	1.00				
Accommodator	.10	1.00			
Diverger	−.05	−.74*	1.00		
Assimilator	−.07	−.22*	−.38*	1.00	
Converger	−.00	−.13	−.23*	−.07	1.00

Pearson correlation
N=132
*$p \leq 0.01$ (Sig. one-tailed)

The descriptive statistics for the whole sample (Table 6) on gender distribution for learning styles reveals that the learning styles of both the females and males were predominantly divergent (female = 54; male = 19), followed by the accommodator learning style (female = 32; male = 8) with the least dominance in the converger learning style (female = 2; male = 4). In the assimilator learning style, the females were more present than the males (females = 8; males= 5). The finding in the current study that females are predominantly divergers or accommodators confirms previous research by Andreou et al. (2008), Peng et al. (2006), Philbin et al. (1995). Given these dominant learning styles, the predominant cognitive styles of the female students in this study would be in the feeling and intuition (CE) domain. The findings pertaining to the male students in the current study are not confirmed by previous research since most of the males' predominant learning styles were similar to the females in this study, namely divergers and accommodators.

Tab. 6: Cross tabulation of learning styles and gender.

	Total learning styles	Gender	Total gender per learning style
Diverger	73	Female	54
		Male	19
Assimilator	13	Female	8
		Male	5
Converger	6	Female	2
		Male	4
Accommodator	40	Female	32
		Male	8

8 Conclusion

A summary of the main findings in terms of learning styles, learning orientations, the relationship between learning styles and academic performance as well as the relationship between learning styles and gender, will be presented in this section together with concluding implications for the students and faculty members.

Learning styles were not equally distributed among the IEMS students participating in this study. The majority (55 per cent) were divergers, followed by accommodators (30 per cent), assimilators (10 per cent) and convergers (5 per cent).

As mentioned previously, the divergers (CE and RO) are the reflectors, acquire knowledge through using their intuition to generate new ideas, and are imaginative and creative. They are able to see the big picture. While the ability to see the bigger picture and multi-task is a strength, these learners need more time to consider and process the different perspectives before taking action, lose sight of detail, and are inclined to become distracted and somewhat disorganised in keeping notes. It is pointed out by Kolb and Kolb (2005: 196) that divergers are likely to specialise in the arts discipline. While this assertion concurs with the creative aspects in organising events or participating in projects, the ability to begin with a project could be challenging because of the many alternatives, and this would complicate decision making. Kolb and Kolb (2005: 196–197) propose that: divergers learn most effectively in groups, benefit from personal feedback, readings, lectures, using analytical models and need time for reflecting prior to responding and enjoy activities such as brainstorming. Concentration is increased by using diagrams, visuals and examples, rather than detailed theory.

The accommodators (AE and CE) prefer to learn through taking action (activists), take risks and acquire knowledge through intuition rather than logical analysis. Accommodators are motivated and energetic learners whose greatest strength is the ability to be fully involved in new experiences, able to take action quickly (work quickly) and rely on information from others. Their strengths could, however, contribute to their not finishing a task because they are involved in too many tasks from a wide range of interests and experiences (Connelly, 2010). These learners will adopt a more shallow orientation to completing assignments and tasks, leave things to the last minute and, like the divergers, need to plan better. This learning style will facilitate "getting the work done" in the event industry, and need leadership roles. Due to their fractured learning approach and task completion, accommodators benefit from group assignments, field work, small group discussions, games, and exploring different ways of accomplishing tasks with other people, especially on projects.

The two least two dominant styles were the assimilators (theorists) (RO and AC) and the convergers (pragmatists) (AC and AE), with the converger being the most under-represented in this study. Assimilators (RO and AC) learn by using multiple sources of information which are logically analysed in a step-by-step process and then on planning and reflecting. Consequently they need time to think and prepare, and find it difficult to complete a task. Assimilators benefit from readings, lectures, case studies, theoretical readings, reflective exercises and using analytical models and need time for reflecting before responding. A systematic analysis of theory in an impersonal learning environment is preferred. On the other hand, Convergers (AC and AE) prefer to learn through solving practical problems, get things done, are results-orientated and need to improve their interpersonal relationships. Convergers learn best through exploring new ideas, simulations, practical assignments and prefer solving technical issues.

Both the divergers and accommodators (dominant learning styles) learn through feelings and intuition rather than abstract conceptualisations (objective facts). This finding is contrary to the research by Joy and Kolb (2009) indicating that the abstract learning orientation (AC) should be dominant in China. This phenomenon could be attributed to the cultural values of the students in China and the role of Confucianism. In contrast, it is interesting to note that in research done in the USA, the dominant learning styles seem to be convergers and assimilators (Lynch et al. 1998: 64). A study done by Vawda (2005: 72) and in the HE context in South Africa confirmed the results of this study for students in the Management sciences, namely that the two dominant learning styles were accommodator and diverger.

The question can thus be posed whether the Faculty members who teach on the IEMS programme at SUIBE should focus on accommodating the two dominant learning preferences, or whether a more balanced approach needs to be considered where learners are developed and stretched to improve their underdeveloped learning style, thereby achieving greater learning versatility and contributing to the development of a student-centred approach. The latter would be more aligned with the government in China's new framework to better cultivate talent and professionals in order to meet the demand of social development in China.

Since the two most dominant learning styles in this study were Divergers and Accommodators, the most dominant learning orientation for both these learning styles was concrete experience (CE). Consequently, the respondents gather and understand information through concrete experience (CE) by means of emotions (feelings and people involved) which represents a receptive experience-based approach to learning rather than through abstract conceptualisation (AC) which represents an analytical conceptual logical approach by using thoughts and facts (objective and factual). The respondents further processed the gathered information primarily through either reflective observation (RO) which indicates reflective learning based on experience (introvert) or active experimentation (AE), indicating that learning takes place by acting out the experience (extrovert) based on taking risks.

Overall there was only one trend in the relationship between learning styles and academic performance, namely that most of the students in each learning style performed at the satisfactory academic performance level. Previous research by Vawda (2005) at a HEI in South Africa could not establish a relationship trend between the learning styles of university students from different faculties and academic performance.

In all the learning styles the females scored higher than their male counterparts. It should be noted that there is a bias in this finding, since most of the students in these cohorts of IEMS students are female. Both the females and the males' dominant learning styles were divergers and accommodators with a concrete experience orientation. The finding pertaining to the males is contrary to previous research and could possibly be explained in terms of an Asian cultural orientation and the relatively smaller number of male students in the cohorts.

A number of limitations with regard to the generalisation of the results of this study need to be mentioned. Firstly, these results were derived from two 2nd year cohorts of the IEMS programme and may not be representative of all the students in the IEMS programme or students in similar programmes at other universities. Secondly, the exploratory and descriptive nature of this study and the use of convenience sampling is limiting. Thirdly, the small number of students who could be classified as convergers (5 per cent) and assimilators (10 per cent) must also be acknowledged. Consequently very little could be said about their performance pat-terns, and the findings in this study pertain mainly to the divergers and accommodators. Fourthly, due to the small sample size, and wide spread of results in the GPA scores, no correlations could be found between learning styles and academic performance, despite previous research indicating that the cognitive prototype, including learning styles, directly influences the students' academic performance.

Despite these limitations, the present study does have implications for the IEMS programme at SUIBE. Firstly, knowledge of the learning styles and increased self-awareness of the strengths and weaknesses of each learning style and the learning orientations provides students with insights into their own conceptual prototype. Consequently students are empowered to identify and address non-productive behaviours and strengthen beneficial behaviours. As a result they should have a more informed sense of control over their aca-demic performance and social integration, which has implications for their approach to learning (surface or deep learning) and career development. Secondly, considering the increased attention being paid to the learning effect as a significant index of quality students in higher education in China since the 1980s, this study provides insights into the learning styles of the selected cohorts in the IEMS programme and some guidance on the appropriate teaching and assessment methods according to the different learning styles. Consequently, being more aware of the ways in which students learn provides the basis for meaningful learning experiences on the IEMS programme at SUIBE and would facilitate the proposed shift in teaching orientation towards a student-centred approach. Thirdly, while it could be argued that Faculty members could use the insights gained to adjust the content and method of instruction to accommodate the most dominant learning styles of the students, it is cautioned that there should a balanced approach across the learning styles. As such, it is suggested that a balanced approach across the learning styles enables greater learning versatility and contributes to the development of a student-centred approach.

Recommendations for future research:

- Further validating the learning styles instrument to the Asian context because of the cultural sensitivity in learning styles;
- Determining the impact of culture on teaching and learning methods;
- Assessing the correlation between learning styles and approaches to learning, including a strategic learning approach;
- Further investigate the correlation between approaches to learning, learning styles and motives as predictors of academic achievement; and
- Administer a culturally sensitive learning styles instrument, including some of the mentioned aspects to all the IEMS students at SUIBE in order to determine the correlation with academic performance more accurately.

9 Literature

Abatso, Yvonne (1982), *Coping strategies: Retaining Black Students in College*, Atlanta, GA: Southern Education Foundation

Andreou, Eleni, Andreou, Georgia and Vlachos, Filipos (2008), 'Learning Styles and Performance in Second Language Tasks', in: *TESOL Quarterly*, 42 (4), pp. 665–74

BK One Corporate Training (2011), *Learning Style Indicator*. Online: http://www.bkone.co.in/LrngStyleIndicator.asp (accessed on 9 September 2014)

Cassidy, Simon and Eachus, Peter (2000), 'Learning Style, Academic Belief Systems, Self-report Student Proficiency and Academic Achievement in Higher Education', in: *Educational Psychology*, 20 (3), pp. 307–22

Chang, Xin, Kang, Ting Hu, and Wang, Pei (2005), 'The Influence of Cognitive and Emotional Factors on University Students' Achievements in English Learning', in: *Psychological Science*, 28 (3), pp. 727–730

Charkins, RJ, O'Toole, Dennis and Wetzel, James (1985), 'Linking Teacher and Student Learning Styles with Student Achievement and Attitutes' in: *The Journal of Economic Education*, 16 (2), pp. 111–120

Collis, Jill and Hussey, Roger (2014), *Business Research: A Practical Guide for Undergraduate and Postgraduate Students*, London: Palgrave MacMillan

Connelly, Ruth (2010), *Additional Information : Unlocking my Learning Potential and Discovering my Learning Style*, Unpublished workshop paper, Student Counselling, Career and Development Centre, Nelson Mandela Metropolitan University, Port Elizabeth, South Africa

Cronbach, Lee and Snow, Richard (1977), *Aptitudes and Instructional Methods: A Handbook for Research on Interactions*, New York: Irvington

Dee, Kay, Nauman, Eric, Livesay, Glen, A and Rice, Janet (2002), 'Research Report: Learning Styles of Biomedical Engineering Students' in: *Journal of Engineering Education*, 20 (8), pp. 110–1106

Diseth, Åge and Martinsen, Øyvind (2003), 'Approaches to Learning, Cognitive Style, and Motives as Predictors of Academic Achievement', in: *Educational Psychology*, 23 (2), pp. 195–207

Drysdale, Maureen, Ross, Johnathan and Schulz, Robert (2001), 'Cognitive Learning Styles and Academic Performance in 19 First-Year University Courses: Successful Students Versus Students at Risk', in: *Journal of Education*, 6 (3), pp. 271–89

Dunn, Rita (1984), 'Learning Style: State of the Science', in: *Theory into Practice*, 23 (1), pp. 10–19

Entwistle, Noel and McCune, Velda (2004), 'Measuring Studying and Learning in Higher Education: Conceptual and Methodological Issues' in: *Educational Psychology Review*, 16 (4), pp. 325–45

Entwistle, Noel and Wilson, John (1977), 'Degrees of Excellence: The Academic Achievemetn Game', in: Cassidy, Simon and Eachus, Peter (2000), 'Learning Style, Academic Belief Systems, Self-report Student Proficiency and Academic Achievement in Higher Education', in: *Educational Psychology*, 20 (3), pp. 307–22

Friedman, Peggy and Alley, Robert (1984), 'Learning/Teaching Styles: Applying the Principles', in: *Theory into Practice*, 23 (1), pp. 77–81

Garavalia, Linda and Gredler, Margaret (2002), 'Prior Achievement, Aptitude, and Use of Learning Strategies as Predictors of College Student Achievement', in: *College Student Journal*, 36 (4), pp. 616–626

Gauss, Sandra (2002), *Personality, Associated Learning Styles and Academic Performance of Third Year Psychology Students*. Unpublished master's thesis, University of Port Elizabeth, South Africa

Hao, De Yong, (2005), 'Socialized Orientation and Cultivation of Qualified Manpower', in: *Educational Research*, 304 (5), pp. 54–57

Huang, Hui Jing and Xin, Tao, (2007), 'Linkage between Teacher's Instructional Behavior in Classroom and Students Achievement', in: *Psychological Development and Education*, (4), pp. 57–62

Hun, Tan Lay, Loy Chong, Kim and Milah, Ram (2013), 'A Study on Predicting Undergraduates' Improvement of Academic Performances Based on their Characteristics of Learning and Approaches at a Private Higher Educational Institution' in: *Procedia – Social and Behavioral Sciences*, 93, pp. 1957–65

Huo, Jin Zhi, Cai, Yan, Zou Yan, Feng, Wei Juan, Zhu, Sheng Tao, Xu, Ping, Geng, Xiao Fang, Zhang Qun, Mao, Dan (1997), 'Research on the interactive influence of motivation, intelligence and personality on academic performance', in: *Chinese Mental Health Journal*, 11(6), pp. 328–330

Hyland, Ken (1993), 'Culture and Learning: A Study of the Learning Style Preferences of Japanese Students' in: *Regional Learning Centre (RELC) Journal*, 24, pp. 69–87

Isemonger, Ian and Sheppard, Chris (2007), 'A Construct-Related Validity Study on a Korean Version of the Perceptual Learning Styles Preference Questionnaire' in: *Educational and Psychological Measurement*, 67 (2), pp. 357–68

Jones, Cheryl, Reichard, Carla and Mokhtari, Kouider (2003), 'Are Students' Learning Styles Discipline Specific?', in: *Community College Journal of Research and Practice*, 27, pp. 363–375

Joy, Simy and Kolb, David (2009), 'Are there Cultural Differences in Learning Style?', in: *Inter-national Journal of Intercultural Relations*, 33 (1), pp. 69–85

Kayes, Christopher (2005), 'Internal Validity and Reliability of Kolb's Learning Style Inventory Version 3 (1999)' in: *Journal of Business and Psychology*, 20 (2), pp. 249–57

Kolb, David (1984), 'Experiential Learning: Experience as the Source of Learning and Development', in: Kolb, Alice and Kolb, David (2005), 'Learning Styles and Learning Spaces: Enhancing Experiential Learning in Higher Education' in: *Academy of Management Learning and Education*, 4 (2), pp. 193–212

Kolb, David (1984), 'Experiential Learning: Experience as the Source of Learning and Development' in: Thomas and Yunyan, Jia (2004), 'Students' Learning Styles and their Correlation with Performance in Architectural design Studio' in: *Design Studies*, 26, pp. 19–34

Kolb, Alice and Kolb, David (2005), 'Learning Styles and Learning Spaces: Enhancing Experiential Learning in Higher Education' in: *Academy of Management Learning and Education*, 4 (2), pp. 193–212

Komarraju, Meera, Karau, Steven, Schmeck, Ronald and Avdic, Alen (2011), 'The Big Five Personaltiy Traits, Learning Styles and Academic Achievement' in: *Personality and Individual Differences*, 51, pp. 472–77

Kvan, Thomas and Yunyan, Jia (2004), 'Students' Learning Styles and their Correlation with Performance in Architectural design Studio' in: *Design Studies*, 26, pp. 19–34

Li, Yan Xia and Lan, Xing (2013), 'Research on the Event Human Resource Development Model from the Perspective of Cross-cultural Competence', in: *Modern Business Trade Industry*, (19), pp. 103–105

Lian, Rong, Yang, Li Xian, and Wu, Lan Hua (2006), 'A Study on the Professional Commitment and Learning Burnout of Undergraduates and their Relationship', in: *Psychological Science*, 29 (1), pp. 47–51

Lu, Gen Shu (2005), 'The Relationship between Learning Style and Academic Performance', In: *Higher Engineering Education Research*, (4), pp. 44–47

Lynch, Thomas G, Woelfl, Nancy, Steele, David J, and Hanssen, Cindy A (1998), 'Learning Style Influences Student Examination Performance', in: *The American Journal of Surgery*, 176, July, pp. 62–66

Marton, Ferrence and Säljö, Roger (1976) 'On Qualitative Differences in Learning: I – Outcome and Process' in: Diseth, Åge and Martinsen, Øyvind (2003), 'Approaches to Learning, Cognitive Style, and Motives as Predictors of Academic Achievement', in: *Educational Psychology*, 23 (2), pp. 195–207

McFarland, (1997), cited in: Vawda, Aamena (2003), *The Learning Styles of First Year University Students*, Unpublished master's thesis, Nelson Mandela Metropolitan University, South Africa

McSorley, Michelle (2002), *The Construct Equivalence of the Motivated Strategies for Learning Questionnaire (MSLQ) for a South African Context*, Unpublished master's thesis, University of Port Elizabeth, South Africa

Nie Jing, Zhao, Ming and Shan, Lin (2000), 'Research on the Influence of Non-intellectual Factors on Academic Performance', in: *China Higher Medical Education*, (2), pp. 47–50

Pan, Mao Yuan and Che, Ru Shan (2009), 'Research on the Positioning and Feature of Provincial Universities and Colleges', in: *China Higher Education Research*, (12), pp. 15–18.

Pedrosa de Jesus, Helena, Almeida, Patricia Albergaria, Teixeira-Dias, Jose Joaquim and Watts, Mike (2006), 'Students' Questions: Building a Bridge between Kolb's Learning Styles and Approaches to Learning', in: *Education and Training*, 48 (2/3), pp. 97–111

Peng, Xian, Ma, Su Hong, and Li, Xiu Ming (2006), 'A Study on the Cognitive Styles and Gender Difference of Normal University Students', in: *China Journal of Health Psychology*, 14 (3), pp. 299–301

Philbin, Marge, Meier, Elizabeth, Huffman, Sherri and Boverie, Patricia (1995), 'A Survey of Gender and Learning Styles' in: *Sex Roles: A Journal of Research*, 32 (7/8), pp. 485–495.

Riordan, Melissa Clare (2002), *A Preliminary Investigation into the Use of the Noncognitive Questionnaire (NCQ) with a Sample of University Applicants in South Africa*. University of Port Elizabeth, South Africa. Online:

http://books.google.co.za/books/about/A_Preliminary_Investigation_Into_the_Use.html?id= QLBRNwAACAAJ&redir_esc=y (accessed on 12 September 2014)

Robotham, David (1999), *The Application of Learning Styles Theory in Higher Education Teaching, Visiting Lecturer in Human Resource Management*, Wolverhampton Business School, University of Wolverhampton, United Kingdom

Rodrigues, Carl (2005), 'Culture as a Determinant of the Importance Level Business Students Place on Ten Teaching/Learning Techniques: A Survey of University Students' in: *Journal of Management Development*, 24 (7), pp. 608–21

Rosander, Pia and Bäckström, Martin, (2012), 'The Unique Contribution of Learning Approaches to Academic Performance, After Controlling for IQ and Personality: Are there Gender Differences?', in: *Learning and Individual Differences*, 22, pp. 820–26

Ruble, Thomas, L and Stout, David, E (1993), 'Learning Styles and End-user Training: An Unwarrented leap of Faith' in: *MIS Quarterly*, 17 (1), pp. 115–118

Schmeck, Ronald, Ribich, Fred and Ramanaiah, Nerella (1977), 'Development of a Self-report Inventory for Assessing Individual Differences in Learning Processes' in: Komarraju, Meera, Karau, Steven, Schmeck, Ronald and Avdic, Alen (2011), 'The Big Five Personaltiy Traits, Learning Styles and Academic Achievement' in: *Personality and Individual Differences*, 51, pp. 472–77

Sun, Rui Jun, Shen, Ruo Meng and Guan, Liu Si (2012), 'Research on the Factors that Influence University Students Learning Effectivity', in: *Journal of National Academy of Education Administration*, (9), pp. 65–71

Tait, Hilary and Entwistle, Noel (1996), 'Identifying Students at Risk through Ineffective Study Strategies' in: *Higher Education*, 31 (1), pp. 97–116

The Chinese State Council (2010), '*Outline of China's National Plan for Medium and Long-term Education Reform and Development (2010–2010)*', Beijing: People's Publishing House.

Tu, Chao Lian (2013), 'Research on the Influence of Affective Factors on Academic Performance', in: *Journal of Xi'an International Studies University*, 21 (3), pp. 62–65

Vawda, Aamena (2005), *The Learning Styles of First Year University Students*, Unpublished master's thesis, Nelson Mandela Metropolitan University, South Africa

Vermunt, Jan (2005), 'Relations between Student Learning Patterns and Personal and Contextual Factors and Academic Performance' in: *Higher Education*, 49 (3), pp. 205–34

Wang, Jing Xin, Zhang, Kuo and Fu, Li Fei (2010), 'Relationship between Professional Adaptability, Learning Burnout and Learning Strategies of College Students', in: *Studies of Psychology and Behavior*, 8 (2), pp. 126–132

Wu, Yue (2004), *Study on Relationship among Undergraduates' Learning Strategy, Cognitive Style of FDI, Learning Style, Study Motivation and Learning Achievement*, Unpublished master's thesis, Shanxi Normal University, China

Xie, Jin Yu and Song, Guo Xue (2005), 'An Analysis on the Students' Possible Employment and their Useable Skills after Education', in: *Nankai Journal (Social Science)*, (2), pp. 85–92

Yin, Lei (2008), 'A Research on the Relationship between Study Attitude and Study Achievement', in: *Psychological Science*, 31 (6), pp. 1471–1473

Zhang, Zhi Hong and Geng, Lan Fang (2009), 'A Positive Research on the Influence of University Students' Learning Attitude on their Academic Performance', in: *Chinese University Teaching*, (10), pp. 87–89

Zhang, Ti Qin, Liu, Jun, Yu, Hong Liang, Jiang, Yan, Xue, Jing (2009), 'Research on graduate employment policy from the perspective of employability', in: *Economic Theory and Policy Studies*, 2(6), pp. 70–86

Zhou, Ju Hong (2007), *Effects of Gender, Culture, Personality and Belief about Language Learning*, Unpublished master's thesis, Xidian University, China

Lecturing key competencies in China and the challenge of transnational education

Steinkuhl, Claudia,
Gray, Clare,
Metz, Annette

在中国传授核心能力以及跨国教育中的挑战

The challenges faced by non-Chinese lecturers teaching in the Sino-German programme International Event Management Shanghai are part of an ongoing process of personal, intercultural and didactic development. Different institutional structures and teaching systems demand a high level of continual reflection by those involved in the organisation, planning and teaching of this transnational programme. The following article emphasises the importance of soft skills for students and graduates. It reflects the experiences and challenges encountered by lecturers teaching key competencies, such as academic writing and intercultural communication, to Chinese students. Cultural and historical differences, which may influence learning styles and require an adaptation of teaching methods, are also considered in this article.

外籍教师在上海对外经济贸易大学中德合作国际会展专业教学期间遇到的挑战，是其持续不断的个人、跨文化和教书育人发展历程中的一部分。在不同的制度体系和教育系统之间成立的跨国合作办学项目，要求每个在组织安排、计划和教学岗位上的参与者不断地进行深度的总结和反省。文章强调了软实力对于在校生和毕业生的重要性，这体现在教师在传授诸如学术写作、跨文化交流等关键能力时的经验和挑战。文化和历史背景的差异可能影响了中国学生的学习模式，这就需要教师据此调整教学方法。这一点在文章中也进行了探讨。

1 Introduction

International Event Management Shanghai, taught at Shanghai University of International Business and Economics (SUIBE) in cooperation with the University of Applied Sciences Osnabrueck, is a Sino-German bachelor degree programme which ends with a joint bachelor degree from both institutions of higher education. Lectures are taught in both Chinese and English and cover subjects ranging from the fundamentals of business management, accounting, services marketing and macroeconomics to specialist modules covering the complete scope of event management. IEMS was initially established in cooperation with the German Academic Exchange Service (DAAD) in 2004.

The so-called flying faculty, the posting of lecturers from the German partner university to Shanghai for block lectures, represents just one of the many features of the IEMS programme. Lecturers from Osnabrueck University of Applied Sciences teach Chinese students from Shanghai University of International Business and Economics specific event and business-related modules for intensive two-week block periods. Although most German lecturers have multiple years of teaching experience in Germany and China, the challenges they encounter are part of an ongoing process which requires continual reflection. Because institutional structures and study organization as well as the teaching and learning cultures are significantly different (Lux 2013), there may still be misunderstandings or even frustration in this intercultural setting, both for the lecturers and the students.

Transnational programmes have become more and more important in the development of German and Chinese higher education systems during the past decades.

> "The basic principle of TNE [Transnational Education] involves the delivery of higher education programmes in a different country from the one where the awarding/overseeing institution is based. Students can study towards a foreign qualification without leaving their country of residence. TNE involves the mobility of academic programmes and providers/institutions across jurisdictional borders to offer education and training opportunities. There is collaboration with a local institution or provider (twinning, franchise, validation, joint and double degree programmes), and it can also involve setting up a satellite operation (branch campus)." (DAAD, 2015)

A number of studies on transnational higher education and useful guides to teaching international students have been published in recent years (Coverdale-Jones 2013; Schumann edt 2012). The goal of this article is not to give further normative suggestions for overcoming intercultural differences between Germany and China in further education. The following article reflects experiences and challenges encountered whilst teaching key competencies such as academic writing and intercultural communication to Chinese students. It also discusses possible reasons for differences, including certain aspects of the historical and social development facing the students in their academic careers. The consideration and comprehension of these differences allows the suitable adaptation of 'German' teaching methods of key competencies in China and may facilitate the answering of the question how a good level of cooperation and interaction between Chinese students and German lecturers can be ensured, despite the obvious intercultural differences. The text also touches upon the continual importance of soft skills in the early careers of graduates and finally discusses the changes in values and attitudes of the new generation of students in China today.

2 Key competencies in higher education

In 2010, Jin Sun conducted a study about the intercultural differences in higher education between China and Germany. The table below shows the general findings of the research.

The results of the survey indicate the vast differences between the German and Chinese higher education systems and the necessity to compare, reflect and adopt core qualities from both systems.

Tab. 1: Dimension of and differences in higher education cultures. (Sun 2010: 274 cited according to Lux 2013: 85)

Dimension of higher education culture	Main differences	
	China	Germany
Access to higher education and degree	Model of strict selection prior to beginning of studies	Model of broad access for prospective students
	Model of guaranteed graduation	Model of strict selection after beginning of studies
Student organisation and administration	Model of third party administration	Model of autonomy and self-administration
Study organisation	Model of centralised study organisation	Model of self-organisation
Orientation of tuition and development of competencies	Unifying and standardising tuition and competence development	Individualising tuition and competence development
Performance requirements and control	Formalised performance requirements and control	Immanent performance requirements and strict performance control
Shaping of social relations and contacts	Model of a socially tight-knit university	Model of socially loosely linked university
Role awareness of lectures	Hierarchical role awareness of lectures	Egalitarian role awareness of lectures
Role awareness of students	Immaturity oriented role awareness of students	Responsibility-oriented role awareness of students

The survey includes interviews with German and Chinese students. Questions concerning the general approach towards their studies have clearly shown that Chinese students regard themselves as being more advanced with regard to purposefulness, effort and persistence. It is also clarifying that German students attach more importance to their intrinsic interests than their Chinese counterparts (Sun 2010). It was emphasised that competencies such as autonomous and critical thinking, creativity, arguing, discussing and presenting are often actively taught in Germany. Furthermore, the degree of interaction during discussions, arguments, presentations or the critical reflection of what has been said by lecturers is usually higher with German students. These are often keen to voice their own opinions, to pose questions, to actively answer any questions which arise in class, or even to criticize a particular subject or statement. Chinese students tend to be more reserved. Respect for age, hierarchy and the significance of education represent key characteristics in traditional Chinese culture. The defined position within society can be traced back to Confucius, who said: "Let the ruler be a ruler, the minister be a minister, the father be a father, and the son be a son" (Chan, 1963: 39). The young are taught at a very early age to keep silent and to listen to and respect their parents and grandparents. They are required to show a high degree of modesty, humbleness, reservation and constraint, and they are taught in a monologic manner, given no room for self-reflection or criticism towards their teacher or the subject. There is a clear definition of roles with very little, if any, room for discussion. Questioning a teacher is regarded as disrespectful and irreverent, both towards the lecturer as well as towards fellow students, who have come to learn from an experienced academic and not to waste time listening to like-minded, inexperienced peers voicing their opinions or even their personal doubts or criticism. Harmonious cooperation and the avoidance of losing face ('Mianzi' in Chinese) play a decisive role in everyday life, including the academic environment. Going unnoticed and belonging to a collective group of harmonious equals is of paramount importance in the undergraduate academic environment. Respect for elders and the more experienced or better-educated is a cultural trait which explains the way the Chinese education system, still characterized by a strong one-way monologue approach, functions. Pupils and students listen to their respected teacher and learn mainly through the concept of repetition. Copying and reproducing are in line with the traditional value of harmony; whereas creativity is not (Faure/Fang 2008: 203). Students frequently learn content by heart, rather than critically reflecting or questioning other people's proposals.

It must be pointed out at this stage that despite a certain generalization of specific structures, characteristics and competencies which may be attributed to German or Chinese students, generalised statements cannot be applied to everybody. German lecturers have often recalled lively and critical interaction with Chinese students.

The promotion of soft skills has become important at some Chinese universities (Sun 2010: 236), including the IEMS partner university in Shanghai, which may very well be attributed to the IEMS programme structure. German higher education has placed great importance on the development of these and other key competencies for many years. Soft skills constitute an important element of curricula at German universities, particularly since the Bologna reform[1]. They often include subjects to promote and develop these skills and often extracurricular seminars and workshops are offered to acquire and train them. Key competencies have played a central role in the political educational views of the OECD since the end of the 1990s. The OECD conceives key competencies to be the personal ability people have to handle complex requirements from all social areas of life (Rychen 2008). In a publication about competencies which are necessary for innovation and research, the organisation announces "A broad range of skills contributes to innovation and 'soft skills' may be increasingly important" (OECD 2011). According to those who hold this view, possessing key competencies can promote individual success as well as societal welfare. Selected skills were recorded empirically in an international comparison in three PISA-Studies in 2000, 2003 and 2006 (Lange 2012).

---

[1] A European-wide harmonisation of study programmes which should lead to increasing transparency and more international mobility of students, Gabler (2014): Wirtschaftslexikon

2.1 Intercultural competencies for students and lecturers in transnational programmes

Having emphasised the importance of key competencies it must clearly be said that acquiring the relevant skills often means changing internalised behaviour. Behavioural patterns, which have developed deeply during primary and secondary socialization phases automatically need to be challenged (Behrend 2007).

For the western observer, China appears to be embracing paradoxes which are difficult to fully comprehend. Hofstede once classified the Chinese as high in collectivism and power distance (Hofstede 1980, 1991; Hofstede and Bond 1988). On the other hand, during the past decades, the Chinese have widely proven to be very entrepreneurial (Weidenbaum 1996; Hofstede and Bond 1988), which may seem to indicate a rather individualistic nature. When walking around the campus at the Chinese partner university, German lecturers often observe the following paradox: on the one hand the campus is filled with small groups of young Chinese students, intensively chatting and laughing whilst strolling around together, but on the other hand those same Chinese students appear almost silent minutes later in class. They sit in lectures, heads down, almost mute, lacking interest, sometimes solemn and often only reacting when spoken to directly.

In this world of apparent ambiguity, the importance of intercultural competency when teaching Chinese students as a foreign lecturer in China is self-explanatory. One well known finding and advice of studies and literature in transnational education programmes is that intercultural behavioural differences will be better understood if lecturers not only focus on learning about and getting to know the foreign culture, but also reflect their own personal culture and background. Anybody teaching in an intercultural setting knows that there are no panaceas or perfected rules for such situations. Applying the basic principle 'when in Rome, do as the Romans do' will not suffice either. Intercultural competency does not consist of avoiding awkward situations or following specific rules. Intercultural competence consists of a high degree of personal openness, a two-way willingness to learn, sensitivity for each other's cultures, tolerance and flexibility as well as the confidence to retain one's own culture and identity whilst learning about the foreign culture. Acquiring intercultural competence is not about giving up one's own identity and taking on another in order to fit in. It is about adjusting one's own perspective and reflecting about the differences between the foreign culture and one's own (Utler & Thomas 2010: 320). Self-reflection and a change of perspective as vital aspects of intercultural competency will lead to an improved sensitization for the foreign culture and a better understanding of the differences between the German and Chinese academic and learning environments. Adopting the appropriate mind-set for the respective intercultural environment is an aspect Christopher Ziguras discusses in his paper about transnational higher education in South East Asia. "If education is conceived as a way of changing students, the educators should accept that they cannot be culturally benign, but invariably promote certain ways of being over others" (Ziguras 2001: 15).

Finding a balance between one's own culture and the foreign culture is an important task for lecturers as well as students in the IEMS programme. Educating these students is not simply about transferring facts and knowledge with a basic willingness to be open and tolerant. The challenges faced by German lecturers teaching key competencies to a group of 20–60 Chinese students of this generation in China are plenty. Chinese students are used to standardised teaching methods with regulated text books and uniform exam structures, whereas German lecturers apply individualistic teaching methods, using personalised scripts and a large variety of examination types (Sun 2010: 242). These significant intercultural educational differences need to be considered closely by lecturers in the programme. Adopting the local frontal teaching methods for the two-week period of a block lecture would be very simple and easily implemented for some lecture topics, but this situation would most probably lead to frustration, at least on the lecturer's part, and is not suited to subjects which are experience-orientated or dependent on active participation by the students. This would also contradict the whole concept and fundamental significance of the entire IEMS programme, which lays great importance on its transnational status and character. Individual or joint presentations, group work, role plays, open discussion groups and other interactive teaching methods all offer the Chinese students a new and more involved insight into the subject areas they cover as IEMS students. However, although German lecturers teaching in Shanghai are required to retain their German teaching methods, introducing the Chinese students to more openness, more room for interaction and in short – the German study culture, the lecturers may ask themselves how they can modify their own teaching methods and to what extent they can acknowledge the practices in China in order to productively add them to their repertoire and find the best-suited methods for all parties (Lux 2013).

Whilst experiencing the 'western' approach to learning, the Chinese students may react with a certain degree of dismay or they may just simply nod and agree with what the lecturer has said. One of the German IEMS lecturers was once overheard saying "Chinese students always say 'yes', even when they do not understand something. Why is that?" This is often found amusing, confusing, sometimes even aggravating. Experience shows that Chinese students may require a 'warm-up phase' before they realise their ability to open up, to join in or to understand the advantage they are being offered by these different methods. They often reply with a simple 'yes', in order to show an initial 'I have noted what you have said and will try and understand it at a later date'. If the student were to say 'no' or to question the lecturer's explanation, both student and teacher would be submitted to embarrassment and a 'loss of face' in front of the whole group. Critically contesting, debating or even questioning topics in class does not conform to the traditional Chinese university teaching methods. According to Sun, lecturers have very clear roles in traditional Chinese further education. They are regarded as teachers, as knowledge-transmitters, as leaders and architects, even as pastors or authorities (Sun 2010: 254). On the other hand, German lecturers play a more egalitarian role. They are perceived as teaching researchers, as supporters and consulting bodies, as specialists in their individual fields, leaving the students more space and personal opportunity to learn and understand topics for themselves, rather than simply learning what the teacher has said. In this case, it is the role of the German lecturer to offer the students a helping hand and to aid them on their way to learning new methods and techniques. Silence in class may initially provoke insecurity or even dismay on the lecturer's part, but it is not necessarily a lack of knowledge or a sign of ignorance on the students' part. It is more likely to stand for the respect for the teacher or the fear of expressing one's personal opinion in front of peers and therefore standing out from the group or crowd. It would then partly be the role of the lecturer to encourage the students to open up and partly the role of the student to grasp and understand the new study and communication skills being introduced by the German lecturer. Chinese students sometimes may appear very passive in class, but experience shows there is often a huge magnitude of knowledge just waiting to be released with time. Often the openness and the courage to express personal ideas, to actively participate or to even criticise may not develop until later on in the IEMS programme, when students are in higher semesters, having gained more experience from German lecturers with more egalitarian teaching methods.

2.2 Academic writing as a key competency for Chinese students

Teaching 'Communication and Key Qualifications' in the IEMS programme includes working on students' academic writing skills. As a German bachelor degree is awarded, students in the IEMS programme conclude their studies with a bachelor thesis that has to meet western/German requirements. To prepare students for this and to develop academic writing skills as a method of gaining, increasing and communicating knowledge, students should practise this kind of work before they are faced with the task of writing their bachelor thesis.

Cultural background, different teaching methods, learning styles and writing traditions have several impacts on students' approach to academic writing. "In ancient China [...] students were typically encouraged to copy the words of their masters" (Zhang 2010 cited according to Li 2012: 581). Nowadays, Chinese students are often blamed for not referencing other people's ideas and thoughts in their assignments (Sun 2010: 148). The textual copying or plagiarism has become an issue of growing concern and has been widely discussed (Li 2012: 569). It would be dishonest to state that German lecturers in the IEMS programme have not been faced with the gap between Chinese and German source-acknowledgement practices. However, experiences at the partner university have shown a very positive development and an increased awareness regarding this topic. Educating Chinese students in academic writing requires an understanding of specific problems, reasons and differences in their approach, some of which are mentioned below.

Academic Writing as a subject has a higher standing in Germany. Trends show that the development of such skills is given more attention than in China (Sun 2010: 156). German students have to deal with academic writing more often during their degree courses than Chinese students. They take part in special academic writing courses and they have higher demands in terms of content and form. In comparison to their Chinese counterparts, German students are not given points just for 'effort'. Because of the requirements in the Chinese system (e. g. same age groups graduating at the same time and identical timetables), academic work is characterized by an above average structural formality compared to the German system. Final assignments do not serve as the acquirement or the diagnosis of competencies; they symbolize the legitimation for the receipt of the certificates for completing a university degree. Standards of quality in academic writing are ensured and protected in the German academic system by giving universities the freedom to award grades and degrees individually and without fixed completion dates for entire intakes.

The reason for the lack of sources in an academic paper is often closely linked with the student's understanding of such a piece of work in general. Instead of considering their papers as individual and creative tasks, their effort often focuses more on the search for standard responses. It appears that the students wish to show that they are capable of finding those exact responses and depict them in their work, rather than quoting the respective source. It is not uncommon that students think their examiners already know the correct responses, making a further reference to the sources apparently superfluous (Sun 2010).

Specific problems or tendencies are noticeable regarding language and writing style. German students often face problems when they are requested to use suitable scientific phrases. Chinese students, who are given tasks to prepare pieces of academic work in English during the

IEMS programme, are faced with a much greater challenge. On the one hand this frequently leads to the use of phrases resembling the source text or not differing from it at all. On the other hand, Chinese students who try to express their statements and ideas more independently often tend to use a narrative and multifaceted style of writing, which often results in an illogical and incomprehensible line of reasoning in the perception of readers with different cultural backgrounds. Understanding this situation may be facilitated if one considers the fact that Chinese and English as languages belong to fundamentally different cultural systems, including different patterns of thinking. The Chinese way of thinking subconsciously influences their academic writing in English significantly. The 'spiral' thinking (Kaplan 1966) for instance leads to a less linear line of argumentation than the straight western one. The frequent use of personal pronouns and modal verbs can be traced back to the fact that the importance of human beings is greatly emphasised, while the distinction between the subject and the object is not. "Man and nature are seen as an organic whole and the unification of subject and object is a major focus" [...] (Ren and Hitchcock 2013). The difficulties which students face during academic work processes in foreign languages have been investigated increasingly recently. Research on language teaching methods includes the recommendation to give students the opportunity to work with positive examples and to gain a variety of writing experiences, obtaining support throughout the entire process. Integrating academic writing into regular lessons is also desirable (Findeisen, Schröder 2012: 541). Therefore, academic linguistic education and the development of a specific goal and question which sets the tone for the structure of an assignment is a vital part of teaching academic writing.

Many German universities place great importance both on academic reading as well as academic writing. Words such as 'interpret', 'evaluate', 'validate', 'question' or 'review' are often used in the western university context when referring to the preparation of papers during the reading phase. When it comes to the actual writing, students are frequently advised to orientate themselves, to create coherent arguments and to illustrate examples, admitting difficulties or any hurdles they have encountered or asking questions as they proceed. Emphasis is also placed on precise sourcing and the inclusion of any ethical relevance or research methods (Cortazzi and Jin 2006). Whilst working with source texts, students in China often have problems evolving their own reading strategies, taking notes, filtering information out of diagrams or statistics and, as already described above, expressing themselves in their own words. Apart from the reasons outlined above, this may be attributed to a diversity of other explanations.

According to a study by ASIA Society, China's students are regarded as the most diligent in the world. They spend twice as much time studying compared to their peers in the USA. In 2009, pupils attending a secondary school in Shanghai came first in an international PISA study in reading competence (OECD 2010). Nonetheless, Chinese media often reports discussions about whether Chinese students are learning the appropriate subject materials. In 2012, Hu Jiangkang, a member of the Chinese Education Ministry, criticized the Chinese 'Test Culture' and demanded a development that trains the imaginative and creative competencies of a single student, instead of simply teaching them to succeed in standardized tests and questionnaires (WirtschaftsWoche Global, 23.04.2012, D18).

In another study, carried out by the International Organisation for Cooperation and Evaluation in 2009, Chinese students only achieved the 17th place out of 21 for creativity (WirtschaftsWoche Global, 23.04.2012, D18) and the last place for fantasy (OECD 2010).

Socio-economic pressure may be one of the main reasons why the reformation of China's school system is so difficult. Bearing in mind the current high unemployment levels of graduates and the exceedingly competitive post-university career situation in China today, students are faced by constant high levels of pressure to succeed and to prove their professional qualities. Although methods of learning have changed and students are enjoying a new variety of teaching experiences, usually the next test is all that counts. However, Hayhoe (2006), who published 'Portraits of Influential Chinese Educators', stated that creative and critical development can be seen in Chinese university education. This statement can be confirmed by lecturers in the IEMS programme, who also observed a noticeable improvement regarding these competencies. According to Martin Cortazzi and Lixian Jin (2013) "The next generation of Chinese students should feel more comfortable with creative and critical ideas". The demand to meet those key expectations has recently been emphasized by Chinese education policies. For example, several Chinese universities now teach Creative Writing as a subject and encourage the development of individual thinking and problem-solving skills (Cortazzi and Jin 2013: 114).

3 The continual importance of key competencies for university graduates

The teaching of key competencies at university is just the beginning of a life-long-learning process. Students graduating from university in China may be primed with newly obtained skills and experiences in both these fields, but do these new competencies suffice for a successful career? "Due to the ever-increasing speed of innovative changes in the economy and society, professionals are faced with new situations and new work contexts over and over again, which they have to master accordingly. Key competencies make employees less dependent on short-term changing requirements of the job market" (Knauf 2003).

German lecturers and German managers working in China share some similar experiences. Managers in China often state difficulties trying to make Chinese employees speak out their own ideas and thoughts (Chen and Tjosvold 2007). Recent business management research indicates the importance of personal identification of a Chinese employee with the manager, in order to be ready to voice his/her thoughts and opinions (Liu, Zhu and Yang 2010). This research shows the importance of a continual learning of soft skills even after the students' graduation. One approach is to learn from best practice voice managers[2], foreign managers who are especially successful in making employees speak up through enhanced personal identification, and to understand how those foreign managers interact with their Chinese employees. Chinese often observe details very carefully when meeting a foreigner for the first time. Their initial tendency is to keep a distance and to observe from afar. They want to get to know the foreigner first; they are interested in what the foreigner has achieved as well as who the foreigner is. The German distinction between private and professional life is not

---

[2] "Discretionary communication of ideas, suggestions, concerns, or opinions about work related issues with the intent to improve organizational or unit functioning", (Morrison 2011: 375)

common in China; Chinese are more interested in getting to know the holistic person, the professional as well as the private side (Metz and Gunkel 2013). Voice managers should not be mistaken as 'soft' managers focusing only on relationships. On the contrary, they have clear expectations, addressing good and poor performance by being very consistent in making decisions and following them up.

This knowledge may be supportive for teaching in a Sino-German study programme. On the one hand it may help to build trust by referring back to hard facts as personal knowledge and achievements. On the other hand it is recommendable to open up about softer aspects, perhaps sharing personal lessons learnt in life. Showing genuine interest and appreciation in China as well as in the Chinese students may help the foreigner build the basis for the personal identification, which in turn will lead to the students also opening up. Genuine respect is the basis necessary for building up trustful relationships. The time spent on this relationship-building in the beginning is well invested as it pays off in the students' real engagement later on.

4 The new generation: A change in values?

The last 35 years, from 1978 until today, brought about tremendous changes which were unique in the 5,000 year history of China (Faure/Fang 2008). The above addressed eminent paradoxes within the Chinese culture have even been enhanced by the fact that the Chinese open door policy, which was started in 1978, encouraged the Chinese to enter into direct contact with foreign cultures and lifestyles. The globalization tendency intensified the tremendous change process and has led to a modernization with direct impact on social behaviour (Faure/Fang 2008). Bearing in mind these paradoxes and changes could strengthen the awareness lecturers have of how important an empathetic and self-reflective approach is before meeting and teaching Chinese students. The Chinese students in the IEMS programme may have been born in a country with a 5,000 year old culture and tradition, but they have experienced dramatic societal change during the course of their lives, which partly contradicts the learnings from that culture and tradition.

Contrary to the traditional upbringing young Chinese students experience as children, being taught to follow and keep silent towards parents and teachers, they are currently noticing huge changes in their daily lives. Observing individuals setting up companies and being highly successful at a young age by implementing completely new, often web-based, business ideas, they are challenging the defined importance of hierarchy and seniority which most Chinese students traditionally learn to adhere to at home and at school. Similar success stories of young Chinese entrepreneurs can be found throughout the country and many Chinese students are asking themselves which direction to take. Should they follow their parents' recommendations to study diligently and follow a traditional path or should they take the examples from young entrepreneurs and try to grab the chance to attempt something new? Who represents their real role model? What is the 'correct' life concept? Many Chinese students may find themselves facing such challenges at the onset of their university careers. They could be questioning the exact traditions which they were brought up with as a child.

The Chinese students taught in the IEMS programme in Shanghai belong to the generation Y. Generation Y, born between the late 1970s and the early 1990s, sometimes referred to as the 'spoilt one-child generation' (Hong-kin-Kwok 2012) or 'Millennial', were the first generation with high familiarity and usage of new media, social networks and other digital technologies (Tyler 2007). They are a generation with diverse personal opinions, with a broader, more international outlook and attitude compared to the previous generation. In other words, they belong to a new generation of students who despite valuing old traditions, values and culture, may be more likely to question exactly these old traditions, values and culture, positioning themselves and making more individual and perhaps even seemingly selfish decisions to promote their own academic careers, their professional goals and their individual future lives. Access to worldwide information has made this generation so different from the previous generation, particularly with respect to international ideas, travelling and personal capital, belongings and wealth. When questioned about their future professional plans, students are often unclear. Some plan to seek a profession clearly outside their degree subject, often mentioning the wish to become self-employed (for example owning coffee shops and restaurants.) Others wish 'to be rich and travel the world' or 'to be rich and not to have to work', without offering any further clarification about which professional activity this fortune should be based on. This is an example of an apparent self-overestimation of generation Y. The importance of the family as an institution has not diminished; it has perhaps changed from being primarily more of a spiritual support to becoming a vital source for the fulfilment of material goals and dreams. A family's role may range from offering help to obtain the latest up-to-date digital devices or funding complete semesters abroad to using the family's personal 'Guanxi' network to support the difficult task of obtaining a satisfactory place of employment.

The further development of attitudes, values and priorities of the above mentioned generation Y and the following generation Z, who were born between the year 2000 and today may lead to a change in self-perception by the students, which in turn will lead to new challenges both for the students and the lecturers in transnational higher education.

5 Literature

Behrendt, Erich (2007): Schlüsselqualifikationen von Wirtschafts- und Sozialwissenschaftlern – ihre Bedeutung für den Arbeitsmarkt und ihre Vermittlung in der Lehre. Vortrag vom 14. Forum Wissenschaft am 16. April 2007. Hamburg

Chan, W. (1963): Analects – A sourcebook in Chinese Philosophy, Princeton University Press

Chen, M.-J. (2002): Transcending paradox: The Chinese middle way perspective, in: Asia Pacific Journal of Management 19, p. 179–199

Chen, M.-J. / Miller, D. (2010): West meets East: Towards an ambicultural approach to management, in: Academy of Management Perspectives, November, p. 17–24

Chen, Y.-F. / Tjosvold, D. (2007): Cross-cultural leadership: Goal interdependence and leader-member relations in foreign ventures in China, in: Journal of international Management 11, p. 417–439

Cortazzi, Martin; Jin, Lixian (2013): Creativity and Criticality – Developing Dialogues of Learning and Thinking with through Synergy with China, in: Tricia Coverdale Jones (ed.) 2013: Transnational Higher Education in the Asian Context. Palgrave Macmillan

Coverdale-Jones, Tricia [ed.] (2013): Transnational Higher Education in the Asian Context. Palgrave Macmillan

Deutscher Akademischer Austausch Dienst (DAAD), German Academic Exchange Service (2015): In Transnationale Bildung. Ziele und Wirkungen, duz Special, Raabe Verlags-GmbH

Faure, Oliver G. / Fang, Tony. (2008): Changing Chinese values: Keeping up with paradoxes, in International Business Review 17, p. 194–207

Findeisen, Renate/Schröder, Jörg (2012): "Aber wie soll man Theorie in der Arbeit einsetzen und mit seiner eigenen Arguemntation verbinden". Beobachtungen zum Schreibwissen chinesischer Studierender in der fremden Sprache Deutsch, in: Informationen Deutsch als Fremdsprache. DAAD

Hayhoe, R. & Liu, J. (2010): Chinas's Universities, Cross Border Education and Dialogue among Civilizations, in: D.W. Chapman; W.K. Cummings & G.A. Postiglione (eds.)

Hofstede, Geert (1980): Motivation, Leadership and Organization: Do American theories apply abroad?, in: Kolb, David / Rubin, Irwin / Osland, Joyce (1991): The organizational behavior reader, 5th ed., Englewood Cliffs: Prentice-Hall, p. 347–368.

Hofstede, Geert (1991): Cultures and Organizations: Software of the Mind, London et al.: McGraw-Hill.

Hofstede, Geert / Bond, M. H. (1988): The Confucius connection: From cultural roots to economic growth, in: Organizational Dynamics 16 (4), p. 4–21

Hong-kin Kwok (2012): The Generation Y's Working Encounter: A Comparative Study of Hong Kong and other Chinese Cities Springer Science+Business Media

Huang, Joanne (2010): China besser verstehen. Interkulturelle Annäherung – Warum Chinesen anders denken und handeln. Huang + Jaumann

Knauf, Helen (2003): Das Konzept der Schlüsselqualifikationen und seine Bedeutung für die Hochschule, in: Knauf, Helen/ Knauf, Marcus (Hg.): Schlüsselqualifikationen praktisch. Veranstaltungen zur Förderung überfachlicher Qualifikationen an deutschen Hochschulen, Bielefeld 2003, S. 11–29

Lange, Elmar (2012): Zur Verbesserung von Schlüsselkompetenzen in universitären Lehrveranstaltungen. ZAF (2012) 45:63–78. Institut für Arbeitsmarkt- und Berufsforschung

Li, Yongyan (2012): Text-Based Plagiarism in Scientific Writing: What Chinese Supervisors think about copying and how to reduce it in students' writing. Springer

Liu, W. / Zhu, R. / Yang, Y. (2010): I warn you because I like you: Voice behavior, employee identifications, and transformational leadership, in: The Leadership Quarterly 21 (1), p. 189–202

Lux, Markus (2013): Challenges and Measures Related to the Integration of Chinese students in Germany – the Activities of a German Foundation, in: Tricia Coverdale Jones (ed.) 2013: Transnational Higher Education in the Asian Context. Palgrave Macmillan

Metz, Annette / Gunkel, M. (2013): China schweigt – Wie westliche Expatriates erfolgreich mit Chinesen kommunizieren, in: Personal Quarterly 4, p. 14–19

Morrison, Elizabeth (2011): Employee Voice Behavior: Integration and Directions for Future Research p. 375, in: The Academy of Management Annals, New York University

OECD 2010): PISA 2009 Ergebnisse. Zusammenfassung

OECD (2011): Skills for innovation and research. Executive summary

Ren, Zhaoying/Hitchcock, Richard (2013): Influences of Chinese Cultural Pattern of Thinking on Discourse Organisation in English Dissertation Writing, in: Tricia Coverdale Jones (ed.) 2013: Transnational Higher Education in the Asian Context. Palgrave Macmillan

Reynolds, S., Valentine, D., (2004): Guide to Cross-Cultural Communication. Pearson Education, New Jersey

Rychen Dominique, S. (2008): OECD – Referenzrahmen für Schlüsselkompetenzen – ein Überblick, in: Kompetenzen der Bildung für nachhaltige Entwicklung. VS Verlag für Sozialwissenschaften | GWV Fachverlage GmbH, Wiesbaden

Schumann, Adelheid (ed.) 2012: Interkulturelle Kommunikation in der Hochschule: Zur Integration internationaler Studierender und Förderung Interkultureller Kompetenz. Transcript Verlag Bielefeld

Sun, Jin 2010: Die Universität als Raum kultureller Grenzerfahrung. Chinesische Studenten an einer deutschen Hochschule. Peter Lang. Frankfurt

Tyler, Kathrin 2007: The tethered generation, in *HR Magazine*, 52 (5), 41.

Utler, A. & Thomas, T. (2010): Critical Incidents und Kulturstandards, in: Weidemann, A, Nothnagel, S. & Straub, J. (eds.) 2010: Wie lehrt man interkulturelle Kompetenz? Transcript Verlag Bielefeld

Weidenbaum, M. (1996): The Chinese family business enterprise, in: California Management Review 38 (4), p. 141–156

WirtschaftsWoche Global. Sonderheft China NR. 01 vom 23.04.2012. Das Knurren der Tigerbabys. D18

Zhang, Yuehong (2010): Chinese journals find 31 % of submissions plagiarized, in: Nature Vol. 467, p 153

Ziguras, Christopher (2001): Educational technology in transnational higher education in South East Asia: the cultural politics of flexible learning, in: Educational Technology & Society 4 (4) 2001

Authors

Dr. Cai, Meng
Cai Meng is Lecturer of Event Management in Shanghai University of International Business and Economics since July 2012. He got his Ph.D. in Human Geography from East China Normal University in June 2012. His research interests mainly focus on low-carbon tourism and sustainable event, which he have published some papers in Tourism Tribune, Tourism Science, Human Geography, China Population Resources and Environment, and Ecological Economy.

Chen, Patrick
Patrick was graduated from Shanghai University, MPA of Shanghai Jiao Tong University. He joined in Shanghai Municipal Tourism Administration on 1998 and worked in Personnel Dept. and International Tourism Promotion Dept. He's in charge of the international marketing and promotion with North American and Europe Market for Shanghai Tourism and focus on international meetings, conferences and incentive travel promotion for the city of Shanghai as well. On behalf of SMTA, Patrick is an active member of ICCA and be the vice chairman of ICCA Asia Pacific Chapter since 2010–2013. He also was appointed as secretary general of ICCA China Committee, Director General of Steering Committee of Shanghai Meetings and conferences Standard Commission. Since 2006, Patrick started to launch "Shanghai Conference Ambassadors" programme on behalf of Shanghai Municipal Tourism Administration, there were 98 conference Ambassadors appointed by SMTA by the end of 2014 who's from 30 industries such as IT, Medicine, Finance, City developing fields etc. and hosted 300 middle to large scale international meetings and conferences in Shanghai.

Chen, Xianjin

Mr. Chen has been engaged in organising international exhibitions since 1984. He obtained an MBA degree after studying in the UK. As a Senior International Economist, he has profound academic knowledge and practical experience. He currently also holds the position of Executive Vice President of UFI, Director of National Technical Committee on Exhibition & Convention, President of Shanghai Convention and Exhibition Industries Association.

From April 2002 to October 2003, he was the Deputy Director of the Bidding Office for World Expo 2010 Shanghai. From 2004 to 2007, he was the President of Shanghai World Exop group, from 2007 to 2010, he was the Deputy Director of Bureau of Shanghai World Expo Coordination, responsible for the affairs of exhibiting, ticket and market development. In 2011 to 2013, as the Vice Chairman of Shanghai Municipal Commission of Commerce, he was responsible for the management and development of exhibition industry in Shanghai.

He was Chair of the UFI Asia/Pacific Chapter from 2006 to 2010. Chen Xianjin has been selected as 2013 President of UFI. He is the first Chinese President of this global association of the exhibition industry.

Chen, Zeyan

Chen Zeyan is the Vice President of China Construction Machinery Association and Senior Vice President and General Secretary of China Convention and Exhibition Society. Born in September, 1945, he graduated from the Mechanical Engineering programme of Beijing University of Technology. Engaged in MICE industry since 1981, he has organised many international exhibitions and led groups to overseas exhibitions. Since 2006, he has been mainly doing researches in MICE economy and has given several speeches on the China Expo Forum for International Cooperation. Due to his extraordinary achievements, he has been appointed as a visiting professor of Shanghai University and as a consultant to many cities. He is currently the Vice Executive Deputy Director of the Steering Committee of China Convention and Exhibition Society. Mr. Chen is also a professional engineer and senior member of Chinese Mechanical Engineering Society.

Dams, Colja M.
Colja M. Dams is a graduated economist and CEO of VOK DAMS, agency for events and live-marketing, based in Wuppertal, Germany. VOK DAMS has eleven offices in Germany, the US, France, China, the Czech Republic, Brazil and Dubai. Since its foundation in 1971, the agency has been one of the international market leaders for events and live-marketing. In China, VOK DAMS was one of the international event pioneers with VOK DAMS Beijing opening in 2004 and VOK DAMS Shanghai following suit in 2009. Whenever he is not visiting one of the numerous events organised by VOK DAMS all over the world or spending time in one of the VOK DAMS offices, Colja lives with his wife and three children in Essen, Germany.

Dr. Ding, Ye
Ding Ye is a lecturer of Event Management in Shanghai University of International Business and Economics. She got her Ph.D. in Shanghai University of Finance and Economics in 2013. Her research interests mainly focus on tourism and event economics, which she has published some papers in Statistics and Decision, and Economic Geography. She also has published some books including Management of Participation in Exhibition (2nd edition) and Analysis Methods and Indicators System of the Event Industry Contribution to the National Economy. She won the 1st Prize of 6th China Exhibition Economy Research Institution in 2014 and Excellent Papers of Shanghai Social and Science Institution in 2013 respectively.

Dr. Ding, Yi
Ding Yi, teaching faculty of the Sino-German joint programme International Event Management Shanghai at Shanghai University of International Business and Economics. She received a Bachelor of Science and a Master of Science in Natural Geography in 1991 and 1994 respectively at East China Normal University, a Master of Art in Conference Management in 2006 at University of Westminster, UK, and then a Doctorate Degree in Economics in 2011 at East China Normal University. She also gained valuable experience in business operation and management in managing a private business in Shanghai from 1994 to 2003.
Her research interests focus on corporate organisation in the event industry. The projects completed recently include The Consulting Report on the Reform of the Management Structure of the Event Branch in Zhejiang China Commodities City Group Co. Ltd (2015), Auditing rules for exhibition statistics (2014), and The Feasibility Report and Working Plan on the 2014 Initial Cultural Licensing Show in China Free Trade Zone (2014).

Du, Jiayi
Du Jiayi graduated from New York University with Master of Science in Travel and Tourism Management and is pursuing her PhD. Degree in Marketing in Shanghai University of Finance and Economics. Jiayi's research interests include sports event, themed events, and strategic marketing. Her published papers include "Sports Event and Shanghai City Brand Marketing", "Situational Analysis of China's Sports Event Integrated Marketing", "Economic Analysis of China's Event Industry" and others.

Prof. Dr. Frey, Andreas
Andreas Frey studied business mathematics at the University of Ulm, Germany, and the University of Wisconsin at Milwaukee, USA. He completed his Ph.D. degree at the University of Ulm in 1995 with a dissertation on point process theory. In 1996 he worked as a postdoctoral fellow at the NTT Multimedia Network Laboratories in Tokyo, Japan. Having been assistant professor at the University of Ulm for the following two years, he then joined Siemens AG as an engineer in the area of mobile communications. In 2004 he became professor for business mathematics and statistics at the University of Applied Sciences Osnabrueck (Hochschule Osnabrueck, Germany), where he co-founded the competence center for "women in leading positions". Since 2013 he is Rector of Nuertingen-Geislingen University (Germany).

Dr. Gaida, Hans-Jürgen
He held various leading positions in the MICE-industry in Berlin, Frankfurt (Messe Frankfurt), Vienna (Wiener Staatsoper), CEO of Halle Münsterland (Convention, Exhibition and Event Centre), CEO of HCC – Hannover Congress Center. He has more than 15 years of experience in event catering as well as large arena catering (Hannover soccer-stadium). He is active as independent consultant for the MICE-industry. Since 1990 he has been lecturing on cultural management, event-catering, management of event venues and destinations at ICCM (Intl. Center for Cultural Management) in Salzburg/Austria, the Intl. Academy for Media and Events in Baden-Baden/Germany, the Cooperative State University in Ravensburg, the University of Applied Sciences Worms, the Reinhold-Würth-Hochschule (University of Applied Sciences) Künzelsau/Heilbronn, and at the Shanghai University of International Business and Economics, SUIBE (former SIFT since 2008). Dr. Gaida is member of MPI and member of the Advisory Board of the Confucius Institute, Hannover/Germany.

Gao, Frankie
Frankie Gao is currently serving as the Managing Director of MCI China, managing operations of two offices in Beijing and Shanghai, and leading his team to carry out main businesses of Association Management & Consulting, Creative Services & Production, Destination Management, Corporate Meeting & Event Management, Professional Conference/-Congress Organization and Performance Improvement Program. Under his leadership, in year 2013, MCI China managed over 600 projects around 86 Chinese cities and 36 international cities bring the company into a new level. Before joining MCI, Frankie Gao established Transworld Tourism Resources, a company in China providing incentive programme and related travel solutions in all aspects. The company, acquired by MCI in 2007, provided the business including performance and programme improvement, incentive travel solutions and events market research. Frankie Gao joined the hospitality industry in 1989, after that, he had been working in marketing and sales with Air China for seven years. In 1998, he was appointed as China Business Development Manager by Tourism Australia, becoming the first local management member appointed by foreign National Tourism Organization in China.

Prof. Dr. rer. pol. Gervers, Susanne
Susanne Gervers teaches tourism management at Nürtingen-Geislingen University, Germany. Her work focuses on the manifold aspects of sustainability and tourism, new social networks and innovation management, creativity, tourism and arts, business ethics, theory and methodology of tourism management. She received her PhD in political theory from Leuphana University Lüneburg in 1996. In the same year she started her own study tour operator business and worked as its CEO for eleven years, until she found again the academic path and became a fellow of the German Society of Tourism Research (DGT) in 2010.

Gray, Clare
Clare Gray, Project Coordinator for International Event Management Shanghai at Osnabrück University of Applied Sciences, Germany. Clare Gray earned her Bachelor's degree from the University of Hull, United Kingdom followed by her Master's degree from the University of Osnabrück Germany, both in Transnational Integrated European Studies. Following 10 years in Sales and Marketing at Tetra GmbH in Melle, Germany and 4 years of self-employment in teaching, she joined Osnabrück University of Applied Sciences in 2009. Clare Gray is a certified Intercultural Trainer and has an advanced qualification in Event Management. She teaches Intercultural Training and part of the Communication and Key Qualifications module to Chinese students both in Shanghai and Osnabrück.

Prof. Dr. Griese, Kai-Michael
Kai-Michael Griese is Professor of Marketing at the University of Applied Science in Osnabrück, where he has been since 2009. He received his Ph.D. in Business Science from the University of Chemnitz in 2002. Since 2011 he is a Visiting Professor at the Shanghai University of International Business and Economics. His research interests center on improving the understanding of sustainable brands and sustainable marketing, mainly through application of consumer research and statistics.

Prof. Dr. Große Ophoff, Markus
Since 2001 Markus Große Ophoff is the Head of the Centre for Environmental Communication of the German Federal Environmental Foundation. He received his Ph.D. in Chemistry from the RWTH Aachen University in 1993. Between 1993 and 2001 he worked at the German Environmental Protection Agency and the German Federal Environmental Foundation. Since 2003 he is a lecturer at the University of Applied Science in Osnabrück. In 2014 he was

appointed as a Professor at the Faculty of business management and social sciences this University. His research interests center on sustainable event management and communication.

Hamid, Noor Ahmad

Noor started his career with Tourism Malaysia where he was involved in international & domestic tourism promotion, media hospitality, meeting & incentive projects and event organising. He was posted to Los Angeles for five years where he was actively involved in the meetings and incentive promotions. After 16 years with Tourism Malaysia, he joined the business sector in event management, sponsorship and innovative tourism projects. He joined ICCA in 2009 and managed to expand the research team in the regional office, making it a Global Research Centre for ICCA. This has enabled comprehensive research projects to be undertaken by the research team based in Kuala Lumpur for the benefit of members worldwide.

Dr. Jin, Quan

Jin Quan is Associate Professor for International Business and Human Resources Management at the Shanghai University of International Business and Economics (since 2003). Her research interests include International HRM, Global Entrepreneurship, Entrepreneurial Team, and Change Management. She teaches International HRM, Entrepreneurial HRM, Global Consulting, and Strategic Management for undergraduate students and graduate students since 2003. Jin Quan got her doctorate in management at the University of Fudan.

Kamphus, Manfred

Manfred Kamphus acted as General Manager of a medium-sized German stand construction company in Shanghai from 2010 to 2013. After attending commercial college and completing his apprenticeship as a wholesale, import and export merchant at Thyssen, Kamphus

Gray, Clare

Clare Gray, Project Coordinator for International Event Management Shanghai at Osnabrück University of Applied Sciences, Germany. Clare Gray earned her Bachelor's degree from the University of Hull, United Kingdom followed by her Master's degree from the University of Osnabrück Germany, both in Transnational Integrated European Studies. Following 10 years in Sales and Marketing at Tetra GmbH in Melle, Germany and 4 years of self-employment in teaching, she joined Osnabrück University of Applied Sciences in 2009. Clare Gray is a certified Intercultural Trainer and has an advanced qualification in Event Management. She teaches Intercultural Training and part of the Communication and Key Qualifications module to Chinese students both in Shanghai and Osnabrück.

Prof. Dr. Griese, Kai-Michael

Kai-Michael Griese is Professor of Marketing at the University of Applied Science in Osnabrück, where he has been since 2009. He received his Ph.D. in Business Science from the University of Chemnitz in 2002. Since 2011 he is a Visiting Professor at the Shanghai University of International Business and Economics. His research interests center on improving the understanding of sustainable brands and sustainable marketing, mainly through application of consumer research and statistics.

Prof. Dr. Große Ophoff, Markus

Since 2001 Markus Große Ophoff is the Head of the Centre for Environmental Communication of the German Federal Environmental Foundation. He received his Ph.D. in Chemistry from the RWTH Aachen University in 1993. Between 1993 and 2001 he worked at the German Environmental Protection Agency and the German Federal Environmental Foundation. Since 2003 he is a lecturer at the University of Applied Science in Osnabrück. In 2014 he was appointed as a Professor at the Faculty of business management and social sciences this University. His research interests center on sustainable event management and communication.

Hamid, Noor Ahmad

Noor started his career with Tourism Malaysia where he was involved in international & domestic tourism promotion, media hospitality, meeting & incentive projects and event organising. He was posted to Los Angeles for five years where he was actively involved in the meetings and incentive promotions. After 16 years with Tourism Malaysia, he joined the business sector in event management, sponsorship and innovative tourism projects. He joined ICCA in 2009 and managed to expand the research team in the regional office, making it a Global Research Centre for ICCA. This has enabled comprehensive research projects to be undertaken by the research team based in Kuala Lumpur for the benefit of members worldwide.

Dr. Jin, Quan

Jin Quan is Associate Professor for International Business and Human Resources Management at the Shanghai University of International Business and Economics (since 2003). Her research interests include International HRM, Global Entrepreneurship, Entrepreneurial Team, and Change Management. She teaches International HRM, Entrepreneurial HRM, Global Consulting, and Strategic Management for undergraduate students and graduate students since 2003. Jin Quan got her doctorate in management at the University of Fudan.

Kamphus, Manfred

Manfred Kamphus acted as General Manager of a medium-sized German stand construction company in Shanghai from 2010 to 2013. After attending commercial college and completing his apprenticeship as a wholesale, import and export merchant at Thyssen, Kamphus studied Business Administration in Duisburg and then changed to Osnabrück University of Applied Sciences after passing his intermediate examination in order to study Event Management. He completed his studies at Osnabrück University of Applied Sciences as a Diplom-Kaufmann (FH) in 2000. In the years that followed, Kamphus assumed a number of functions in the agency and trade fair environment. He became Key Account Manager at Expotechnik Heinz Soschinski GmbH in Frankfurt in 2007. After spending three years in Germany, he was given the opportunity to lead the Expotechnik branch in China in 2010. Expotechnik founded its first branch abroad in Atlanta, USA as early as 1985. This was followed by branches in Mexico, Singapore and Japan, and its first own branch in China – in the booming city of Shanghai – in 2002.

Kaur-Lahrmann, Ravinder
Ravinder Kaur-Lahrmann is Senior Lecturer in the School of Business at Osnabrueck University of Applied Sciences, Germany. Studied at Coventry University gained a BSc (Hons) in European Engineering and then an MSc in Manufacturing Engineering and Management. Currently lecturing in the subject group Management, main modules being Strategic Management, Cultural Management and Management Concepts and Tools.Research interests include, the evolution of management practices, the diffusion of management knowledge internationalisation strategies of organisations and the cultural management within the work place.

Koetter, Harald
Harald Koetter, Director Division Public Relations & Trade Fairs Germany, Association of the German Trade Fair Industry (AUMA), Berlin, Germany Studied economics in Muenster. With AUMA since 1980: First as Manager in the Division Trade Fairs Germany, 1989 as Director of the Public Relations Department. Since 2006 Director Division Public Relations & Trade Fairs Germany. Furthermore since 2006 Managing Director FKM – the Society for Voluntary Control of Fair and Exhibition Statistics. Has published various articles on the exhibition industry, holds regular lectures at associations and companies in Germany and abroad.

Dr. Li, Yanxia

Li Yanxia is a faculty in International Event Management Shanghai (IEMS), Shanghai University of International Business and Economics. She got her PHD in Management from Fudan University in 2010. Her research interests comprise human resource development and management in event industry, international event management (particularly the internalisation of Chinese trade fair companies), and organisational behaviour. Her research has been published in many journals in China, the Academy of Management Proceedings and International Association of Chinese Management Research Proceedings. Now one of her books is in print. For her work on organisational behaviour, she received substantial projects funding in both China and Germany. Dr. Li has teaching experience in Economics, human resource management, research methodology and leadership on the BSc and MSc-level.

Dr. Louw, Lynette

Lynette Louw, appointed in the Raymond Ackerman Chair of Management, Department of Management and the Deputy Dean, Faculty of Commerce at Rhodes University in Grahamstown, South Africa. She obtained her Doctor Commercii in Business Management at the University of Port Elizabeth in South Africa. She is the recipient of research awards, serves on journal editorial boards, co-author and editor of Management and Strategic Management textbooks. Lynette has delivered numerous national and international conference papers and published widely in academic journals. Her areas of speciality include Strategic management, International Organisational Behaviour, Intercultural and Cross-cultural management. International teaching experience includes Germany, Netherland and China, P.R.

Louw, Mattheus
Mattheus Louw is a senior lecturer in the Department of Management at Rhodes University in Grahamstown, South Africa. He obtained his MBA degree at the Stellenbosch University in South Africa. He is currently a director of the Southern African Institute for Management Sciences. He has delivered numerous papers at national and international conferences and published in academic journals. He is the co-author of a Management textbook and has contributed towards an e-learning Human Resource Management textbook. His areas of speciality include Human Resource Management, Strategic Management, International Organisational behaviour. International teaching experience includes Germany, Netherland and China, P.R.

Lu, Margaret Kwai Ting
Margaret received her Bachelor's degree in Arts from the University of Malaya. Upon graduation, she started her career as a Translator at the High Commission of India, Kuala Lumpur. In 2010, she made a career shift from the diplomatic body to the non-profit arena, as a Membership Development Executive at the ICCA Asia Pacific Regional Office.

Mao, Daben
Chief Executive Officer of Wuhan Sungoal Exhibition Co. Ltd since June, 2015. He has been engaged in the event industry for more than twenty years, and headed many large-scale enterprises, including state offices, state-owned companies, joint ventures and China branch of German-based exhibition companies. He graduated from the MBA programme of California State University.

Prof. Dr. Mayer, Peter
Peter Mayer studied business administration and economics at the universities of Frankfurt and Milwaukee and completed his doctorate degree at the Goethe University of Frankfurt. From 1994 to 2001, he was resident representative of the German Friedrich-Ebert-Foundation in Accra / Ghana and Seoul / South Korea. In 2001 he became professor for international economics at University of Applied Sciences Osnabrück, teaching economics, economic policy and international economics. Since then he taught courses at the University of Wisconsin-Oshkosh / USA, Shanghai University of International Business and Economics, University of Business / Vilinius / Lithuania and Nelson Mandela Metropolitan University in Port Elizabeth / South Africa. From 2003 to 2007 he was Dean of the Faculty for Business Management and Social Sciences and Vice-President for International Affairs of the University of Applied Sciences Osnabrueck. He published numerous articles on higher education management and on economic development issues, with a special focus on East Asian affairs. He is co-editor of two books on challenges in higher education in Asia and Africa.

Dr. Metz, Annette
She earned her PhD in International Management from Leuphana University in Lueneburg (D), her Master's degree in European Marketing Management from Brunel University (GB), and her Bachelor's degree in European Business Studies from Osnabrueck University of Applied Sciences (D). Following purchasing/sales/marketing positions in trading business and a position as senior consultant within a Swiss consulting company, Annette Metz co-founded the HR consulting company CONBEN Deutschland GmbH in Duesseldorf. In 2004 she relocated to Shanghai to support CONBEN customers in China and South East Asia. In her work as HR consultant she supports management teams of international companies in HR related development topics, mainly leadership and team development. She has been teaching part of the Communication and Key Qualification s module to Chinese students in Shanghai for five years.

Prof. Dr. Milewicz, Chad
Chad Milewicz is Associate Professor of Marketing at the University of Southern Indiana in the United States. His expertise is in marketing strategy and professional selling. His research is published in several journals, including Industrial Marketing Management, Management Research Review, Marketing Management Journal, Journal of Political Marketing, and Marketing Education Review. In addition to research, he teaches undergraduate and MBA classes and consults cities and non-profit organisations on marketing.

Müller-Martin, Rolf
He was working 30 years for Lufthansa German Airlines in various positions: based in Hong Kong as Advertising Manager Far East for 8 years, as Marketing Manager for Mexico and South America for 5 years and from 1990 till 2001 he was in charge of all fairs and exhibitions worldwide, including all subsidiary companies in the Lufthansa group. In between he was member of the organisation team for EXPO 92 in Seville/Spain and EXPO 2000 in Hanover/Germany. 2002 he opened the German office for the British exhibition design company HBM and since 2008 he is representing the German fair construction company Rhino as Manager International Consulting. He was lecturing at the International Congress Academy in Karlsruhe, at the European Media and Event Academy and at the Messe Frankfurt Academy. Since 2006 he is involved in the Sino-German project IEMS International Event Management Shanghai. He is also the co-author of the leading trade book "Successful Participations at Trade Fairs", published 2001 in Germany by Cornelsen in Berlin.

Prof. Quan, Hua
Professor Quan, currently Dean of the Tourism and Event Management School, Shanghai University of International Business and Economics (SUIBE), is also a PhD supervisor in

Shanghai University of Finance and Economics, a member of the Expert Committee of Shanghai Tourism Development Research Centre, an expert consultant with Hunan Chamber of Commerce, Tourism Branch, and a council member of Regional Tourism Professional Commission in the Regional Science Association of China, and an assessment expert with Scenic Spot Office under the Ministry of Water Resources of the People's Republic of China.

Prof. Dr. Schinnenburg, Heike
Heike Schinnenburg is Full Professor for Business Administration and Human Resources Management at the University of Applied Science in Osnabrueck (since 2002). Her research interests include International HRM with a special focus on Asia, Global Talent Management, Career Development, and Change Management. She teaches quite regularly at partner universities in Asia (China, India, Indonesia) was part of the team for the IEMS programme since 2006. Due to her experiences as HR Director of a wholesale company and as business consultant before her professorship she is interested in combining theory and practical implications for strategic and daily challenges in HRM. Heike Schinnenburg got her doctorate in economics at the University of Hanover.

Schultze, Matthias
Matthias Schultze is the Managing Director of the GCB German Convention Bureau e.V.. The GCB is the central marketing organisation representing the conference and convention interests of meeting destination Germany. Matthias Schultze studied business management at Heidelberg Hotel Management School and worked for Brenner's Park Hotel in Baden-Baden, Hotel Le Bristol in Paris, Bayerischer Hof in Munich and Hilton International. He has been an executive board member of the World Conference Centre Bonn – the convention centre incorporating the former German parliament buildings in Bonn. Matthias Schultze has held the position as Vice President of the European Association of Event Centres (EVVC) and for several years he was a member of the GCB's marketing committee.

Prof. Schwägermann, Helmut

Helmut Schwägermann is Director of the International Event Research Institute Shanghai/Osnabrück and Professor for Business Management and Event Management at the University of Applied Sciences Osnabrück. He was heading the study programme Event Management & Business Events in Osnabrück between 2000 and 2014, is founder of the Bachelor Programme International Event Management Shanghai (IEMS) and was its Programme Director from 2003 to 2015. Schwägermann studied economics in Kiel and is involved in the event industry since more than 35 years. Between 1978 and 1995 he held several management positions in marketing, sales and management at Messe Berlin and was Director of the International Congress Centre ICC Berlin in the 1990-ies. Between 1996 and 2006 he was managing director of ConEcon Management & Marketing GmbH, a strategic consultancy company for the international event industry, based in Berlin.Throughout his career Schwägermann has been actively involved in several national and international associations of the event industry. Schwägermann published numerous articles and consults companies and organisations in the international event industry.

Seifert, Frank

Frank Seifert had 40 years of experience and expertise in the national and international congress and trade fair business. Frank started his career in 1971 at Messe Berlin, where he was Director of Marketing Messe Berlin from 1976 to 1984. From 1984 to 1986 he held the position of Marketing Director and Sales International Congress Centre ICC Berlin. During this period (1983), as a pioneer in the German trade fair industry, he organised 'CAMP Beijing', a trade show and conference on computer graphics, in Beijing.He was a shareholder and Managing Director of 'Direct Communication Ltd.' Berlin from 1986 to 1997. From 1997, Frank was the owner and Managing Director of Congress- & Messe-Marketing International, an internationally operating service and consulting company in the area of trade fairs and congresses. Frank was a member of the board of ICCA (International Congress and Convention Association) from 1991 to 1997. He also started lecturing on the Management of Congresses module for International Event Management Shanghai (IEMS) in 2009.
Frank Seifert passed away in March 2015.

Spinger, Marco
Marco Spinger, Director Division Global Markets, Association of the German Trade Fair Industry (AUMA), Berlin, Germany. Studied law in Kiel. Since 1998 certified lawyer. With AUMA since 1997: Assistant to CEO followed by the post of Manager Legal Affairs. Since 2004 as Director of Division Global Markets. Gives lectures at chambers, associations, holds seminars and speaks at national and international congresses. Author of various publications.

Steinkuhl, Claudia
Claudia Steinkuhl, lecturer in Communication and Key Competencies at Osnabrück University of Applied Sciences, Germany (HSOS). She earned her Bachelor's degree in Business Management from Osnabrück University of Applied Sciences, followed by her Master's degree in European Marketing Management from Brunel University, London and an advanced qualification from Hamburg University in Communication Psychology. Following different positions in industry, Claudia Steinkuhl has been employed at Osnabrück University of Applied Sciences, where she has been responsible for the coordination of international study programmes and has been teaching Communication and Key Qualifications in German and Chinese study programmes for more than ten years.

Tang, Jiani
Tang Jiani is a graduated student of Shanghai University of International Business and Economics, where she studied Exhibition Industry and Event Management from 2010 to 2014. Now she is pursuing her master degree of Business Finance and Accounting in Warwick Business School of University of Warwick and will finished it 2016.

Walk, Marlene
Marlene Walk is an Assistant Professor at the School of Public and Environmental Affairs at Indiana University-Purdue University, Indianapolis (USA). In 2015, she received her Ph.D. in Social Welfare from the University of Pennsylvania (USA). Her research interests focus on how individuals react to and act during organisational change as well as on the management of human resources in nonprofit organisations. Marlene is the recipient of the 2013 Association for Research on Nonprofit Organization and Voluntary Action (ARNOVA) Emerging Scholar Award and the 2015 Academy of Management (AOM) Organization Development and Change Division Best Paper Based on a Dissertation Award. Marlene holds a social work degree from the University of Applied Sciences Hildesheim (Germany, 2004) and an M.A. in Nonprofit Management from the University of Applied Sciences Osnabrück (Germany, 2009).

Xie, Jia
Xia Jia, currently teaching as a lecturer of business school, Suzhou University of Science and Technology, is also a doctoral candidate in Shanghai University of Finance and Economics majoring in Management of Tourism Destination. The leading area of study is tourism quality management and hotel management.

Zhang, Li

Zhang Li, lecturer of IEMS Programme, Tourism and Event Management School, Shanghai University of International Business and Economics, doctor candidate majoring in tourism management at Fudan University. During the last few years many articles about the Mega-event marketing, travelling behaviour of Chinese travellers have been published including the textbook "Introduction to the MICE Industry of China", hosted and participated many research projects including "A Comparative Study of Event Industry Development Between China and Germany", "Event Industry's Development Planning of Yulin, Guangxi Province", "The development strategies of Shanghai International Resort". In 2009, the teaching research about "Exploration and innovation of talent training mode majoring in Event Management" got the First Prize of Education Achievement in Shanghai, 2009 by Shanghai Municipal Education Commission.

Dr. Zhao, Lei

Zhao Lei is a Senior Lecturer in the Department of Tourism Management at Zhejiang University of Technology. He received his Ph.D. degree from Shanghai University of Economics and Finance. He specialises in tourism economy, with special interests in the impact of tourism development on economic growth.